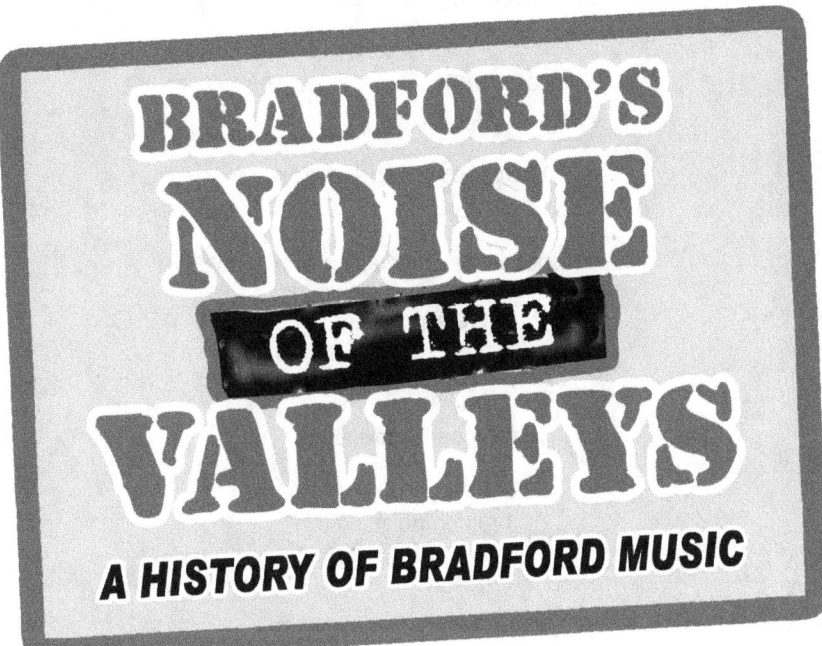

A HISTORY OF BRADFORD MUSIC

VOLUME 3.1 • 1999 - 2003
GARY CAVANAGH AND MATT WEBSTER

LS ARTS BOOKS
A Bradford Noise Production

Dedicated to all the musicians who are no longer with us, by Gary.

Dedicated to Spock's Knee, by Matt.

Bradford 2025 Edition

First published in the United Kingdom in 2025 by
LS Arts Publishing
West Yorkshire

Leeds Streets Ltd

www.leeds-streets.uk

bradfordnoise.com
mutiny2000.com

© 2025 by Gary Cavanagh and Matt Webster

The Authors hereby assert their moral rights to be identified as the Authors of the Work.

Written and researched by Gary Cavanagh and Matt Webster
Graphic design by Matt Webster
Layout by Matt Webster and Gary Cavanagh
Family trees drawn by Gary Cavanagh
with bits moved around by Matt Webster!

All images in this book are copyright of the original creators.

All rights reserved. No part of this publication may be reproduced, stored in a retrieval system, or transmitted, in any form or by any means, electronic, mechanical, photocopying, recording or otherwise, without the prior permission of the publisher and copyright holders.

British Library Cataloguing in Publication Data
A catalogue record for this book is available from the British Library

ISBN 978-1-7391481-5-7

Printed in the UK by Lightning Source

FOREWORD

Extraordinary and encyclopedic, this unique project now reaches its third volume. There can be no other city that has had its musical history recorded in quite such microscopic detail. In creating this comprehensive collage, Gary Cavanagh and Matt Webster have given us the complete picture. Through their dogged determination, we have profiles of every active band and musician associated with Bradford and its surrounding area since the 1960s. As well as photos, publicity material, and discographies, we get comprehensive histories via numerous rock family trees illustrating the changing line-ups of band after band, alongside the other activities of each member.

In addition to this new book, which in itself is the first of two volumes, the pair have revised, expanded, and updated volumes one and two. Much of the content of the first volume, for example, was gleaned by Gary trawling painstakingly through library records of the Telegraph and Argus, other local papers, as well as fanzines and other printed sources. Many of these reports contained inaccuracies. Back then, there was no internet, Wikipedia, or social media. Nowadays, access to reliable first-hand accounts and detailed research by both band members and fans has provided them with a wealth of detail. Contacting individual musicians is also much easier, and they've made extensive use of other sources, notably Google, Discogs, and Facebook pages. These two comprehensively improved volumes are also newly available.

It's worth noting that, while each book in this series covers a different period, many bands associated with a particular era have continued to record and perform, and so have an ongoing story that can be followed from book to book.

Released alongside this book are three CDs: one of folk music, one of rock-metal bands, and one of indie rock. All told, Gary and Matt have so far released a total of 22 CD albums, which offer readers the chance to hear recordings by many of the artists covered in the three books. More CDs are already in the pipeline, including a dance CD to tie in with part two of book three.

Book three, volume two, will probably be the last of this series to be compiled by Gary and Matt. However, they plan to pass that baton on to a couple of younger people who are more directly involved with the recent and current music scene in the Bradford area. If so, expect this to evolve into an ongoing venture. Let's hope so.

Nick Toczek
May 2025

We know what you did, We know where you live

Bradford is in some ways still a small town, surrounded by a number of smaller townships that all merge into the city as we know it today. Situated at its centre is a natural bowl provided by the great valleys of the rivers Aire and Wharfe.

Since 1974 Bradford has been enlarged to a metropolitan district, taking in the townships of Shipley, Bingley, Haworth, Keighley and Ilkley, making it the seventh largest urban/rural conurbation in the UK.

This edition is the third volume (at least the first half) of *Bradford's Noise Of Valleys*. *Volume 3.1* covers the years 1999 to 2003 in two chapters, and a third chapter which focuses on the folk and world music scene from 1999 to 2009. The decision to publish the book in two parts was taken due to the large page count and overall cost of producing one long volume. The second half will cover 2004-06 and 2007-09 in two chapters, plus a separate chapter covering Bradford's dance scene between 1999 and 2009. *Volume 3.2* will appear in the not-too-distant future, all being well.

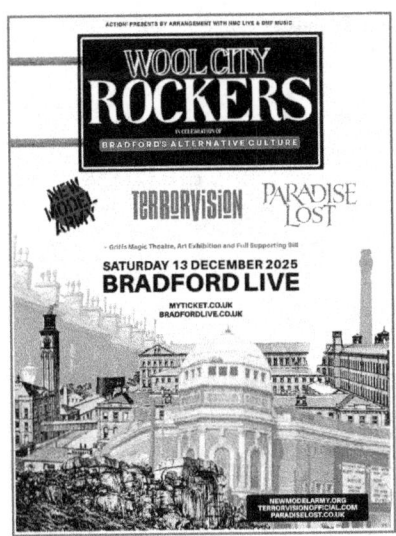

Once again, we hope to showcase the vast amount of talent from numerous different musical genres that Bradford has produced over the years.

At the time of publication, Bradford is the UK's *City Of Culture*. A major new venue, Bradford Live, has finally opened after years of renovation and a long-running campaign to save what was The Gaumont and later The Odeon cinema.

A few things seem to be coming full circle. The Bradford Live *Wool City Rockers* promoted gig is named after the 1979 Nick Toczek fanzine and promoted by long-time Bradford music manager Andy Farrow. The poster features three bands, New Model Army, Terrorvision and Paradise Lost, and one DJ show, Griff's Magic Theatre. These artists have traversed the decades and the pages of all three of our *Bradford's Noise Of The Valleys* books.

Is this a new dawn for Bradford? After the loss of so many venues over the years, we hope the new Bradford Live will become a major venue for touring bands and big-name artists in the future and put Bradford firmly back on the map as a major music city.

Gary Cavanagh
Matt Webster
Bradford,
May 2025

www.bradfordnoise.com

How to read the Rock Family Trees

Just in case anybody has difficulties in understanding the Rock Family Trees, below is a basic key on how to read them. Firstly they are read downwards and in chronological order by year date. Year dates in closed brackets indicate the years a band was active, and the rear end open brackets denotes that no information is available as to when the band ceased to be active.

Symbols and abbreviations

#2 etc – denotes the 2nd incarnation of a band
voc – vocals
gtr – guitar
drm – drums
keyd – keyboards
harm – harmonica
hamm – hammond organ
trump – trumpet and so on
- - - ! denotes an occasional guest or studio member

(RIP 2000) – As a mark of respect for the fallen, this denotes the year known of the individual's passing.

CONTENTS

Preface 1-8
Bradford Noise: The Story So Far Reviews • R2 • Telegraph & Argus • Jumbo Records • The Missing Music CDs • Leeds Noise Of The Valleys

Chapter 1: 1999-2000 9-72
Intro: Northern Scream • Ooberman • Tony Pensavalle • #Crime • IdiotBox • Nursery • Daisy Cutter • Indiqa • Water • Mad For It • Red Sky Coven • Loved Ones • Nato Goes To War • Alpine Movement • Rock/Heavy Metal Scene • Hypnosis • Conquest Of Steel • Khang • The Belonging • The Enchanted • Bloodstream • Parallel Or 90 • Shandyland • The Sound Of The Suburbs • The 1 In 12 Club • Danbert • MayDay '99 • Gigs: May-June • Eviction Of 120 Rats • The Devils • Enslaved Records • Ebola • Film Nights • Gigs: July-Sept • Kids Club • Lunatics Tournament • 1in12 Publications • Bradford • Aid For Kosova • Decade Of Dissidence • Gigs: Oct-Dec • Hive • Crisis #3 • Big Issue In The North • City Stride To The Premiership • Bradford Festival '99 • Bradford Poets • Local History Walks • Another Love Affair • Bingley Music Live • Smokie Man Goes Solo • Three Men & A Bass • Hendrix Honoured • Blowdry • Battle Of Seattle • • 200 • Flat Back Floor • Lene Martin • NMA & Joolz • Refugees • Skiver • Jennifer Robertson • Warm • Bradford Trades Council • Lifeforce • 1 In 12 Club Gigs: Jan-May • Taking Control • Gigs: July-Aug • 1in12 AFC • Carpe Noctum • Gigs: Oct • Guide To DIY • Gigs: Nov • Sawn Off • Drama Collective • Gigs: Dec • Death Of A Member • Tribute To Smokie • Losing Control • Nikki Stuart & Girl Thing • Mariko • Green #2 • Bradford Festival 2000 • Linton Kwesi Johnson • Mela • Without PrejudicevChris Sharp • T&A Page Changes Hands • Myrtle Park Bingley Live • Love Affair New Album • Goad • Puzzle Hall Festival • Embrace • Lapdog • Mutiny 2000 • White Abbey Road • Gardeners Of Eden • Shiny Beast • Angelo Palladino • Moota • Frantic • Elvis Taxi • Year Dot • Supersonic • Jazz Mutiny • Grim • Solar • Mutiny 2000 Band • DJ Lynda • The Negatives • Keighley Scene • Circus

Chapter 2: 2001-2003 73-130
Bradford Film Festival • Brazil • Rampage • Scatter • Local Books • 1 In 12 Club 2001 • Chumbas • Gigs: Feb-Mar • 20 Years • WEA • Beyond TV • Gigs: Apr-May • Inspectors • KMP • Heavyfest • Silverburn • MayDay • Bradford Bad Lad / Book • Gigs: June-July • Boxed-In • Reason To Believe • Bookworms • Alternative World Cup • Gigs: Aug-Oct • Out Of The Void • Losing • The Battle • Baba Yaga • Gigs: Nov-Dec • Bradford Festival • Zico • Kwai Chang Caine • Andy Wells • July 7/8 Riot • Artscene • Bottom • Twin Towers 9/11 • Parva • Playing The Field • Barbara Moore • Peel Gets An Honorary Degree • Keighley Scene • Breene • Wet Paint • Driven Down • 2002 • EMI • Gareth Gates • 8th Bradford Film Festival • WW1 Plaque • The Empress • Reeved • Jack Magazine • Voltage Records • Franz Ferdinand • Falconetti • 1 In 12 Club Gigs: Feb-April • Humanfly • Dezerter • Mayday • Angola 3 • 1 In 12 AGM • Anti-Monachist Celebrations • Heavyfest II • Gigs: May-July • Gigs: Aug-Oct • Radical Cheerleaders • Gigs: Nov-Dec • Bradford Festival Wharf Rats • Ginger Fringe Festivals • Soup Bowl Press • Simon Ellis • His Girl Friday • Loom • Bradford Embassy • Laika Dog/Malibu Stacey • Girls Aloud • Keighley Scene • Random Hand • The Return Of Skeletal Family • The Pipers • Fatal Joy • Operator Six • 2003 • Priestley Centre • Justin Sullivan Solo Single • Tortoise Waltz • The Iraq War • Paradise Lost 20th Anniversary • Threshold Shift • 1 In 12 Club Gigs: Jan-April • Ninepound Note • Mayday • Bradford Anarchist Group • The Birth Of BNOTV • Gigs: June-July • Heavyfest III • Gigs: Aug-Oct • Gigs: Nov-Dec • Darwin • Los Guys • Bradford Festival • Gentlemen's Pistols • Trial • That Fucking Tank • Natalie Goodair • Sally Dawson • Pulse Radio's Battle Of The Bands • Finapple • Judgement Day Fesival • Accolade • Beautiful Daze Urban Walk • This Et Al • Bradford In Focus • Film Festi • Keighley Scene • Exoteric • Don Gaudiosi & Hush • Black Horse Fairy

Chapter 3: Bradford Folk 1999-2009 131-166
Intro • Folk Rarities • Janet Jones • Jovial Crew • Look Records • Barbara Young • Quare Fellas • Bradford Folk Club • Steve Tilston • Tim Moon & The Yorkshire Miracle • Arrin • Gary Boyle's Crosstown Traffic • Jon Harvison • Fiona-Kate Roberts • Topic Folk Club 1999-2009 • Gael Force • Honeyhole • Zydeco Funk Butchers • Bradford Fowk/Bracken Haley Sisters • RDB • Jason McNiff • Keith Christmas At The Topic • Tim Moon • Performance Express • Keighley Scene • Kitchen Songs • Fay Hield • Eddie Lawler • Karl Dallas • Roy Bailey • Chumba Folk • Hall Brothers • Shaun T Hunter • Wilful Missing • Demon Barbers • Nigel Garry • The Melborn • Folk At The 1 In 12 • Unfinished Drawings • Abi Lovelle • Captain Hotknives • Sketch • Sex Patels • The Family Elan • James Dey • Julie Felix • Two Madre • Laura Groves • Jazz/Blues/World Music • Jimmy Cliffe • John Lee Hooker • Jools Holland • Annie Whitehead • Al Dimeola • Peter Green • Zoot Money • Midnight Train • Clare Teal • Alan Wormald Band • Off The Wall • John Etheridge • Huddersfield Jazz • Jed's Blues Band/Maureen Galvin • Threads Orchestra • Jonathan Brigg • Welcome Home Sexy • Chantel McGregor • Jo Dunwell • Berkana • Huigan Quartet • The 309s • The Bad Shepherds • Roger Davies • Queensbury Music Festival • Beehive Poets • Cleckheaton Folk Festival • Saltaire Live • Jonathan Taylor • Raise Your Banners

References/Bibliography   167-170
If it's wrong, blame the source!

Index Of Bands On Trees   171-176
From Abyss to Zydeco Funk Butchers

Afterwords   177-195
About The Authors • Acknowledgements • RIP Page • About the CDs for Volume 3 • The Missing Music CDs • Leeds Noise Of The Valleys CDs

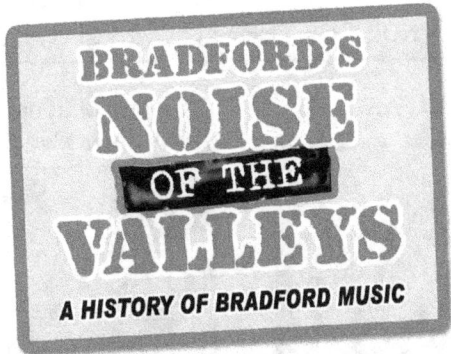

PREFACE

Ok, we admit it, it's been a while... After the publication of *Bradford's Noise Of The Valleys Volume One* in 2009, we carried straight on with the second volume, which took a mere four years! In 2013, Volume Two and a new edition of Volume One were published by Mutiny 2000 Publications.

A lot has happened since then, both in the world in general and in everyone's personal lives. We've had the joys of austerity, Brexit, Donald Trump, Boris Johnson, Covid-19, lockdowns, wars in the East and West and, er, Donald Trump again to shake everything up. Both authors have had health issues to deal with. Well we are getting on a bit, especially Gary.

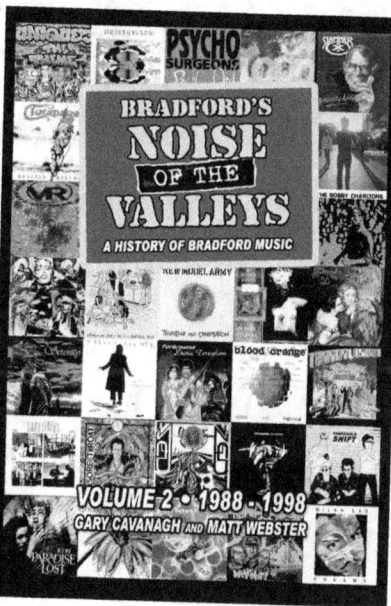

Gary also took time out to 'manage' a reformed Bradford anarcho-punk band he had always loved. We almost put their come-back EP out on vinyl.

And speaking of vinyl, Matt Webster was heavily involved with his Signia Alpha band project. Started just before lockdown, Matt began recording sessions with former band mates and new friends, initially in conjunction with poet Nick Toczek. Remote recording allowed musicians, now spread far and wide, to contribute. As of 2025, Signia Alpha have released four vinyl albums and a 12-inch EP featuring a few of the names in this book.

We also produced a stream of Missing Music CDs, did a few live appearances at spoken word events. and even a Bradford's Noise Of The Valleys pub quiz!

And the world has moved on a bit. Gary started this project by scanning through old copies of the T&A on microfiche in Bradford Library and cobbling together info from the details on bands' cassette tapes. He interviewed countless musicians, some with notoriously poor recolective powers. Some of whom had forgotten the name of the bass player in the third lineup of a band that split up thirty years before! We now have resources like Wikipedia, Discogs, Facebook and band websites, packed with potentially useful info.

But the primary source material from people is still the main source of material. Hoarded photos, flyers, posters, and press cuttings still form a large part of these books. All scanned in one at a time and tidied up. And, of course, band members first hand info.

We do our best to record this accurately, checking for secondary sources where we can. As a result, we have revised, expanded and updated Bradford's Noise Of The Valleys Volumes 1 & 2.

We have once again used the latest available listings from the *2016-2022 Record Collector's Rare Record Guides* (RCRGG) for those artists whose product is now deemed collectable

As the online resources become more plentiful, our primary research sources are diminishing. It struck us when reading through this volume, started 12 years ago, how many people we have lost along the way. The talented souls who were kind enough to share their passion for music with us

This book is dedicated to them.

BRADFORD NOISE - THE STORY SO FAR...

Bradford's Noise of The Valleys Volume Two was published in November 2013 and was launched with a book signing event at Bradford's prestigious Waterstone's Bookshop in December.

Promotional events for the book included an appearance by the authors in the Spoken Word Tent at the fith *Deer Shed Festival* in the summer of 2014.

Gary and Matt presented a *Bradford's Noise Of The Valleys Pub Quiz* at the Black Swan, Thornton

Road, Bradford, in November 2014, where the audience had the chance to win numerous Bradford Noise goodies, including CDs, books, t-shirts, sweatshirts and the fabulous Bradford Noise beer mat!

The following year the pair appeared at The Hop, Saltaire, as part of the *2015 Saltaire Festival* on September 14.

Over the years, Gary has given talks about the books and CDs at various venues, including Bradford Library (twice), Keighley Library, Bradford University (three times) and Leeds Metropolitan University.

SPOKEN WORD

Once more The Guardian's Dave Simpson curates another great spoken word line-up, including a-bit-a-football.

The Fallen On The Fall

Ever wondered what it's like to be dumped out of a Transit van in a Swedish forest or find yourself in the middle of a mass punch-up onstage? Anyone who has played in The Fall would know. This unique panel assembles four generations of former Fall musicians - Steve and Paul Hanley, Mile Leigh and 'Funky' Si Wolstencroft - and discusses life in and out of Mark E. Smith's legendary John Peel favourites. Compered by Dave Simpson, whose own acclaimed, revelation-packed book The Fallen was burned by Mark E. Smith.

Marching On Together - Heidi Heigh

Book shops shelves bulge with books about the sport but very few are written by women, never mind offer a female fan's perspective. Heidi Haigh talks to The Last Champions author Dave Simpson about her book Follow Me And Leeds United and her 40 year odyssey as a female following a male-dominated sport. Expect a unique view on everything from chanting to pies, and much discussion of Leeds United then and now, and the increasing impact of women on the so-called 'beautiful game.'

Bring The Bradford Noise - Gary Cavanagh and Matt Webster

Bradford isn't always thought of as a music capital, but Gary Cavanagh and Matt Webster's Bradford's Noise Of The Valleys books present a compulsive case that puts that right. Here, with art and visuals, they explore decades of Bradford music, literally thousands of musicians and unearth a few surprises among Bradford's musical exports - which take in everyone from Smokey to Whatever Happened To The Likely Lads, Ade Edmonson's spoof rockers Bad News to a band called Midnight Hearse.

PREFACE 1999 - 2003

The books and CDs were reviewed in various publications, a few of which are presented here. From left to right: *Record Collector Magazine*, *RnR Magazine*, *Yorkshire Post* (bottom) and the *Telegraph & Argus* (over).

Noise Of The Valleys: A History Of Bradford Rock And Pop Volume 2: 1988-1998

Gary Cavanagh & Matt Webster

★★★★

Mutiny 2000, £25
ISBN 978 0 992675516, 300 pages

Anyone recall the song Over The Berlin Wall?

Back in the mid-80s this writer lived in Yorkshire: six months in Leeds and eight in Bradford. Bands ranging from Creation Roots to Ghost Dance gigged on the local scene, while Leeds University played host to the likes of The Christians.

The first volume of this forensic analysis of the Bradford scene came out in 2008 and covered the 60s to 1988. This addition explores the following 10 years, covering the hardcore, dance, indie, folk and metal scenes, along with crucial local bands including Terrorvision and My Dying Bride. As with the previous volume, band biographies are detailed and passionately written, and the authors have included extensive family trees, photos, handbills, newspaper cuttings and even *Rare Record Price Guide* valuations. Well-known Bradford venues are also featured, including the 1 In 12 Club, which showcased all manner of bands and labels, both local and national.

Readers curious for more can also buy a lovingly compiled 4CD set of Bradford music from the period – now if only I could remember the name of my favourite band from the area. They sounded like Pet Shop Boys with a singing guitarist.

Ian Shirley

Record Collector 426, April 2014

BRADFORD'S NOISE OF THE VALLEYS VOLUME 2
Gary Cavanagh and Matt Webster

(MUTINY 2000 PUBLICATIONS/BRADFORD NOISE PRODUCTIONS) www.bradfordnoise.com

ISBN 978 0992675516 Softcover. 300 pp

In 2009, Cavanagh and Webster produced their first book covering the Bradford music scene in minute detail – every demo, gig, and change in band line-up that they could find for the years 1967-1987. Now, thirty pages thicker, comes their coverage of 1988-1998. The last book was accompanied by six CDs. This one comes with another six. They're truly excellent and astonishingly varied, amply illustrating how worthwhile the book is.

This whole project's exemplary – an urban museum of popular music. For completists, volume three's underway. When it's done, no city will have had its music scene as comprehensively researched, compiled and published as Bradford. On the CDs alone, you get reggae to Cajun, heavy rock to bhangra, indie to folk, pure pop to rap, electro to punk, and more.

In the book, amid photos, flyers, press cuttings, rock family trees, and picture sleeves, are all the hopes, struggles, successes and failures of the hundreds of individuals who collaborated in 4,000 days and nights of rehearsing, gigging and recording that helped to keep the city alive and on the cultural map. Above all, this is a glorious record of human faith, endeavour, creativity, ambition, entertainment and kick-ass memories.

Nick Toczek

Various artists – Leeds Noise of the Valleys 1978-1987
Review by Duncan Seaman

Compiled by Gary Cavanagh and Matt Webster, who have also curated volumes of 'missing music' from Bradford, this CD explores a fertile period in Leeds's musical history that gave the world Soft Cell, Sisters of Mercy, Chumbawamba and Gang of Four. A companion to Richard Rouska's book *It Ain't Peters and Lee*, the 21 tracks here show how wiry post-punk, in particular, flourished in the city thanks to the likes of The Mekons, Delta 5, The Expelaires and Girls At Our Best!. By 1982, that had given way to the darker grooves of Sisters of Mercy and March Violets, in whose gothic stead followed Red Lorry Yellow Lorry. Leading an electronic strand were Soft Cell and Music For Pleasure, while flying the anarchist flag were Chumbawamba. Visit bradfordnoise.com

Yorkshire Post, April 2023

VARIOUS
★★★★★

Bradford's Noise Of The Valleys: The Missing Music 3 & 4

(BRADFORD NOISE) www.bradfordnoise.com

Matt Webster and Gary Cavanagh have produced two books the size of old phone directories and twelve twenty-track albums in their quest to document the entire history of popular music in the Bradford area. They're now working on book three and here are their thirteenth and fourteenth albums.

This smartly wrapped fold-out package offers another thirty-nine tracks from artists they missed out last time around, many of them excellent.

CD3 (1966-88) kicks off with US blues veteran Champion Jack Dupree who lived in nearby Halifax. Variety's the key: there's Root & Jenny Jackson's ace 1969 legendary take on blues-soul classic 'Lean On Me'; psych-folk 'Sorcerers' by Jan Dukes De Grey; classy 1980 heavy rock from Dawnwatcher; 1984 punk rage from Anti System; wild mid-80s Asian percussion from Anjana and reggae from Jab Jab.

CD4 (1989-1998) opens brilliantly with 'Early Learning' by Twice Around The Houses, followed by class stuff from Gorgeous; Beer Beast (magnificently mangling 'Ilkley Moor'); Mannix; Anita Madigan; Rattlesnake Shake; Zed; My Dying Bride – and even Smokie with Roy Chubby Brown asking *'Who the f*** is Alice?'* Numerous rarities and undiscovered gold, all from the city that beat Chelsea by four goals to two!

Nick Toczek

1999 - 2003 BRADFORD'S NOISE OF THE VALLEYS VOLUME 3 PART 1

CITY'S MUSIC OF THE PAST

REMEMBER WHEN

MUSIC historians Gary Cavanagh and Matt Webster have taken time out from working on a third volume of their books exploring Bradford's music scene to release a new CD compilation.

The pair have delved into local music history in their books, Bradford's Noise of the Valleys. The fifth edition of their Missing Music CDs presents more 'missing' tracks from artists born or based in Bradford, including Kiki Dee and Smokie - before they were known as Smokie.

"It seems the older stuff is becoming more popular as we go on; as more people find the books we're getting more older stuff sent in from periods we've already covered, but it's of no less importance or relevance than anything published so far," says Matt. "As a result, we feel duty bound to put out these Missing Music CDs every now and again. It's fun for us to hear it all too."

The CD covers a 30-year period of changing music styles, beginning with classic Sixties sounds, veering into the local folk scene then cantering into Seventies pop - including an early incarnation of Smokie and Kiki Dee, the first Bradford female singer to have a

SOUNDS OF THE PAST: Music historians Gary Cavanagh and Matt Webster

Number One hit - followed by late 1970s New Wave and 80s and 90s pop and rock. Among the rarities are former Turner Prize winner Elizabeth Price, from Bradford, who was in Oxford-based indie band Talulah Gosh.

"As we write and research Volume 3, which will take the story from 1999 to 2009, a lot of older material which we knew about but couldn't find or, in some cases, knew

nothing about, keeps turning up," says Gary. "We do our best to include this 'missing music' as extra CDs and update the story of these bands and songs in the preface of the next volume of the books. This is part of Bradford's musical legacy - it's simply too good to be lost to posterity and deserves to be heard by a wider audience."

Gary and Matt find their 'missing music' searching second-hand

record stores and websites and also have tracks sent to them. "Matt's a genius at audio restoration and digital editing," says Gary. "We can usually make a scratched old seven-inch single or hiss-filled cassette sound like a freshly recorded song, or as close as we can get."

Volume One of the book covers 1967 to 1987, Volume Two 1988 to 1998, and Volume Three takes the story from 1999 to 2009.

Missing Music 5 includes: Three Good Reasons singing Beatles classic Nowhere Man, which topped the Dutch charts in 1966; Pretty Girl by Hogsnort Rupert's Original Flagon Band, featuring Bradford's Ian Terry (1970); Rivington Pike's Wish A Little Love (1972), a collectable single by Bradford Cabaret band featuring Mike Berry of Lorraine & The Baht'ats; Lonely Long Lady (1973) by Kindness, the second incarnation of Bradford rockers Smokie; Jovial Crew by Keighley folk band Johnny Lad (1973) Rock Show(1980) by Cleckheaton new wave band Excel; Kiki Dee and Elton John's 1976 hit Don't Go Breaking My Heart; and Silver Screen Girls (1980), the only single by short-lived Queensbury band Photograph.

● For more about the CD, visit bradfordnoise.com

Emma Clayton

LONG-LOST SONGS FROM CITY'S POP MUSIC PAST

Emma Clayton on an album of Bradford's "missing music", from sitcom song to City anthem

4

There are now 22 CDs worth of music collected to accompany the books. The first four CDs were released with *Bradford's Noise Of The Valleys Volume One*, followed by two *Missing Music* CDs collecting songs we didn't have available at the time the first set was released. both *The Missing Music* and *The Missing Music 2* cover the period of the first book, 1967-1987.

Bradford's Noise Of The Valleys Volume 2 was accompanied by a 6 CD box set which featured different genres. Following that, a double CD set - *The Missing Music 3 & 4* was released in 2014 with a selection of recently found tracks and lost classics from the period covered by the first two books to date

The Missing Music series continued with The Missing Music 5 (2016),The Missing Music 6 (2019), The Missing Music 7 (2023), The Missing Music 8 (2024), The Missing Music 9 Indie/Pop! (2025).

There are also two CDs with music from a small town we discovered just outside Bradford, called Leeds. *Leeds Noise Of The Valleys CD 1* and *Leeds Noise Of The Valleys CD 2* are also available to the discerning enthusiast.

Tracklistings for all Bradford Noise CDs appear at the back of this book.

Various – Bradford's Noise of the Valleys: The Missing Music 3&4 (Bradford Noise Records) bradfordnoise.com
Gary Cavanagh knows how to make big pictures on a limited canvas. He has previously run the record label for Bradford's autonomous venue the 1in12 Club – a shining beacon of resourcefulness and a DIY spirit. This edition of Noise from the Valleys collects forgotten singles and overlooked album tracks recorded in Bradford from 1966 to 1998. Renegade bluesman Champion Jack Dupree settled outside of Halifax long enough to open up this bizarre, eclectic comp. Spacerockers Vex are literally out-of-this-world with Project Alien Emotion while Anti System's punk-metal crossover, Guido's synthpop and Bradford Kids' saccharine Christmas Song highlight the hopeless endeavour of defining a 1980s sound. Short-lived quirksters Mash-M push boundaries, as quick as hair metallers Lost Weekend erect them. My Dying Bride are my fave 90s contribution, although the gypsy lounge of L'Orchestre du Cafe and the madcap Trip and Stumble's Ovaltinies song run close seconds. Sometimes you can get lost in the present and retro is too selective, but Noise from the Valleys gives a panoramic view of Bradford's music scene and a taste of its beauty and diversity.

VARIOUS
★★★★

Bradford's Noise Of The Valleys – The Missing Music 5, 1966-1996
(BRADFORD NOISE) www.bradfordnoise.com

Matt Webster and Gary Cavanagh continue their exhaustive documentation of Bradford's musical past (with a third book and a sixteenth CD now in preparation). This fifteenth CD offers an extraordinary variety via twenty-four tracks recorded between 1966 and 1996. Among the familiar are local girl Kiki Dee alongside Elton John on their hit, 'Don't Go Breaking My Heart', Talulah Gosh with the twee-pop 'Beatnik Boy', The Godfathers (drummer from Bradford) with 'She Gives Me Love' and nearly-men The Invaders offering 'Rock Methodology'.

Of the heavy rockers Kindness impress with their Free-style 'Lonely Long Lady' while Stormtrooper turn it up several notches on 'Grind'n'Heat'. There's folk: Jovial Crew's seafaring Irish sing-along 'Johnny Lad', the pure voice of Janet Jones on 'Silver Coin', Hebric's rousing version of the traditional 'Blow The Candles Out' and a jaunty, Jethro Tull-ish instrumental 'Imaginary Lady' from Titan.

The post-punk tracks are among the best on here. They include The Donkeys with their punch-pop 'Four Letters', the should-have-made-it-big Silver Screen Girls with their excellent 'Photograph', Excel sounding very Bay City Rollers on 'Rock Show' and Clouded Fish sounding sharp on 'Expect'. Few cities have their music culture so remembered. Lucky Bradford!
Nick Toczek

Double dose of regional tracks

ALBUM

Gary Cavanagh, who has released another album of tracks by local bands that spans four decades

MUSIC historians have released another album of songs recorded by Keighley and Bradford acts over four decades.

The Missing Music 3 and 4 is a double CD of 'lost' tracks from bands and solo performers in a range of styles, including heavy rock, folk and goth.

Many of the songs have not been heard for years, but have been rescued from the collections of former band members and fans of yesteryear.

Among Keighley bands featured are Dawnwatcher – the town's biggest act of the late 70s – thrash outfit Mannix and hard rockers Rattlesnake Shake.

They rub shoulders with acts like Joolz, with War Of Attrition, and top Bradford band Smokie.

Liz Narey, who performs at Keighley acoustic nights, has contributed her 1982 recording *Ships Out Of Sligo*.

The album has been compiled by Gary Cavanagh and Matt Webster, who are halfway through writing a four-volume history of the district's music scene.

Gary released the first volume of Bradford's Noise Of The Valleys several years ago, chronicling the golden years of Bradford's music scene up to the late 1980s. A second volume with Matt Webster, covering the 10 years from 1988, was reeased last year.

Between the two books Gary and Matt released *The Missing Music 1 and 2*, featuring many of the tracks they could not find before publication.

And now – as the pair continue writing a third volume covering up to 2009 – they have released a second double album of newly-recovered tracks.

As par of this research, the pair are appealing to *Keighley News* readers for information on The Pipers and The Undecided, who for several years were both major players on the Keighley music scene. Email matt@bradfordnoise.com if you are able to help.

The Noise Of The Valleys books and CDs are on sale at Keighley Musicians Centre in Russell Street.

Do you have a leisure story? get in touch by e-mail via david.knights @keighleynews.co.uk

Keighley News, 2013

VARIOUS
★★★★

Bradford's Noise Of The Valleys – The Missing Music 6, 1966-1996
(BRADFORD NOISE) www.bradfordnoise.com

Matt Webster and Gary Cavanagh continue their exhaustive documentation of Bradford's musical past (third book and sixteenth CD imminent). This fifteenth CD has true gems among its twenty-four tracks from 1966 to 1996.

There are interesting tracks featuring local guitar legends Allan Holdsworth and John Verity alongside songs from many nearly-bands including second single 'Stay' from Fassbender/Russell (one-hit wonders with their debut 'Twilight Café'), 'Eastern Eyes' from Anglo-Asian outfit Boys From The East, 'One Fine Morning' from U.S. soul singer (relocated to Yorkshire) Tommy Hunt, and Stormer's 'My Home Town' recorded for Ringo Starr's Ring O' Records.

Surprisingly, opening track 'Dear Mother, Love Albert' from *The Likely Lads* star, Rodney Bewes (co-written with Manfred Mann's Mike Hugg) is a stand-out, as are singles from both Skeletal Family ('She Cries Alone') and New Model Army ('Green & Grey').

However, tracks twelve to sixteen are pure gold. They are the bass'n'drums-heavy 'Kissed To Pieces' by The Headmen, the funky 'New Musical Testament' by Joy, the heavy dub of Rootsman's 'Tremors', the marvellous 'Mask' by singer-guitarist Jon Harrison, and, from Grim, the unforgettable 'F***kin' Weird, Mate' featuring the line '[You're] so thick you can't blink quick.'

Nick Toczek

R'n'R 79, Jan/Feb 2020

VARIOUS

★★★★★

Leeds – Noise Of The Valleys
(BRADFORD NOISE) www.bradfordnoise.com

With their third encyclopaedic book nearing completion and countless CDs released, all platforming Bradford music, author-archivists Matt Webster and Gary Cavanagh take a timely detour to reference Leeds, less than ten miles away. These twenty-one tracks testify to the crucial role Leeds played in redefining pop culture between 1978 and 1987.

The Mekons' 'Never Been In A Riot' shakes the comfort out of punk. Gang Of Four's 'Love Like Anthrax' proves an exercise in musical deconstruction. Delta 5's 'Mind Your Own Business' is infectiously edgy. 'Alice' shows Sisters Of Mercy at their iconoclastic peak. Ditto for their underrated sidekicks, The March Violets. The Three Johns never disappoint. Chumbawamba make musical resistance marvellous. Akimbo offer proto-rap. Age Of Chance are percussively perfect.

There's blatant commerciality, too. Expelaires pump pure reggae-fied pop punk. Music For Pleasure create lo-fi lovability, as do Soft Cell with their compulsive camp cover of 'Tainted Love'. Girls At Our Best! are joyously just that.

Genre greats include jazz-rock perfection via The Volunteers' 'Francis' and Upside Down's 'Dead Man's Clothes', space-rock from Dance Chapter, slices of pub-rock-swallows-punk from Knife Edge and Salvation, shlock-rock from The Batfish Boys, solid soul from Zoot And The Roots, and full-fat funk from Son Of Sam.

Nick Toczek

Below are two staff recommendations from the Jumbo Records website, from 2023 and 2024.

Gary Kavanagh is now well known for his incredible books that delve into the bands and musical trees of Bradford music and releases, he's a grafter and a do'er and after reading Richard Rouska's great book on the Leeds music scene he realised that there wasn't any great Leeds retrospective comps available so he did one himself! This is a cracking comp with some amazing tracks from the post-punk/DIY/goth scenes from 1978-1987. Highlights for me include the awesome Son Of Sam, Salvation, Danse Chapter and Expelaires.

Staff Recommendations

Gary Cavanagh has done it again, delving like the music obsessive he is, deep down into the Leeds music scene and coming up with more treasure. From post-punk, rock n roll, indie pop, goth and jazzy joints this uncovers some great talents that mainly didn't ever get the spotlight and a few who massively did.

A heroic effort from the ever dependable, hardworking grafter who has done such an amazing scene documenting the Bradford scene that he surely needs to be recognised for his efforts...Sir Cavanagh awaits.

By Matt Bradshaw

CHAPTER 1: 1999-2000

It's time to party like it's 1999! The new millennium dawned, that once unimaginable year by which time we were all supposed to be living in unbridled luxury, riding around in flying cars with robots seeing to our every need and taking regular holidays on the moon or Mars. However, in this fair city of Bradford, things were not quite like that just yet.

These fabulous futuristic events had not reached The Boy And Barrell (above) on Westgate which was still enjoying regular Karaoke nights and had hardly changed since it was seen in the classic 1959 film *Room At The Top*, adapted from the novel by Bingley author John Braine. (1)

At the beginning of the year, a new bunch of local bands emerged on the scene, including **Parky** (from Baildon), **Suburban Fish** and **Mantra**.

A NORTHERN SCREAM

Fagley based label In Yer Face Records (run by Blade frontman Billy Allen) released its fifth compilation CD, *A Northern Scream*, in early 1999, featuring mainly Bradford, Halifax and Leeds based bands.

The four Bradford bands showcased were Blade, Quantico, The Jon Does and **Substance**.

Baildon based rock band **Quantico** contributed the track *Shall I Lie?* which was taken from their recent five-track demo *Into The Night*.

During their appearance on local Bradford Community Broadcasting show *Cable Beat* the band were surprised to find out that their session was being listened to in the USA when they were emailed on air by history teacher Michael Littman in Florida to say he was enjoying their music.

The Jon Does track *Major League* appeared on *A Northern Scream Volume 1* and a second track of theirs appeared on the later *Volume 2*.

The band managed to finance two cassette EPs, *Funhog*, in September 1998, and *The Same Old Story*, in May 1999 both recorded at Pots'n'Panz Studio on Manchester Road.

A local pop-punk five-piece, they were led by Dan on vocals and Phil on lead guitar. They had supported the likes of UK Subs and The Vibrators and were regulars at Rio's.

OOBERMAN

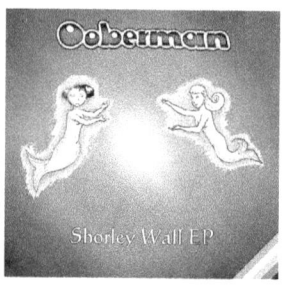

Ooberman singer Dan Popplewell and guitarist Andy Flett met at Buttershaw School in Bradford in 1988 and formed the band The Forestry Commission, with Andy's younger brother Steve on bass.

The band split after Dan moved to Liverpool, followed by Steve in 1992 and then Andy in 1997, where Ooberman were formed after the addition of drummer Alan Kelly and Liverpool lass Sophia Churney on vocals and keyboards.

Their quirky mix of humorous and touching lyrics and experimental indie-pop style won them the 1997 BT Merseyside Arts Award for Best Newcomers shortly after playing their first gigs and recording some demos.

Blur's Graham Coxon was impressed enough to release their first single *Sugar Bum / Tears From A Willow* on his Transcopic label in 1998.

Their next release was the *Shorley Wall EP*, on Tugboat Records, after which they signed to Independiente Records to release the single *Blossoms Falling*, which was their highest UK chart hit, reaching number 39.

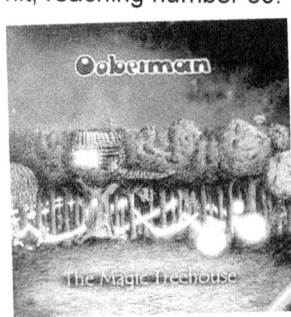

In 1999 they released their debut LP, *The Magic Treehouse*, on Independiente Records. The album was produced by Stephen Street who was known for his work with the likes of Blur and Morrissey.

Four singles were released to promote the album, including new versions of *Shorley Wall*, which reached number 47, and *Tears From A Willow*, 62.

In 2000 the band began work on their second album, the more experimental and introspective *Hey Petrunko*, which took three years to complete.

The single *Dolphin Blue* was released on the Rough Trade label in December 2000.

They released a mini LP and single, both called *Running Girl*, in 2001. The EP *Bluebell Morning* and the single *Beany Bean* followed in 2002, all on Dan Popplewell's own Rotodisc label.

Hey Petrunko was finally finished and released in 2003 alongside the single *First Day Of The Holidays* both on Rotodisc. The band folded soon after.

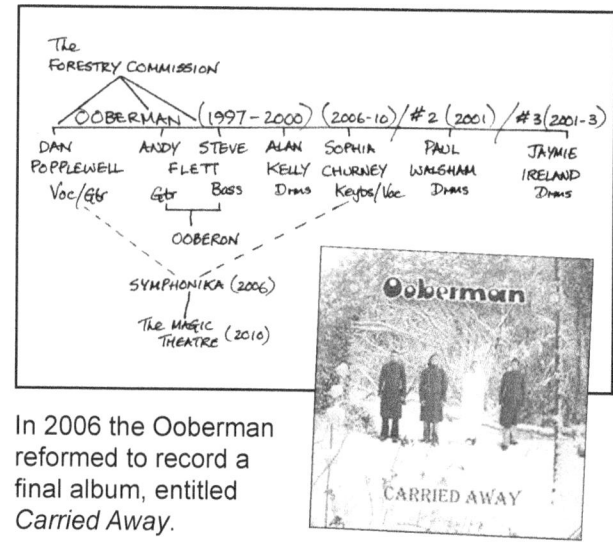

In 2006 the Ooberman reformed to record a final album, entitled *Carried Away*.

The bands' related activities include an orchestral side-project by Dan Popplewell as Symphonika entitled *The Snow Queen* which featured the Royal Liverpool Philharmonic Orchestra and also had Sophia Churney on vocals, released on Rotodisc in 2007.

In February 2007 Bradford brothers Andy and Steve Flett released the album *Waiting For The Sonic Boom* under the name Ooberon. The album featured other members of Ooberman on various tracks.

The last Ooberman release to date came out in September 2007 and was a collection of rare recordings made over the band's lifetime, *The Lost Tapes - Rare Recordings 1991-2007*.

Dan and Sophia released the album *London Town* in 2010, under the name The Magic Theatre.

Diamond of a record by Tony the local lad...

With his exotic name and bronzed looks, Tony Pensavalle should really be from somewhere like Bologna rather than Bolton Woods.

His crooning voice is pure easy listening and owes plenty to people like another Tony - Bennett - and his idol Neil Diamond. There's even a silky version of Love On The Rocks here.

Recorded at Carl Stipetic's In A City studio in Bradford, *On Days Like These* (TFP CD001) features 17 favourites ranging from oldies like Nat King Cole's Unforgettable to covers of more modern smoothies like George Michael.

SMOOTHIE: *Tony Pensaville*

It is on sale at Virgin Megastore and at all of Tony's gigs. You can catch him at Manningham Ward Labour Club tonight, Clayton Heights Working Men's Club tomorrow, the Victoria in Allerton on March 11, the Gable End in Bradford Moor on March 16 and the Jade Palace in Rawdon on March 26.

He also has other bookings in February and March throughout the region.

CRIME

This goth ensemble had been together for over ten years on the local scene, but only played sporadically.

By early 1999 the band had released the self produced CD single, *Defiance*, which was available at their gigs.

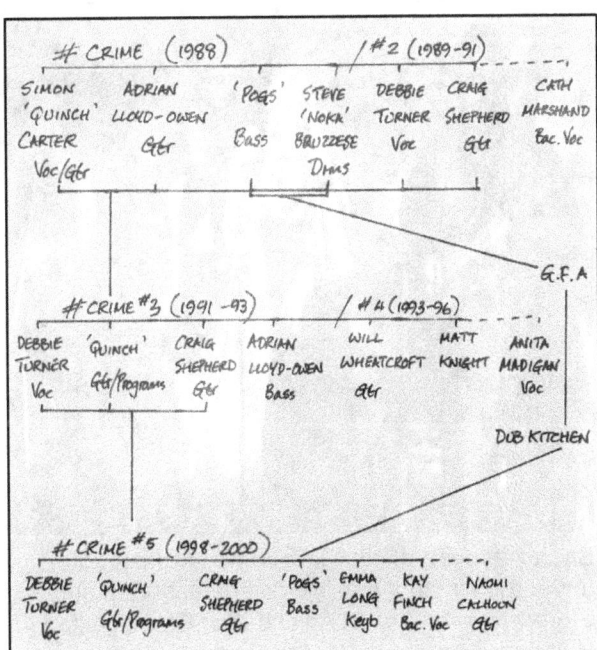

On the January 30 1999, local rock act Terrorvision scored a No 2 hit in the singles chart with *Tequila* on their Total Vegas label. It stayed in the charts for ten weeks. The track was inspired by the 1958 hit of the same name, originally done by The Champs, and original writer Chuck Rio is co-credited on the Terrorvision version of song. The single was produced by Edwyn Collins, formerly of Scottish band Orange Juice, and appears on their fourth album, *Shaving Peaches*.

IDIOTBOX

IdiotBox formed at the end of 1998 when newly-relocated Durham band That Man There found themselves in need of a bass player and singer. They recruited former Bullweek bass player Rick Bolton, and quickly changed direction from their Sarah Records-influenced indie-pop sound to the quirky pop/rock style they have since become known for.

The original IdiotBox line-up of Rick Bolton (guitar/vocals), Mickey Motorvator (bass), and remaining That Man There players Adam Cockburn (guitar) and Gaz Pugh (drums) recorded a three-song demo, but within a year or so, Mickey had left, and Adam had been replaced by Ben Holden (who went on to form This Et Al, and Dolphins) and Steven Wilson (This Et Al, Dinosaur Pile-Up, Hawk Eyes) became the new drummer, with Gaz moving to bass. This band recorded another five-song demo and played a memorable set in front of hundreds at a festival in Bradford's Centenary Square in 2000.

Shortly afterwards, this line-up had broken up under the strain of musical differences. Ben and Ste left to form This Et Al, and Idiot Box recruited Hull-based drummer Kristian Barford, but another extended period of short-term guitarists ensured the band were unable to capitalise on their burgeoning success despite writing some of their best material.

Eventually, Kris left, and was replaced by one-time (and major IdiotBox influence) Cardiacs drummer Mark Cawthra. In 2003, the band attempted to record their debut album at Mark's home studio, but the departure of long-standing bass player Gaz (who joined Bradford punks Lowlife UK), then-guitarist Ben Holden (who had briefly rejoined), and the loss of the recordings themselves, knocked the band back yet again.

IdiotBox regrouped with the return of Kris (drums) and Gaz (bass), along with Russ Petcher on guitar, seeing another burst of great material. Russ left within six months, and the band responded with an expanded line-up with former Western Dance and Bullweek bassist Ade Clark, and the addition of keyboards played by newcomer Rebecca Stubbs, while Gaz moved to guitar.

In 2013 they released their first vinyl 7 inch single, *Valentine / Figurine,* on clear vinyl on former Negatives bass player Bob Robinson's London based label Curious Fox Records.

Their self-titled 12-track debut album, recorded at Voltage Studios, was released in 2016. The track *Drop Dead Darling* appeared on a *Vive Le Rock Magazine* cover-mounted CD comp later that year.

Sadly, Rick Bolton passed away in 2018.

In 2025, as a tribute to Rick, former guitarist/bassist/drummer Gareth Pugh released an album of previously unrecorded songs by the band on which he sang and played all the instuments. *WXYZ Is Zhe Yew FXWk* by IdiotBox was released on Bandcamp.

> **9. IDIOTBOX – Drop Dead Darling**
> Bradford's Idiot-Box have been around for some time, gigging solidly and counting Mark Cawthra of the Cardiacs as a former member. Taken from their self-titled debut album, this alt-rock tune is undeniably infectious and fun.

CHAPTER 1 — 1999 - 2000

IDIOT BOX / YEAR DOT / KWAI CHANG CAINE

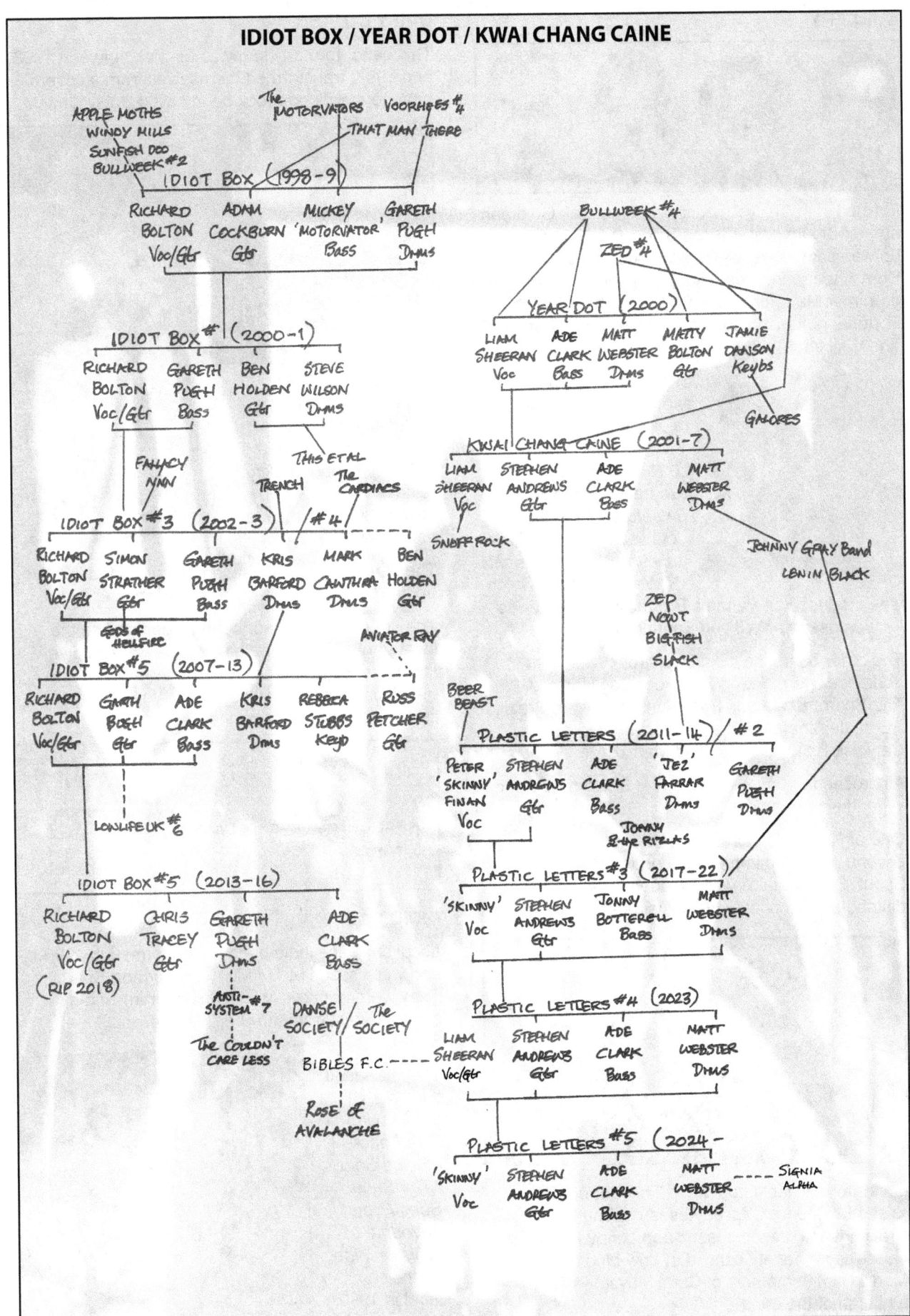

NURSERY

Formed in 1997 by American guitarist Zak Goldman and ex-Bloom singer Innes Stiles, the Nursery line-up was soon completed by the addition of bassist Dom Sheard, from defunct local band Green, and drummer Matt Fortune (younger brother of 'Fluff' Fortune, guitarist of local Pink Floyd cover band Off The Wall fame).

The band produced two demo tapes, before releasing a three track self titled CD. In 2001, they contributed two tracks, *8 pm* and *Sweetbread,* to the double compilation CD *Junction 47- The Cream Of West Yorkshire* which was produced by Panama Productions, the Leeds venue Joseph's Well and Sponge Studios.

The other bands on the CD, all from West Yorkshire, were; Being 747, Four Day Hombre, The Scaramanga Six, Parisman, Mr Shiraz. Brazil, AEon, Japanare, Mama Scuba, Lorimer, 5' 4", Catylyst, Eightysix, Visa and Mariko.

All proceeds from the CD went to St Gemma's and Wheatfields Hospices.

One of Nursery's tracks *Spectacle,* from their second demo, so impressed London based Talent Scout agency that is was included on a CD being distributed amongst industry insiders.

On March 19, local pop group **The Gillettes** raised £2,609 for Cancer Research. The trio, Craig Joseph, Jason Joseph and Lenny Raymond, performed a benefit concert at Low Moor Working Men's Club in memory of Carol Maystone, who was a big fan of the band.

DAISY CUTTER

This band, formerly know as Mr Mak between 1993 and 1997, transformed themselves from a covers band to a slick pop rock band called Daisy Cutter.

After 1997, the band were writing their own material, and the result was their debut CD album, *Perfect Landing*, released on their own Glass House label in early 1999.

The album was self financed and recorded locally at the Potz'n'Panz Studios on Manchester Road.

They managed a minor coup by persuading the local Virgin Megastore to stock the CD and give them their own 'listening post' in the shop where the album was on play repeatedly for customers to listen to through headphones.

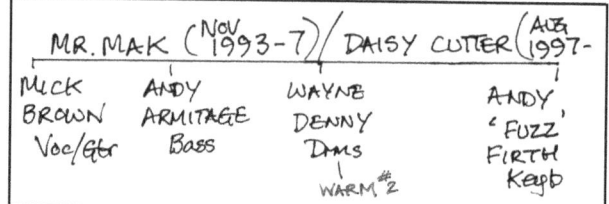

INDIQA

Local six-piece indie band Indiqa formed in 1998 and were based at Try Mills on Thornton Road. They were apparently 'big in Rotheram' and had some interest from the Stereo MC's label Gee Street.

They released a 4 track CD EP, *Praying To A Fence / Flying Solo / The Shoe Song / Your Favourite Word Is Mine*, on their own label in 1999.

CHAPTER 1   1999 - 2000

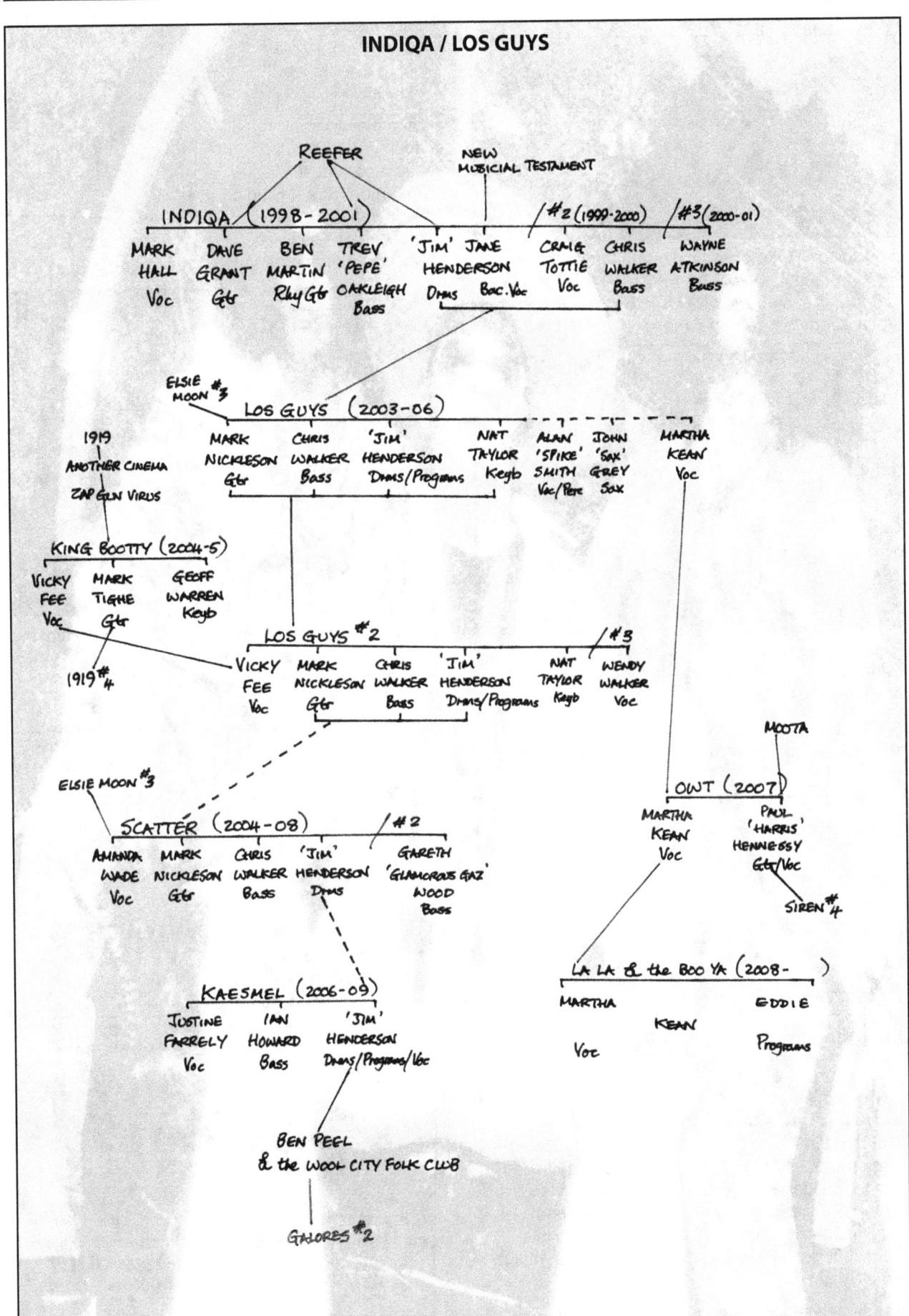

15

WATER

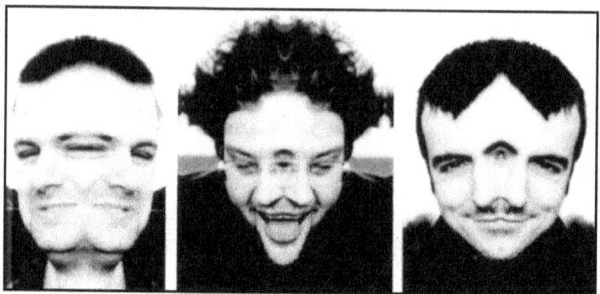

Four-piece Wyke-based indie-pop band, Water, were formed in 1995. They recorded a four-song demo at Sunny Bank Studios in Ripponden which got a good review from Simon Ashberry in the T&A.

They played around the local music scene at venues like The Love Apple and the Duchess Of York in Leeds.

Water appeared at the Music In The Sun Festival at the Don Valley Stadium, Sheffield, where Cleopatra and Chaka Demus & Pliars were also on the bill.

The band headlined a free all-dayer at the Beehive pub on Westgate, on June 24th 1999, organised by their managers Joe and Alan as Shandyland, in support of the Bradford Festival. The other seven local indie-pop bands on that day from 2 till late were Flat Back Four, Facelift, Slide, Radius, Indiqa, Nursery and Lapdog.

Singer Jez left in 1999 and the band continued as a three-piece with guitarist David Hemmingway taking over as lead vocalist.

Their eleven-track album, *Monkey Steps*, was recorded at Beaumont Street Studios, Huddersfield. It was released on CD in 2000 on the Belle Records label and was 'handmade in Halifax'.

Water folded in 2001 and singer David Hemingway went on the play solo under the name Sol Gravy before reuniting with Ruchard Furness and Mark Redman as the first line-up of the band Galores.

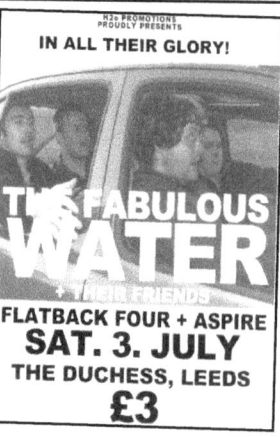

CHAPTER 1 — 1999 - 2000

WATER / NURSERY / LABORATORY NOISE

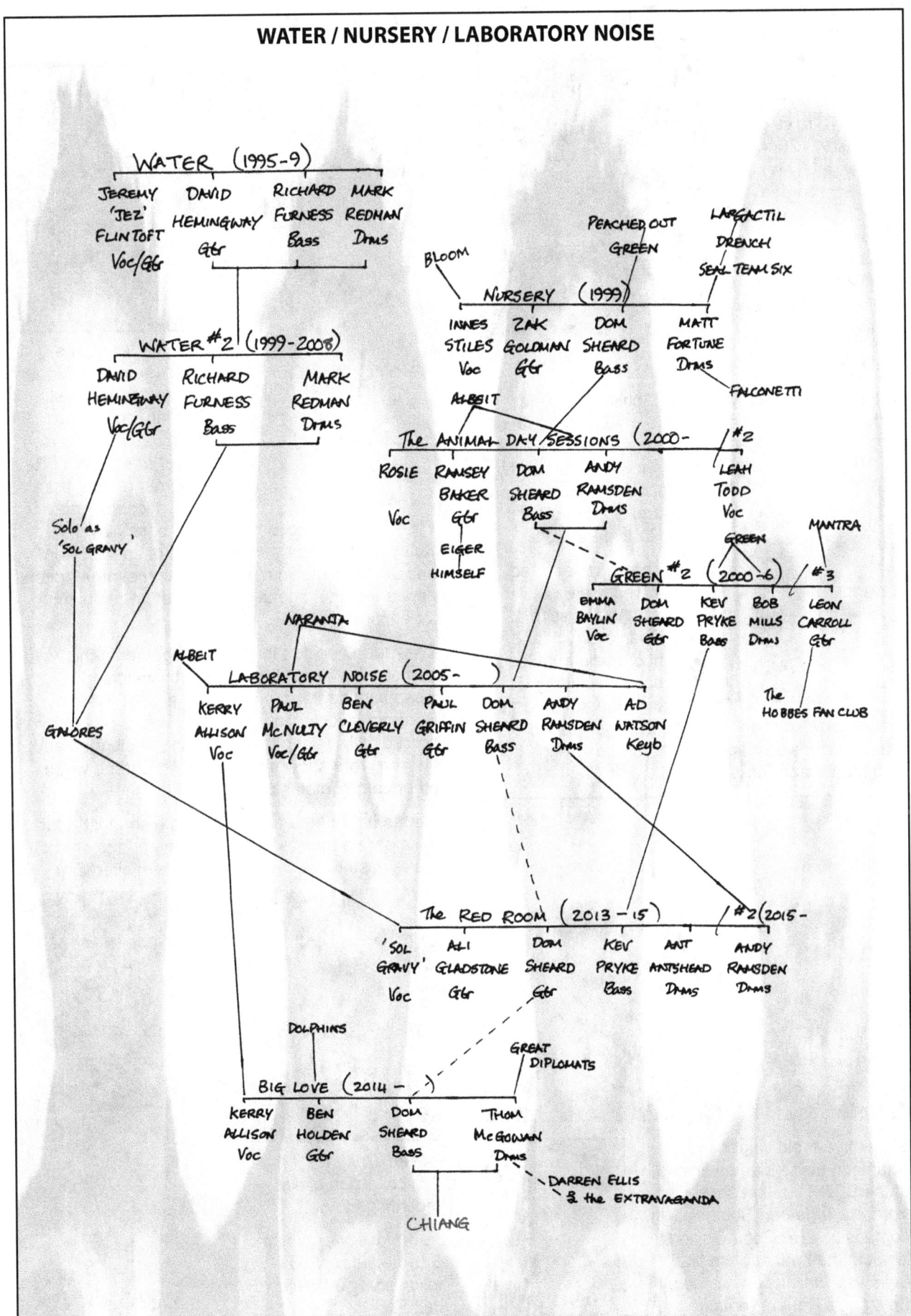

Bradford Bulls' Robbie Paul and singer Anita Madigan made a guest appearance on St Luke's Hospital Radio 573 to celebrate the station's 20th anniversay. The pair had just recorded a version of the disco classic *Ain't No Stopping Us Now* with Robbie's brother and team mate Henry Paul.

MAD FOR IT

Not to be confused with the ITV children's series of the same name which ran from 1998-2000, this short-lived cable TV show was hosted by singer Anita Madigan and Bradford Bull's Robbie Paul.

The show featured interviews with comedians such as Charlie Chuck and had music from local bands including Us, which featured former Architect guitarist and Voltage Studios supremo Tim Walker alongside Happiness Ad/Blood Orange duo Rob Moore and Ricky Howard.

Sixteen year old singer Jodie Adamson made it to the final of the BBC TV talent show *Get Your Act Together*. She her own composition *He Got It Going On* for both the heat and the final of the show, which was hosted by Boyzone's Ronan Keating

RED SKY COVEN

This quartet of was made up of New Model Army frontman Justin Sullivan, poet Joolz Denby and Kent based singer and guitarist Rev Hammer (solo artist also known for working with The Levellers), accompanied by bass player Brett Selby. They performed a mixture of spoken word and acoustic music numbers, with the three writers appearing on stage separately before teaming up for encores.

The group decided to perform together in this format after being disillusioned by watching disappointing performances on a night out at a Bradford folk club in the 1980s. They performed sporadically, taking their travelling unplugged and spoken word show on tour around Europe when other commitments allowed.

In March 1999 the quartet began a short UK tour to celebrate their tenth anniversary and to promote the release of their double CD album, *Red Sky Coven, Volumes 1 & 2*, a collection of live recordings to date.

Red Sky Coven Volume 3 came out on 2001 followed by a *Volume 5* in 2009.

THE LOVED ONES

Another local band who had been around for quite a few years but only played intermittently were The Loved Ones. The band featured former 1919 vocalist Ian Tilleard and original Somebody's Brother guitarist Vince Deary. They released their quirky, self-produced album, *Self Destruction For Beginners*, on CD in 2006.

Three members of the band later continued as Henry's Radio with former Vex bassist Rik Ironmonger.

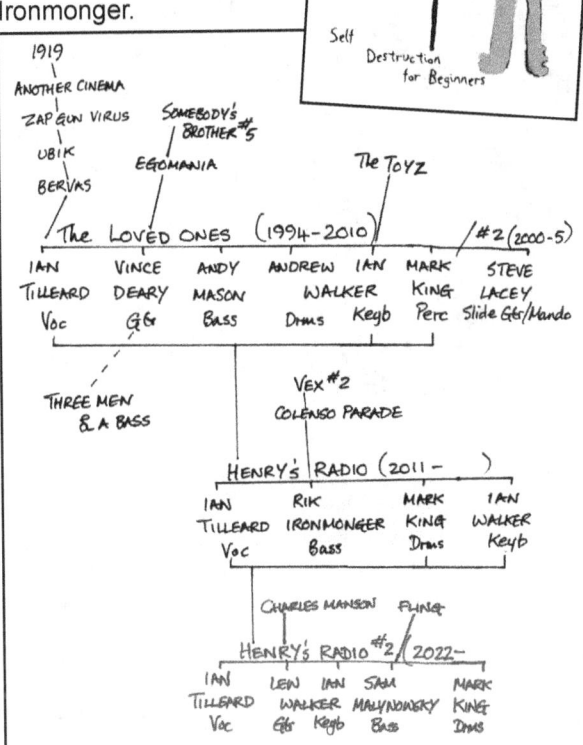

ALPINE MOVEMENT

This six-piece local indie band with rap and dance influences started in 1998 and played many gigs locally until they initially split in 2003.

They produced a four song CD featuring the tracks *Homeless / Do You Wanna Get Down? / Satellite / Get Down* in 2001.

Alpine Movement made a short comeback in 2009 with a new dtrummer on board.

They later continued under the name of Vandal Supreme.

NATO GOES TO WAR

On March 24, 1999, for the first time in its 50 year history, the North Atlantic Treaty Organisation (NATO) Pact countries went to war by bombing Serbia in reaction to its attacks on the former Yugoslavian province of Kosova.

Serbian President Slobodan Milosevic's nationalist forces had carried out 'ethnic cleansing' massacres between 15-17 January at Recak, near the Kosovan capital Pristina, against mainly Muslim victims. Nato planes flew over 3,000 bombing missions between March-June forcing the Serbs into an extensive system of underground shelters, a relic of the Tito era.

After 80 days of aerial bombing by NATO, Serbia was forced to surrender and NATO peace keepers moved in to Kosova and refugees returned to their homeland. (2)

THE ROCK / HEAVY METAL SCENE

Bradford has long been a haven for heavy rockers. From the late 1960s to the end of the twentieth century, Bradford had a strong and healthy stream of bands plying their wears on the local rock-metal scene. In addition to the resurgence of heavy rock with the New Wave Of British Heavy Metal (NWOBHM) in the late 1990s, there also developed a range of crossover sub-genre styles such as thrash, stoner, doom, dark and pagan metal.

HYPNOSIS

Formed in 1993, this local band set about fusing the groove of 1970s rock with the sharp riffs of old school thrash metal, producing ever increasing dynamic overtones.

The result of over ten years of constant writing, recording and gigging in bars, clubs and venues in the North and Midlands of England led to several line-up changes.

In 2005 they released their ten track self-titled *Hypnosis* album on CD, recorded at Dewsbury's Academy Studios.

Their track *Unopposed* featured on the Bradford Council sponsored compilation CD *Bradford A2E*, released in 2009.

CONQUEST OF STEEL

Formed in 1997, Conquest Of Steel would become one of the finest exponents of Bradford metal.

Their self-released four-track EP *Priests Of Metal*, released in 1998, gained them many fans who loved

the 'old school' values of their metal style, and the track *Steel Is The Law* became a live anthem.

2003 saw the release of *Stadiums Of Steel*, a split 12" EP featuring three tracks each from Conquest Of Steel and Evanesance.

In 2004, the band released their debut self-titled album on their No Face Records label and in 2006 released the five-track *May Your Blade Never Dull EP* which included tracks from the *Priests Of Metal EP* and new songs.

The band's second album, *Hammer & Fist*, came out the following year, again on their No Face label, followed by their third album, *Storm Sword: Rise Of The Dead Queen*, in 2009.

By 2011, Conquest Of Steel were an established band, regularly touring the UK and Europe, as they released the four-track 7" EP *Victorious In Defeat* in a gatefold sleeve. Their fourth and final album was 2013's *Of Fire & Steel* which came out on CD and red vinyl.

The band finally called it a day in after seventeen years glorying in being true 'metalheads'. (3)

In their final year, Conquest Of Steel played a number of big metal festivals including the three-day 'Kin Hell Festival at Vox, New Craven Gate, Leeds, on May 4, 2014, and Bloodstock in Walton Upon Trent on August 9, headlined by Megadeth, Emperor and Saxon.

CHAPTER 1 — 1999 - 2000

CONQUEST OF STEEL / THE BELONGING

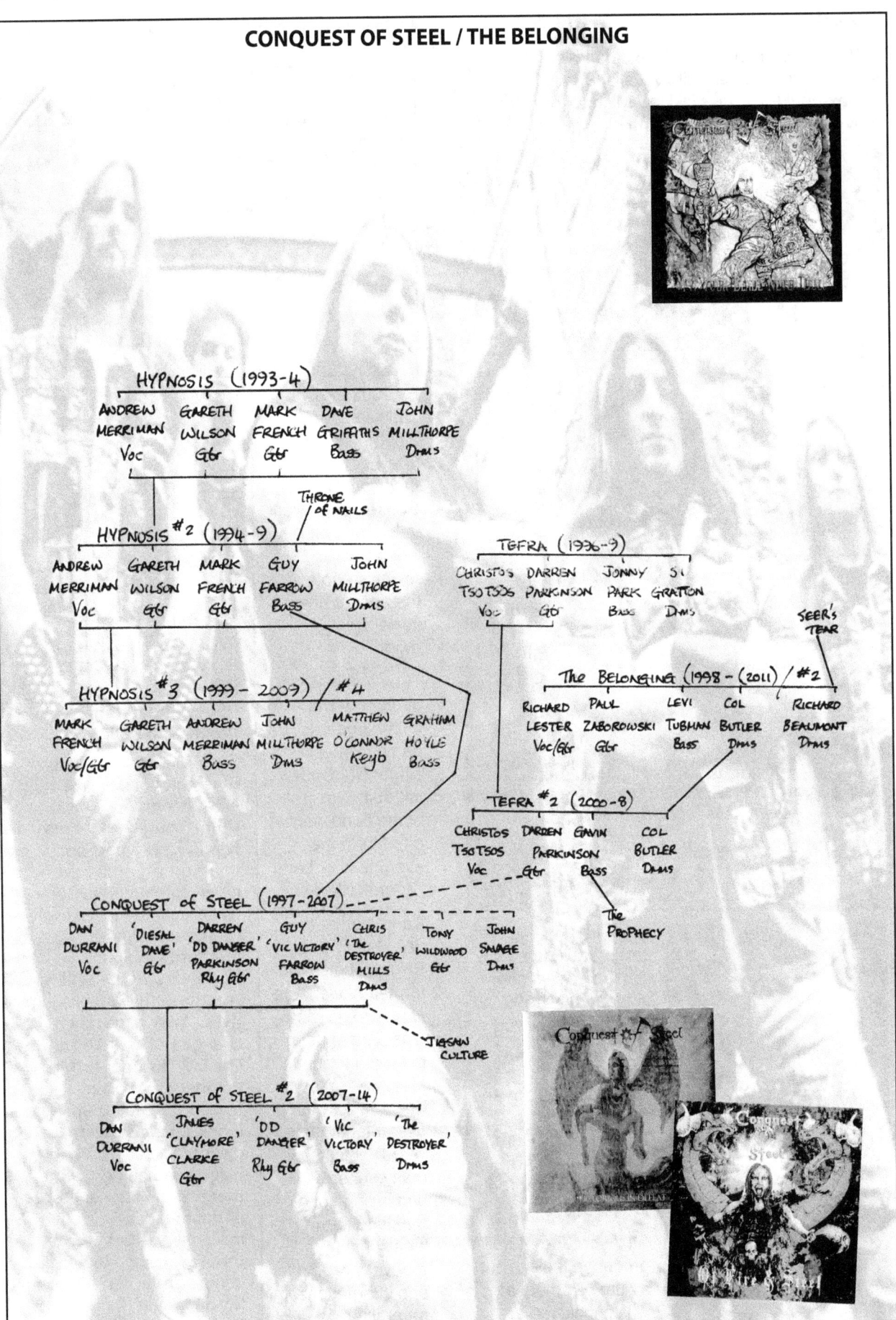

KHANG

In 1997, three members of the defunct band Serenity joined forces with vocalist Bryan Outlaw and ex-Foul Play bassist 'Daz' Miah to form the heavy-stoner-doom metal band Khang.

They released a four-track demo cassette, recorded in June 1998, at Academy Studios in Dewsbury. The tracks were *It Was Me / Flower Thing / Deep Inside* and *So Cold Inside*.

A full-on grinding rock three-track demo CD *Got To Love It* soon appeared in 1999, as the band stabilized their line-up and played with the likes of Orange Goblin and the US stoner-rock trio Karma To Burn from Morgantown, West Virginia at Rio's in April, 2000.

That year they also produced their debut album, *Premeditated*, which included an inspiring cover version of Leafhound's *Stagnant Pools*.

By 2002, the band's second album, *Worship The Evil*, on their own Bionic Conker label, was unleashed on the world to mixed reviews - note the poor review in *Kerrang!* (4) (right).

They completed another demo in 2003 before parting ways with singer Bry Outlaw in 2004. The rest of the band went on to form the even heavier band Lazarus Blackstar.

Band members Lee Baines and Bri Talbot also formed *None More Heavy* to promote gigs. They put on the regular annual *Heavy Fests* at The 1 In 12 Club over the next few years, which saw many superb and inspirational bands from the 'heavy riffing, groove rock' UK and international fraternity.

Khang
Worship The Evil
(Bionic Conker BC001CD)
KK
Debut album from Bradford metallers.

STONER ROCK has, in its time, thrown up some truly great bands.
Unfortunately, that time was five years ago, and those great bands have either split up (Kyuss) or wised up and moved away (Monster Magnet). Bradford's Khang, however, are true believers. Trouble is, they aren't Kyuss. They're not even Orange Goblin. 'Worship The Evil' is stoner-rock-by-numbers: the sort of fuzzed-up, thumbs-in-belt-loops boogie metal that gives pints of cider and black a bad name. Granted, there are occasional flashes of doom-laden malevolence, but even those are ruined by vocalist Bryan's grimly flat sub-John Garcia drone. (*DE*)

CHAPTER 1 — 1999 - 2000

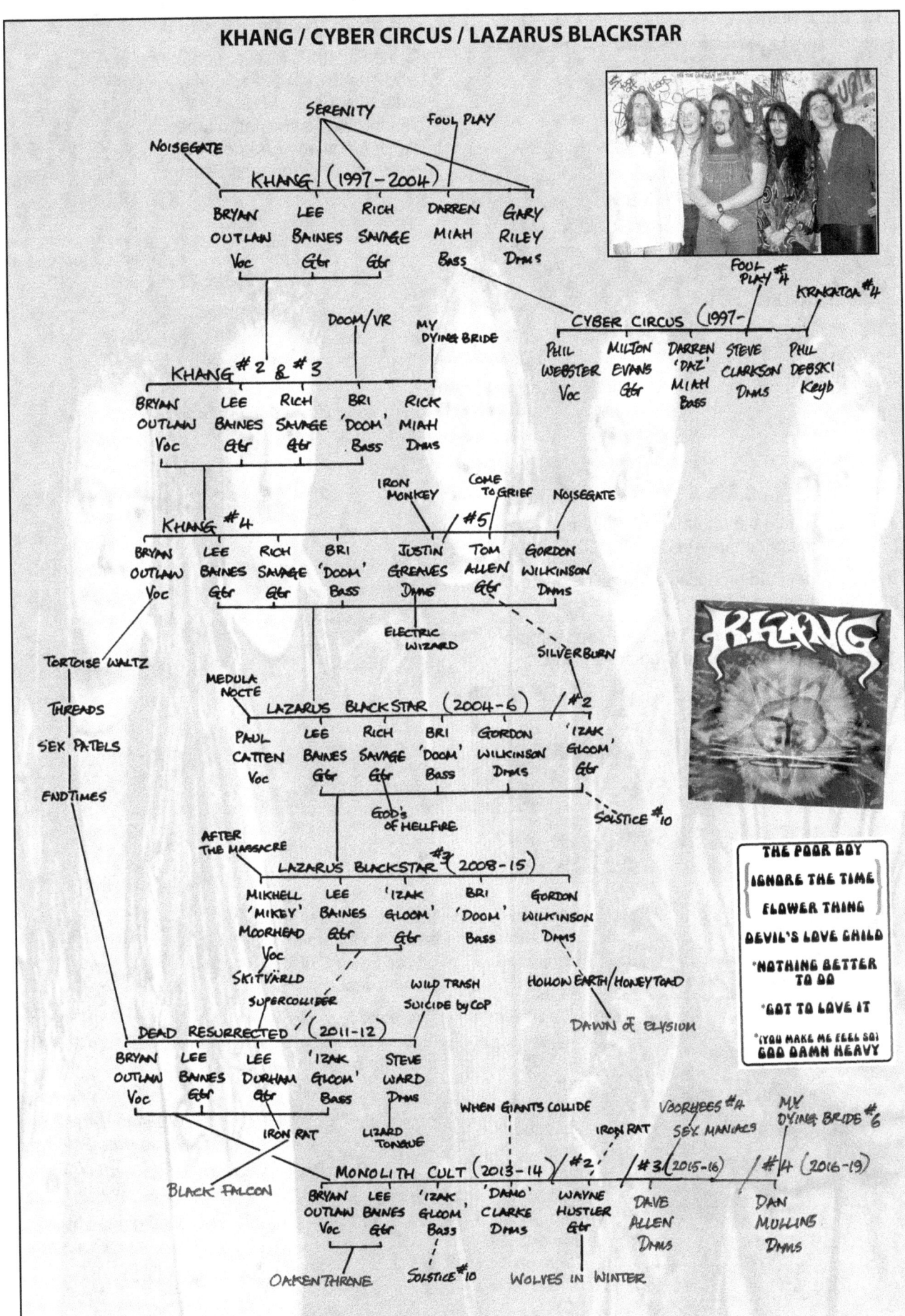

23

THE BELONGING

This black metal band formed in 1998, and produced their first three-track demo CD in 2001.

By 2003, they had produced a four-song demo entitled *Dreaming Darkness*.

Their first album, *Setting The Scene,* appeared in 2005. It was recorded at Bradford's In-A-City

Studios and released on the band's own label.

Ashes Of The Fallen Throne in 2008 became the band's second full length CD album. The Belonging's third, *An Immortal Creation,* came out in 2011.

THE ENCHANTED

Formed in 1997, local pagan metal band The Enchanted originally featured a female lead vocalist. They produced two demo tapes, *Pagan Metal* and *Freedom To Perceive* (1999) on their Sinister Realms label.

By 2000 guitarist Robb Phillpots had taken over lead vocal duties as the band released their first, self-titled album on CD on their own Sinister Realms label.

The band recorded their second CD, *Trust In Death & Rebirth*, in 2002, released again on their Sinister Realms label.

Their 2004 four-track EP, *For Those Who Fall*, was recorded by Tim Walker at Voltage Studios.

The band gigged heavily on the local rock scene, especially at Rio's and The Empress on Sunbridge Road.

CHAPTER 1 — 1999–2000

THE ENCHANTED

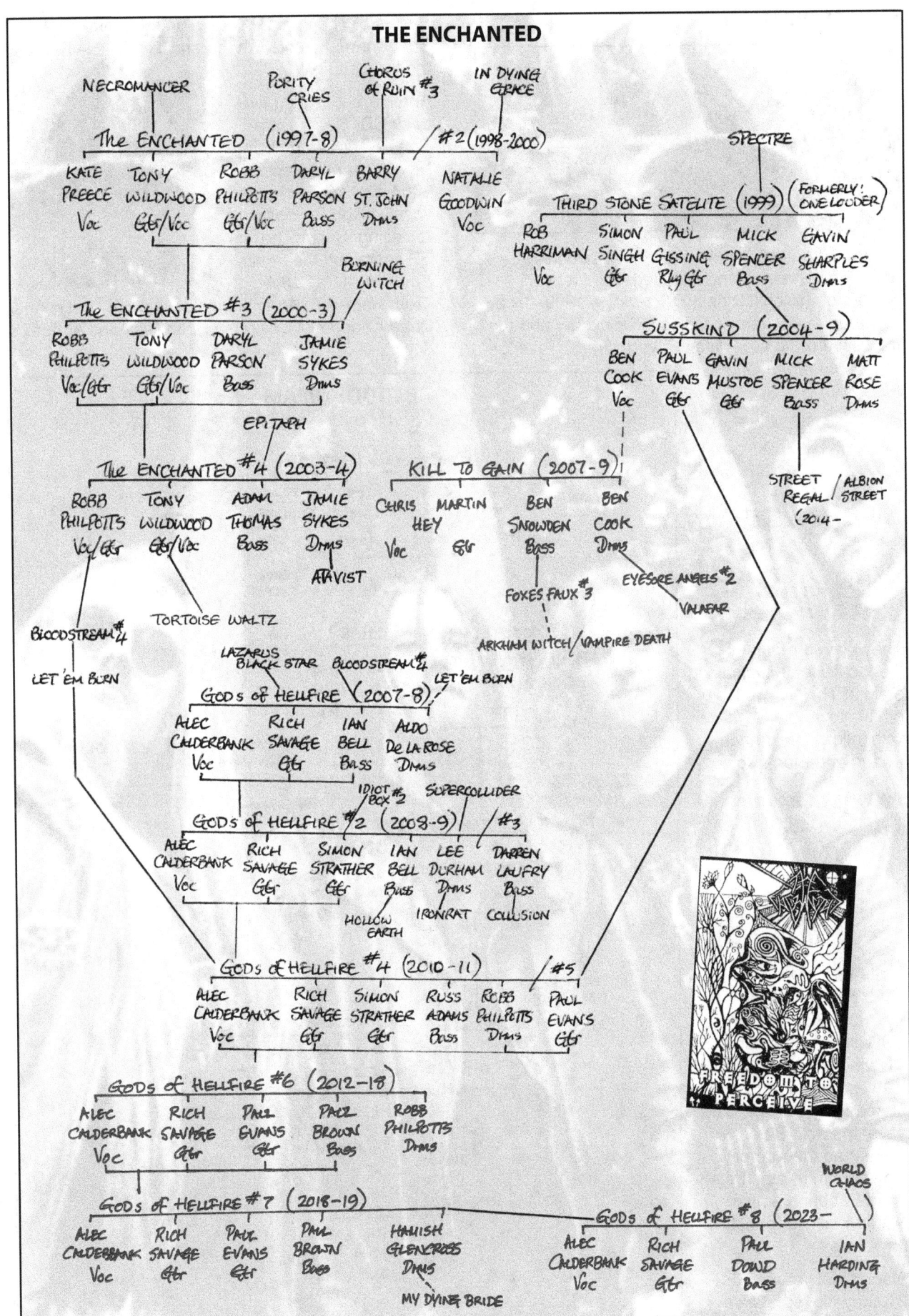

Freedom to Perceive

BLOODSTREAM

Another Bradford metal band that formed in 1997 were Bloodstream, who released their first self-issued four-track CD demo, *Scarlet*, in 1999. It was recorded at Academy Studios in Dewsbury and the tracks were *Slow Decline / Poverty Trap / Revenge Not Hate / Alone Once More*.

They played regularly on the local scene, including a gig at The 1 In 12 Club on 26 November 1999 with fellow local bands Khang and Black Rock.

By 2002, Bloodtream had released their first CD album, *Black Storm Harvest*, again recorded at Academy Studios. The seventh track, *Blood & Sand*, had the former Nottingham thrash metal band Sabbat member Martin Walkyier guesting on vocals.

Also in that year, on June 21, they played at *Heavy Fest III* at The 1 In 12 Club, along with two other Bradford metal acts, Khang and The Enchanted, on the ten band bill.

Another self-issued five-track CD, *Death-Hate-Speed,* appeared during November and December 2004, with ex-Enchanted vocalist Rob Philpotts replacing 'Brick'. The EP contained the tracks *Epiphany / Day 13 / From Hatred To Ahes* alongside two cover versions; Dead Kennedys' *California Uber Alles* and Anthrax's *Only*.

BLOODSTREAM

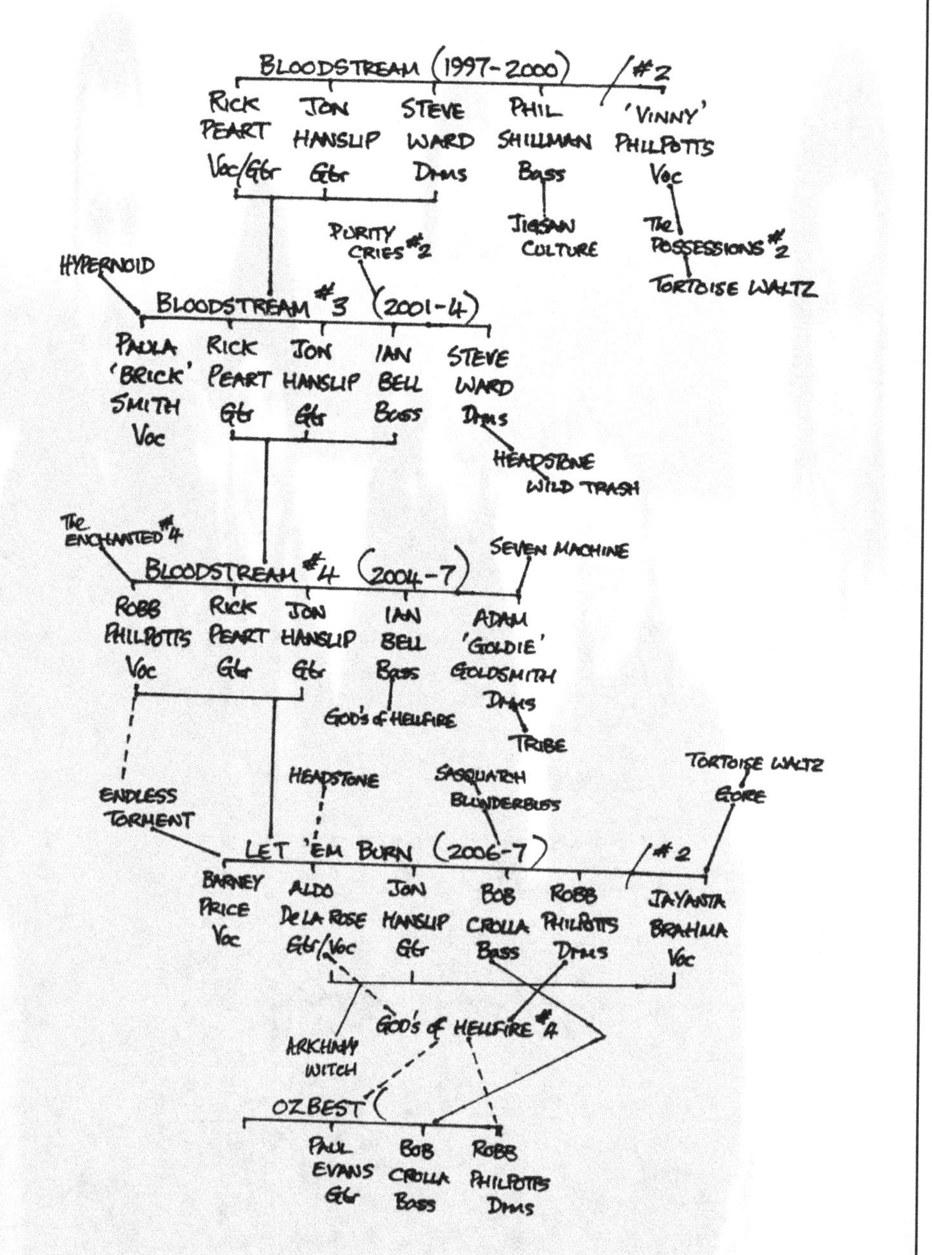

[Hand-drawn band lineup chart:]

BLOODSTREAM (1997-2000) #2
- Rick Peart — Voc/Gtr
- Jon Hanslip — Gtr
- Steve Ward — Dms
- Phil Shillman — Bass
- 'Vinny' Philpotts — Voc

Connections: Hypernoid, Purity Cries #2, Jigsaw Culture, The Possessions #2, Tortoise Waltz

BLOODSTREAM #3 (2001-4)
- Paula 'Brick' Smith — Voc
- Rick Peart — Gtr
- Jon Hanslip — Gtr
- Ian Bell — Bass
- Steve Ward — Dms

Connections: Headstone, Wild Trash

BLOODSTREAM #4 (2004-7)
- Robb Philpotts — Voc
- Rick Peart — Gtr
- Jon Hanslip — Gtr
- Ian Bell — Bass
- Adam 'Goldie' Goldsmith — Dms

Connections: The Enchanted #4, Seven Machine, God's of Hellfire, Tribe, Endless Torment, Headstone, Sasquatch, Blunderbuss, Tortoise Waltz, Gore

LET 'EM BURN (2006-7) #2
- Barney Price — Voc
- Aldo De La Rose — Gtr/Voc
- Jon Hanslip — Gtr
- Bob Crolla — Bass
- Robb Philpotts — Dms
- Jayanta Brahma — Voc

Connections: God's of Hellfire #4, Arkham Witch

OZBEST
- Paul Evans — Gtr
- Bob Crolla — Bass
- Robb Philpotts — Dms

PARALLEL OR 90° (PO 90)

Formed in 1998, this five-piece prog rock band included former Beats Working / Fall Guys / Bantus guitarist Gareth Harwood and former GFDD / Minister Of Noise keyboardist Andy Tillison whose albums had appeared on Peaceville Records in the early 1990s. Andy Tillison was also the house engineer at Lion Studios, Leeds, where many Bradford based bands recorded demos in the 1980s and '90s.

In early April 1999, the band released their third self-issued CD, *Time Capsule*.

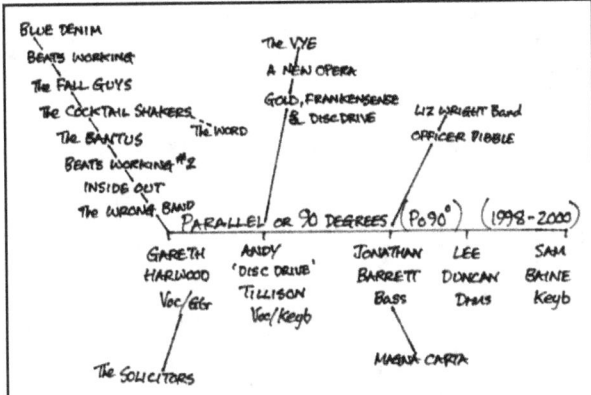

SHANDYLAND

Promoters Joe Fabian and Alan Gill started their monthly showcase event *Shandyland* at the New Beehive on Westgate as an opportunity for up-and-coming Bradford talent. *Shandyland* was also a forum for the other arts, including acts like Skipton artist Sean, showcasing his painting pandemonium.

In March, the Wigan based folk-punksters The Transads (whose debut album *Shandyland* was the inspiration for the monthly event) were the headliners. Wyke based band Water, managed by Joe and Alan, were the support for the event.

In April, local indie outfit Facelift were the headliners with fellow local acoustic five-piece Shiny Beast as support. Admission was £2.

SOUND OF THE SUBURBS

On the evening of April 3, 1999, Channel 4 broadcast the Bradford episode of their new music TV series *Sound Of The Suburbs* (presumably named after the title of No 12 chart hit for The Members in 1979).

The programme was hosted by legendary DJ John Peel and was filmed locally the previous summer. It featured interviews with people like Dean Cavanagh of Glamorous Hooligan, Aki from Fundamental (picture above), dance act VSI, indie band Ripcord and Lianne Hall, formerly of Witchknot / Hiphuggers, who now performed solo.

The half-hour programme started with Peel having a discussion with Aki in the Sweet Centre on Lumb Lane, which then cut to an interview with Bhangra musician Mangal Singh at Sagu Motors at the back of the University. Local indie band Ripcord were filmed at Hebden Bridge Trades Club, then Dean Cavanagh was interviewed in a derelict Manningham Mills before fourteen-year-old singer Jade Doherty and Peter Miller of VSI were filmed at Undercliffe Cemetery. The final piece was an interview with ex-Witchknot singer Lianne Hall at her converted bus/home at the site on Claremont.

The show produced a nine-track compilation CD sampler costing £2.99. The Bradford contribution was the track *Cosy* by Lianne Hall.

John Peel returned to Bradford on April 24 to take part in a birthday party for St Peter's Church on Moorehead Lane, Shipley, invited by the vicar Reverend Chris Edmondson in celebration of the Church's 90th anniversary. He helped hand out the raffle prizes during the afternoon and later was seen in Fanny's bar in Saltaire.

1999 - 2000 BRADFORD'S NOISE OF THE VALLEYS VOLUME 3 PART 1

SAND / THE INSPECTORS / THIS ET AL / HARMACY / DOLPHINS

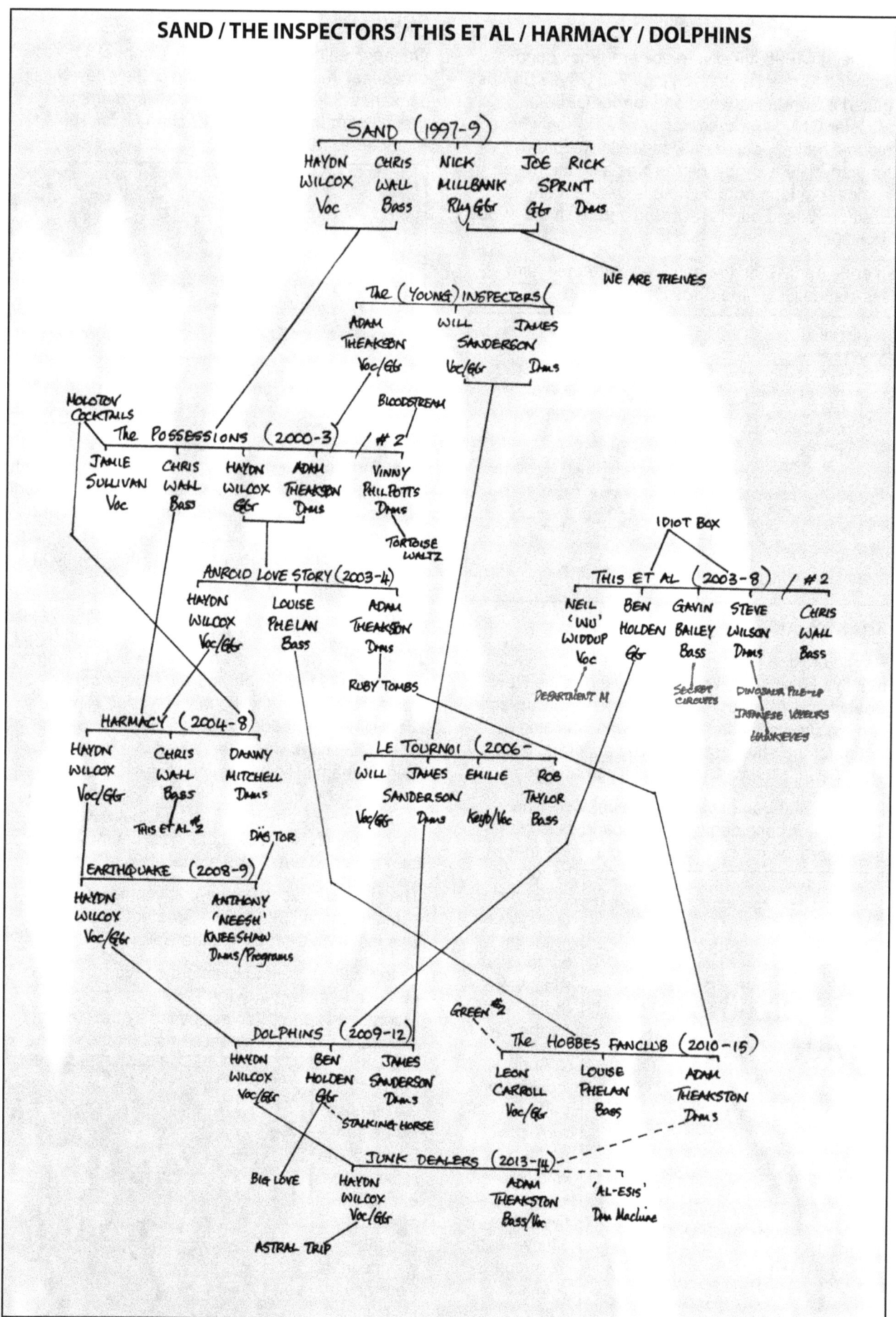

CHAPTER 1 — 1999 - 2000

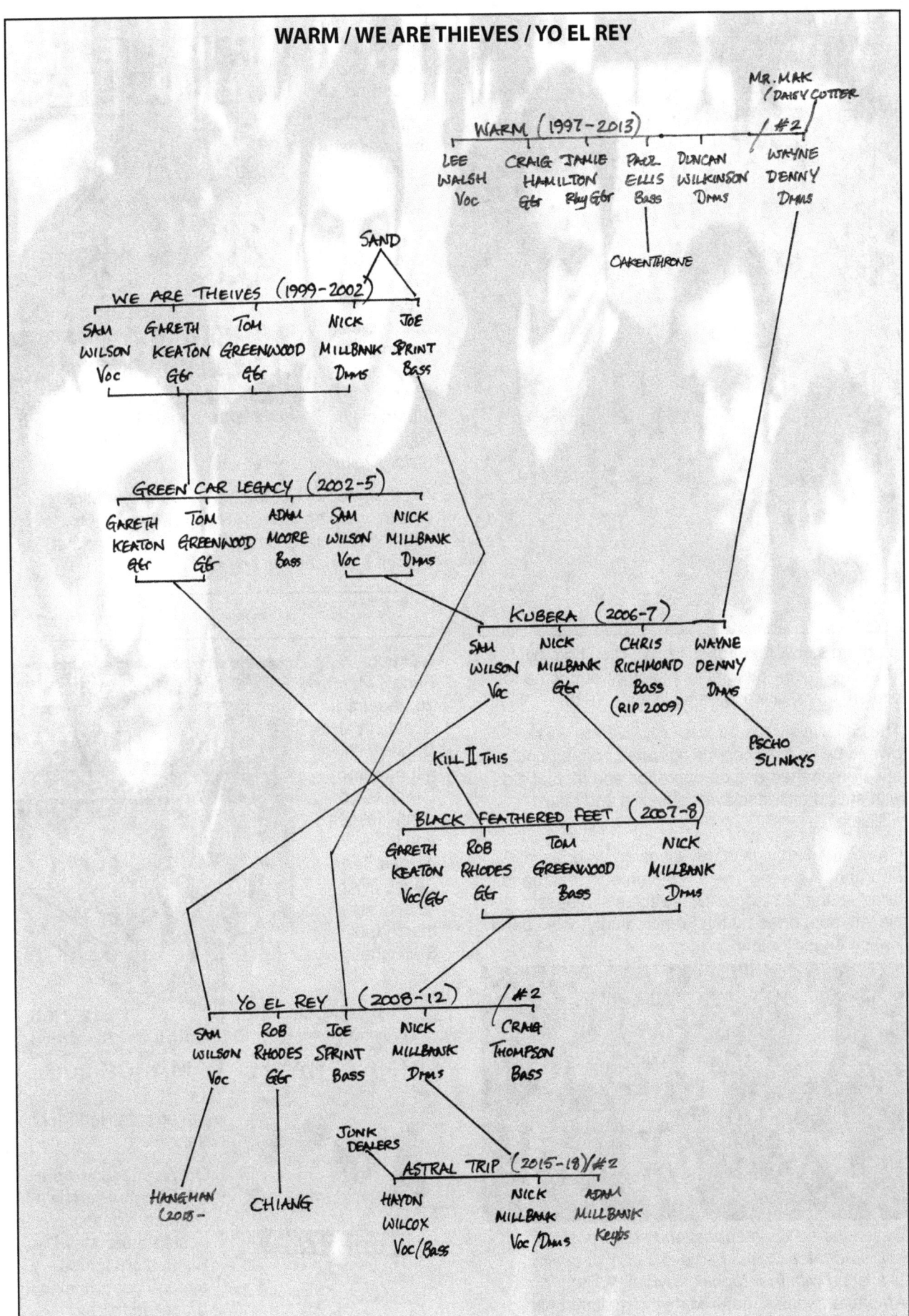

THE 1 IN 12 CLUB

Courtesy of Guiseppe Lambertino

Bradford's now legendary 1 In 12 Club had, by 1999, been operating at its Albion Street home for eleven years, since opening in June 1988.

The collectively run three-storey building was owned by its membership operated on the principles of self-management, co-operation and mutual aid with strong anti-fascist/racist/sexist and statist policies.

One of the first gigs of 1999 was on Wednesday, February 10, when The Amphetameanies, a band billed as the '20 legged Glaswegian ska beast' played, supported by the French quirky-noise band Happy Anger (below).

Described as *"...an upbeat and humorously self-derogatory band, purveyors of high quality ska laced with foot-tapping rhythms"*, The Amphetameanies featured rhythm guitarist Alex Kapranos who went on to form Franz Ferdinand. (5)

During 1999, they released their debut 7" single *Last Night / Suzie The Muppet* on F&J Records, pressing only 600 copies making it now very sought after. An album called *Right Line In Nylons* followed a year later.

Another member of the band, trumpeter Mick Cooke, went on to be in Glasgow based folk-influenced Belle & Sebastian (named after the French story about a boy and his dog).

```
AMPHETAMEANIES
99 F&J Records SHAG024   Last Night/Suzie The Muppet Ltd (7" p/s 600 pressed) ......8
```

A gig on Friday, March 26, featured Scottish band Debris with support from Leeds band John Holmes and local heroes Beer Beast. In April, local noise merchants Stalingrad played with Red Right Hand.

On Wednesday, April 14, Chumbawamba's Danbert Nobacon hosted a pre-May Day Bingo night for the second year running to a packed top bar.

CHAPTER 1 — 1999 - 2000

Number's up for popster Danbert this Mayday

MAYPOLE-ITICAL: *Danbert at last year's bingo*

Danbert Nobacon of West Yorkshire political popsters Chumbawamba, kicks off the build-up to this year's traditional May Day celebrations at Bradford's 1 in 12 Club next week.

Nobacon, who shot to notoriety after drenching Deputy Prime Minister John Prescott with water at the Brits awards last year, will once again call the numbers at a prize Bingo night on Wednesday at 8.30pm.

The evening is planned as a curtain-raiser for a weekend of festivities to celebrate May Day, formerly a big day in the Trade Union calendar but seldom celebrated in Britain today.

In Bradford, the tradition was revived three years ago by the 1 in 12 Club. Its Pete Chapman said: "The move to Reclaim May Day in this country as a celebration for ordinary working class people began in 1996, when a group of 43 people went from Bradford to Barcelona.

"We discovered that May Day is still celebrated on a massive scale throughout the rest of the world."

This year's Bradford events include a light-hearted Reclaim May Day march through Bradford city centre on Saturday May 1, starting at 1pm at the Infirmary Fields and a weekend of football featuring touring teams from Germany and Belgium.

On Friday 16, American hardcore band Code 13, fronted by Maximum Rocknroll columnist Felix Von Havoc, graced the 1 In 12 stage. They were supported by the German band Ebola, Newcastle's Sawn Off and John Holmes.

MAY DAY 1999

For the third year running, the Club held a weekend of events celebrating Mayday, starting on Saturday, May 1 with the annual parade from Infirmary Fields with attendant police protection through town on the designated route leading to Centenary Square.

An afternoon of entertainment was enjoyed by all present, then back up to the Club for an evening of craziness with the Slinky Malinki cabaret.

The next day saw a gig featuring Leeds band Canvas. There was also an historical discussion about the 1906 Klondike land occupations off Whetley Lane.

The third play, The Uses Of Disorder, was performed over the weekend by the Club's Drama Collective at the Priestley Centre for the Arts (Playhouse) off Leeds Road. The play was part of director Noel Batstone's trilogy of anarchist plays and was a futuristic portrayal of society.

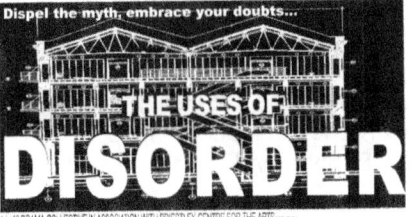

The 1 In 12 football team again hosted a Friday Night Disco as a precursor to that weekend's tournament held at Northcliffe Park, near Shipley. (7) Twelve teams turned up, including teams from Germany (Hanau FC) and Belgium (Lunatics FC), plus teams from Bristol (Easton Cowboys), Norwich (Athletico Cowtower - 1998 winners), York (Boca Ark), Leeds (Republica Highland & White Stag) and for the second year running a women's team from Bradford University. After some hard-fought matches, the final on Sunday was a gruelling contest between the 1 In 12 Club and the White Stag who won on penalties after a 0-0 draw.

THE 1 IN 12 CLUB GIGS MAY/JUNE 1999

Wednesday, May 12: Decrepit - A US band from Seattle, supported by Accion Directa from Brazil.

Friday, May 21: Slide / Honeytrap.

Saturday, May 22: Sasquatch - A five-piece dub reggae band.

Wednesday, May 26: Hard To Swallow / Withdrawn / Rauschen.

Thursday, June 10: Tequila Girls - folk/punk from Sweden, and local boys The Next World.

Sunday, June 13: Hellnation - A US band, supported by French 'grindcore' band Vomit For Breakfast from St. Etienne and UK's Temper / Scalplock / Urko.

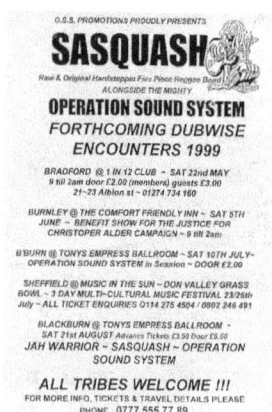

EVICTION OF 120 RATS

The Leeds squat at 120 Meanwood Road (next door to The Globe pub) was a block of three derelict houses knocked through, that had gained its name from the profusion of local rats in the neighbourhood.

The squat had begun around 1993 and was made up of a 'tribe of urban punk warriors' which included the French members of the band Headache who'd originally settled in Bradford and got involved in The 1 In 12 Club. Over the years, the Club had organised many benefits to raise money to help the 'Rats' squatters, and many local and out-of-town bands played there during 1995 and '96, but by June 1999 it was under threat of eviction.

THE DEVILS

Formed around 1998 as a kind of local supergroup from members of Doom, Stalingrad and Scatha.

'Fronted by two screaming singers, no one was safe from their brutal mix of intense hardcore and old school metal-edge, with intelligent samples.' (8)

Doom's lead singer Wayne replaced Pete and played his first gig with the band in April 2002 in Nottingham.

In 2003, they recorded their only album, *How I Learned To Stop Worrying & Forget The Bomb*, at the 1 In 12 studio. It was released on CD by Nottingham label In At The Deep End Records.

CHAPTER 1 — 1999 - 2000

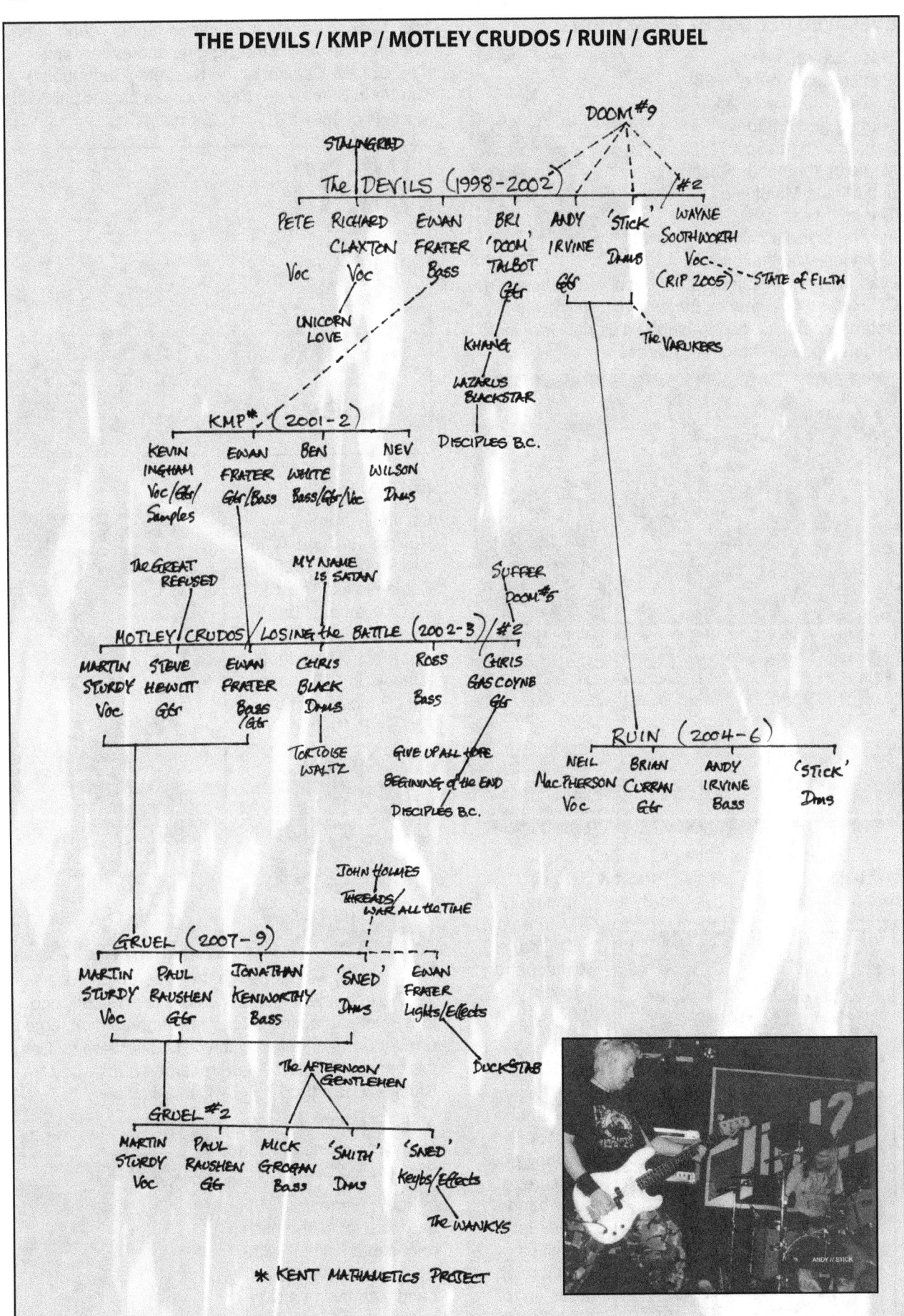

ENSLAVED RECORDS / PROMOTIONS

This local record label was started around 1998 by Club members Nick Loaring and Anthony Palmer with the split 7" single by the bands Shank and Minute Manifesto. The next year, 1999, they released a split LP by Minute Manifesto and Urko, and a 10" split by Cruel Face and Subcut. The CD *Refuse To Kneel* by Belfast band My Name Is Satan, which included Kabinboy guitarist Gary in the line-up, was there next release.

In 2000, the label put out a one-sided 7" single by Ebola. Another 7" single, *Thrash & Burn* by Swedish band DS-13 (Demon System), and an LP/CD, *Threefold* by Dagda, a Belfast band, followed in 2002.

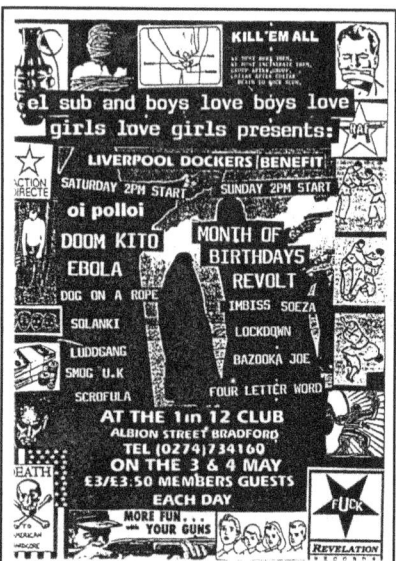

Promoting gigs at The 1 In 12 Club as *'elsubo louso'* or El Sub they gave exposure to many bands on their label, as well as other foreign bands up to 2008.

Nick Loaring settled in Shipley with his young family and later began promoting gigs and events as *The Golden Cabinet* at the Kirkgate (Community) Centre in Shipley, to great success and acclaim with reviews of shows in *The Guardian*.

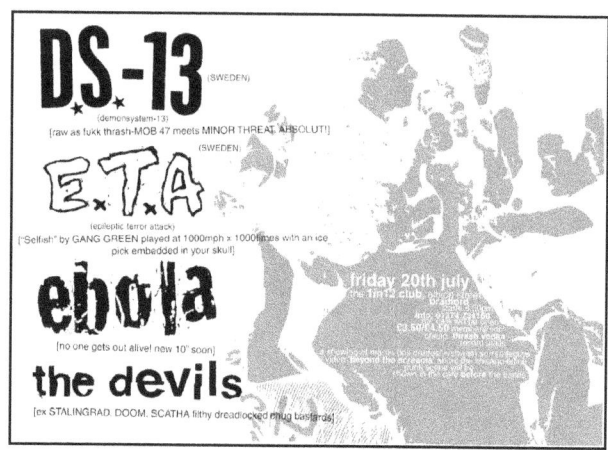

EBOLA

Originally from Newcastle-Upon-Tyne and formed in 1995, Ebola played The 1 In 12 Club at least three times between 1996 and 1998. Their debut release, in 1996, was the LP *Incubation* on Flat Earth Records.

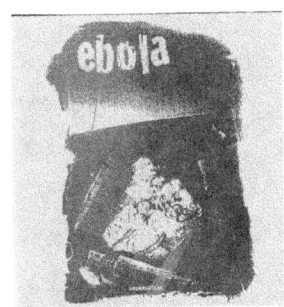

Nick Loaring was added to their line-up on vocals in 1997, strengthening the Bradford connection, and they released a nine-track 7" EP *Imprecation*, again on Flat Earth, in a fold-out lyric booklet sleeve. Both the band's LP and 7" were recorded a In-A-City Studios in Bradford, run by Carl Stipetic.

A one-sided 7" single was released on Enslaved Records in 2000.

In 2003, German hardcore label Totenschiff released a split LP with Ebola and Newcastle band Jinn taking a side each.

CHAPTER 1 — 1999 - 2000

FILM NIGHTS

During July, the 1 In 12 organised a weekly Wednesday Film Night showing *Pulp Fiction*, *Reds* and *The Battle Of Algiers* in the cafe/library.

Club members also set up the *1 In 12 Kidz Club* on a Saturday afternoon, run by members for their own small children, which was run every week up to about 2003/4.

JULY - SEPTEMBER GIGS

Saturday, July 10: An Allday Hardcore Festival with End Of Century Party - an emo/hardcore band from Tampa, Florida, USA, supported by Zemezluc, from the Czech Republic. Plus Dog On A Rope / Extinction Of Mankind / Active Minds / Cath O'Connor Sound / Deisal vs Steam.

Friday, July 23: The Tone / Hobhadod

Wednesday, August 4: Khang / Dying Son / The Enchanted / Project R

Saturday, August 28: UK Players / Lenin & McArthy

Saturday, September 4: Uncurbed (from Sweden), supported by Hellkrusher / Scalplock / Cress

Friday, September 10: Parky, a local Baildon rock band.

Friday, September 17: A Benefit Cabaret Night with Thom The World Poet (from the US) / Alex / Wolfy / Pete The Poet / Schultz-Dickie duo.

Saturday, September 25: Dog On A Rope / Freaks Union

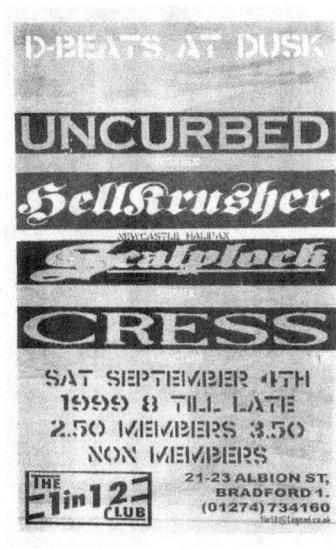

1 in 12 Kids Club

"If the kids are united, they will never be divided."

The spirit of co-operation and self-management that has guided Bradford's 1 in 12 Club throughout its eighteen year history is in safe hands as Bradford kids start to get themselves organised! Now well into its second month, the 1 in 12 Kids Club is every Saturday, 11.30 - 3.00pm.]With a toddlers climbing frame, tunnels, trampoline, see-saw, face-painting, play-dough and lots of other activities - the whole middle floor of the Club is given over to the kids! The mums and dads, grandparents and friends are all expected to pitch in, helping the children set up the equipment and get the room ready, organise the activities and tidy up afterwards.

The kids decide on what happens and what doesn't, they make the decisions! Who said democracy was for the over-18s? The atmosphere is unique, this do-it-yourself with the kids in charge.

And while the adults adjust to being told what to do for a change they can take solace in a pint of real ale or fresh coffee from the bar, have a bite to eat in the cheap vegetarian cafe, or of course throw in their lot with the kids and have their face painted all over by a group of four year olds!

Indeed this is as much for parents as it is about kids. With more and more pubs shutting their doors to families and most cafes, however welcoming, short on things for kids to do, 'Kids Club' is a modest attempt to offer something new and valuable to our city - a safe, child-centred, but grown-up friendly space in the centre of town. Come down one Saturday, take a break from the shopping and get involved!

Kids Club: " a modest attempt ro offer something new"

LUNATICS TOURNAMENT (BELGIUM)

The 1 In 12 football team travelled to Belgium for the Lunatics Tournament between the 13 and 15 August at their Berendrect Woods site outside Antwerp. The site had three football pitches, a large camping area, a large marquee with a bar and stage (for riotous drinking and music after a day's playing) and a food kitchen area not far from the toilet and shower block.

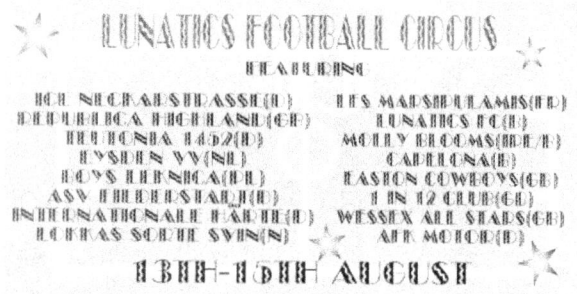

This socially conscious international tournament had attracted sixteen teams from all over Europe: 5 German, 4 English, 3 Belgian (including our hosts -The Lunas), plus Dutch, French, Polish and Norwegian teams.

After a hard-fought day of football, everyone retired to the beer marquee for a night of entertainment from two bands, Scale Sheer Surface and the duo Rocket Freudental, plus local DJs, well into the early hours. On Sunday morning, with many a hangover, the remaining teams fought on to the final, which turned out to be a West Yorkshire affair between the 1 In 12 and Leeds team Republica Highland. The match ended 0-0, but the 1 In 12 were victorious, winning the penalty shoot-out 5-3!

More riotous celebrations were forthcoming after the receiving of the trophy (9), making it another long night, with the team returning home by ferry the next day.

1 IN 12 PUBLICATIONS

The Publications Collective produced its next book, a collection of thirty-seven lyrical poems entitled *Whatever Else - Love Songs To Friends* by Pete Chapman, local performing Poet and bar staff manager at the Club. Some of the poems had rather interesting titles like; *Likely Lads, Virgin's Lament, Mystic Messiah, Sex For Beginners* and *Perfect Buzz*.

RED AND BLACK UNITE

Leeds free magazine *Panic!* (run by Richard Rouska) gave The 1 In 12 Club some complimentary reviews in it's September #58 and November #59 issues, stating - *'...For real agit-pop, it is Yorkshire's top hot spot for the politically active. Be you Socialist or Anarchist this is the place to hang out. Be you Homophobic, racist, sexist, right wing or otherwise THIS is not the club for you.*

The 1 In 12 is volunteer run and if you are interested in helping out, they'd like to hear from you, pay a visit for a wealth of hardcore punk n'rock acts plus a anarcho-socialist friendly environment that survives despite Blair, Thatcher et al.'

BRADFORD AID FOR KOSOVA

After the fall of Communism in the Eastern Bloc Countries of Europe during 1989-90, came the total disintegration of the state of Yugoslavia as its separate republics and autonomous zones descended into civil war and ethnic cleansing. (See map below)

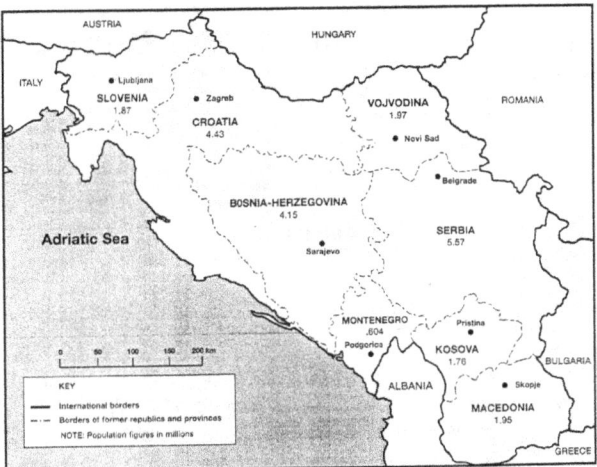

By 1991, Slovenia and Croatia had declared themselves independent. While the Bosnian war raged on between 1992-95, in the UK the Workers Aid for Bosnia was formed to send convoys of aid to the distressed.

The book *Taking Sides: Against Ethnic Cleansing In Bosnia* (1998), published by the Workers Aid group in Leeds and edited by three volunteers; Geoff Robinson, Bob Myers and John Davies, describes the turmoil of the convoys journeys and the situation on the ground seen by the volunteers.

Fast forward to 1998 and the Serbian state who had invaded Kosova in February 1989 with the Yugoslav Army, was intensifying its ethnic cleansing, resisted by the Kosovan Liberation Army (KLA) who had formed in 1996 to protect the mainly muslim population. After several massacres by Serb 'Otpor' police paramilitaries in early 1999 and masses of evidence of systematic intimidation, Nato declared war on Serbia in April.

In Bradford, the Aid For Kosova group was set up in 1998 by Geoff Robinson (veteran of Aid To Bosnia), Mandy Farrar, Sajjad Shah and Amanda Mortimer. Supported by local Labour MP Marsha Singh and meeting every Sunday at the 1 In 12 Club, it quickly gained support and much needed aid in the form of blankets, dried foodstuffs and hygiene and medical supplies for the proposed convoys.

Thursday, April 29, 1999
Telegraph & Argus

DELIGHT: *Geoff Robinson and Mandy Farrar ring up the amounts needed for Kosovo*

Kosovo charity overwhelmed

Generous Bradfordians have overwhelmed a charity with donated goods for Kosovan refugees.

Now the Bradford Aid for Kosova group is desperately trying to find a local company willing to donate a 7.5 tonne lorry, so they can drive the much needed supplies to Macedonia in a convoy.

The group has been delighted with the response to its appeal and is close to raising its £1,500 cash target.

It has also received a mountain of goods such as clothes and blankets at its James Street base but now just need a set of wheels so the convoy can set off on May 4.

Geoff Robinson, the veteran of five previous aid missions to the region, said: "People seem to think we will be driving through bandit country, but that's not the case.

"We will be within the EU until the Greek border and then will have a variety of escorts after that."

Two 1 In 12 Club members, Rachel and Cameron, with Dave Redhead, a Workers Aid volunteer, set off in a car on the 23 December 1998 with money (10) raised after being denied "aid visas", arriving in Belgrade (Serbia) on the night of the 26th.

The first lorry of aid from Bradford, joined a convoy leaving Manchester on 20 June 1999, en-route to Skopje and its neighbouring refugee camps, where 2,000 people in one camp had the use of three sinks for washing and toilets were a hole in the ground.

DECADE OF DISSIDENCE

> V/A - "Decade Of Dissidence—Worst Of The 1 In 12 Club Vol 14/15" CD
> This record is a DIY project created by a non-profit making record collective. They record the bands that play in their club and put out benefit compilations. This volume is a benefit for the people of Kosovo. There are 22 bands on this, but some of them are better than others. DOG ON A ROPE, from Amsterdam, play punk in the vein of ZOUNDS, and HAPPY ANGER remind me of the MOB. EXTINCTION OF MANKIND play hardcore from the UK. CRESS are CRASS sound-a-likes, and VOORHEES plays really fast hardcore. Overall, this comp is OK, but it is for a really good cause. Volume 12/13 looks like it would be much better. (SR)
> (1 In 12, 21-23 Albion St., Bradford, BD1 2LY, UK)
>
> M.R.R. DEC. 1999

In October 1999 came the first 1 In 12 Record Collective release for four years with the double CD album *A Decade Of Dissidence - The Worst Of The 1 In 12 Club Volume 14/15*, intended as a benefit for the people of Kosova.

> **'DECADE OF DISSIDENCE'**
> Worst of THE 1in12 CLUB Vol 14/15
> DAWSON HEALTH HAZARD WITCHKNOT DOG ON A ROPE CONCLUDE HEADACHE GLUE JIMMY SAVILLE'S WHEELCHAIR REVOLT STALINGRAD MANFAT CRESS BLOODSUCKINGFREAKS JOHN HOLMES SAWN OFF EXTINCTION OF MANKIND KITO HARD TO SWALLOW VOORHEES POLARIS HAPPY ANGER MONTH OF BIRTHDAYS
> A Benefit for the people of Kosova

The CD's front cover was a reproduction of a painting of a gig at the Club by Pete Osmond of *Land Of Treason* distro and was packaged with a twenty-eight-page booklet including a page for each of the twenty-two bands featured.

The booklet was laid out by Richard Claxton, the singer in Stalingrad and later The Devils. (10)

The album was a celebration of the Club's decade at Albion Street. The range of music was some of the cream of the UK's punk/hardcore scene as well as two foreign bands - Happy Anger from France and Japan's Conclude, who had all played The 1 In 12 Club between August 1992 and February 1999.

Radio One DJ John Peel was sent a copy, (he now had the full set of *Worst Of The 1 In 12* releases!) and favourable reviews were forthcoming from *Fracture* and US zines *Maximum Rocknroll*, *Heartattack* and *Slug & Lettuce*.

> **SLUG & LETTUCE #64**
> **v/a DECADE OF DISSIDENCE - WORST OF THE 1IN12 CLUB VOL 14/15 CD** A good compilation with a great deal of variety. But for the most part this stays on the more political/extreme (buzzword) size of the tracks. Some of my favorites on this were Blood Sucking Freaks, Cress, E.O.M, Revolt and Voorhees. But that's only naming a few. And it's not mentioning the best thing about this; Health Hazard doing a Motorhead cover! What else do you need to know? Oh yeah, I won't forget about Stalingrad, Sawn Off or John Holmes, but I'm not listing all the bands. So go get yourself a copy. (1in12 Records / 21-23 Albion St. / Bradford / BD1 2LY / UK) (-Ja

> **FRACTURE #9** OCT '99.
>
> **V/A - "Decade Of... Worst Of the 1 In 12 vol 14/15" CD/ 73:20.**
> Why is it called Volume 14/15 when it is only one CD? Why not just call it one or the other. Anyway I saw this on one of the lists in a recent "mailout" and thought to myself that I must get that, so lo and behold Dave pops one into the post for me to review, ah isn't he kind? I can tell you I was more than chuffed to receive this. This comp is actually a benefit for the people of Kosova. So while DAWSON's dark, sombre track played in the background I decided to read the information that is printed in the centre of the booklet. It's quite interesting but hey, you are going to have to buy the CD and read it for yourselves. There's a mammoth 22 bands on it, most of them being pretty darn heavy and the actual sound quality of the recordings of their songs are second to none, so let me say that there are no shoddy recordings on this. Now I said that the bands were heavy, well this doesn't imply that they sound like each other - they all have their own characteristics. The bands on the comp are HEALTH HAZARD (doing a MOTORHEAD cover), DOG ON A ROPE (more mellower than any of the bands on this), WITCHNOT (more mellow stuff, but different), CONCLUDE (definitely new to me), GLUE, HEADACHE, JIMMY SAVILLE'S WHEELCHAIR, REVOLT, STALINGRAD, MANFAT, KITO, CRESS, BLOOD SUCKING FREAKS, SAWN OFF, EXTINCTION OF MANKIND, HARD TO SWALLOW, VOORHEES, HAPPY ANGER (from France), MONTH OF BIRTHDAYS (definitely not heavy), JOHN HOLMES and a very surprisingly harsh and heavy track from POLARIS. The booklet contains a page by each band, which mostly contains their lyrics and artwork. I think this is an ace comp and a worthy benefit. £5 (UK), $12 (WORLD) Post-paid. (MH)

CHAPTER 1 1999 - 2000

GIGS OCTOBER - DECEMBER

Saturday, October 2: Spirit Caravan (from USA) / Hangnail / Khang

Spirit Caravan were a trio from Maryland, led by cult underground guitarist Scott 'Wino' Weinmich who had formerly played in St. Vitus and The Obsessed. At this time the band had a new five-track CD out called Dreamwheel on Meteor City Records.

Wednesday, October 6: Phobia / Unruh, both from the US, supported by local acts State Of Filth and Stalingrad.

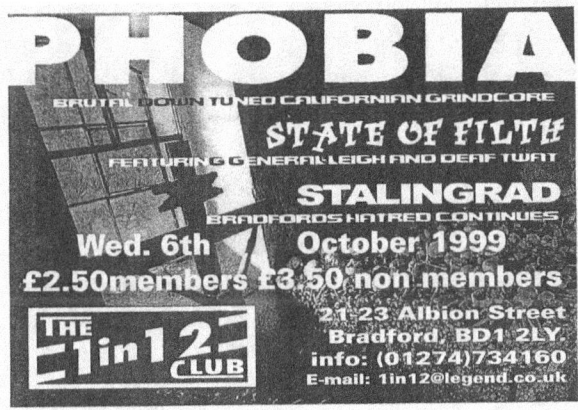

Phobia were a 'grindcore/ doom' band from Orange County, California on their first European tour. Unruh were from Tempe, Arizona and were promoting a new CD Setting Fire To Sinking Ships out on Pessimiser Records.

Friday, October 8: Raging Speed Horn/ Ninth Circle / Khang.

Saturday, October 9: the return of the Ska Au Go Go disco.

Friday, October 15: Kabinboy, from Belfast / John Holmes / Canvas.

Saturday, October 16: Brother Inferior, from the US / Debris / Skank / Police Bastards.

/ Bloodstream / Khang

Saturday, November 27: start of a weekend festival with: Scatha / Hard To Swallow / Voorhees / Imbalance / Month Of Birthdays / Diesal Vs Steam and Creutzfeldt and Tupamaros from Germany.

Sunday, November 28: Endstand, from Finland / Stalingrad / Unborn / Spy Vs Spy / Propagumbies / All Is Lost / Carver / Symbiosis.

Saturday, December 4: Neurostar (ex-Zounds) / Hobmadod.

Saturday, December 1: Hellchild, from Japan / Ebola

Friday, December 31: The Crap Disco, run by 1 in 12 AFC.

Saturday, October 23: the return of the Slinki Malinki cabaret night.

Thursday, October 28: Catharsis. a hardcore band from North Carolina, USA, supported by French band Brent and Autumn Year.

Friday, November 26: Black Rock

THE HIVE

In June 1997, several Club members set up a housing co-operative in an old, previously squatted, Victorian terraced house on Spring Gardens, off Manningham Lane. They gained support for their co-op from Radical Routes, a mutual aid organisation made up of worker and housing co-operatives.

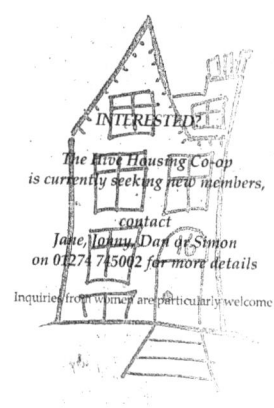

From then on they put into practice the ideals of cooperative living, direct democracy (decisions on running the house were made at regular meetings by consensus), self-reliance and lots and lots of parties. Club members have changed over the years, but there are still members living there today.

CRISIS #3

In November / December 1999, there were two crisis meetings, on Sunday 21st and Sunday 5th to discuss the present financial difficulty. The Club had previously had such meetings in 1990 and 1994 and had settled all the debts at that time.

Inevitably, the never-ending struggle to meet the financial obligations of running a building the size of Albion Street has often imposed a dreary obsession with creating enough revenue to survive.

New strategies were planned, more donations sought, and events organised to stave off the crisis.

Scottish band Disaffect produced the CD *Discography* of all their tracks from 7-inch's, split EPs and their LP *Chained To Morality* as a benefit for the 1 In 12. They urged people to organise events in their own area to show support for the Club, if not, then visit and join as a member.

BIG ISSUE IN THE NORTH

In May 1999, an article appeared in the homeless magazine *Big Issue In The North* discussing the plight of the local Asian population in Manningham who were suffering another series of sustained attacks by far-right organised groups.

The area was synonymous with riots, prostitution and racial tension, images the community has been fighting for years to shake off, not least since the 1995 and 1997 ITV series Band Of Gold, written by Leeds dramatist Kay Mellor and starring Geraldine James, Scottish singer Barbara Dickson, Cathy Tyson and Samantha Morton, had made the area recognisable with its fictionalised story of prostitutes in Bradford.

The article entitled *Standing Firm Against Evil* discussed how prominent local black and Asian politicians had been sent stencilled statements threatening bomb attacks, all after a recent nail-bomb attack in Brixton.

"These are sick, weak, desperate people, but it is only a minuscule number involved. It is quite clear that the vast majority of people in Bradford are anti-racist, the black, Asian and white people are comfortable with each other."

At the 1 in 12 Club, a base for Bradford's anti-racists, anarchists and socialists, the mood is not as confident. Its members have borne the brunt of Combat 18 (far right group) activities in the area.

"I live in Manningham and we are all quite worried about what is going on," said a member who asked not to be named as he'd already been the victim of racist threats. "The whole situation is polarising opinion, last night I had a row with some white guys in a pub who said the bombers had the right idea. This is a racist society and people like Combat 18 and the White Wolves are a lunatic fringe. Here in Bradford, it is becoming like an apartheid state. The Asian community is becoming separated, everyone pretends everyone gets on but it is not true. Scratch the surface and you'll find all sorts of problems."

Yet, despite such dramatic warnings, many other Manningham residents are keen to stress how relaxed the area is. Whatever comes of the present panic and however the community responds to it, something positive can grow from the atmosphere of fear and intimidation. The response lies in ordinary people, sharpen up on anti-racism, show our opposition and we must look to the future. (12)

CHAPTER 1 — 1999 - 2000

CITY STRIDE TO THE PREMIERSHIP

Final Table:

	P	W	D	L	F	A	Pt
Sunderland	46	31	12	3	91	28	105
Bradford City	46	26	9	11	82	47	87
Ipswich	46	26	8	12	69	32	86
Birmingham	46	23	12	11	66	37	81
Watford	46	21	14	11	65	56	77
Bolton	46	20	16	10	78	59	76
Wolverhampton	46	19	16	11	64	43	73
Sheff Utd	46	18	13	15	71	66	67
Norwich	46	15	17	14	62	61	62
Huddersfield	46	15	16	15	62	71	61
Grimsby	46	17	10	19	40	52	61
West Brom	46	16	11	19	69	76	59
Barnsley	46	14	17	15	59	56	59
Crystal Palace	46	14	16	16	58	71	58
Tranmere	46	12	20	14	63	61	56
Stockport	46	12	17	17	49	60	53
Swindon	46	13	11	22	59	81	50
Crewe	46	12	12	22	54	78	48
Portsmouth	46	11	14	21	57	73	47
QPR	46	12	11	23	52	61	47
Port Vale	46	13	8	25	45	75	47
Bury	46	10	17	19	35	60	47
Oxford Utd	46	10	14	22	48	71	44
Bristol City	46	9	15	22	57	80	42

On the 9th May, Bradford City beat Wolverhampton Wanderers 3-2 to finish second in Division 1, gaining automatic promotion to the Premier League (which had started in 1992), a return to 'top-flight' football after an absence of seventy-seven years.

Led by Manager Paul Jewell (an ex-City striker who scored 56 goals between 1988 and 1996) and captained by Leeds lad Stuart McCall (pictured below) who'd galvanised the midfield and inspired the team to reach the dizzying heights of the Premier League. Stuart was on his second spell at City, he'd started his footballing career there from 1982-88, making 300 appearances and scoring 49 goals, before moving to Everton (1988-91, 201 appearances, 10 goals) then Glasgow Rangers (1991-98, 265 appearances, 19 goals and winning 40 Scottish caps) before returning to City.

During the 1999-2000 season, despite some major name signings to strengthen the team (Benito Carbone, Dan Petrescu, Dean Saunders, Stan Collymore and Chris Waddle) City found the transition hard work only just surviving relegation finishing 17th, with 9 wins, 9 draws and 20 games lost and only scoring 38 goals. Unfortunately, the next season, 2000-2001, City were relegated finishing bottom of the league with only 5 wins and 30 goals. It would be a few more years until the team had success and achievements to celebrate again.

In 1999, the Club's fanzine *The City Gent* was celebrating its fifteenth anniversary and is still going strong to this day. (13)

BRADFORD FESTIVAL 1999

The twelfth annual Bradford Festival began on June 26, running until July 18. Besides the usual and regular events like the Lord Mayor's Carnival Parade, the Street Festival and the Mela at Peel Park, there was the Bradford Comedy Festival in Centenary Square, featuring Bradford's own Mary Unfaithful (Jayne Tunnicliffe) among the artists.

Cafe Bradford, also in Centenary Square, was open throughout the Festival and many local acts performed, including Dancing Fly (pictured below)

a band which included former members of the local reggae band Jab Jab.

It culminated in three free 'Big Nights', on July 15/16/17, as a venue for thousands of music fans to enjoy some of the hottest acts in a variety of musical styles.

African superstar Femi Kuti from Nigeria (carrying on the tradition began by his father Fela, the originator of Afrobeat) played on the 16th, supported by Liverpudlian poet Levi Tafari.

On Saturday 17th, Transglobal Underground brought their dance sound with support from the Japanese Kobayakawa Suigan Taiko Ensemble drummers, who in their colourful masks and costumes brought a glimpse of another world.

The Mela weekend of the 3rd and 4th attracted an estimated audience of over 150,000 attending Europe's largest Asian-oriented event. Among the top performers were Asian Dub Foundation (who only managed to play 3-4 numbers, before leaving the stage in a hail of cans thrown by rival Asian gangs in the crowd), Stereo Nation, Jazzy B - the crown prince of British Bhangra (pictured above), Snake Davis and South Africa's Black Umfolosi.

Among two new features at that year's Festival were:

The Bradford Poets

Started as an open group that met on a Monday night at the New Beehive Inn on Westgate, they provided a programme of readings, read-alongs

and critical but constructive workshops of members' poetry, as well as producing and publishing pamphlets and anthologies of their work.

Local History Walks

On Monday, July 5, in celebration of Bradford Resource Centre's (BRC) twentieth anniversary, a historical walk entitled *Routes Of Resistance* was organised and led by Gary Cavanagh.

BRADFORD RESOURCE CENTRE
Resources For Democracy

The walk around Bradford started at BRC's first home in Little Horton and did the circuit of the city before finishing at the centre's new home in Little Germany. It took in many sites of Bradford's rich heritage of resistance in political, social and community struggles, showing the city's proud history of fighting for a fairer and more equitable society. (14)

After the success of the first walk, further walks for BRC took place in 2000 and 2001, also six Urban walks were organised for Gingerbread between 1999-2003 while Bradford University's Peace Studies Department commissioned walks from 2001-2005.

A German textbook for secondary school pupils learning English featured an entire chapter about Bradford's famous Mela, used in teaching about multi-cultural Britain, published by the Berlin firm Cornelsen. Festival press officer and Festival Radio presenter Rob Walsh showed off the book in the T&A (pictured below).

ANOTHER LOVE AFFAIR

During August, Bradford lad Michael Jackson, the former bassist with 1960s pop band The Love Affair, had negotiated with Sony Music an out-of-court settlement (which took account of sales of CDs and the band's inclusion on compilation albums) of a windfall of unpaid royalties. This was mainly for the No 1 single *Everlasting Love*, which had been at the top of the charts in February 1968 for two weeks before Manfred Mann's *The Mighty Quinn* single had replaced it, and at present was enjoying a revival thanks to being used on McDonald's and Coca Cola TV ad campaigns.

Michael had left the band in April 1970 and was currently running his own training and marketing company, Jackson Consultancy in Bingley. He, along with former Love Affair drummer Maurice 'Mo' Bacon and keyboardist Morgan Fisher (who'd also been in Mott the Hoople between 1973-74) went into a Leeds Studio to record a new track entitled *It's A Love Affair*, which took them around fourteen hours. They hoped to get a distribution deal and raise money for charity, on behalf of the Bradford Royal Infirmary's Ward Z Specialist Unit dealing in rare blood disorders.

BINGLEY MUSIC LIVE

On September 4 & 5 at Myrtle Park, Bingley, a Free two-day pop music event was organised by Bradford Council's Recreation Service along with Pulse and West Yorkshire Classic Gold radio stations. Originally a three-day event that started in 1991, by 1998 it had become a two-day event. That year's Saturday line-up were three covers bands, 'Ang About, Abba Gold and BC Sweet who played Sweet's 1970s glam rock hits like the chart-topping *Blockbuster*.

On Sunday, the line-up was made up of three chart-hopeful pop acts. Male group Point Break got to No 29 with *Do We Rock*, released on the Eternal label in October 1999, and reached No 7 in January the next year with *Stand Tough*. Female group 21st Century Girls (pictured) had a No 16 hit in June '99 with *21st Century Girls* on EMI Records.

Finally, the female group Fierce, who had four top thirty hits between 1999 and 2000 including their No 3 single *Sweet Love 2K* (a cover of the Anita Baker 1970s disco hit) in February 2000.

SMOKIE MAN GOES SOLO

Former Smokie guitarist Alan Silson launched his solo career in September 1999. Based in Ilkley, he set up his own record label, Ilkley Moortown, and was recruiting musicians to form a backing band.

Alan had already had a taste of performing under his own name when the previous year he was a guest musician on Suzi Quatro's European tour. *"I was a special guest and came on to do about half a dozen songs, it was more frightening than going on with Smokie."*

Meanwhile, Smokie continued with former guitar tech Mick McConnell replacing Alan.

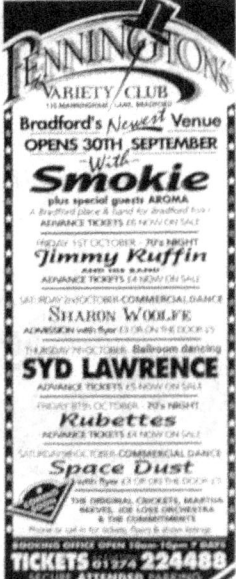

THREE MEN & A BASS

Local group Three Men & A Bass had recently performed their mix of jazz/swing/reggae and rock'n'roll in front of thousands of revellers at Sir Elton John's two concerts at Harewood House in Leeds. The promoters, Marshall Arts, were so impressed by the five-piece group that they wanted them to play at after-show parties for a series of gigs in the next year by performers including Michael Jackson, Tina Turner and Bon Jovi. The group had formed in Clayton in 1993 as a trio before expanding to a five-piece.

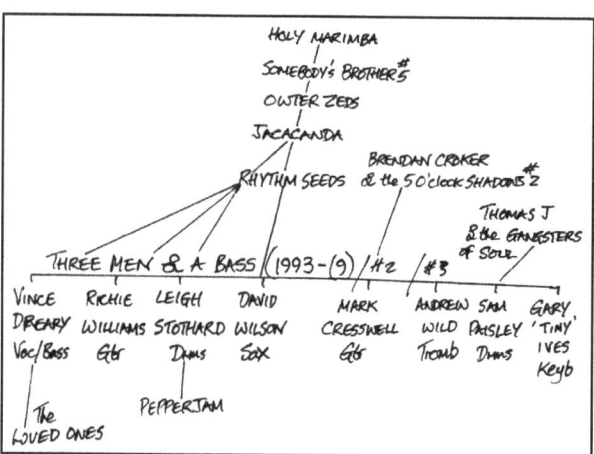

HENDRIX HONOURED

On Sunday, September 14, English Heritage honoured American guitarist Jimi Hendrix with a historic Blue Plaque at 23, Brook Street (next door to that marking the former address of Composer G. F. Handel) in London's Mayfair. This was the first time a contemporary musician had been honoured by English Heritage, and Jimi had lived at the address between 1968-69 with his girlfriend Kathy Etchingham.

At the unveiling by fellow musician Pete Townshend of The Who, was Jimi's former bassist Noel Redding as well as other friends, musicians, fans and the media making a crowd of a couple of hundred in the closed-off street.

THE FILM BLOW DRY

During Sept-October the film *Blow Dry* (originally entitled *Never Better*) was filmed at Bradford City Hall, Dewsbury, Batley and Marsden in Colne Valley.

The film was a social comedy, set in the 1970s, about the highs and lows of a regional hairdressing competition set in Keighley. A local councillor decides to put the town on the map by negotiating the rights to the world's biggest competition for 'crimpers & snippers', but first has to overcome obstacles in the local corridors of power.

Written by Keighley lad Simon Beaufoy (who had famously written the screenplay for the film *The Full Monty*) it starred Alan Rickman, Natasha Richardson and Warren Clarke, who played the Lord Mayor of Keighley (pictured), plus great character actors David Bradley and Bill Nighy.

It was a shame that none of the filming was done in Keighley itself. This book's author though did manage to get a day's filming as an extra in a funeral scene shot in Dewsbury which did appear in the finished film and not on the cutting room floor.

The film was officially released in March 2001.

THE BATTLE OF SEATTLE

On November 30, 1999, the city of Seattle on the northwestern seaboard of the USA, saw 50-100,000 anti-capitalist / globalisation protesters on its streets, to disrupt and delay the summit of the World Trade Organisation (WTO) conference at the Sheraton Hotel.

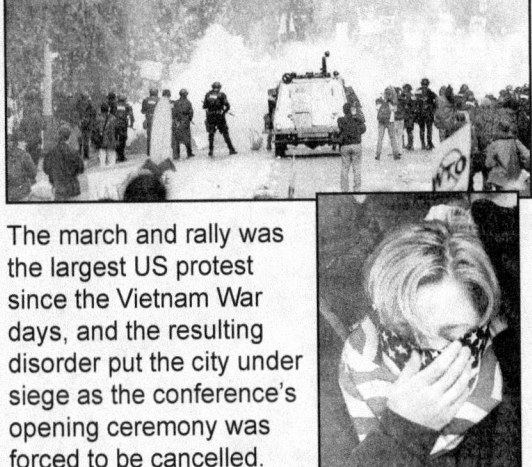

The march and rally was the largest US protest since the Vietnam War days, and the resulting disorder put the city under siege as the conference's opening ceremony was forced to be cancelled.

Among the thousands of demonstrators was a wide range of different struggles from environmentalists, labour unions, farmers, church and consumer groups, steel workers, loggers, human rights activists, Tibetan monks, Zappatistas and anarchists as well as the Body Shop's Anita Roddick.

'The protesters say that the WTO presides over the world trading system that is skewed in favour of rich countries and multinational companies, that it harms the environment and acts against the interest of consumers.'

The local riot police used tear gas and rubber sting pellets as demonstrators attacked shops and commercial premises like Gap, Starbucks, McDonalds and the Bank of America. The US Security Agencies (including the FBI and CIA) were present as US President Bill Clinton was due to arrive for talks on December 1.

In London, near Euston station a *Reclaim The Streets* rally was organised to tie-in with the WTO demonstration, as 2,000 clashed with police in a two hour battle, resulting in one police van being set alight, forty people arrested and seven hospitalised, including one police officer.

CREATION ROOTS ALBUM

Bradford's premier and popular reggae band Creation Roots, had released their first 7" single, *Selassie I Lives*, in 1989. Two 12 inches: *No Way / Selassie I Lives*, *Dread Down Deh / Christmas In The Ghetto*, also came out that year on Quatro World Music. Their EP, *Girls / Pye Pye Lovin'*, was released on the band's own Graphics label in 1992 and were popular songs in their live set.

They appeared on TV on the BBC2 programme *Out Of Our Heads* and the Channel 4 Ruby Wax Show, *Wax On Wheels*.

Their only album, *Troddin*, contained eleven tracks. It was produced by 'Mad Professor' Ariwa and came out in late 1999 on CD on the band's own Graphics label, distributed by Jet Star Productions.

The band finally called it a day in 2003, the year after the untimely death of their MC, Mikey Roots.

KEIGHLEY SCENE

The town's local music scene was developing all the time, with new bands continually emerging, including Rhino, The Undecided, Demonix, Soulfish and Johnny & The Poorboys.

RHINO

Formed in 1989 as a no-nonsense pub rock covers band, Rhino were drawn from members of Keighley's premier NWOBHM band Dawnwatcher. Because of the pedigree of the band, they became an instant success on the pub circuit, selling 250 of their t-shirts at a tenner a pop in the first month. The band continued for around fourteen years before calling it a day, with three of them going on to form the band Glamnation. (15)

THE UNCECIDED

Another local band were The Undecided, who had been around since 1997. They recorded their first four-track demo cassette, *2 am*, at Blue Noise Studios, based at The Mill in Bradford.

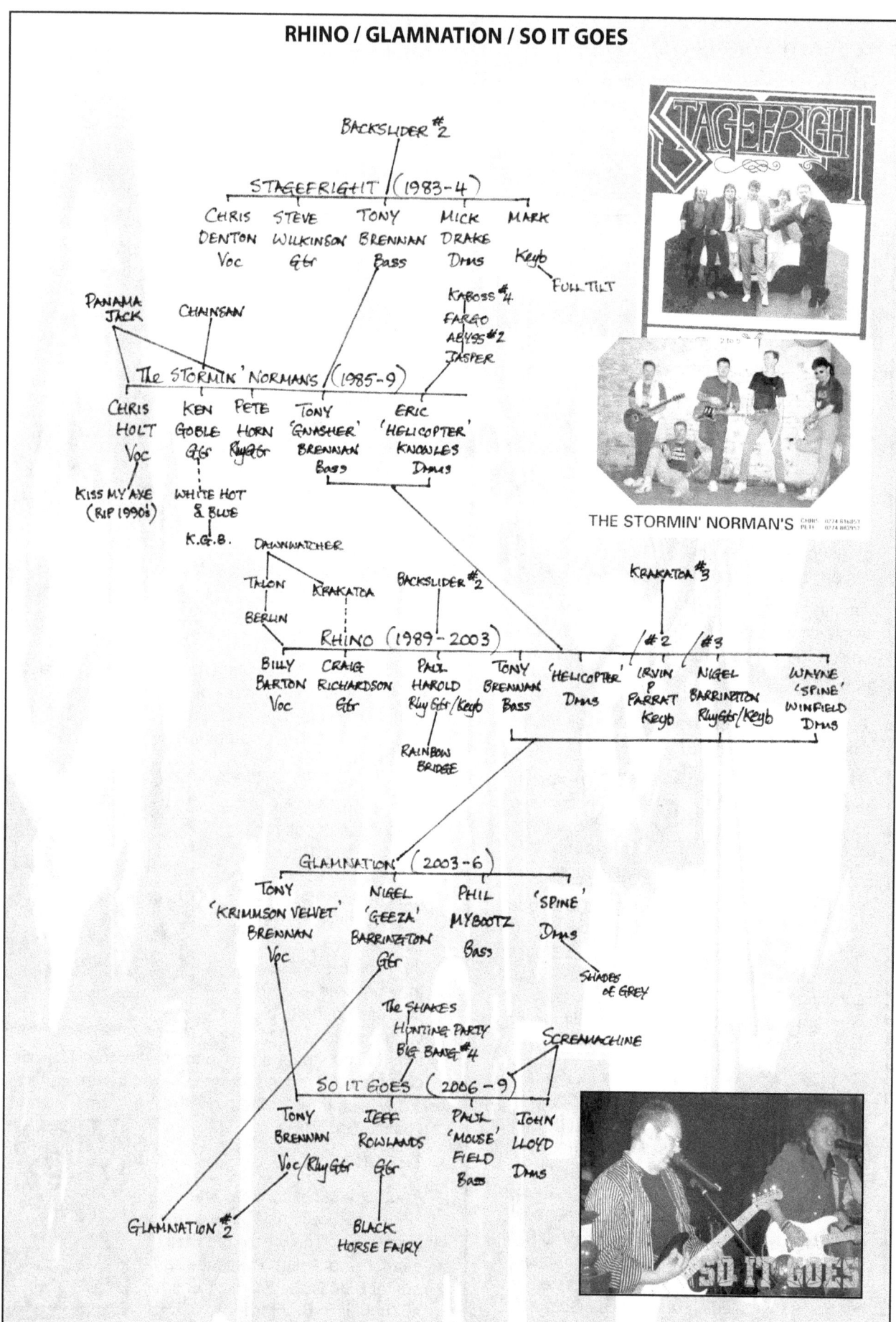

CHAPTER 1 — 1999 - 2000

THE UNDECIDED / SOUNDS OF SWAMI / CITUSK

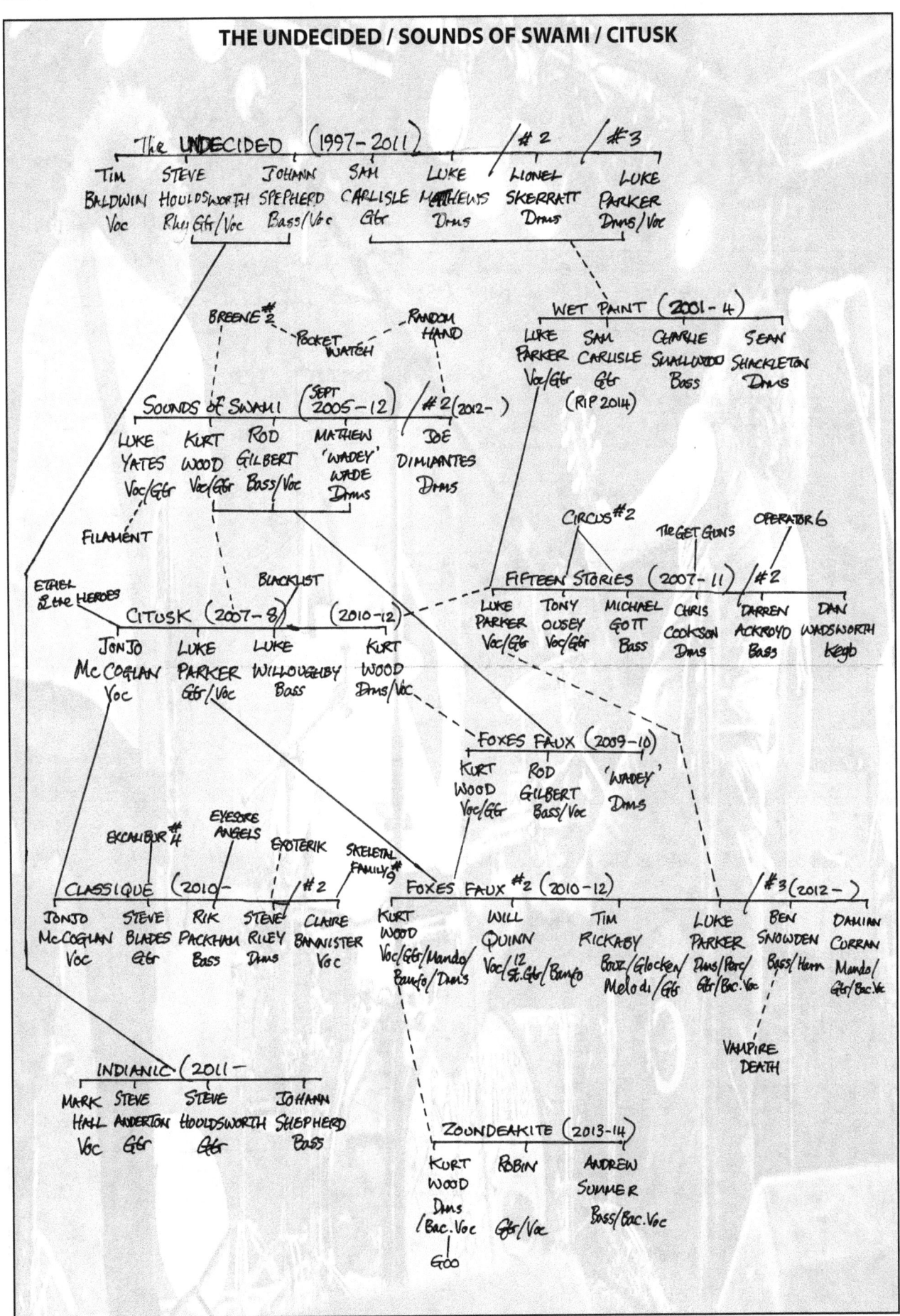

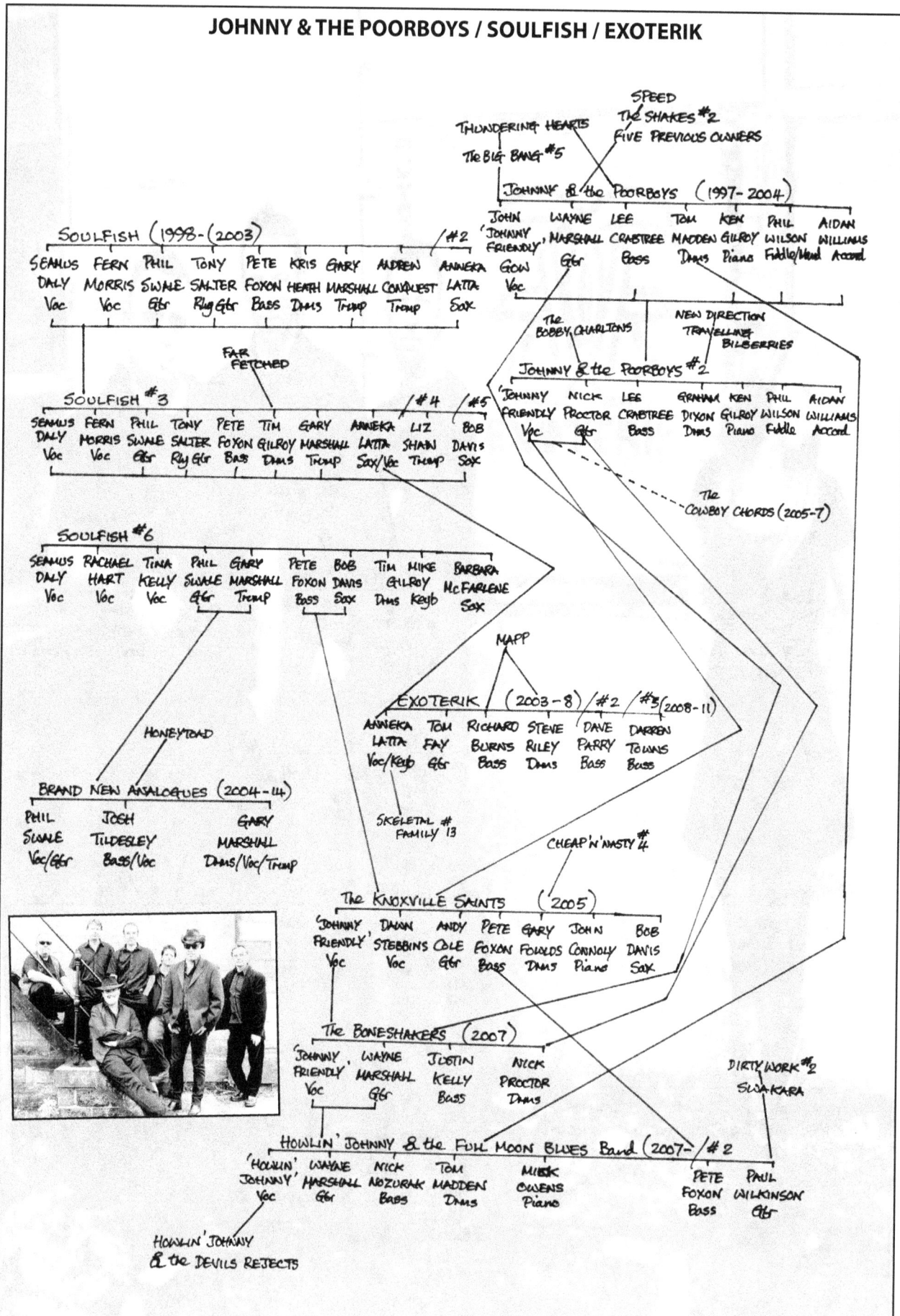

DEMONIX / IRONSTORM / LAMP OF THOTH

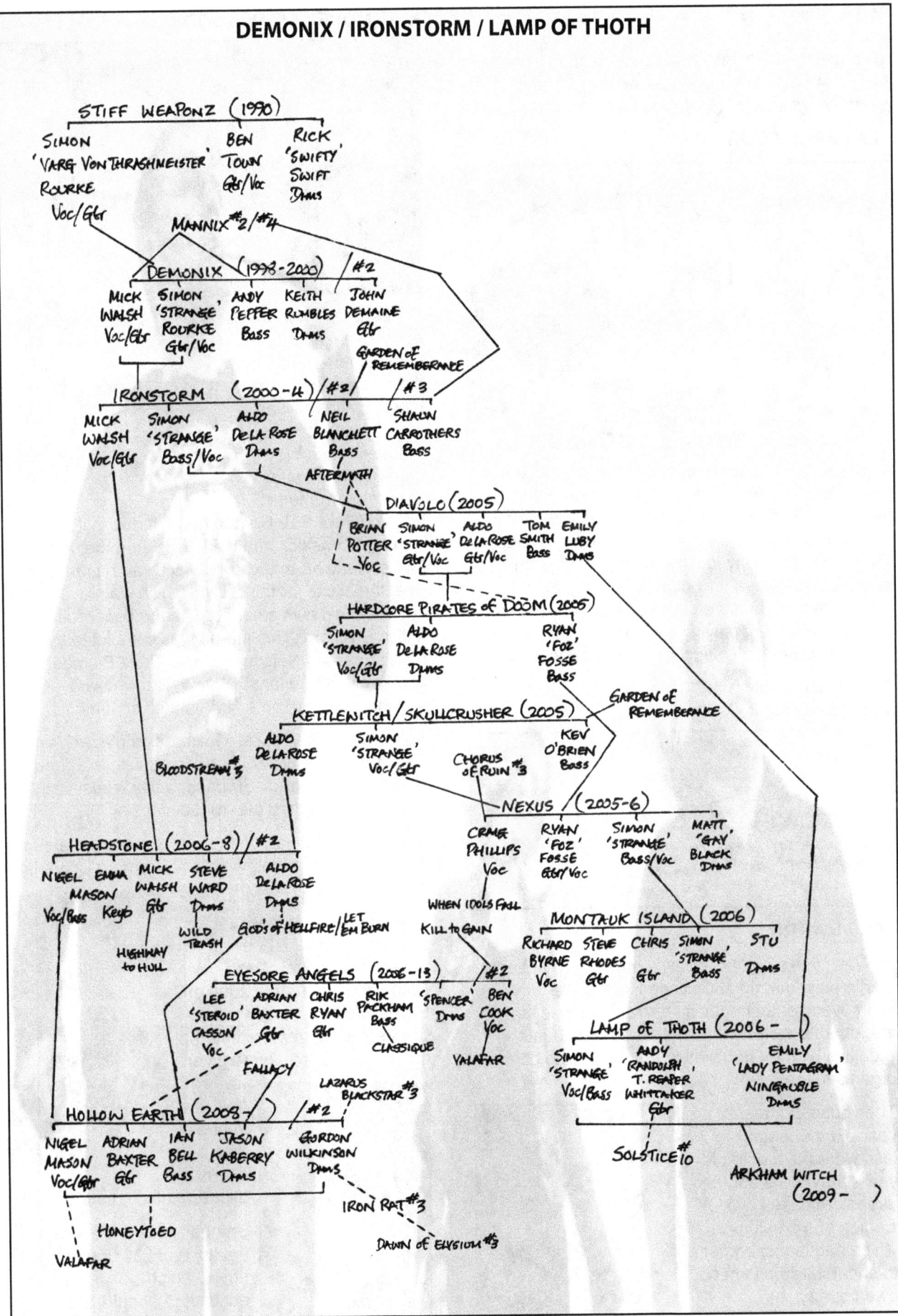

At the dawn of the 21st century, as the world worried about the possibility of a technological Millennium shutdown - all that was blaring from Gary's stereo's speakers was the prog classic 21st *Century Schizoid Man* by King Crimson. (16)

FLAT BACK FOUR

Amongst many a band formed in the late 1990s were Flat Back Four. Reconstructed from the remains of Twister 5 (1995-7), by May 1999, they were a five-piece once again, with a new guitarist They didn't do many local gigs (except regularly at McRory's) instead concentrating on gigs in Manchester and London. A rare local appearance in May '99 saw them playing a Shandyland promotion at the New Beehive, supported by Bullweek.

Their debut eight-track CD was entitled *20 Seconds*, and recorded at In-A-City Studios.

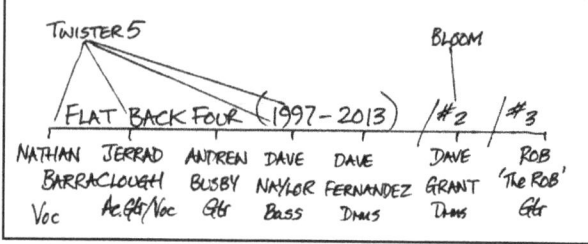

LENE MARTIN

On Valentine's night, Norway's hottest export Lene Martin played a gig at Chicago Rock Cafe - a short-lived venue on the side street to the left of the Alhambra. Her show was broadcast country-wide live by the radio station Pulse FM who had organised the event.

The young eighteen-year-old had been discovered a couple of years previously and had already released two singles and an album, which had launched her to superstardom in her own country.

NEW MODEL ARMY & JOOLZ

In February, New Model Army released their latest album, *Eight,* on their own Attack Attack label. Justin Sullivan was the only original member left in the current line-up after long-term drummer and co-writer Rob Heaton had left due to ill health. Former Homesick and Kill II This drummer and New Model Army drum tech Michael Dean had taken over the sticks for this album which was recorded in the band's own studio on the top floor of The Mill in Bradford. The line-up was completed by regular bassist Nelson, guitarist Dave Blomberg and keyboard/guitarist Dean White who was also making his debut on a NMA studio album.

Former Nine Below Zero Harmonica player Mark Feltham, who'd previously worked with the band, guested on the track *Someone Like Jesus*, while Joolz had designed the front cover.

On March 4, as part of a tour promoting the album, NMA played a hometown gig at Bradford University, their first in five years.

Around the same time, Joolz was promoting the release of her debut novel *Stone Baby*, due out in April 2000 on Harper Collins. Glossy promo booklets which reproduced the first three chapters were given away free at venues and events all around the country.

She had received an advance of £30,000 for the novel, which was a dark and edgy story about a stand-up comedienne whose boyfriend was a serial killer. Joolz had drawn heavily on her own experiences as a live performer over many a year.

The novel won Joolz the Crime Writers' Association Debut Dagger award.

> **REFUGEES / ASYLUM SEEKERS**
>
> Bradford as a city has a proud tradition of welcoming refugees/asylum seekers and people of different nationalities. After the recent war in former Yugoslavia, a group of twelve families from Kosova were welcomed to Shipley and housed in a former residential home. At the time, these refugees were waiting anxiously for news of when they could return home.
>
> Local figures suggested that around 140 asylum seekers had settled in the city by the end of March 2000.

Local alternative Doom metal heroes Paradise Lost played Rio's on February 24, admission was £7.50 in advance on the door. The band's recent album release, *Host,* had come out in 1999.

SKIVER

This five-piece band had formed in 1996 when they all met at Bradford University. They were led by guitarist Jim Storer and drummer Steve Sowden (who were both employed at Bradford-based computer software developer Atlantic EC in Little Germany). The band didn't play their first official gig until March 2000 at Queens Hall.

JENNIFER ROBERTSON

Sixteen-year-old Jenny, a pupil at Skipton Girl's High School, beat off hundreds of other hopefuls to perform live at a concert at the Greenwich Millennium Dome. The event, co-sponsored by the Dome management and Marks & Spencer, called *Voices Of Promise*, was a platform to find new songwriting talent. It was hosted by Emma Ledden and Steve Wilson of the BBC's hit show Live & Kicking. Jenny joined twenty-one other lucky winners from 2000 entries from all over the country.

Jenny sang her own composition *The Guiding Hand Of Tomorrow*, backed vocally by school friends in front of the 3,500 crowd. *'The concert was a spectacular event, a showcase of the incredible songwriting and performing talent from these schools,'* said Maggie Semple director of the Dome's management company.

WARM

Local band Warm played a gig at the Attic in Cowgate, Edinburgh on April 28, the night before the Rugby League Challenge Cup Final. The band and coach loads of other fans had made the trip north to see the Bradford Bulls play Leeds Rhinos in the final at the Murrayfield ground as Wembley, the usual venue, was under redevelopment. The Bulls won on the day over the Rhinos 24-18.

Warm were the first band to sign to the Bradford-based Skylark Records who released their debut single *Need I Say / New Man* in 2000. The band produced a second four-track CD EP with the tracks *Take Me Away / Monday Comedown / Prayer For The Lonely and Feel It In The Music* on the same label later that year.

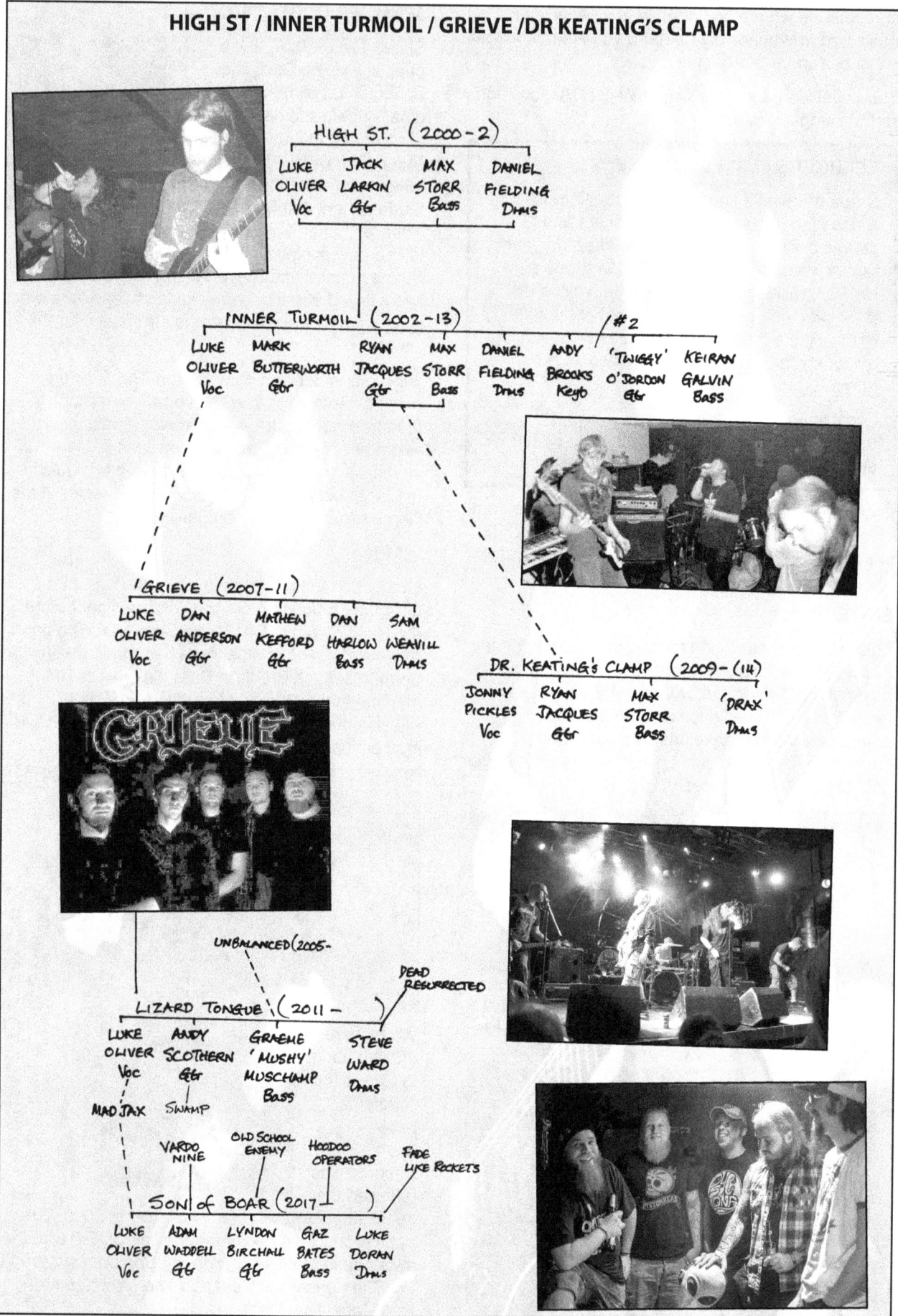

BRADFORD'S TRADES COUNCIL

Between Friday 28 and Sunday 30 April 2000, Bradford's Trade Union Council organised two public events as part of their *A Weekend To Remember*. On Friday there was an open gathering in Forster Square to commemorate Worker's Memorial Day, the scene of a tramway disaster in the late 1800s.

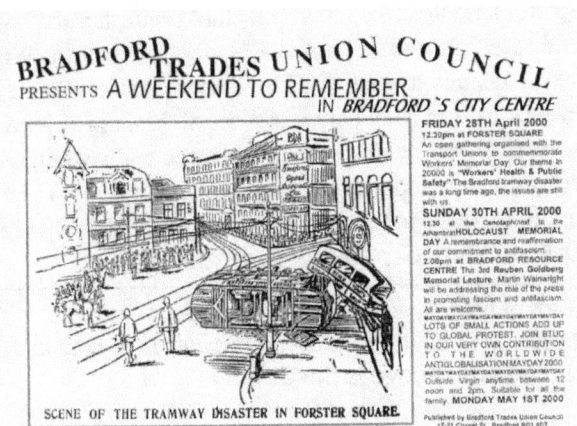

On Sunday at 12.30, a Holocaust Memorial Day was held at the Cenotaph (next to the Alhambra) in remembrance and as a reaffirmation of the commitment to anti-fascism. At 2 o'clock there was the third *Reuben Goldberg Memorial Lecture* by Martin Wainwright, who addressed the role of the press in promoting fascism and anti-fascism at the Resource Centre in Little Germany.

LIFEFORCE

During April and May, preparation work was underway on the new National Millennium Faith Centre (Lifeforce) housed in the old Post Office building in Forster Square. The £5 million attraction was designed to celebrate and explain humankind's history of religious belief.

The Lifeforce team employed around fifteen people in the restaurant, shop and ticketing office, as well as film-makers like Bev Jenkinson and Craig Ferguson (pictured) who recorded the lives of the city's top sports people, looking into their backgrounds and how they managed to succeed in their careers. They also planned to film local firefighters and wanted to hear from people doing other kinds of work for the exhibition.

When the centre opened it selected specific films to be shown via interactive touchscreen monitors. Another major exhibition was the Bradford Observatory which looked at the achievements of famous Bradfordians, such as Sir Titus Salt. The official opening was on July 28. The centre had only 63 paying visitors in the first week and by September, even with free entry, it only had 600+ visitors a week. In February 2001 the centre closed due to insolvency.

1 IN 12 CLUB 2000

On February 10, the Club held the first in a series of meetings by the Mayday Discussion Group, entitled *History As Progress?* The meetings were held on the second Thursday of every month at 8 pm.

GIGS JANUARY - MAY 2000

Saturday, February 19: An all-dayer with Dog On A Rope / John Holmes (both from Leeds) / State Of Filth / Violent Affray and others.

Friday, February 25: Worm from Chesterfield, supported by Eighty Six / Fig 4.0

Saturday, March 11: Honeyrider / Hiphuggers

Friday, March 14: A None More Heavy promotion featuring the Belfast band Kabinboy supported by local heavy rock act Khang.

Thursday, May 4 : Canvas from Leeds / Enchanted / Dropnose / Dead Man's Fingers

Saturday, May 6: Another None More Heavy promotion featuring Sloth / Khang / Dukes Of Nothing

May 26: Dutch band Insult (who were promoting their new CD album The Mosh Pit Is Our Sabbath on Dutch label Balowski Records) / BSE / Urko / Sawn Off

of organising, working in cooperation and taking control over the basic areas of their lives.

> *1 IN 12 CLUB*
> *21/23 Albion St., Bradford, West Yorkshire, BD1*
> *Phone number: 01274-734160*
> *E-mail: 1in12@go-legend.net*
> *Website: http://www.legend.otg.uk/~1in12*
>
> Anarchist collective run social club, venue, library, bar and cafe. Their main "political" campaign over the last year has been around CCTV. They organise a week's events around May Day in Bradford. Main priority & objectives of the club are to promote and sustain all activities based on mutual aid, co-operation & solidarity. Also produce a magazine called KDIS (Knee Deep In Shit). *See local groups section.*

During June, the *Agitator* magazine compiled a directory of all the autonomous centres in Britain and Ireland, above is the description of the Club.

That month's meeting by The 1 In 12 Club's Mayday Discussion Group showed a short video called *Sleepless In Seattle* and an eye-witness account of the anti-WTO event of November 30, 1999, in Seattle, USA.

TAKING CONTROL

On Saturday, April 8, from 10 am til 5 in the afternoon, the Club ran a day of practical workshops under the heading Taking Control. The joint event was organised by the 1 In 12 and Radical Routes (a national network of Co-ops) via the Hive Housing Co-op. With the cafe open and the kidz club active, visitors could be informed and inspired by workshops promoting alternative ways

On Friday, July 14, the T&A produced an article about the Club's new practice room and future recording studio. Various club members had worked very hard renovating and kitting out a space in the cellar area for the project.

A chance to record

Bradford's 1 in 12 Club is opening its own recording studio and band practice room.

Phase one - the practice room - is now open for business for musicians to rehearse for £3 an hour.

Club member Stick said: "Bands used to practise in the gig room which is far from ideal acoustically. We also used to get a lot of complaints from adjoining businesses through the day."

Phase two will involve building an adjoining recording studio at the club in Albion Street, Bradford, which will enable tracks to be recorded live for future compilation albums.

GIGS: JULY - AUGUST 2000

Saturday/Sunday July 15 /16: A two-day festival of hardcore featuring The Unknown (from USA), Facedown (from Belgium), three Belfast bands Dagda, Kabinboy and Redneck Manifesto, Liverpool's Imbalance, Leeds bands Canvas, Polaris, John Holmes and Month Of Birthdays, also Scarper, Urko, Debt, Red Monkey, Split Red, Sawn Off, Noise Jihad and the Aalborg.

Sunday, July 23: Percy (a band from Hull that included former Housemartin's drummer Hugh Whittaker)

Friday, July 28: Another *None More Heavy* promotion with London band Sally / Khang

Tuesday, August 1: From Denmark hardcore band Heads Up / Joe Ninety / The Autumn Year (a Leeds based Emo band featuring members of Canvas and Dropnose)

Friday, August 17: Symbiosis / Grover /Fig 4.0 / The Autumn Year

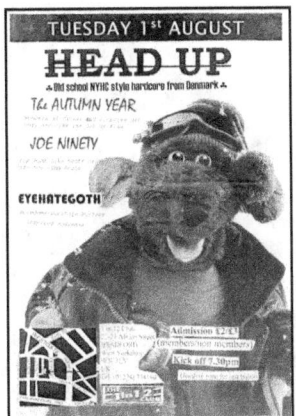

Thursday, August 31: Victims (from Sweden) supported by Scarborough's Active Minds.

1 IN 12 AFC

The 1 In 12 Club's football team had joined the Saturday Grattan League for the 1993-94 season, and by the year 2000 were still mid-table in Division 2. After original manager Steve Jackson there had been Rob Murphy (of Dog On A Rope fame), then joint managers Craig Williams and Gareth James, before a new cabal of Steve Tandy, former Anti-System guitarist Dom Watts and Rob 'Kito' Hallowes.

After a home win of 3-2 in early February 2000 over Smiling Mule in the quarter-finals of the League's Supplementary Cup, the lads in red and black were drawn against a Brook Hansen side for a semi-final at Apperly Bridge on April 1. Despite a 2-0 advantage at half time with strikes from Craig and Imran, in the end, the Club lost 4-3 to Brook Hansen in an entertaining and hard-fought match which became the high point of that season.

In that year's Mayday tournament, held in Leeds under the supervision of comrades Republica Highland, the club beat Republica 3-1 with goals from Shiz, Gary Cavanagh and Kev Poppleton.

The year 2000, also saw the Club's team squad enlarged with an influx of new younger players, and they were able to field a team in the Bradford Sunday Alliance League, starting in Division 4A. The Sunday Alliance League had 105 teams in nine divisions, the Club over the years gradually rose to Division 3A by 2004 and Division 2A by 2006.

In 2001, the club played at the Easton Cowboys organised Alternative World Cup tournament in Thorncombe, Dorset... and won the final.

By 2002, besides running two football teams, the Club fielded its first cricket side in a friendly match at Tadcaster, losing by 71 runs. The cricket team flourished and encouraged members' youngsters into the squad and still play regularly to this day.

Tuesday, October 30, 2001
Telegraph & Argus

LEAGUE CUP: *Upset for Premier team*

Mail Coach are given their cards

by BRIAN CRAVEN
T&A Sports Reporter

Division One strugglers One In Twelve knocked Premier Division Mail Coach out of the League Cup at the second round stage.

Mail Coach, who sacrificed ground advantage, fell behind when One In Twelve midfielder and club secretary Craig Williams scored from close range. John McNally soon had Mail Coach level but Williams restored One In Twelve's lead and Naeem Mohamed then put them 3-1 up at the break.

Mail Coach hit back through Ian Brame before Williams completed a good afternoon's work with his hat-trick and his side's fourth goal.

Mail Coach's Phill Lunn made it 4-3 right on the whistle, but the day belonged to the One In Twelve side.

BRADFORD SUNDAY ALLIANCE DIVISION 2A

	P	W	D	L	F	A	Pts
Relay Rec Rvrs	22	20	2	0	101	19	62
Greengates Alb	22	15	4	3	75	42	49
Farmers	22	14	2	6	75	45	44
Bradford Ukrainian	22	12	2	8	58	50	38
White Swan	22	10	4	8	51	55	36
Fountain	22	10	2	10	53	47	32
Druids	22	9	2	11	52	70	29
One in Twelve	22	6	4	12	44	70	22
Hare & Hounds	21	5	3	13	47	60	18
Wyke Wndrs Res	22	6	1	15	40	72	18
George & Dragon	22	5	2	15	35	65	17
Bankfoot Lions	21	4	2	15	54	90	14

CARPE NOCTUM

After a launch night in 1999 at the Club, *Carpe Noctum* (seize the night) began regular monthly disco nights with member and DJ Howard G Vodka playing a mixture of goth, darkwave, electro and industrial music. They also began putting on bands, such as Saints Of Eden, who were formerly in Fields Of The Nephilim, on Saturday, September 23, 2000. During 2001, more bands played at the monthly nights, like Amila on June 16, and Mechanical Cabaret / Katscan / Squid on October 5.

Carpe Noctum also put on an unofficial after-show party for the Infest Festival which was the annual goth/darkwave/experimental festival held at Bradford University. The party, whilst being chaotic, set a path for more organised collaborations in future years.

In 2002, with the monthly gigs going strong and after a proper Infest after-show party, *Carpe Noctum* released a budget-priced CD compilation entitled *New Blood Volume One* to celebrate their third birthday. The CD was sold for £2 and contained fifteen tracks mainly by bands that had played at their club nights. Also that year they started a Saturday afternoon get-together at the Exchange Bar on Market Street (under Waterstone's) predictably called *Carpe Diem* (seize the day).

Key *Carpe Noctum* promoted gigs at The 1 In 12 Club during the period 2003-2005 included; The Scary Bitches / Screaming Banshee Aircrew end-of-year gig, who again highlighted on August 9, 2004, with Zombina & The Skeletones; and on November 13, 2004 Killing Miranda (pictured) who'd released their CD album *Transgression By Numbers* on the Noise Kontrol label the previous year.

During 2005, 616 Abortions (formerly the Squids), Dead Filmstar, Action Directe from Leeds, Inkubus Sukkubus and on July 5, Cauda Pavonis (deathrock from Bristol) / Rhombus / Mourning For Autumn all graced the 1 In 12 stage.

The *Carpe Noctum* collective team decided to move on after its fifth year at the Club and the next year re-launched as a monthly club night at the New Beehive Inn, although they returned to the 1 In 12 for their New Year's Eve bash.

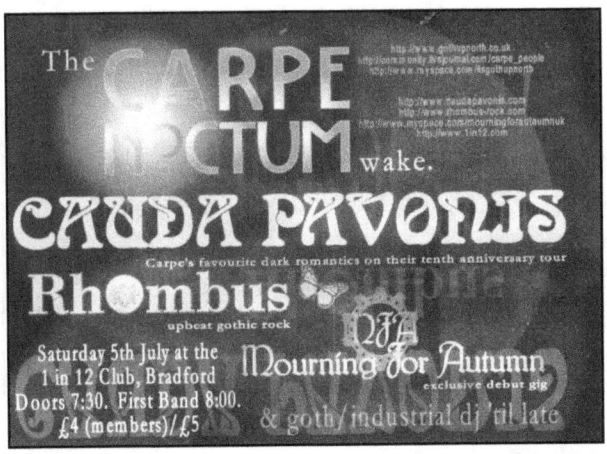

Over the next few years, the *Carpe Noctum* team continued their *Goth Up North* scene at the Mannville Arms and the Zuu Bar before moving to the Gasworks.

In 2015 they started their monthly residency at the Library in Leeds, where it continued for many years.

GIGS AT THE 1 IN 12 CLUB : OCTOBER 2000

Saturday, October 7: An International DIY All-dayer with thirteen bands including Bane (USA), Endstand and Manifesto Jukebox (from Finland), The Get Up & Go'ers (Sweden), Beezwax (Norway) and Winchester 73 (Germany).

Friday, October 13: Violent Design a metal band from Huddersfield.

Thursday, October 19th: The return of Submission Hold from Canada who'd played the Club in 1998 and were promoting their CD *Progress... As If Survival Mattered* a compilation of all their vinyl and cassette releases co-released on the local Flat

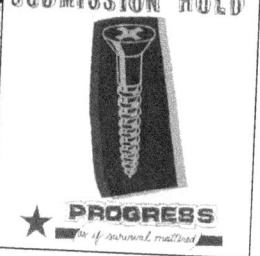

Earth label. On the night they were supported by Newcastle's Red Monkey.

An afternoon gig on Sunday, October 22 featured Skimmer, returning from their third Japanese tour / Vibracathedral Orchestra (improvised jazz-noise-rock) / Fig 4.0 (from Leeds) / Final Conclusion for £2.50 (£3.50 non-members).

On Halloween Night, The 1 In 12 Club's Kidz Klub held a special party for members' kids and produced a leaflet which included a word search puzzle, short ghost stories, jokes and a potted history of the origins of Halloween.

A GUIDE TO UK DIY PROMOTERS

The fanzine *Fracture* ran an article on UK DIY promoters as a guide to booking a UK tour in its November issue #13. Below is an extract:
"Promoters are the unsung heroes of the underground scene... plastering posters on walls away from the baleful eye of the CCTV. Problem is – it's not easy to find them outside of where you live, true some such as the Just One Life and STE collectives (Brighton and Southampton respectively) and the awe-inspiring 1 In 12 Club in Bradford have become institutions in their own right. But by and large, finding out who put on gigs where can be very tricky indeed."

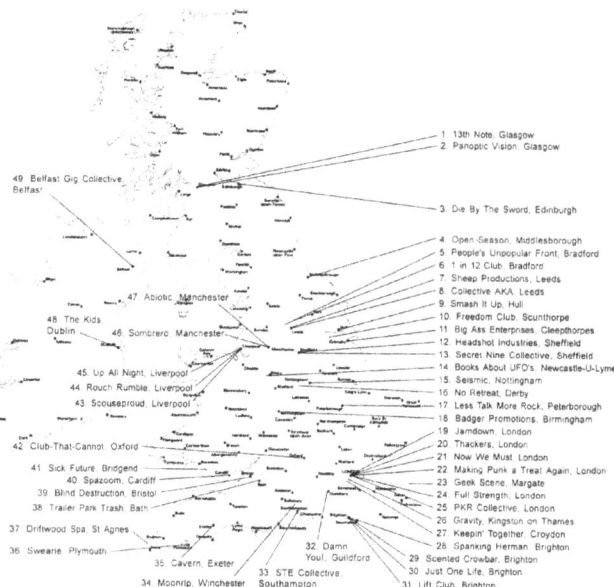

#6 — 1 IN 12 CLUB

Contact: Whoever answers the phone!
Address: 21-23 Albion St, Bradford, BD1 2LY
Telephone: 01274 734160
Email: 1in12@go-legend.co.uk
Web: www.legend.org.uk/~1in12
Feed: Yes
Sleep: Yes
Payment: Phone to find out
Other: A club autonomously run by its members. Has 3 floors: gig room, bar and cafe. There are many different people who put gigs on here. If you phone up to ask if you can get a gig make sure you ask for your name to be forwarded to the Sunday meeting. This way we can make sure someone who likes your band can sort out the gig.

The May Day Discussion Group's November monthly meeting on Thursday the 11th was called *A Touch Of Class*, an open discussion about class in the 1990s and beyond with a screening of a recent episode of the TV sitcom *The Royle Family*, written by Caroline Aherne.

GIGS: NOVEMBER

Friday, November 3: Herod, a new local indie rock band who released the six-track demo, *Champion The Cause*, in 2002.

Saturday, November 25: Bug Central / Homebrew / External Menace / Kismet HC / Debris / Sawn Off / Nailbiter / Stress / Eggraid / I.O.D. which was a benefit gig for Rape Crisis and Women's Aid.

Wednesday, November 29: Another *None More Heavy Promotions* gig with the return of US trio Spirit Caravan supported by Dutch band Beaver who'd released their five-track CD *Lodge* on the Man's Ruin Records label the previous year.

SAWN OFF

Although a Newcastle based band, they did play rather a lot at the 1 In 12 Club and were released on the local Flat Earth Record label. Below is a review in the rock magazine *Terrorizer* in November 2000, which erroneously classes Sawn Off as a Bradford grind punk band!

SAWN OFF
'Sawn Off'
FLAT EARTH

Sawn Off are typically Bradford grind punk. Call that narrowminded or lazy labelling but then again we all know what Californian Power Violence is. Okay, what exactly is Bradford grind? Nothing really. Just a band from Bradford that plays grind of some awesome power. We're talking short, fast, loud and very crusty slabs of brutality with intelligent lyrics, a dogdy rendition of the Sweeney theme tune, a Judas Priest cover and a cool photo of Carter on the sleeve. What more do you want? How about incredible drum rolls and quickfire melodic breaks last heard on a No Comment record; but other listeners will refer to anyone from Discharge to Doom. Whatever. It's all good stuff. As is usual, the main letdown is the less than dynamic production which lacks the meat to emphasis some of the band's thick riffs. Is this release timely? With a change in line up, are we going to experience a new phase in Sawn Off's plan of attack or is it business as usual? I wouldn't mind the latter but it could get a little too boring. Sawn Off can do better. They will do better. Twenty six songs in twenty six minutes. Neat. 7 [SK]

DRAMA COLLECTIVE

The 1 In 12 Drama Collective was originally set-up in 1997, when *The Haymarket Incident*, the first of a trio of plays written and directed by club member Noel Batstone was performed for the annual *Reclaiming Mayday* week. The two other plays *Durruti* and *The Uses Of Disorder* were performed in 1998 and 1999 respectively.

After around six weeks of rehearsals, the drama collective were ready to perform a new play, a murder-mystery farce called *Murder In The Library*, on three consecutive nights, Friday, December 1 to Sunday, December 3, 2000, on the gig floor at the Club. The play was in two parts and had a fifteen-minute interval. A cast of ten players was directed by member Lyn Gunn who also wrote the play. Great fun was had by all the actors, the performances were packed for each night and everyone thoroughly enjoyed themselves.

GIGS: DECEMBER

The only gig in December at the 1 In 12 Club was on Wednesday 13 which was a triple bill featuring Finnish political punk called Pax Americana supported by Scottish crust band Fastard and Sawn Off.

DEATH OF MICK ALLISON

The body of Michael Allison (pictured), former drummer in Stalingrad and Beer Beast who mysteriously disappeared after a Christmas party, was discovered in Shipley Canal on February 7, 2001. Mick, who lived on St Paul's Road in Manningham, was last seen on December 22, 2000, after enjoying a Christmas drink in the Noble Comb pub in Shipley with work colleagues from Pace. He was due to join his sister and her family in Southport for the holidays but never turned up.

After a major investigation, with more than 100 posters appealing for information put around Shipley, Frizinghall and Manningham, the police were alerted by a member of the public who spotted the body in the canal about a mile from the Noble Comb pub. His death was not treated as suspicious, although the exact circumstances of how he died remain a mystery. (17)

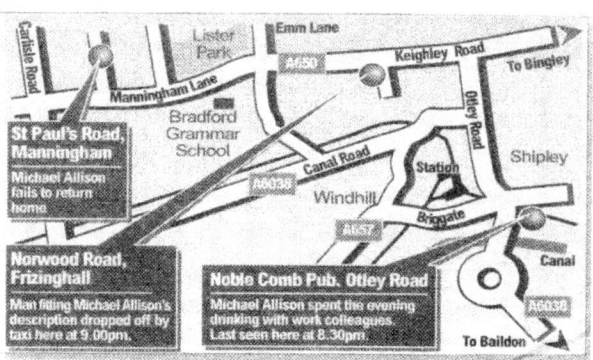

After the Second World War, in 1946, there were around 15,000 TV sets in the UK. By the year 2000 the number had risen to 55 million.

A TRIBUTE TO SMOKEY

A twelve-track CD entitled *A Tribute To Smokey* came out in 2000. It was by a group of uncredited session/studio guys who had mastered the Smokie sound, called the Bradford Boys. Ten of the cover tracks were from Smokie's top twenty hits, including one No 3 and three No 5's with the No 34 song *Take Good Care Of My Baby*. The twelfth and final track was a cover of Percy Sledge's *When A Man Loves A Woman*.

LOSING CONTROL

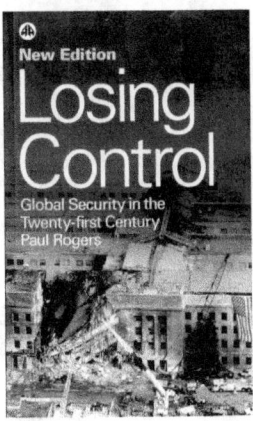

In 2000, Professor Paul Rogers of Bradford University's Department of Peace Studies published his book *Losing Control: Global Security In The 21st Century* on Pluto Press. The book looked at the world since the end of the Cold War and analysed the Western powers' perceptions of security and the real insecurities of growing inequality and unsustainability.

Professor Rogers, who had been Head of Department (1993-99) taught courses on international security, arms control and political violence for twenty years. He was a frequent TV commentator on international security issues and the book was a product in part of innumerable discussions and arguments with past and present students, as well as many shared views with development and peace activists.

The Department of Peace Studies was established in 1973-74, following an initiative from the Society Of Friends (Quakers). With close to 200 postgraduate students from more than 35 countries, it is the world's largest university peace studies department - a leading world centre for peace and conflict research. It is one of the UK's leading centres for politics and international studies and its research has a substantial impact in Britain and many other countries.

NIKKI STUART & GIRL THING

Talented local girl Nikki Stuart seemed poised for stardom after beating the 2,500 other girls who had auditioned to join the five-piece female pop group Girl Thing. Three of the other four girls, Michelle, Jodi and Linzi were British and the fourth, Anika, was Dutch.

They were the brainchild of Chris Herbert, who had helped launch the UK's most influential and successful female vocal group the Spice Girls, who went on to have nine chart topping singles. Girl Thing

were obviously trying to emulate them but unfortunately fell short of that kind of success. They did have two top twenty hits, *Last One Standing* reached No 8 in July, and *Girls On Top* topped out at No 25 in November 2000, Last One Standing which reached No 8 and, both on RCA Records.

MARIKO

Pudsey based sleeze-rockers Mariko (formerly known as Resin) were named after a top Japanese model of the 1970s. The band produced a three track demo CD in May 2000, with their songs *User Friendly, Elvis Loves Us* and *End Of The Week*. The CD was produced by Chris Langdon who was the brother of Royston and Anthony of Leeds band Spacehog.

MARIKO (2000 -			(formerly RESIN)	
PAUL	DAN	JOHN	GLEN	BILLY
GAUTREY	JACKSON	EMSLEY	JONES	MITCHELL
Voc	Gtr	Gtr	Bass	Drums

GREEN #2

Dom Sheard (pictured), Former bassist of Nursery, reactivated his old band Green (1996-99) in 2000, while still working with the band The Animal Day Sessions. Green #2 added new female singer Emma Baylin along with the old rhythm section of Kev and Rob and the band gigged extensively locally over the next few years. They added a fifth member at some point, ex-Mantra guitarist Leon Carrol. In 2007 they released a self-promoted three-track CD, *One, Two / Cry Harder / Martha's Harbour*.

BRADFORD FESTIVAL 2000

Bradford Festival 2000 ran for five weeks from Monday, May 19 to Sunday, July 2. Many local venues hosted events from literary evenings to live music to comedy shows, alongside main events at Centenary Square.

The square was a daily arena for daily live music, with *Cafe Bradford* hosting acts including The Cheb Hooray Band, L'Orchestre Du Cafe, Pete White's Suitcase Circus from 19-21 June in the afternoon.

World In A City hosted evening gigs in the square where Linton Kwesi Johnson & Dennis, Bovell Dub Band and Bradford's Creation Roots played on Thursday 22 June, Sharon King and Colin Reid on Friday 23 and Thomas Mapfumo & The Blacks Unlimited and Yat Kha performed on Saturday 24 June.

LINTON KWESI JOHNSON

"Ingland is a Bitch...You've got to learn how to survive in it" is a quote from a song by Linton Kwesi Johnson that best expresses his uncompromising scorn of racist British culture.

You have been watching
Linton Kwesi Johnson
at one of the live literature events in this year's Bradford Festival.

Linton had arrived in London from Jamaica aged eleven, and as a teenager had joined the British equivalent of the Black Panther party. He became one of the first black Britons to get a degree in sociology at London University's Goldsmith College.

His debut LP *Dread Beat An' Blood* was released in 1978 on Island Records. At the Festival Linton was promoting his latest album *More Time*, released in 1998 on his own LKJ Records label.

Bradford's music pubs and clubs hosted numerous gigs throughout the fortnight, including The Melborn (Bussard, Keiran Halpin, Howling Whippets, Halibop, Shiny Beast, Jed's Blues Band), Macrory's Bar (L'Orchestre Du Cafe, Angelo Palladino, Still Jumpin'), The Love Apple (Balladeers & Chancers, Aura), The New Beehive (Songs Of Resistance with Roy Bailey).

The Spring Bank Holiday from Saturday 27 – Monday 29 of May became a three-day live music event at Centenary Square, sponsored and covered by BBC Music Live, and featured a host of Bradford talent alongside *'international stars and national legends'*.

Saturday, May 27 saw Bradford acts Juke Joint (pictured above), Us, Purity Cries, and The House Band play alongside 7 Hours, Big Rory, Inztants Theatre, Tegenwind, Kuladu and headliner, award-winning saxophonist Andy Sheppard.

Stars of French American roots music, La Bottine Souriante, who had headlined festivals all over the world, took to the top slot on the Sunday show, preceded by Bradford's Cajun Aces, Macumba, Bedlam Oz, Skokiaan, Rent, Opera North, Bassa Bassa, Inztants Theatre and Tegenwind.

Bradford legends Smokie closed the whole event on the Monday night, topping a bill that included Doris & The Dinner Ladies with The Big Bloody Soul Band, The Primitives, Nachda Punjab Dancers, Beat This! By Drumcall, Elephant Talk and The Howling Whippets - fronted by Denny Austin and featuring young, talented blues guitarist Chantel McGregor.

At the same time, the usual colourful mix of street performers entertained crowds of shoppers along the main shopping thoroughfares.

On Saturday, July 1, Macrory's Bar hosted its annual *Ginger Fringe Festival* (named after bar owner Ian Austin's vibrant hair!). A stage set up in the hotel's car park hosted local bands.

BRADFORD MELA

For the third year running the Bradford Mela (a traditional Asian fair of music, dance and food) was held at Peel Park on Saturday 1 & Sunday 2 July. It had earned a global reputation and between 35-60,000 people were believed to have attended over the weekend, despite torrential rain on the Saturday.

The main attractions were Asian artist Talvin Singh, folk singer Shaukat Ali, pioneering band Joi, bhangra band The Sahotas and rap band Fundamental (pictured) which featured ex-Southern Death Cult drummer Aki Nawaz.

The final act on the Sunday, The Sahotas, were on the main stage when someone threw a plastic bottle at the band. A band member swore at the crowd, which inflamed a certain section of youths in the audience.

"The mela was then shut down early by the Police, with festival organisers' permission, after youths lobbed more missiles at performers. Afterwards, officers in riot gear were needed to break up a large crowd of youths who had gathered in the street outside Peel Park on Cliffe Road. Eleven people were arrested on public order offences." (19)

WITHOUT PREJUDICE

The trio Without Prejudice consisted of Craig Sowden, Mark Higgins and Matt Jennings who had been performing their mix of reggae, ska and soul covers since 1997. (18)

On Saturday, July 29, they were asked to play a gig at Pennington's on Manningham Lane for the ticket price of £2.

The band flew in to play the one-off gig, as they were in the middle of their fourth summer season in Ibiza, where they played between April and October. The Pennington's entertainments manager Gareth Cawood was so eager to book them that the venue paid their airfares for the flying visit.

Keyboardist Matt Jennings would also play with the eight-piece soul covers band Planet Soul before joining the Pleasure Seekers in 2001.

CHRIS SHARP

Windhill-based singer-songwriter Chris Sharp had been about since 1989, with his five-piece Chris Sharp Project, working on material at Dave King's Engine Rooms studio and co-writing songs with ex-Voyager UK keyboardist Andy Wells.

In 1994, he was the first artist to appear on the BBC TV show *Kilroy* singing his song *Jealousy*.

During the next two years, Chris and the band gigged all over the UK, before he took a break between 1996 and 2000.

In August 2000 he was back, releasing his debut CD album *Secrets Of The Heart* on his own Delirium Records label. The thirteen-track album was recorded over two years and featured guest artists such as former FM keyboardist Phil 'Didge Digital' Manchester and vocalist Anita Madigan. Anita provided 'doo-wop' backing vocals for his song *Crazy For The Heart* which she later reprised on Terrorvision's *Oblivion*

single, which was recorded at the same studio.

Radio 2 DJ Steve Wright championed Chris's track *You & Me* on his show.

Chris performed songs from his album as a duo with guitarist Dave Johnson. They played a gig at the New Furnace on Halifax Road on Friday, August 4, 2000.

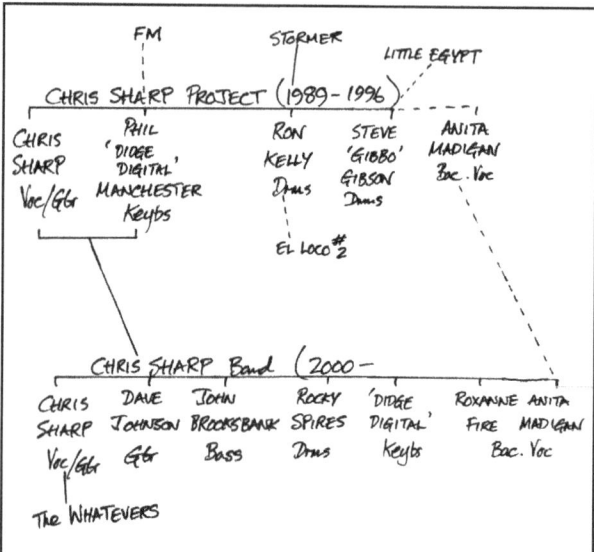

T&A MUSIC PAGE CHANGES HANDS

In September 2000, long-standing columnist Simon Ashberry relinquished the *Telegraph & Argus*' traditional Friday rock and pop page to journalist Jim Jack, having written the page for almost ten years. Simon later took his love and knowledge of music over to BCB Radio where he presented a long-running music show, Bradford Beat.

MYRTLE PARK, BINGLEY LIVE

The annual free event at Bingley's Myrtle Park on Saturday, September 2, featured Tamla Motown soul star Edwin Starr, whose most famous hit single was *War*.

He played to around 15,000 people at the event, organised by Bradford Council and Pulse Radio.

LOVE AFFAIR NEW ALBUM

On September 4, Love Affair released a fourteen-track anthology album on CD, *No Strings: Every Now And Then,* on the Angel Air label.

It was their first release in nearly thirty years and included a sixteen-page booklet charting the band's history.

The album avoided their most well-known songs, instead, it focussed on their obscure B sides and album tracks. The CD included the band's newly composed and recorded track *It's A Love Affair* and four previously unreleased tracks from 1966.

On Friday, September 15, Belfast boy Van (The Man) Morrison, ex-singer of 1960s beat group Them, played a sell-out concert at St George's.

GOAD

Goad were a four-piece eclectic indie-funk-rock band from the Clayton area. The band had an international feel as their guitarist was Italian, the bassist Ukrainian and the drummer was Polish.

They had only been together since July 2000, but soon put a three-track demo out with songs entitled *The Road / Orange Quilt / Why Am I Me?*

On Sunday, October 8, Goad, played the Love Apple supported by **Skiver**.

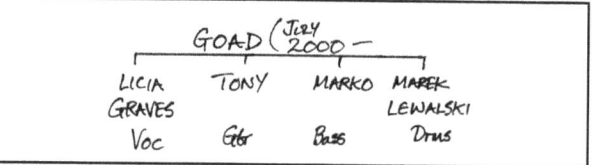

PUZZLE HALL FESTIVAL

The eighth annual free festival took place at the Puzzle Inn in Sowerby Bridge on Friday, August 25. The four-day festival included the three-piece Stipetic from Bradford, led by guitarist Carl Stipetic with his two brothers.

Other bands and artists performing were; Halifax lad The Shirt, rock band Slightly Alien, The Gecko's (all teachers), jazz band Tongue & Groove, three-piece Fez, folk-rock from Imaginary Friends, Manchester-based band Pocket Central, Des Horsfall's Fallen Horses, and folk stars Joe Stead and Peter Coe.

The band **Coastal Dune** was formed by recent graduates from Durham University. The line-up included guitarist Jonathan Heasley from Keighley. They played a gig at Bradford University on November 6.

EMBRACE

After touring Thailand, Japan and Europe, the band returned to St George's Hall to do a hometown gig as part of their seventeen-date UK tour on Tuesday, November 7.

Embrace were promoting their second album, *Drawn From Memory*, which contained eleven tracks, three of which had already been released as singles. In March, *You're Not Alone* reached No 14, in June, *Save Me* got to No 29 and, in August, *I Wouldn't Wanna Happen To You* reached No 23, all on the Hut record label through Virgin Records.

Embrace, who formed in 1997, had a run of four top twenty hit singles between 1997-98. The No 6 hit *Come Back To What You Know* was their highest chart entry.

LAPDOG

Formed in August 1998, this local band (three local lads and the guitarist from Ossett) were keenly sponsored by Voltage Records who wanted to sign them. They recorded their three-track EP *Breathing Is Optional: Nick Drake / Parasite / Mellowbrickroad* at Voltage Studios in November 2000 and sold it for £3.

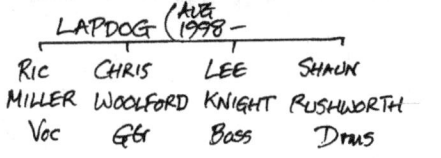

Arcane were a four-piece indie rock band, made up of 18 years-olds who were all still at school. They played a gig at the Chicago Rock Cafe on Great Horton Road on November 27.

The year 2000 saw the sad death of singer Ian Dury. He had several top twenty hit singles during the late 1970s with his band Ian Dury & The Blockheads, most famously a No 1 with *Hit Me With Your Rhythm Stick*.

Daily Mutiny
No 2 Friday 25 December 1998

Catnap calamity causes cancellation chaos at Christmas concert collaboration!

TOO MUCH SHERRY IN THE TRIFLE!

DISAPPOINTMENT today as hopes of a ZED reunion at the annual Bradford Ex-Rock Stars Christmas Dinner were dashed when bassist Jont 'Captain' Scarlet and guitarist Nogsy 'Simon' Nolan nodded off after Christmas dinner.

Reports that the non-appearance of the former ZED men was due to an excess of sherry in the trifle were strongly denied earlier today by a Mutiny 2000 spokesman.

However, this reporter can exclusively reveal that over *1 tenth of a bottle* of notorious party drink *Harvey's Bristol Cream* was inserted into the trifle by person or persons unknown!

The pair were later seen downing *at least two portions each* before tucking into the cheese and biscuits.

The cheese board was reported to include a variety of *foreign cheese* as well as locally sourced..., who shared a notorious bachelor pad with the accused, Mr Nolan was recently coming out of Boots trying to conceal a...

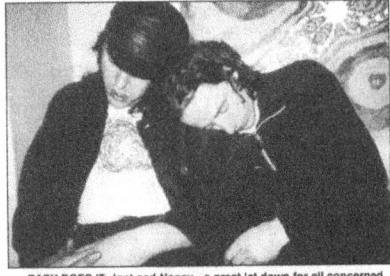

EASY DOES IT: Jont and Nogsy - a great let down for all concerned

NO TREK FOR STAR
More disappointment for Bradford utility

ALSO AVAILABLE FROM MUTINY 2000

ZED - A DOLLAR AND A DREAM - ZEDLP1
ZED - THE ARTICLES OF CAPTAIN MISSION - ZEDLP2
WESTERN DANCE - WESTERN DANCE - WD2001
GARDENERS OF EDEN - ALBUM - GARD01

...AND COMING SOON - ALBUMS FROM
JAZZ MUTINY
SHINY BEAST
MOOTA
YEAR DOT
PRIMATE

ZED - MUTINY 2000 - ZEDLP3
ZED - TWELVE DAYS IN A BUNKER - M2KZL1
MUTINY 2000 VOLUME 2

MUTINY 2000

In January 1997, Bradford rockers Zed rented a rehearsal space on the top floor of a mill on Thornton Road in Bradford, which later became a nightclub (The Mill). At that time, the top floor was an open space apart from an already built unit occupied by the legendary Bradford psychedelic DJ and light show Griff's Magic Theatre.

In 1998, Zed guitarist Crispian Baker developed cluster headaches, a debilitating neurological condition that sadly led to his death in 2015. This was another reason Zed decided to create a studio and label.

Jont and Matt joined forces with like-minded musician friends (notably Mark 'Moota' Appleyard, Harris, Chad Meade and former New Model Army drummer Rob Heaton) and pooled gear and skills to build and equip a studio with a 32-channel mixing desk and 16-track analogue tape machine. They named the studio and label after the last album, Mutiny 2000.

It was also intended to be a label in the mould of Motown, where musicians could be chosen from a pool to record on different projects, although this concept was never fully realised.

WHITE ABBEY ROAD

By the end of the year, the studio released its first compilation album, *White Abbey Road*, with tracks recorded by bands and acts that used the studio. It was recorded mainly by Rob Heaton and Matt Webster and put together with Zed bassist Jont.

Matt Webster designed a spoof newspaper, *The Daily Mutiny*, that was supposed to accompany the album. Also given away with early copies was a free yellow plastic duck. Several bin liners full of ducks were rescued from the set of ITV's detective drama, *A Touch Of Frost*, starring David Jason, which ended up at The Mill.

There was a launch gig for the album at The Mill on November 4, 2000. at which every band on the album played.

GARDENERS OF EDEN

After leaving New Model Army, drummer Rob Heaton began writing and recording his own material. Joined by various friends (including former NMA bassist Stuart Morrow and Kill 2 This guitarist Rob Rhodes), Rob recorded numerous tracks in his own attic Righteous Sound Studio under the banner of The Gardeners Of Eden. He completed an album's worth of material which remains unreleased apart from the songs that appeared on both Mutiny 2000 compilations. *Motherfucker* and *My Name Is Bill* were on *White Abbey Road*, and *Bradford 6 am* appeared on *Soup Bowl Press*.

FRANTIC

Former Dub Kitchen singer Fran Jones teamed up with former New Model Army rhythm section Rob Heaton and Stuart Morrow to record some of her songs. Her track *Move Me* appeared on both Mutiny 2000 CD compilations.

SHINY BEAST

This acoustic band was based around the songs of former Nowt/Grim singer/guitarist Harris. Joining Harris were his cousin Sean Dillon on guitar, Greg Brauns on djembe, and Tooth Fairy duo Bela Emerson and John Gray on cello and saxophone. They played regularly on the local pub circuit at venues like MacRory's Bar and The Melborn and were featured on a Channel 4 new music documentary series *Sound Of The Suburbs*.

Their tracks *Ed Wood* and *Watching Rain* were featured on the album.

ANGELO PALLADINO

London-born Rawden-based blues singer Angelo Palladino was in the process of recording an album produced by Matt Webster when White Abbey Road was released. Tracks *Just Can't Sleep* and *The Restless Road* were included on the album. Angelo was backed by his two-piece acoustic band The Paisanos, which comprised Bradford's Sean Dillon on guitar and Leeds-based Lee Abbott on double bass.

SUPERSONIC

This was a short-lived studio project with DJ Chad Meade, drummer Simon Mawson, guitarist Muzz and James 'Atko' Atkinson on vocals. They put together the track *Supersonic* for the album.

MOOTA

Former Handful Of Dance bassist Marki 'Moota' Appleyard formed this band, originally called Clutch Trouble, after writing a full set of songs on acoustic guitar. En route to a radio session for *The Bradford Beat* at BCB, their original bass player leapt out of the van and ran off into the sunset. After this, Marki renamed the band after his nickname, 'Moota' and recruited new members to add to the lineup of Brett Paley on bongos, Jim Bob on drums. Former Zed duo Jont on bass and Simon 'Nogsy' Nolan on guitar joined and Moota began gigging.

By the time they recorded the songs *Let It Shine* and *Like A Fish*, produced by Rob Heaton, for *White Abbey Road*, former Howling Whippet and Somebody's Brother drummer Timmy Nuttall had joined. John Gray played sax on the session.

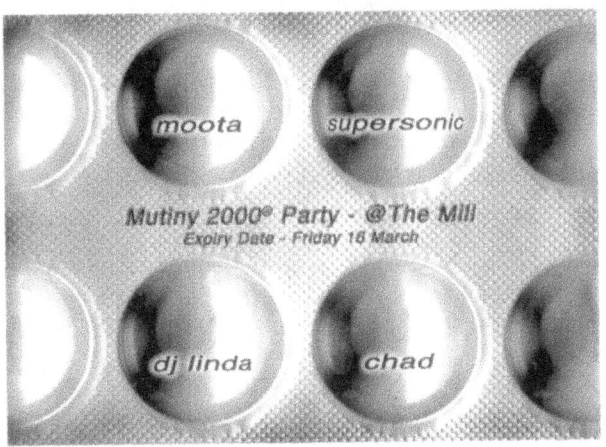

They became regulars on the local circuit, playing at MacRory's, The Melborn and the Love Apple as well as gigs in London.

In 2001 they began recording their *Music From The Big Blue Vein* album at Mutiny 2000 Studios, engineered and co-produced by Matt Webster. Simon Nolan had relocated to Sheffield and his place was taken by another former Zed and Handful Of Dance man, Harris.

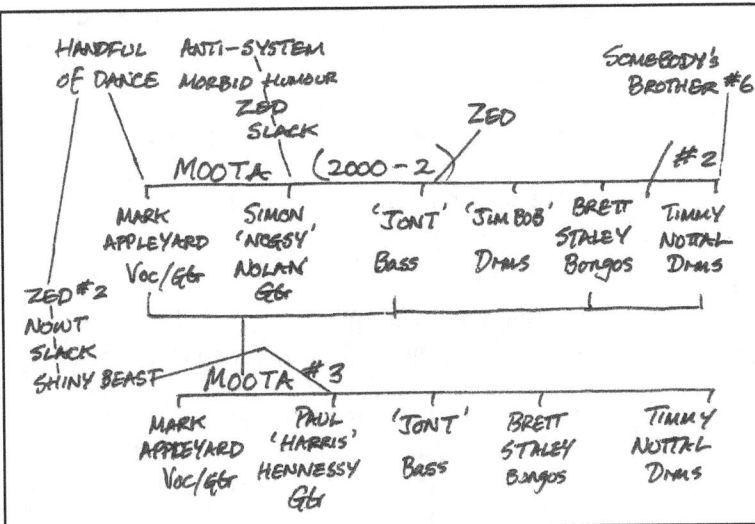

The album also featured a number of guests on various tracks including Adam Bennett, John Gray, Sean Dillon, Bela Emerson, Greg Brauns, Gill Bennett, Cunny and Jez Farrar. After shows to promote the album including a Mutiny 2000 party at The Mill on Friday, March 16, 2002, with Supersonic and DJ's Chad and Linda Sprogis.

Moota came to an end when Marki and his family emigrated to Australia.

ELVIS TAXI

Friends and members of numerous Bradford bands like Somebody's Brother and Howling Whippets formed their own band. They named themselves Elvis Taxi after a local cab firm based in Little Horton Green. The four were also regulars on the Bradford jam circuit at venues like The Peel, The Melborn and MacRory's.

The band shared lead vocals between guitarist Greg Brauns, bassist Sean Dillon and drummer Jake Riley. Their only recording session, produced by Rob Heaton, yielded two songs for the White Abbey Road - *Stopwatch*, sung by Greg, and *Hypocrite*, sung by Jake.

Two of the band, guitarist Dave Ledgard and drummer Jake Riley were also members of Leeds indie band Dragster. When Dragster vocalist and songwriter Craig Brauns (younger brother of Greg) was signed to Island Records in 2002, the Elvis Taxi line-up joined him to become the band Zico.

JAZZ MUTINY

This side project was born from improvised studio test sessions at Mutiny 2000 Studios and was based around the trio of Rob Heaton on drums, John Gray on saxophone and Jont on bass. Guitarists Rob Rhodes and Dave Legard also played on some tracks and Bela Emerson on cello.

A whole album's worth of material was recorded by the band. Two of their tracks featured on the compilation, *Police Cars* and *Banana*, which was a collaboration with ranting poet Dave 'Little Brother' Stockell. The best of all the sessions was later released as an album on Mutiny 2000 Records in 2005 as a tribute to Rob Heaton.

Their only live performance came at the *White Abbey Road* album launch at The Mill in 2020 although enough material was recorded to compile an album which was released in 2005.

SOLAR

Solar was a one-off project by singer Tony Perks. On the track *Discord And Gravity* he was backed by Dave Ledgard, Sean Dillon, John Gray, and Rob Heaton, who played drums and lead guitar and also produced the track.

GRIM

Bradford's Grim contributed their title track, *Grim*, to the album. Harris took the lead vocals and guitar on this track, with Adam Bennett on guitar, Jont on bass and Matt Webster on drums.

YEAR DOT

Former Western Dance bandmates Liam Sheeran (pictured), Ade Clark (recently of Bullweek) and Matt Webster reunited to form Year Dot. Also joining the line-up were two other past Bullweek members, Matt Bolton on guitar and Jamie Dawson on keyboards.

The band recorded several songs, two of these, *Girlington* and *Tea Party*, were released on the compilation. Year Dot only actually played one gig, the *White Abbey Road* album launch party at The Mill before Liam, Ade and Matt were joined by their former Western Dance guitarist Stephen Andrews to become Kwai Chang Caine.

MUTINY 2000 BAND

As well as being a studio and a label, Mutiny 2000 was also an occasional live event. Born from weekly jams in the studio throughout 1998 and 1999, the band was a loose collective that played two live gigs at The Mill.

The line-up included drummers Matt Webster and Rob Heaton, bassist Jont, guitarists including Harris, Sean Dillon, Rob Rhodes, Nat Brewer, and Dave Ledgard, saxophonist John Gray and Bela Emerson on cello. Rob Heaton prepared a tape of audio clips and film quotes that played over the band's industrial-type improvised grooves. A version of the line-up recorded the song *Day After Day* for the album.

DJ LINDA

Bradford DJ Linda Sprogis' piano instrumental, *Bradford Lullaby* - played by Jenny Outhwaite, was the last track on the album. Lynda was very well known on the punk/new wave/indie circuit around Bradford during the eighties and nineties, DJing at many venues including Benson's, The Spotted House and The Smithy.

CHAPTER 1 — 1999 - 2000

Courtesy of the Telegraph & Argus

ENTERTAINMENT
Friday, December 22, 2000 — Telegraph & Argus

Abbey Christmas from Mutiny 2000

In juke boxes throughout the city this winter you will be able to, should you wish, flip past Frank Sinatra's homage to the Big Apple and hear a touching tribute to...Girlington?

Bradford's own 'Abbey Road' studio, Mutiny 2000, has just released a compilation of tracks by some of the district's most promising unsigned talent.

Based, actually, in Thornton Road ("but White Abbey Road, which is nearby, sounds much better"), the firm is the brainchild of sound engineer and producer Matt Webster, and former New Model Army drummer Rob Eaton.

White Abbey Road, the first, 20-track compilation volume in a series, includes a host of unusual

ROCK & POP
with JIM JACK

delights including Banana, Like A Fish and Bradford Lullaby; not to mention Year Dot's urban hymn to Girlington....

Matt, who drums on the track, explained the motivation behind what the promotional magazine that comes with the album describes as "the world's first song about Bradford's beautiful district."

"The singer, Liam Sheeran, works in Girlington and it's about him getting stuck there and trying to call up his girlfriend to come and get him out!

"We're a new record label, recording studio and promotions company, and all the bands that are recording their own albums with us have contributed to this compilation.

"There's all kinds of sounds on there because we'll take on anybody, it's not restricted to any style of music as long as it's good."

The 16-track analogue studio, which has 48-channel computer mixing facilities, opened around a year ago.

It also boasts its own team of 'utility musicians', including Matt and Rob themselves, who can work with the recording artists.

And then there's the live side of things, which Matt is passionate about: "I don't think there's anything happening live in Bradford at the moment," he argues.

YOU'RE ALWAYS IN FASHION WITH WHITE ABBEY ROAD

TALENT SPOTTER: *Jeremy Nigel, member of Mutiny 2000, the label's own band, with the CD compilation of tracks by some of the district's most promising unsigned talent.*

"It's dead after we lost the Queen's Hall, with a lot of bands going through to Leeds to play, but we're hoping to do something to rectify that.

"We're lining up some multi-group gigs for the New Year, where four bands will play with shared headlines.

"The idea is to have it all in hand so we can produce, promote and do the art work for everything and we don't have to rely on anybody else."

White Abbey Road is available from System Records in North Parade, priced £10 which includes a copy of the witty New Mutiny Express 'newspaper'.

Matt insists there are plenty of more surreal, and eclectic, offerings to come.

"It's going to be a continuing thing. We've already started recording the next one and bands will be bringing out their own albums soon, all through our label."

e-mail: jim.jack @newsquest.bradford.co.uk

Mutiny 2000 studio photos by Richard Ingham

THE NEGATIVES

In December 2000, the original line-up of The Negatives, minus singer Dave Wilcox, teamed up with the Bradford City fanzine *City Gent* to release a CD EP to celebrate Bradford City's promotion to the Premier League.

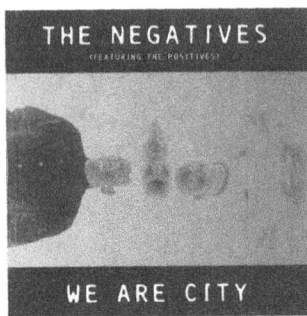

The EP was entitled *We Are City* and contained three tracks. *We Are City* was a reworking of their song *We're From Bradford, Claret And Amber Fever* was a reworking of their earlier song *Little Green Man Fever* and *Valley Of The Rising Son* was a reworking of the traditional *House Of The Rising Sun,* a song the band used to cover.

The vocals were provided by the feature writers from the fanzine, under the guise of The Positives, which comprised Dave Pendleton, Mark Harrison and Chris Harrison, with Mark Neale on whistle. It was recorded by Carl Stipetic, at his In-A-City Studios.

The band's drummer Tino, an ardent City fan, had co-written the song in the 1970s and hoped it would be the new pre-match theme tune. The single went on sale at the club's Up Front store for £3.99.

After reuniting for the single, the band dispersed, as bassist Bob Robinson and guitarist Pete Stobbs no longer lived in Bradford. Drummer Tino Palmer decided to continue playing with a new line-up of The Negatives.

Tino's new Negatives released the CD album *Brain Damage* in 2002, the mini album *Wool City Rockers* in 2004 and *The Negatives... Say* CD EP in 2005, all on their own Not From London label. These releases were a mix of old songs written by the original band with some new tracks written by the current version.

Towards the end of the decade, Tino decided not to carry on with the new Negatives. However, guitarist Rick continued with a version of the band called The Negatives UK, still performing songs by the original band.

In 2014, Spanish label Paramecium Records re-released The Negatives' 1979 single, *Stake Out / Love Is Not Real*, housed in a reproduction of the original handwritten sleeve.

A further vinyl release, *The Bradford EP*, followed in 2016. Side 1 featured two tracks, *We're From Bradford* and *Little Green Man Fever*, recorded in 1978 with original singer Dave Wilcox, who passed away in 2006. For side two, the original surviving members Pete Stobbs, Bob Robinson and Tino Palmer recorded two songs from the same period that hadn't been recorded at the time, *No Alternative* and *World War 3*.

DAILY EXPRESS SATURDAY JANUARY 13 2001

Fame at last for the punk accountant

Rebel band find success 20 years on

BY BOB McGOWAN

SUCCESS has finally caught up with punk band The Negatives – more than 20 years after their only record flopped.

The double A-side single cost the group just £89 to make in 1979 and got nowhere in the charts. Now collectors are paying up to £350 a copy.

The band, who split up after failing to make an impact, have got back together to exploit their belated fame. But when they met up again for the first time in 20 years they found they were not the rebellious youths they once were.

Bass guitarist Bob Robinson, 42, is now an accountant, drummer Tino Palmer is a confectionery wholesaler and lead guitarist Pete Stubbs works with the disabled.

The group minus singer Dave Wilcox who could not be traced – now have three tracks out on a compilation album for punk label Detour Records. They have even been back in the studio, recording the official song for their home football team, Bradford City.

Bob, who now lives in Cambridge, said he was shocked when he found out how much their first single was selling for.

"It's a strange story. I got a phone call from Tino who said a record company had got hold of the single and wanted to put it on a compilation album. It sounded like a wind-up to me but it seems this record is very collectable, particularly in Japan.

"They auctioned one of our singles over the Internet and it eventually went for £350 to a guy from Sweden.

"If somebody had told me it was worth a fiver I would have believed them. We were quite big in our own back garden and that was it. We had a year or two where we gigged around Yorkshire and Lancashire and then we split up.

"In a way I think if the single had sold 10,000 copies and made it to number 50 in the charts it would probably only be worth three quid. But a lack of success can make something more valuable. The nice thing is I have four or five friends back in Bradford who've got copies and they say they wouldn't dream of selling them no matter what they're worth."

Dizzy Holmes, boss of West Sussex-based Detour Records, said: "I came across The Negatives in about 1983 when I started collecting punk records.

"They were big in their own town, but didn't expand out of Bradford.

ROLLING BACK THE YEARS: Accountant Bob Robinson with suit, briefcase and guitar, is reliving his youth, left, as a punk musician with his band The Negatives

They're a solid punk group with attitude. They sang about stuff they believed in, that was happening round them."

The two original tracks from The Negatives' 1979 single – Love Is Not Real and Stakeout – plus an un-released song, We Are From Bradford, are on the Detour Records album Bored Teenagers Volume Two.

Mr Holmes said: "Punk always goes around. Every time the big bands are re-issued collectors get fed up buying the same stuff in different sleeves.

"We try to put out smaller bands who should have been just as big at the time."

CHAPTER 1 — 1999 - 2000

THE NEGATIVES

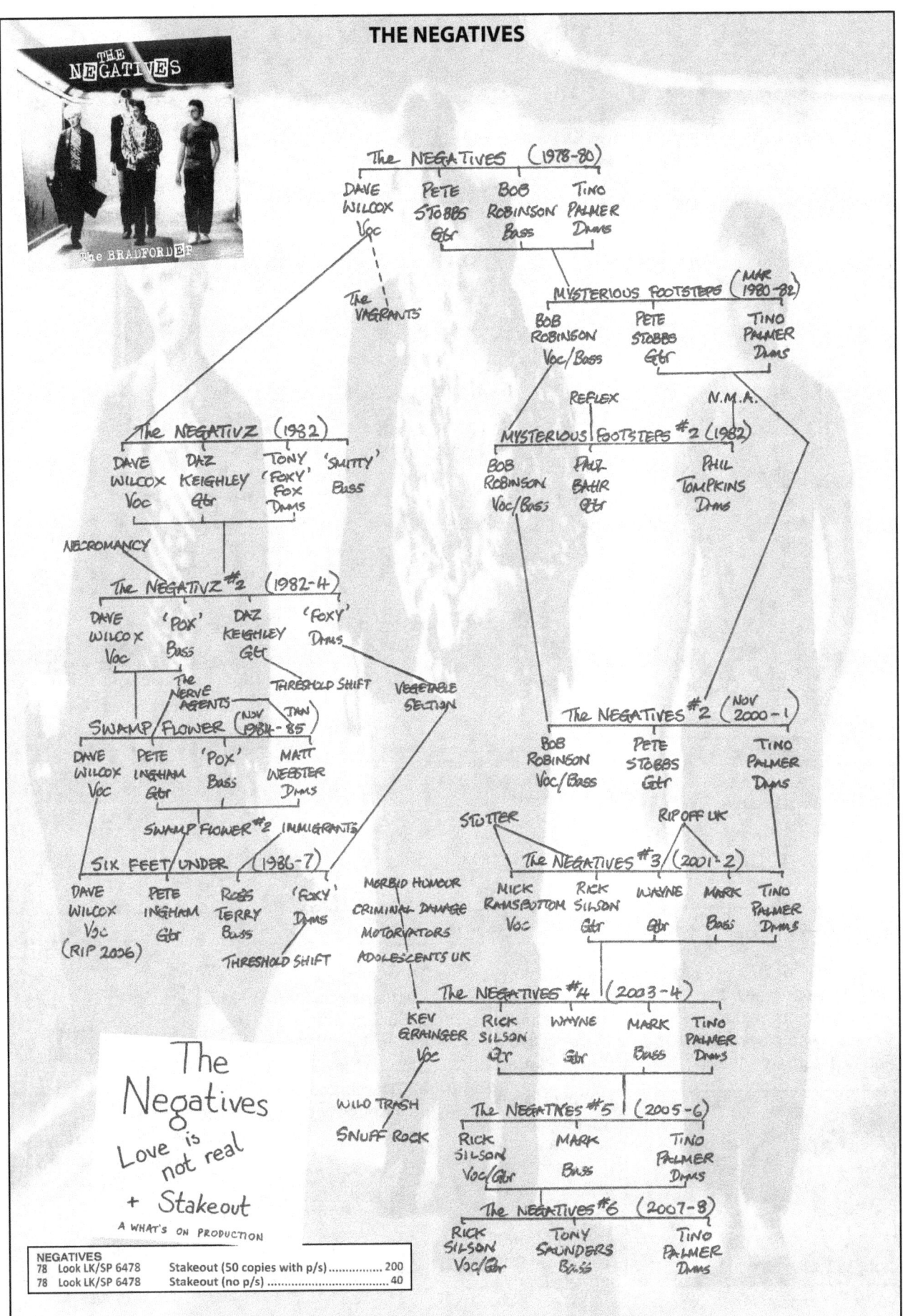

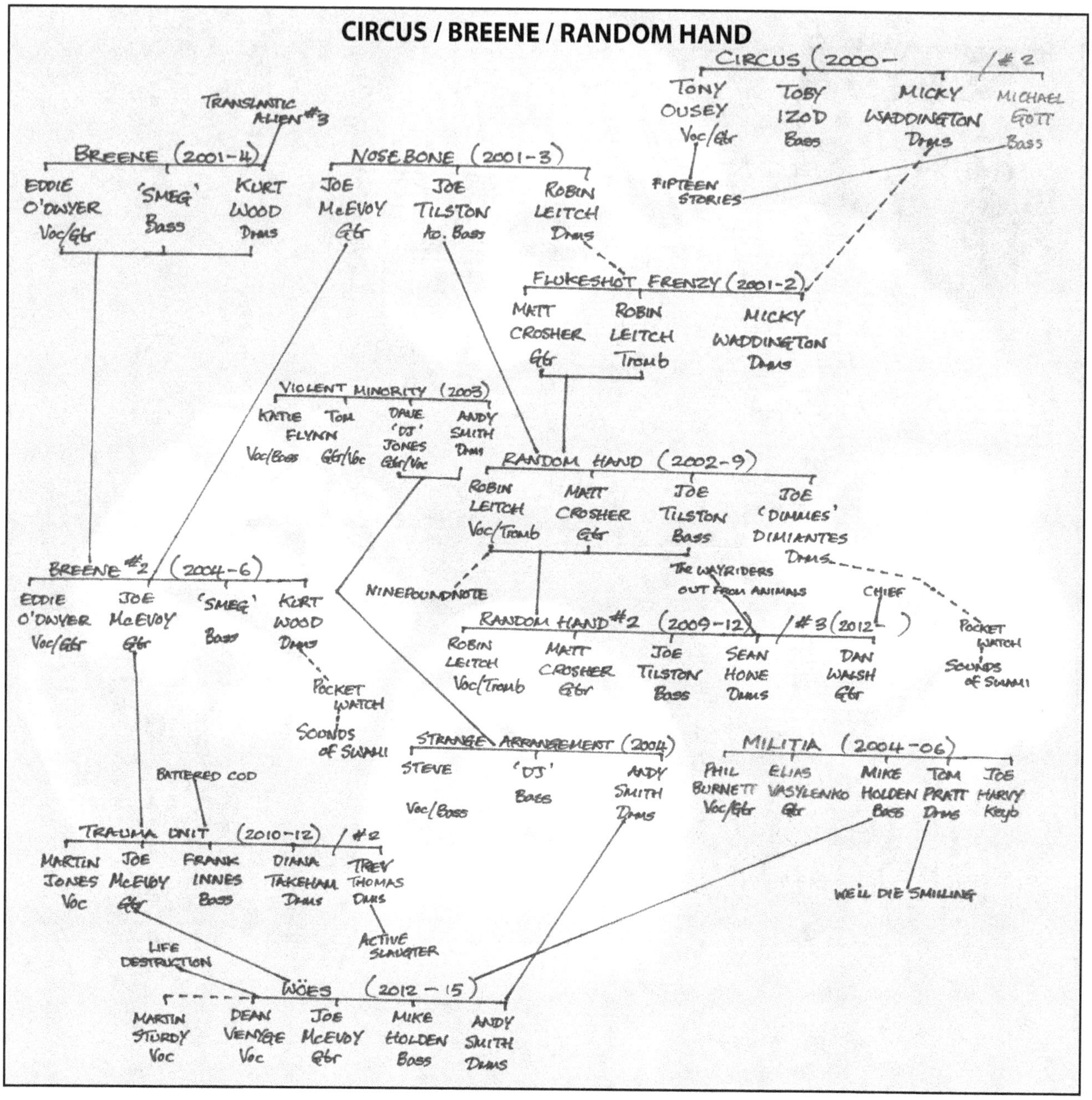

CIRCUS / BREENE / RANDOM HAND

[Band lineage/family tree diagram showing the following bands and members:]

Circus (2000–) / #2 — Tony Ousey (Voc/Gtr), Toby Izod (Bass), Micky Waddington (Drms), Michael Gott (Bass) — Fifteen Stories

Breene (2001-4) — Eddie O'Dwyer (Voc/Gtr), 'Smeg' (Bass), Kurt Wood (Drms) — Translantic Alien #3

Nosebone (2001-3) — Joe McEvoy (Gtr), Joe Tilston (Ac. Bass), Robin Leitch (Drms)

Flukeshot Frenzy (2001-2) — Matt Crosher (Gtr), Robin Leitch (Tromb), Micky Waddington (Drms)

Violent Minority (2003) — Katie Flynn (Voc/Bass), Tom (Gtr/Vbc), Dave 'DJ' Jones (Gtr/Voc), Andy Smith (Drms)

Random Hand (2002-9) — Robin Leitch (Voc/Tromb), Matt Crosher (Gtr), Joe Tilston (Bass), Joe 'Dimmies' Dimiantes (Drms)

Breene #2 (2004-6) — Eddie O'Dwyer (Voc/Gtr), Joe McEvoy (Gtr), 'Smeg' (Bass), Kurt Wood (Drms) — Ninepoundnote, Pocket Watch, Sounds of Swami

Random Hand #2 (2009-12) / #3 (2012–) — Robin Leitch (Voc/Tromb), Matt Crosher (Gtr), Joe Tilston (Bass), Sean Howe (Drms), Dan Walsh (Gtr) — The Wayriders, Out From Animals, Chief, Pocket Watch, Sounds of Swami

Strange Arrangement (2004) — Steve (Voc/Bass), 'DJ' (Bass), Andy Smith (Drms)

Militia (2004-06) — Phil Burnett (Voc/Gtr), Elias Vasylenko (Gtr), Mike Holden (Bass), Tom Pratt (Drms), Joe Harvy (Keyb) — We'll Die Smiling

Trauma Unit (2010-12) / #2 — Martin Jones (Voc), Joe McEvoy (Gtr), Frank Innes (Bass), Diana Takehall (Drms), Trev Thomas (Drms) — Life Destruction, Active Slaughter, Battered Cod

Wöes (2012-15) — Martin Sturdy (Voc), Dean Venyge (Voc), Joe McEvoy (Gtr), Mike Holden (Bass), Andy Smith (Drms)

KEIGHLEY SCENE

At the close of 2000, the local scene in Keighley was still seeing new bands emerge, including **Ironstorm** - formed from the ashes of Demonix, **Aspire** - who played at Liverpool's Cavern Club on Friday, February 11, 2000, and club band **Platinum**.

Hollow Horse - (pictured) became a four-piece act after having formed as a duo in 1997 with Roger Cannon and former Chaos vocalist/bassist Gary Kaye.

CIRCUS

The young trio Circus formed in 2000. They played at The 1 In 12 Club on May 25, 2001, with another new Keighley band, **Nosebone**. On September 8, Circus played the North's leading rock venue, Bradford's Rio's. They returned to The 1 In 12 Club in March 2002, after releasing a ten-track CD called *Quarantine*.

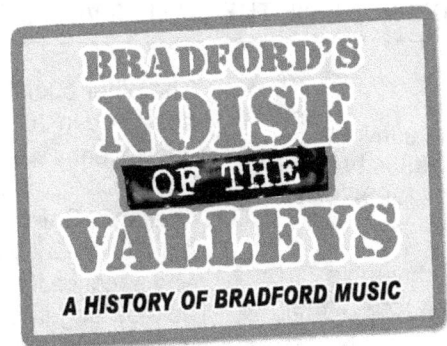

CHAPTER 2: 2001-2003

At the start of January 2001, Bradford Council announced that it was putting in a bid for the 2008 *European Capital Of Culture*. If successful, the city would look forward to potential economic regeneration.

Bradford's 7th Film Festival took place between March 1-17 at the National Museum Of Photography, Film & Television. Amongst the 100 films shown there was a new print of Stanley Kubrick's *2001: A Space Odyssey* and *Enemy At The Gates,* the epic tale of World War Two snipers during the siege of Stalingrad, starring Jude Law, Ed Harris and Rachel Weisz. There was a retrospective on the French comedian Jacques Tati entitled *Comedy Of Silence* with his *Monsieur Hulot* films.

On March 9, Bradford's prodigal sons Smokie played St George's Hall. When they returned to play the encore *Living Next Door To Alice*, the lads all came on stage proudly wearing Bradford City shirts.

BRAZIL

During March, local band Brazil, who were based in Doncaster, described their full-on guitar pop/rock as 'future-wave'. They released their EP *This Is Future Wave* at the same time as their track *School Daze* appeared on the Fierce Panda label's EP *Cheffing & Blinding*. The EP was a sampler with Brazil and five other bands. Both releases were selling well at the local Virgin music store.

In 2003, the band had the track *Pornstar* featured on the compilation CD *Underground Vol 2* put out on the Daily Star newspaper's Peoplesound label.

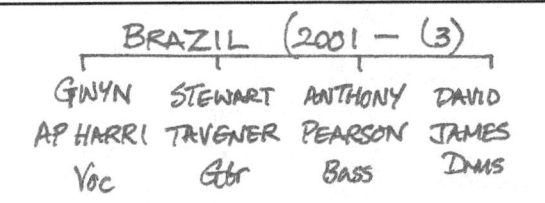

In March, two other new bands appeared, both with Steve 'Tappa' Hawthorn on the drum stool; **Model 13,** who released a five-track EP called *California Foreplay* on their own Average Joe Records, and the five-piece **Fugoo**.

RAMPAGE

On Sunday, April 15th, more than one hundred youths rioted in the Lidget Green area, torching cars and throwing petrol bombs. The violence was believed to have started at the Coach House pub, where a Hindu wedding party was taking place. Suddenly, two groups of Asian youths spilled onto the street and continued fighting.

Three men (two white, one Asian) were arrested after the violent clashes, which saw eight people injured and three pubs (the Coach House, the Second West and the Oddfellows) damaged-one the Second West set on fire-and several cars torched in the Coach House car park. (1)

SCATTER

Bradford lad Chris Hladowski had been in local band Thurser / Mundane in the late 1990s before he teamed up with Alex Neilson as Aste (1999-2001) while studying in Glasgow.

In 2001, they formed the 8-11 piece ensemble Scatter, playing experimental jazz-folk rock. Other members were from the local Glasgow scene, including Chris' sister Stephanie on vocals. The band's bassist was Blackpool lad Nick McCarthy, who would soon help form the band Franz Ferdinand.

They played at least two gigs on the same bill as Franz Ferdinand, at the Chateaux on December 6, 2002, and as part of the lineup at the event *Cells Out*, in February 2003.

In May 2003, they released their debut CD *Surprisingly Sing Stupendous Love* on the Leicester Pickled Egg Records. (2) Nicky

McCarthy, while now firmly with Franz Ferdinand, continued his commitment to the band by playing on the album.

A second album, *The Mountain Announces* (2006), appeared on Blank Tapes. It contained a few traditional numbers like *Dowie Derns Of Yarrow* and *She Moves Through The Fayre*.

LOCAL BOOKS

Bradford's literary prowess had long been established by the Bronte sisters and the plays and novels of JB Priestley. (3)

In 2001, two new books were published by Bradford authors. The first was the debut of Bill Broady, *In This Block There Lives A Slag*, published by Flamingo, which is a riveting collection of thirteen short stories set in Bradford and around Yorkshire. Bill's debut novel, *Eternity Is Temporary*, was published by Portobello Books in 2006.

The other book that appeared in 2001 was Joolz Denby's second novel, *Corazon*. Published by HarperCollins, this was a thriller about betrayal and sacrifice. In her acknowledgements, Joolz gave thanks to various people, including was 1 In 12 member Sarah Strong, who ran a body-piercing and tattoo parlour on Ivegate.

Over the next few years, two other authors produced books of note. T&A reporter Jim Greenhalf published a biting critique of Bradford in his *It's A Mean Old Scene: A History Of Modern Bradford From 1974*. The book was published by Dave Tipon of Frizinghall's Redbeck Press in 2003.

The first novel from forty-year-old Bradford-born writer and part-time postman Robert Craig, *Cover To Cover*, also came out in 2003. Robert's second novel, *More Like Wrestling Than Dancing* - an eye-opening expose of the single life, followed in 2004. Both were published by Weidenfeld & Nicholson.

THE 1 IN 12 CLUB 2001

On Wednesday, February 14, long time 1 In 12 comrades Chumbawamba had an evening showing of a film about the band, entitled *Well*

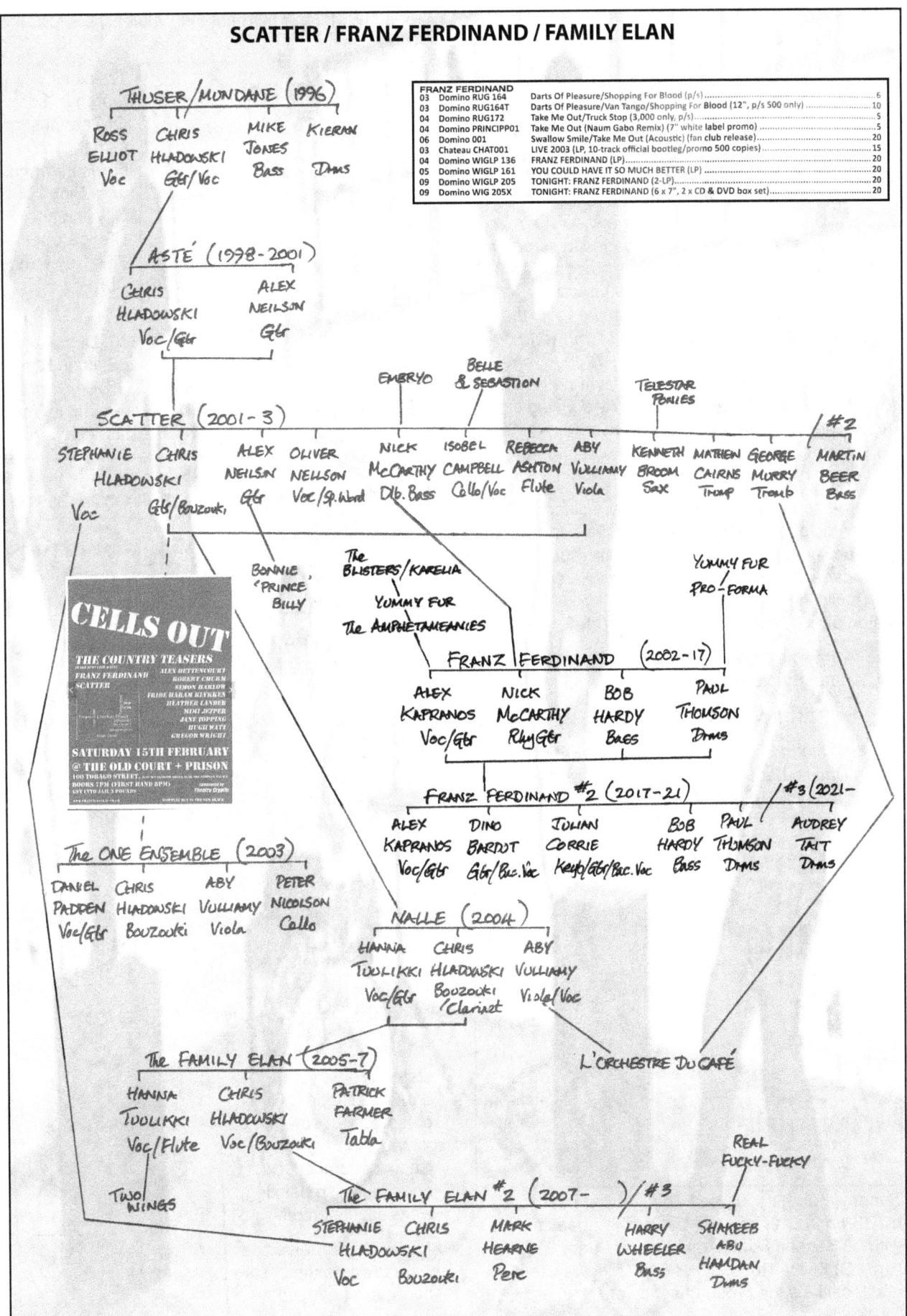

Done, Now Sod Off, at Leeds Metropolitan University. The leaflet that advertised the film described it as a *"potted and often hilarious history of Chumbawamba. Footage and interviews from the last two decades retrace the early days of communal living and involvement in the Miners' Strike of 84-85, their survival through the Thatcher years and the barrage of bad press to surface in the nineties wiser but unrepentant. This is the unlikely tale of a band who spent more time shoplifting than jamming and somehow managed to scrape a living from making radical music in a conservative culture. With the uncanny knack of upsetting people and 'shooting themselves in the foot', they surprised themselves and the rest of the world by selling 5 million albums in America. Tagged "one-hit wonders" they ensured they'd never be invited to another award ceremony again by dousing the deputy prime minister at The Brit Awards in 1998. This is an ongoing punk rock saga in an age of manufactured bands."*

The free screening was followed by a discussion with participation from members of the band who answered questions raised by the film, such as; does capitalism stunt creativity? Can we subvert the music industry? Do you sell out if you sign to a major label? What is the meaning of life?

The event was organised by the University's School Of Cultural Studies.

GIGS: FEBRURY - MARCH

The first gig of 2001 was on Thursday, February 15, when Danish band Amdi Petersens Arme played, supported by S.T.F. and Leeds band Fig.4.0.

Sunday, February 18, was an all-dayer, headlined by US band Dragboy and Liverpool's Imbalance, with 30 Seconds Until Armageddon / Sawn Off / Army Of Flying Robots / HHH / Parade Of Enemies and local lads the (Young) Inspectors.

Tuesday, March 4: Greenland Whalefishers / Blue Arsed Flies

Thursday, March 8: Songs Of Zarathustra (American hardcore band from Sioux City, Indiana) / Tangarora / This Day Must Die

Friday, March 30: Dumbstruck / Skipton band Driven Down and again The Inspectors.

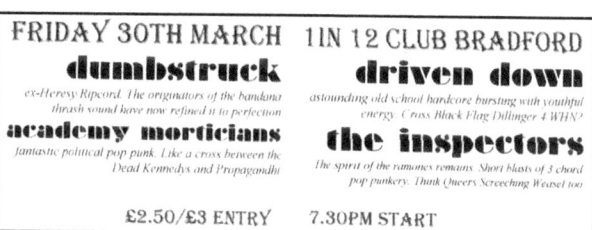

TWENTY YEARS OF SELF MANAGEMENT, MUSIC AND MAYHEM

The year 2001 was the twentieth year of the Club's existence. Two weeks of events were organised to celebrate this and the annual Mayday festivities.

Among the earliest events was an auction on Sunday, February 25, when thirty donated items including a car stereo (not stolen), a mobile phone, two computers, a sofa, a magazine rack, Chumbawamba CDs, and a surprise painting, were auctioned off.

All the money raised went towards the costs of organising Mayday.

WORKERS EDUCATIONAL ASSOCIATION (WEA)

The Club's Library Collective established itself as a branch of the WEA and organised a series of ten weekly courses. The first two started on March 1, *Wine Appreciation* by Lin Gunn and *A History Of Popular Music* by Gary Cavanagh. (4)

Self-education has always been integral to the politics of the 1 In 12. Previous courses on Spanish, Internet and Banner Making had taken place and these new courses were part of that tradition.

BEYOND TV

Saturday, April 17, saw the launch of a Leeds-Bradford Indymedia event, with four workshops in the afternoon. In the evening there was an experimental performance of films with musical interludes by a new Manchester beat combo.

Telegraph & Argus Wednesday, March 14, 2001

It's party time for 1 in 12 Club

Bradford's libertarian social centre – the 1 in 12 Club – celebrates its 20th birthday this year.

And a range of celebratory events covering May Day are being put together to mark the occasion.

They include a range of gigs from hardcore punk to radical folk music, a special party, an exhibition of Anarchist Artworks, a weekend football tournament and the production of a new play by Chumbawamba's Alice Nutter.

The 1 in 12 Club was originally set up by members of the Claimants Union in 1981.

That April, the TUC held a national 'march against unemployment' through Bradford, and the then Conservative Government published the Raynor Report which stated that "1 in 12" claimants were "defrauding the state".

Soon afterwards the Claimants Union organised their first Bradford gig under the banner of the "1 in 12 Club" – which later grew and got premises in Albion Street in the city centre.

CHEERS: *Members of music and social club celebrate with own beer*

HERE'S TO US: *Club official Matt Hannan with a pint of Red and Black which will be unveiled at the club's anniversary on Friday*

Raising a glass to the future

Members of Bradford's 1 in 12 club will be toasting 20 years of music and mayhem – with their own beer.

Pints of Red and Black, brewed in Otley, will be unveiled at the club's anniversary celebrations on Friday.

The club owes its name to the Government's 1981 Raynor Report, which claimed one in every 12 benefit claimants were defrauding the state.

As well as giving advice, the club produced its own newsletter and organised weekly gigs, socials and benefits in a room above a city-centre pub.

Membership rocketed to more than a thousand and the club, which made its headquarters in Albion Street, Bradford, in 1986, began to establish itself on the musical scene building close ties to bands like New Model Army and Chumbawamba.

Matt Hannan, of Great Horton, joined the club in 1985, and worked there between 1986-88.

He said: "The pressure to succumb to capitalistic and exploitative methods has never been far away. But the club has survived, constantly reinventing itself, challenging assumptions and expectations and going in new and exciting directions."

GIGS: APRIL-MAY

Thursday, April 5: Disorder / Pheromones / and local metal act Needlecord.

Tuesday, April 8: Norwegian band Crash / Babies 3 / and another local act, KMP

Tuesday, May 1: Bleeding Hearts / Devils / Pheromones

Friday, May 25 : Circus / Nosebone

THE (YOUNG) INSPECTORS

This local punk trio of Will (vocals/guitar), James (drums/vocals) and Adam (vocals/guitar) (5) blended the influences of The Clash and The Ruts with the modern sounds of Dillinger Four and The Alkaline Trio. The band were regulars at The 1 In 12 Club during the 1999-2003 period. Adam Theakstone went on to play with The Possessions, Android Love Story and Ruby Tombs.

KENT MATHEMATICS PROJECT (KMP)

This band was started by guitarist/bassist Ewan Frater, who was studying at Bradford University, and a group of fellow students. Ewan was also the bassist in local band The Devils and would later play in Motley Crudos / Losing The Battle (2002-03) with Bingley lad Martin Sturdy on vocals. Together, Martin and Ewan organised gigs at the 1 In 12 under various entities such as *Infinite Monkey, Peace, Pot And Headshot, The Kids Just Wanna Rock* and *Bingo Handjob Presents*.

HEAVYFEST

On Saturday, April 28, the promotion collective *None More Heavy*, in association with *Bingo Handjob*, put on a stoner/metal all-dayer called Heavyfest. Starting at noon, eleven bands graced the Club stage, Kabinboy and Cosmonaut from Northern Ireland, Sloth from London, Blackrock from Nottingham, Nightmare Vision from Wigan, Blessed Realm from Co. Durham, Evil Knievil, Leeds' bands John Holmes and Tangaroa plus local bands Khang and Silverburn.

SILVERBURN

The band formed in December 2000 as a groove-based stoner/doom band that included guitarist Tom Allen, who was also in Khang, and ex-Chorus of Ruin guitarist Izak. They played their first gig in February 2001. By the end of March, they had recorded their four-track demo *Godisnowhere*.

After a storming set at Heavyfest, they played Leeds' Dungeonfest on Saturday, July 21, before recording two tracks for a Voltage Records compilation. *The Aural Quagmire (AQ): The Very Best Of Voltage Studios Volume 1* came out in 2002, with seven bands having two tracks each. Besides Warrington band Caine and 1,000 Things, the other five bands on this release were from Bradford – Darwin, Purity Cries, IdiotBox, Worm and Silverburn (who were called Burn Horizon).

At this time, the band went through brief name changes, first to Stonegate, then Burn Horizon, before reverting to Silverburn for the rest of their existence.

In August 2005, they recorded another demo at Voltage Studios. *A Thousand Years* contained five tracks; *Setting Sun / Godlike & 10 Miles Wide / A Thousand Years / The Missing / Soul Erosion*.

The band called it a day in 2007, with most members moving on to other projects.

MAYDAY 2001

The ten days of celebrating Mayday kicked off on Friday, April 27 with the Artworks Exhibition. This was followed by the 20th-anniversary party with the 1 In 12 Disco Allstars, a loose collection of Club members from various local bands, and Baghdaddies, with a buffet meal available from the cafe.

CHAPTER 2 — 2001 - 2003

SILVERBURN / IRON RAT

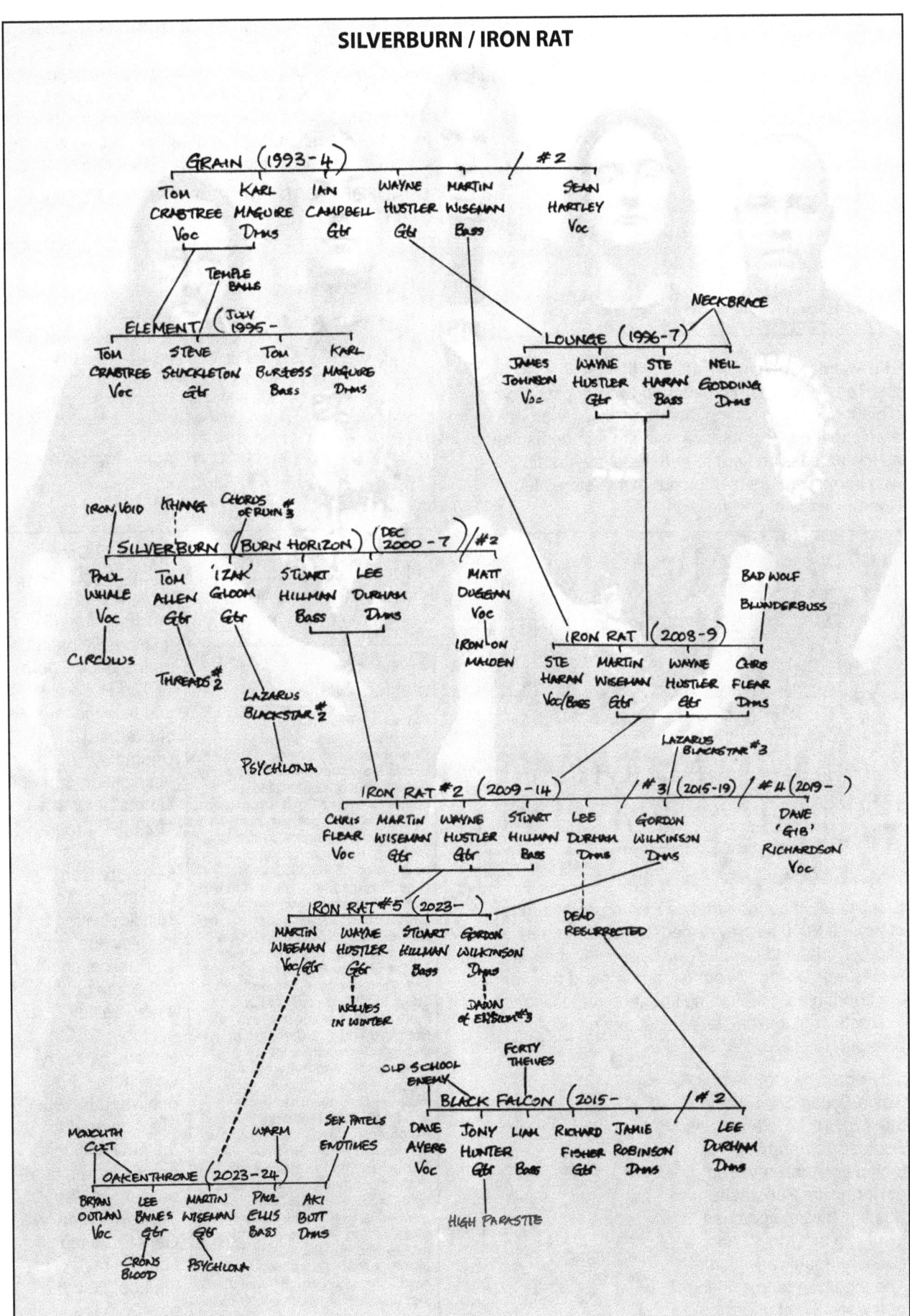

> **Anarchist Artworks 2001**
> to celebrate 20 years of self-management,
> music and mayhem at
> **1 in 12 Club, 21-23 Albion Street
> Bradford, West Yorkshire, BD1 2LY, U.K.**
>
> During April 2001 we will be holding various events including an 'art' show in the 1 in 12 Club itself. This will consist of flyposting up artwork that reflects the creativity of people involved in producing anarchist inspired 'zines/ books/ record covers/cartoons/posters for gigs or campaigns/photos of demos/squats/ bands/ banners etc.
>
> So do send us copies of your artwork or photos - good quality photocopies or prints please - **NOT** your one and only original piece of work because we can't afford to send stuff back - sorry! Plus some info. about why the artwork was produced and where it has been used.
>
> Any donations of artwork to be used for publicity during the 20th anniversary celebrations are also welcome. Please let us know if we can reproduce your work on posters/flyers etc. relating to the weeks events.

The Mayday march on Tuesday the 1st was led by the Red & Black Drummers and two people carrying a giant phoenix heading the procession. A larger than usual police presence failed to dampen spirits as the procession kept alive the Mayday tradition with some workers leaning out of five-storey high workplaces to cheer them on.

Elsewhere, in London that day, an organised mob of around 6000 heavily armed thugs went on a carefully planned rampage against anti-capitalist protesters. Like their counterparts around the world, the London police seem hell-bent on protecting the interests of global capital against any possibility of disruption.

On Friday the 4th, there was a *Footie Social*, before the *4th 1 In 12 International Football Tournament* took place that weekend at Northcliffe Park, near Shipley. It was organised jointly by the 1 In 12 and Leeds' Republica Highland. The other ten teams taking part were: The Lunatics from Belgium, Bristol comrades Easton Cowboys, Norwich's Athletico Cowtower, York's Boca Ark, Leeds' White Stag, Menston Rangers, Hebden Bridge Aliens, Kick It (Racism) Out, Republica Women and Bradford Ukrainians. After a hard-fought competition, the eventual winners on Sunday were The Lunatics, the team from Belgium.

BRADFORD BAD LAD PLAY / ROOM AT THE BOTTOM BOOK

> **BRADFORD BAD LAD** 10 - 12 May 2001
> A play by Alice Nutter performed by the 1 in 12 Drama Collective
>
>
>
> A black comedy showing the thirties as a time of violence, possibilities and necessary criminality. Based loosely on the true story of Bradford's Harry Goldthorpe and the Quebec St unemployment centre, Bradford Bad Lad is a comic romp with a serious underbelly. The Great Depression is famous for its Hunger Marches but Harry Goldthorpe and his mates stayed in Bradford and stole chickens and forged coins to feed themselves. This is the flip side to the image of the unemployed shuffling their feet singing Buddy Can You Spare A Dime.
>
> HARRY GOLDTHORPE Ticket prices £5.00 full £4.00 conc.

Over three nights, May 10-12, the 1 In 12 Drama Collective staged their fourth Mayday play at the Priestley Centre For The Arts. *Bradford Bad Lad* was written by Chumbawamba's Alice Nutter. (6) It is loosely based on the book *Room At The Bottom* and tells the tale of Bradford's Unemployed Association during the hunger years 1929-39, through the eyes of its secretary Harry Goldthorpe. To coincide with the play, the 1 In 12 Publications Collective published a new edition of *Room At The Bottom*, by Harry Goldthorpe, first published in 1959. The foreword to the new edition and a biographical account of Harry's life was written by Gary Cavanagh. Left is a review of the book and the play from the Metro.

> **THEATRE**
> **bradford bad lad**
>
> Written by Alice Nutter of subversive chart toppers Chumbawamba, Bradford Bad Lad is a black comedy inspired by the exploits of colourful local character Harry Goldthorpe. Responsible for setting up an unemployed workers' centre in Bradford during the economic depression of the 1930s, Goldthorpe's grass-roots activism won him many friends among the downtrodden locals but attracted the suspicion of the authorities who eventually imprisoned him for tarring and feathering a police spy. Performed by amateur group The 1 In 12 Drama Collective, to mark the 20th anniversary of Bradford's 1 In 12 Club, the play is Nutter's first venture into scriptwriting and features sets made by fellow Chumbawamba member Dunstan Bruce. The band have long held an interest in Goldthorpe, financing a reprint of his autobiography Room At The Bottom during the 1980s as part of their ongoing mission to shed light on the world's overlooked troublemakers. Nutter believes that Goldthorpe's moral ambiguity makes him no less worthy of attention. 'Goldthorpe was a local hero,' she says. 'But he was also just like the rest of us – flawed.'
>
> *Rosie Wild*

GIGS AT THE 1 IN 12 CLUB: JUNE-JULY

Friday, June 1: Hardcore metal from Flood

Friday, June 8: Mrs Pilgrim / Saab 77 / Propulsion Family Picnic

Saturday, June 9: The boys who ran None More Heavy presented US band, Goatsnake / Sloth /Khang

Thursday, June 14: Diablo 66

Saturday, June 16: Amilia, put on by *Carpe Noctum*

Sunday, June 17: Sunday School Hardcore presented 30 Seconds Until Armageddon / In The Clear / Fig 4.0 / KMP

As part of that year's Bradford Festival, the last two Fridays in June and the first one in July were given over to special gigs organised by Dave 'Little Brother' Stockell the ranting poet under his BCB radio show Open Mind University banner.

Friday, June 22: Mrs Pilgrim / Funk Butchers / Bri Outlaw / Little Brother

Friday, June 29: Loved Ones / L'Orchestra Du Cafe /Four Sandwiches Short / Little Brother

Friday, July 6: Nowt / Tim Moon / Pete The Poet Chapman / Little Brother

Friday, July 20: Swedish Hardcore Thrash from DS-13 and ETA plus local act The Devils

Tuesday, July 24: Unkind – hardcore from Finland.
Saturday July 28: Shank

BOXED IN

Formed in 2001 by former Sawn Off members, with the addition of ex-Ebola vocalist Nick Loaring, Boxed In were based in Bradford and Newcastle and became regulars at the 1 In 12 over the next couple of years.

In 2003, they released the 7" single *Boxed In* on Busted Heads Records, as well as the split CD album *Life's Fast So, Haul Ass* with the Finnish band Unkind. In 2005, they released another 7" single on Headfirst Records and the CD compilation album *(2001-05)* on Flat Earth Records.

EBOLA / SAWN OFF / BOXED IN

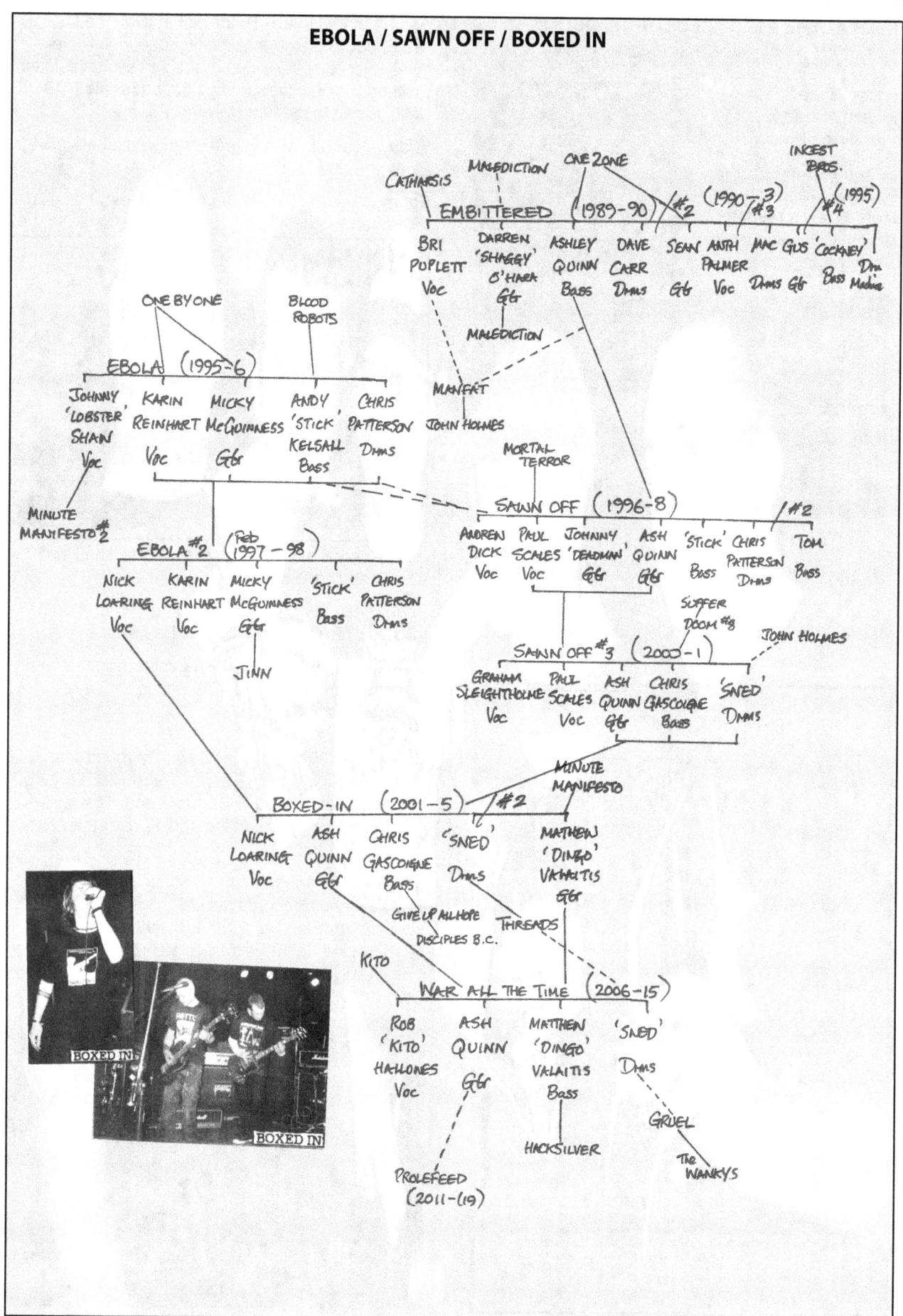

REASON TO BELIEVE FANZINE

The July edition of the free fanzine Reason To Believe #2 was a special edition with twelve pages devoted to The 1 In 12 club. Various Club members discussed their opinions of the Club's major collectives:-

Gords (of Hard To Swallow) recounted the experience of the Mayday Parade, Sarah talked about the artwork exhibition, banner making and drumming workshops.

Julia described the work of the Peasant's Collective. Martin and Pete discussed the merits of the Drama collective, Russ explained the Club's history from a hardcore punk perspective and Ewan enthused on the new Sunday School hardcore gigs.

Stick talked about the new practice room/ studio, and Rob and Dom commented on the 1 In 12 football team. Lastly, Tony was interviewed regarding the Publications and KDIS online activities.

BOOKWORMS

Formed in 2001 by long-time club member Pete 'the Poet' Chapman, and incorporating many other Club members over the years, Bookworms were very active on the Club's cabaret scene and also did many benefit gigs for various good causes.

By April 2010, the group were in their sixth incarnation when they released the CD album *Sex, Death And Architecture* on the Club's 1 In 12 Records (Cat No 12016).

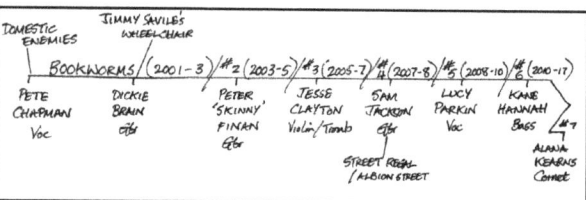

ALTERNATIVE WORLD CUP

The second Alternative World Cup was organised again by Bristol's Eastern Cowboys FC. The three-day festival of football, music and much more besides, took place at Thorncomb in Dorset, on August 23-26.

Twenty amateur teams from England, Scotland, Germany, Belgium, Poland, Denmark, and Austria took part. The aim was to bring together people from around the world through sport and socialising.

The 1 In 12 team went off to participate and, unbelievably, won the tournament, beating Easton Cowboys 1-0 in the final, with midfielder Craig Williams scoring from the penalty spot!

After returning to Bradford, the trophy was lost for a while as each team member had an opportunity to keep it at their home. It now sits in pride of place in the cabinet in the upstairs bar.

GIGS AT THE 1 IN 12 CLUB: AUG-OCT

Friday, August 3 – Local bands Water / Roy

Saturday, August 4 – An all-dayer with Shank / Tangaroa / Kervorkian Solution / Narcosis / Beer Beast / D-Rail / Sermon of Hypocrisy

Friday August 10 – French band from Paris, Cria Cuervos / Baba Yaga

Sunday, August 12 – Gertrude / Baba Yaga

Thursday, August 16 – Scottish band Scatha

Friday, August 24 - The return of US band Catharsis / Newborn from Hungary

Tuesday, August 28 - Irish bands Easpa Measa / Puget Sounds

Friday, August 31 – Lysis / MFR / Sibling

Saturday, September 8 – Beer Beast / Bry Outlaw / Pheramones / Tosca

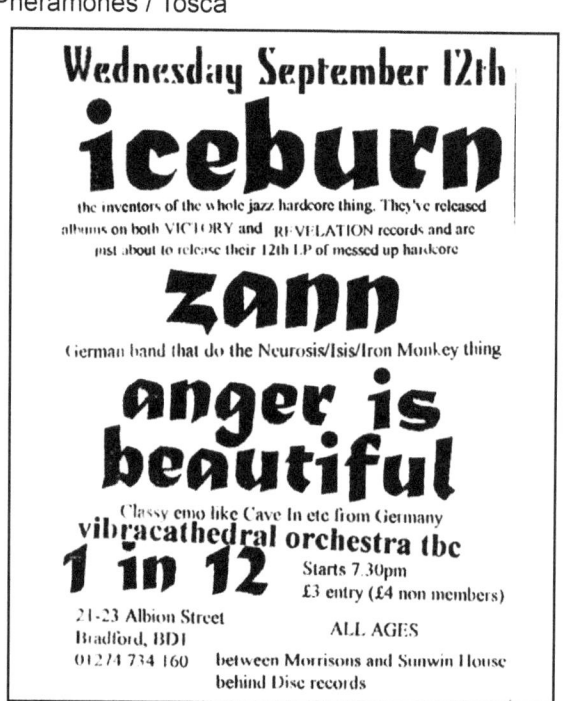

Wednesday, September 12 – US band Iceburn from Salt Lake City, Utah who had started in 1991, with a unique style of jazz meets heavy metal/punk. Their fourth album, 1996's Mediavolution on Revelation Records was highly regarded. They were supported by two German bands Zann and Anger Is Beautiful.

Wednesday, October 3 – The return of US grindcore legends Phobia / Khang

Friday, October 5 – *Carpe Noctum*'s second birthday party – Mechanical Cabaret / Katscan / Squid

Saturday/Sunday, October 13/14 – Two day all dayers with US bands Creation Is Crucifixion and Good Clean Fun

Sunday, October 21 – US band Harum Sacrum / Baba Yaga / Anarchy Spanky

Monday, October 22 – Skimmer / Vibracathedral Orchestra / Fig 4.0 / Final Conclusion

Friday, October 26 – A Gary Numan tribute band

OUT FROM THE VOID

The November 2001 issue of the Japanese fanzine *Out From The Void* contained sixteen pages devoted to The 1 In 12 Club. It included an interview with members Alec & Sarah (of Suffer & Witchknot respectively) and an article on Peaceville band Axegrinder.

LOSING THE BATTLE / MOTLEY CRUDOS

Formed by KMP bassist Ewan Frater with vocalist Martin Sturdy, the band also included former My Name Is Satan drummer Chris Black. They became regulars at gigs and all-dayers over the next couple of years at the Club.

BABA YAGA

Baba Yaga were an all-female quartet, formed in 1996 as an off-shoot of the 'riot grrrl' movement band Witchknot.

They appeared at The 1 In 12 Club three times during 2001 and the same number in 2002. They played a final gig at the Club in March 2007.

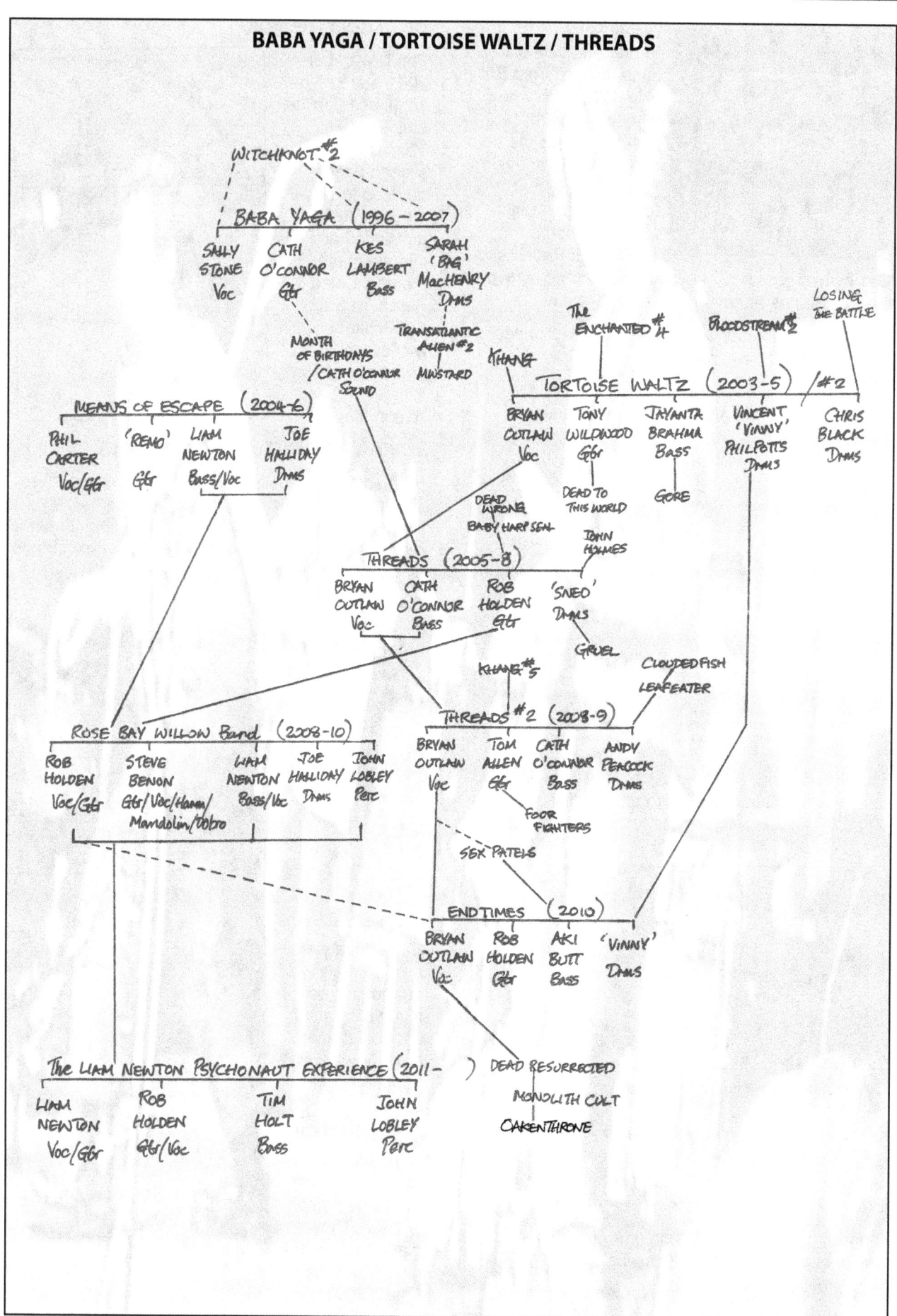

CHAPTER 2   2001 - 2003

GIGS: NOVEMBER - DECEMBER

November 4 – US band 3D House Of Beef / Khang / Parade of Enemies

3D House Of Beef were made up of ex-members of Goatsnake.

November 12 – A *Sunday Skool Matinee* gig from 3-7 with Spanish band Cementerio Show / Scalplock / Narcosis

November 15 – Extreme Noise from Swiss group Schimpfluch Gruppe / Bilge Pump

November 22 – US band Tragedy, formed in 1999 in Portland, Oregon from ex-members of His Hero Is Gone / Convinced (from Sweden) / Deadman's Fingers / Sendmore Paramedics / Motley Crudos

December 19 – *The Annual 1 In 12 Club Xmas Alldayer* with Urko / Sawn-Off / John Holms / Cress / Bilge Pump / Eradicate / Ex-Cathedra

By the end of 2001, the 1 In 12 had hosted some of the best underground haedcore punk bands from all over the world.

BRADFORD FESTIVAL 2001

The fourteenth annual Bradford Festival started on Friday, June 22 in Centenary Square. The festival lasted for sixteen days with three weekends of fabulous celebrations ending on July 7.

The Street Festival saw acts from Poland, Les Obsessionnels (pictured) from France, Australians Bedlam Oz, plus Skinning The Cat, Mind The Gap and Roxy's Toolbox. Various venues were used for a wealth of music including the Love Apple, Beehive, Macrory's Bar, Melborn Hotel, The 1 In 12 Club, Penningtons and Chicago Rock Cafe for Jazz.

The Mela provided music, theatre, comedy, fashion and dance as well as a host of international acts such as Congolese singer Sam Mangwama, Algerian singer Adel Ali Slimani, the band Zubop, Poland's 40 dancers and musicians Zespol Piesni Tranca Zieni Cieszynskiej, Morrocan band MoMo, Pakistan's Rizwan Muazzam Qawwali and bhangra band Anakhi.

On Tuesday, June 26, the third *Routes Of Resistance* walk around the city, organised by Gary Cavanagh, started at midday.

On July 6-7, the *World In A City* finale was staged in Centenary Square for free. It was compered by Peadar Long and featured jazz artist Gilad Atzmon & The Orient House Ensemble (pictured),

Tarika from Madagascar, Scottish act Shooglenify, Canada's Barachois, Sierra Maestra from Cuba. Saturday's final act was the UK's Dreadzone who played a mix of dub and dance before the firework display ended the festival.

After fifteen years of being run by local organisers, Bradford Festival was taken over by two new out of town organisers – Robin Morley and Neil Butler.

ZICO

Former Dragster vocalist Craig Brauns was signed by Island Records in 2001 and put together a band including former Dragster members guitarist Dave Ledgard and drummer Jake Riley alongside his brother, guitarist Greg Brauns, and bassist Sean Dillon. Thus, Zico were born, named after the famous Brazilian footballer.

Dave Ledgard, Greg Brauns and Sean Dillon in action at MacRory's Bar. Photo by Richard Ingham.

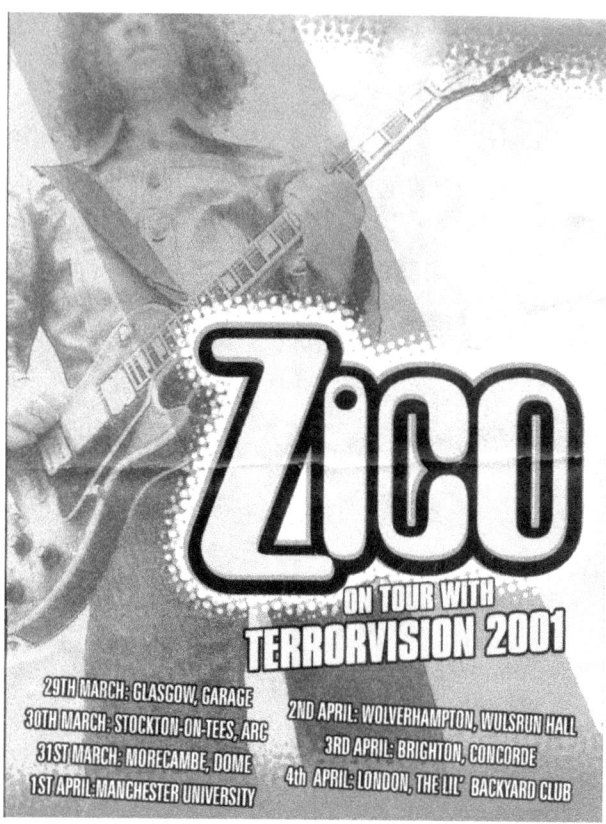

After rehearsing a set of Craig's songs, the band set off on a spring tour with Terrovision and played a few showcase London gigs.

Zico recorded a full album at Wales' famous Rockfield Studios. The album was held back by Island founder Chris Blackwell who thought the album 'too rocky' in the era when bands like Coldplay were coming to the fore. Despite being remixed with more emphasis on the acoustic guitars, the LP was never released. Zico were dropped from the label after being on the books for two years and playing a number of prestigious gigs.

Craig continued to play live as a solo artist and as part of various duos as well as fronting the band Long Shadow Family with brother Greg. In 2024 he released a solo album *Craig Brauns Vol 1*.

Guitarist Dave Ledgard has been a member of Hebden Bridge's long-running ska band The Owter Zeds since the mid-2000s. Sean Dillon was a member of funk band Vonderplanetz and continues to perform live with various musicians including regular jam sessions with his cousin Harris at venues Al's Mars Bar in Saltaire.

KWAI CHANG CAINE

This band reunited the longest-serving lineup of '80s alternative punk act Western Dance who were also known as indie rockers Primate in the '90s.

They released a self-titled CD EP containing four songs, *Kwai Chang Caine / God Luv Ya / Pussy Galore / Pop Fiction* on Mutiny 2000 Records in 2002. Two of the tracks were included on the Mutiny CD compilation *White Abbey Road*.

Their album *The Ones That Never Learn* was co-produced with former New Model Army drummer Rob Heaton, and released in 2002.

Half the tracks for their second album, *Reel To Real Life*, were recorded in the studio but left at the rough mix stage after the reel-to-reel tape machine broke down. For the rest of the songs, the drums were taken from a live recording from MacRory's Bar made by Rob Heaton in 2004, with guitars and vocals re-recorded in 2006.

After Kwai Chang Caine's gig in Centenary Square as part of the 2004 *Fresh Milk* event, the band went on hiatus due to health issues.

They played as Kwai Chang Caine for the final time at the memorial gig for Negatives singer Dave Wilcox in April 2007.

The same lineup played as Western Dance for a 30th Anniversary gig at the Underground in Bradford on November 25, 2016. They also released a 'best of' album entitled *30*, which was available at the gig.

In 2020, as Western Dance they released a lockdown-inspired 7-inch single, *In The Distance / This Is Your...* on red and yellow vinyl.

The four reunited once again in 2023 as the fourth incarnation of punk / new wave covers band Plastic Letters. This meant that Liam, Ade, Steve and Matt had played together in five different decades.

Apart from their involvement with Plastic Letters, Liam and Ade gigged and recorded together as Bibles FC. Ade also played bass for IdiotBox, Paul Gilmartins's version of The Dance Society/The Society and, in 2025, joined Rose Of Avalanche.

Matt recorded a series of vinyl albums as Signia Alpha with guest musicians, including Stephen Andrews, Mark Cranmer, Simon Nolan, Wulf Ingham, Chris Walsh, Keith Jafrate, Harris, and The Damned's Paul Gray. The LPs *Shooting The Messenger (2020)*, *Walking The Tightrope (2021)* and *The Columbus Memoirs (2022)* were collaborations with poet Nick Toczek. The *Entropy* LP followed in 2023 and *Wonderland* in 2025, both with lead vocals by Matt, Harris, Nogsy and others.

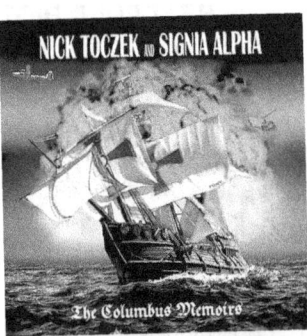

ANDY WELLS

Former keyboardist with local rock bands Baby Tuckoo, Verity and Voyager UK, Andy Wells released the ten-track CD album *Lost The Will To Play* in 2001, recorded at his own Hydeaway Studios in Wyke. He was helped out by Tony Drake on guitar, ex-Baby Tucoo bassist Paul 'Smiggy' Smith and Yogi on bass, and Kev on drums.

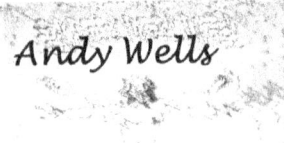

He followed up with the four-track CD EP *Humanized* in 2003, with Tony and Oliver Drake on guitar and drums and with 'Smiggy' again on bass. The four tracks were *Mr Majestic / Waiting For The Night / Unknown Soldier / Unknown Soldier (Edit)*.

ARTSCENE

At the time, *Artscene* was the only free monthly listings magazine in Yorkshire, published by Yorkshire Arts. The July / August edition had articles on Dominic Ibbotson, *Artscene*'s artist in residence, and the Leeds band The Mekons' new project *Oooh! (Out Of Our Heads)*. The launch for their new album took place at the Wardrobe in Leeds on July 13 and featured a giant spinning head.

BOTTOM

Local lad Ade Edmundson and the late Rik Mayall released the video of their sell-out tour, *Bottom: 2001: An Arse Oddity*. The two former *Comic Strip* actors and Bad News members, reprised their alter-egos of 'Richie & Eddie' from their TV series, "...the saddest pair of no-hope losers the world has ever known."

The pair had appeared in the comedy film *Guest House Paradiso* in 1999, where Richie & Eddie were in charge of the UK's cheapest hotel, throwing their shoddy practices into utterly bizarre mayhem. The film was directed by Edmundson and also starred Vincent Cassel and Simon Pegg.

THE BRADFORD RIOT JULY 2001

On July 7, a demo organised by the Anti-Nazi League took place in Centenary Square. Over 500 people attended in order to oppose a rumoured march by the neo-fascist National Front (NF). The police were in heavy attendance, monitoring the crowds with video teams, although the demonstration was peaceful. At around 4.30, on Ivegate, a right-wing rabble began shouting abuse at Asian youth. Fighting began and escalated when an Asian man was stabbed. This incident became the spark that started the ensuing riot.

Asian youth clashed with the police as more rumours emerged of right-wing activists set to attack local mosques. The police forced people out of the city centre, up to the top of town and up Westgate to White Abbey Road as stones and petrol bombs rained down.

The rioters attacked and set fire to various pubs in the Manningham district, including the Upper Globe and the Bavaria. The Mercedes car dealership on Oak Lane was also burnt out.

The Muslim youth of Bradford had staged the biggest riot on Britain's mainland for 16 years, causing £27 million of damage. Over the next months, 297 men were identified on video and arrested, many were sentenced to between 4-5 years and more than 200 police officers suffered some form of injury during the conflict. (7)

In 2006, Channel 4 produced the TV docu-drama called *Bradford Riots*.

TWIN TOWERS 9/11 (SEPTEMBER 11, 2001)

On Tuesday, September 11, 2001 (9/11 in American parlance), shortly before 9 am, an American Airlines Boeing 767, flying from Boston with eleven crew and 81 passengers, was flown into the north tower of the World Trade Centre in New York. Eighteen minutes later, a second AA Boeing 757, from Washington, with six crew and 58 passengers, was flown into the building's south tower. Shortly after 10 am, the World Trade Centre began to collapse, with both towers reduced to rubble and scattering debris and dust across the city.

Within an hour, a third plane hit the Pentagon in Washington, causing part of the building to collapse. A fourth plane crashed near Somerset, Pennsylvania. There was a total of 266 people on board the four planes, hijacked by 19 men of Middle Eastern origin.

The world watched these televised events in real time, as the gruesome atrocity of death and destruction unfolded. The initial death toll of workers trapped in the towers, those killed under the collapse, rescue workers and passengers and crew was estimated at over 6,000, but later on, the official death toll was 2,976.

A 'war on terrorism' was soon declared, with the atrocity attributed to Al-Qaeda and Osama Bin Laden who was taking sanctuary in Afghanistan, controlled by the Taliban. (8)

"For the first time in history, war was declared on an abstract noun." (9)

President GW Bush addressed a joint session of Congress and the American people on September 20, saying: *"Our war on terror begins with Al-Qaeda, but it does not end there. It will not end until every terrorist group of global reach has been found, stopped and defeated."* (10)

After the attacks, the US State Department people – Paul Wolfowitz, Donald Rumsfeld, Dick Cheney and Condoleeza Rice suggested that Al-Qaeda/ Osman Bin Laden had hatched the plot. This led to the bombing of thirty sites in October 2001, then 'Operation Enduring Freedom' the invasion of Afghanistan in November. The US, with allied support (including Britain), linked up with the Northern Alliance and Anti-Taliban forces in retaking the capital Kabal and began the hunt for Bin Laden in the fortified caves of the Tora-Bora mountains.

PARVA

This indie-rock band was formed as Runston Parva in 2000, by Menston lads Nick Hodgson, Andrew White and Keighley-born Ricky Wilson. The name was a deliberate misspelling of the small East Yorkshire hamlet of Ruston Parva. The band shortened their name to Parva after failing to obtain a record deal and added the additional members Simon Rix and Nick Barnes, both from Menston.

They managed to get a deal with the Mantra label, an offshoot of Beggars Banquet and released four singles and an album between 2001-03. The first single *Heavy / Panic Attack* appeared in September 2001 on 7", 12" and CD formats, the other three singles *Hessles / Put Me On The Cover Of Your Magazine*, *Good Bad, Right Wrong / Vending Machine* and *Television / Take My Wife* came out in 2002. Their eleven-track album, 22, which contained all the singles' A-sides, was released in 2003 before the band were dropped by Mantra.

The band decided to aim for a longer-term record deal and started afresh with new songs and a new name - The Kaiser Chiefs.

PLAYING THE FIELD

In early September, the BBC's drama series *Playing The Field* came to town to film at Bradford City's Valley Parade stadium. The series was about a women's football team called the Castlefield Blues Author Gary Cavanagh managed to get a day's filming as an extra at a primary school in Pudsey, playing an inmate in a prison dinner queue!

BARBARA MOORE

In 2001, Japanese EM Records, based in Osaka, released the double CD collection *Sing Sweet Barbara: 1966-1990* by Bradford lass Barbara Moore. The renowned scat-jazz singer, pianist and composer had started in the 1960s as a 'first call' studio backing singer, guesting on loads of albums including Anita Kerr, Stanley Butcher, Dudley Moore, Mark Wirtz and Chico Arnes.

She was famously the voice on the signature tune for the TV series *The Saint*, starring Roger Moore. She released several collectable library records on the De Wolfe label such as *Vocal Shades & Tones* (1972) and *Bright & Shining* (1981) on Sylvester.

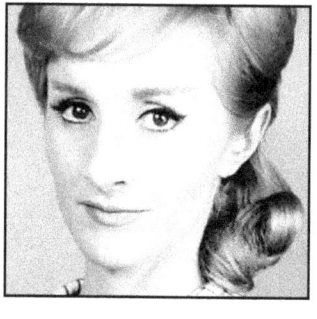

With nearly 300 compositions to her name, and as a composer/arranger, her voice has graced at least eight film soundtracks from *Modesty Blaise* (1966) to *The Snowman* (1983).

On the first CD, of the seventeen tracks, two were from her *A Little Moore Barbara* (1967) album, six from *Vocal Shades & Tones* and five from *Bright & Shining*. The second CD had eight tracks from the film *Sinai* and eight advert jingles, recorded for Toshiba, Renault, Moulinex and others.

Sadly, Barbara passed away on August 27, 2021, at the age of 89.

In November 2001, a new local band **Xi** released a demo CD entitled *Learning* and played a gig at the Empress pub on December 8th.

PEEL GETS A HONORARY DEGREE

In December, the University of Bradford presented BBC Radio 1 DJ John Peel with an honorary degree. The presentation ceremony coincided with the twenty-first anniversary of the university's student radio station, RamAir, which was treated to a live broadcast by Dr Peel.

KEIGHLEY SCENE

On the local Keighly scene, four new bands formed.

BREENE

A very young trio, who played gigs at The 1 In 12 Club and Love Apple in Bradford as well as gigs in and around Keighley. They augmented to a quartet in 2004 with the addition of former Nosebone guitarist Joe McEvoy.

WET PAINT

The Undecided members Sam Carlisle and Luke Parker formed Wet Paint in 2001 as a side project. They played locally including at the 1 In 12 Club and at Liverpool's Cavern Club. By 2003, they had released a debut EP *Seriously Thou* on CD.

In 2004, the band reached the third round of the TV show *Pop Idol* but were kicked off by Simon Cowell after performing their version of *Sweet Dreams*. He described it as *"...a satanic cult performing a chant"*.

DRIVEN DOWN

A Skipton band formed in 2001, they played regularly at 1 In 12 all-dayers. In 2002, they released the album *Skipton Factor* on CD.

DRIVEN DOWN (2001–

ASH MILLER	ALEX DOBSON	ANDY WIGGAN
Voc	Gtr Bass	Drums

A band called **Nosebone** were also on the scene.

EMI

In the early months of 2002, UK record company EMI cancelled the contract of US singer Mariah Carey with a £38 million pay-off. By March 21, 1,800 staff at EMI were sacked and 400 B-listed artists booted off the label.

At this time, the music industry worldwide was worth $40 billion a year, with the big five, Universal, Time/Warner, Sony, EMI, and BMG Bertelsmann producing 70% of all record and CD releases. In 2003, the industry announced a 12.6% slump in sales of recorded music (Sony lost $132 million) due to MP3/Napster downloads and internet piracy. Sony then merged with German media giant BMG Bertelsmann, making four big music companies. (11)

GARETH GATES

Seventeen-year-old East Bowling lad Gareth Gates fought his way to the final of the TV pop talent show *Pop Idol* on Saturday, February 9, 2002.

The former Bradford Cathedral chorister had battled against his speech impediment and had appeared on *Steps To The Stars* in 1999. He auditioned for *Pop Idol* in Manchester in the summer of 2001, in front of a judging panel of Simon Cowell, Pete Waterman, DJ Dr Fox and Niki Chapman. (12)

As the twenty-three-week TV series proceeded to its finale, letters were rolling into Bradford's central post office from all over the world addressed to Gareth Gates, Bradford. The GPO staff just passed them along to Gareth's Dad, Paul, who just happened to be a postman.

"For most of the series, which was drawing more than ten million viewers, Gareth had been the favourite. His angelic looks, tender voice, and chronic stutter (speech impediment) have combined to make him the idol of teenage girls and possibly their mothers and grandmothers too..." (13)

After the voting closed with eight and a half million votes, Gareth narrowly missed out to winner Will Young. Both artists were signed to Spice Girls' guru Simon Fuller's 19 Management company and were given a record deal with BMG.

Within weeks of the final, Gareth's version of the Everly Brothers' *Unchained Melody*, released on March 30, 2002, had knocked Will Young off the number one spot in the UK charts.

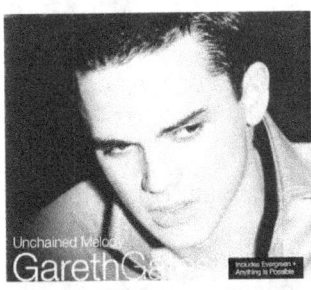

During July and October of that year, Gareth had two more No 1 chart toppers. *Anyone Of Us (Stupid Mistake)* was followed by the double A side, *Suspicious Minds* and a cover of The Beatles' *The Long And Winding Road*, a duet with Will Young. A final single that year, *What My Heart Wants To Say* (also the title of his debut album), reached No 5 in December.

In 2003, he continued to have chart success. His fourth No 1 hit was a *Comic Relief* charity single with BBC TV comedy family *The Kumars*. Gareth took the song *Spirit In The Sky* to the number one position for the third time. It had originally been a hit for American singer Norman Greenbaum, reaching No 1 in April 1970, and later a Number 1 for UK band Doctor & The Medics in 1986.

Two more singles charted. *Sunshine* (No 3) and *Say It Isn't So* (No 4) were taken from Gareth's second album *Go Your Own Way*.

Gareth began a close working relationship with singer Judie Tzuke in 2004, gigging and writing songs together. He returned to the single charts in 2007, with *Changes* (No 14) and *Angel On My Shoulder* (No 22) both from his third album *Pictures Of The Other Side*.

In 2011, Gareth set up the *Gates Academy Of Performing Arts* at Dixon's City Academy, welcoming every child and teaching 5-16-year-olds the three essentials - singing, dancing and acting.

He appeared on the second series of the ITV show *The Big Reunion* in 2013, in the five-piece 'supergroup' 5th Story with *Coronation Street* actor Adam Ricketts, Dane Bowers from Another Level, Kenzie from Blazin' Squad and Anthony 'Kavana' Kavanagh.

Gareth was still gigging with his guitarist Pete Rinaldi, playing Bingley Arts Centre in 2013/2014 and playing a pre-match entertainment at Odsal alongside members from his academy on September 6, 2014. Gareth is a big Bradford Bulls fan, and this was their final home game of the season, against Widnes.

Gareth has the distinct honour of being the only Bradfordian to have had four No 1 chart hits. The other Bradford artists to reach number one in the UK single charts, Kiki Dee, Tasmin Archer and The Crowd, only managed one each.

BRADFORD FILM FESTIVAL 2002

The eighth Bradford Film Festival took place between March 8 and 23, 2002. Highlights included a gala premiere of *The Count Of Monte Cristo*, and the Polish film *Quo Vadis*, directed by Jerzy Kawalerowicz.

Scattered throughout the festival program were the traditional themes of Focus America and Window On The World with a new theme of *Eurovisions* concentrating on the superb films emerging from across the Channel.

There was a career retrospective of one of the UK's greatest actors, Richard Burton, under the title: *Lion Of The Welsh: Richard Burton (1925-1984)*. Amongst the ten films shown were *Look Back In Anger* (1959), *Becket* (1964), *Where Eagles Dare* (1968), the WW2 thriller with Clint Eastwood, and his last film, a remake of George Orwell's dystopian book *1984* (1984).

Two new bands appeared at the beginning of 2002, **Green Car Legacy** and **Inner Turmoil**.

WW1 PLAQUE

On March 21, in the northern French village of Hebuterne, a plaque was erected to commemorate the forty-four men of the Bradford Pals battalion who had died near there during the July 1916 Battle Of The Somme. On the first day of the month-long battle over 600,000 British troops were killed or wounded.

THE EMPRESS

The Empress public house on Sunbridge Road, with a downstairs bar on Aldermonbury, had started putting on Saturday night rock and heavy metal gigs in the late 1990s. Nottingham's Iron Monkey supported by Leeds' Canvas played on October 31, 1997. By the early noughties, local bands like Bloodstream, The Enchanted, Khang, Silverburn and Purity Cries had played there. The reformed Negatives played in 2001, as did the new band Xi on March 2, 2002.

The notorious original Empress Hotel was on Tyrrel Street but was demolished in the early 1970s to make way for Provincial House. That building was in turn demolished in September 2002 to make way for the complex of restaurants/ bars and the new central library, looking out onto Centenary Square.

The modern Empress had reopened in April 1980. It shut down in 2004, was demolished in November 2005, and the site was converted into a Tesco superstore with apartments above.

REEVED

This local metal band was formed by guitarist Alec Marlow with Paul Gooding, a former Dawnraiser guitarist. They produced a three-track CD *Anybody Local*, with the tracks *Everybody Knows / World Keeps Turning / Solo*, in October 2002. It had been recorded and engineered by Tim Walker at Voltage Studios.

JACK MAGAZINE

The first issue of this new men's magazine appeared in April 2002, with the tagline, '*...an orgy of war, animals, fashion, genius and cool!*'.

Its editor-in-chief was the Leeds lad and former *Attack On Bzag* fanzine / *NME* scribe James Brown. James had also worked on the magazine *Loaded* and was CEO of I Feel Good Ltd, the publishers of *Viz*, *Bizarre* and *Fortean Times*.

With investigative journalist and author Jon Ronson among the writers, the debut issue had articles on Martin Scorsese, Uri Geller, Mountains and motel sex, spread among an abundance of high-end adverts for Honda, Audi, Gucci, Prado, Burberry, etc.

In 2003, James sold his *I Feel Good* publishing company for £6.4 Million, before becoming a cultural commentator as presenter of *I Predict A Riot* for the Bravo TV channel. (14)

CHAPTER 2 — 2001 - 2003

REEVED / WILD TRASH / SUICIDE BY COP / THE DRASTICS / SNUFF ROCK

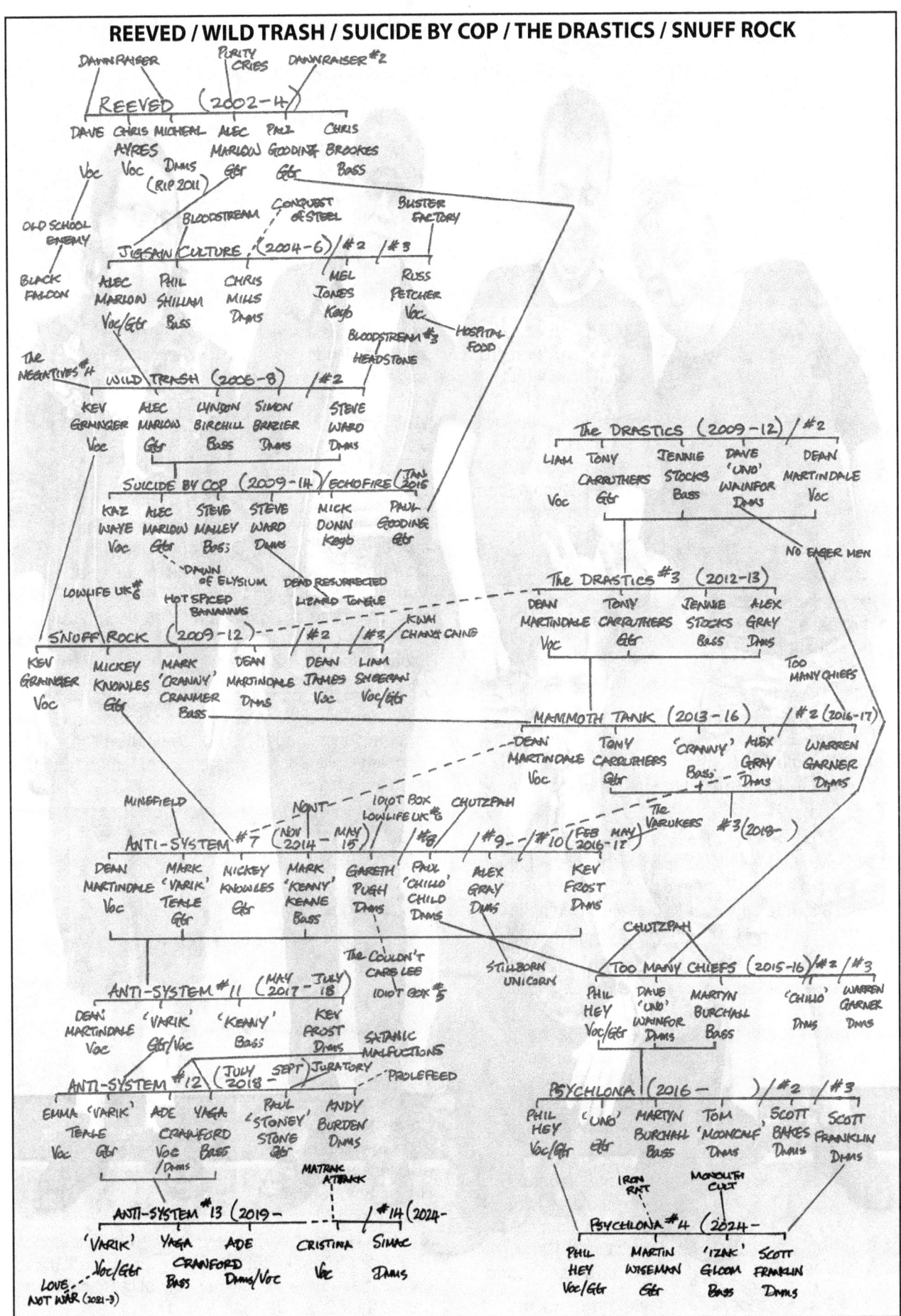

VOLTAGE RECORDS / STUDIOS

This local indie record label had been formed in 1988, by Tim Walker and Paul Cunningham of the rock band Harlequyn. Their first release was the band's debut album *The Order Of The Golden Dawn* in 1989, followed by a 12" EP, *More Than Before,* and CD album *Poets & Thieves* by the next incarnation of the band, now called Architect, in 1991/92.

Tim and Paul had taken over the four-track studio facilities at the Flexible Response Studios in Little Germany in 1987. With the closure of Flexible Response, they relocated to premises behind the recently demolished Theatre Royal.

Since moving their studio from the Theatre Workshops off Manningham Lane to their current location at St Stephen's Mill, Ripley Street, off Manchester Road, the studio has become the most successful recording studio with rehearsal facilities in West Yorkshire, now run by Tim on his own.

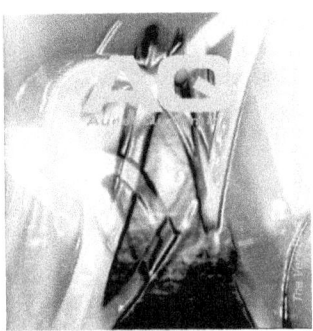

The 2002, compilation CD *AQ: Aural Quagmire* had tracks by local bands Idiot Box, Burn Horizon, Purity Cries, Darwin and Tim's band Worm.

Over the years, the label has released over twenty albums and singles, which are distributed via PHD distribution.

Between 2003-06, the label produced three compilation CDs entitled *Gnarley Dude 1-3*, featuring UK /USA bands promoting skateboard-related bands. At least six local bands appeared on them, including Tortoise Wall, This Et Al, White Light Parade, The Touch, Lowlife UK, and Worm.

The label released albums by numerous bands including Camp Boyz; *Our Soul* (1998), The Downfall; *Transporter* (2005) Worm; *Integral Virus* (1998, 2004) and *Hate* (2004), Arthritic Foot Soldiers: *Tales Of A Drunken Generation* (2004), Yo El Rey, (2013), Iron Rat; *Monument* (2015), and IdiotBox *Idiotbox* (2016).

Apart from the recording studio, Voltage also has video production facilities and has produced videos for bands including My Dying Bride, Iron Rat, Monolith Cult, Ghost Dance, Psychlona and Bad Boy Chiller Crew.

Tim joined a reformed version of Ghost Dance with singer Anne-Marie Hurst in 2021 in a line-up that also included former Harlequyn members Dave Wood (drums) and Phil Noble (bass). They recorded the album, *The Silent Shout* in 2023 at Voltage Studios. Ghost Dance played the Rebellion Festival in Blackpool as part of their 2023 UK tour.

FRANZ FERDINAND

Franz Ferdinand are a post-punk/pop band formed in Glasgow in 2002. The name comes from the Arch Duke who was assassinated in Sarajevo in 1914, the event which sparked the First World War, although the band named themselves after the racehorse of the same name.

Although originally based in Glasgow, none of the four original members are from the city. Their bassist Robert 'Bob' Hardy was from Wyke, Bradford, and was in his third year at the prestigious Glasgow School of Art Fine Art department.

Bob was the final member of the quartet, having been persuaded by guitarist Alex Kapranos to learn to play the bass on a borrowed guitar. (15)

Within a short space of time, they were making inroads on the lively Glasgow art and music scene, playing at first at 'art shows' in friends' flats, then at the student union's Vic bar at the School of Art. After gigs around Glasgow and Edinburgh and a successful trip to London, the band were courted by hoards of record company A& R people and finally signed to Laurence Bell's London-based indie label Domino.

The band's debut release, *Darts Of Pleasure*, was a five-track EP which came out in 2004. This was followed by their debut album, *Franz Ferdinand*, which was

recorded in Malmo, Sweden and produced by Tove Johansson. It reached No 3 in the album charts and went on to sell over five million copies.

The first single to be taken from the album, *Take Me Out*, reached No 3 in the single charts.

Their second album, *You Could Have It So Much Better*, released in 2005, went to the No 1 top spot, while their third album *Tonight* (2009), reached No 2 in the album charts.

Two other albums *Right Thoughts, Right Words, Right Action* (2013) and a limited edition two LP set *Live* (2014), have cemented the band's global success.

In 2015 Franz Ferdinand joined forces with brothers Ron & Russ Mael from the 1970s pop/rock band Sparks to form supergroup FFS. Sparks were best known for their No 2 hit single *This Town Ain't Big Enough For The Both Of Us*, from their *Kimono My House* LP on Island Records in 1974. They played that year's Glastonbury festival as FFS and released an album of the same title, as well as the singles *Johnny Delusional, Call Girl*, and *Police Encounters*.

In 2016, as part of *30 Days, 50 Songs* - a project criticising the presidency of Donald Trump, Franz Ferdinand released a new song *Demagogue*.

After a line-up change, Franz Ferdinand recorded the album *Always Ascending* in 2018. Now a five-piece, the band, still with Bradford lad Bob Hardy on bass, embarked on a world tour.

In 2022, the track *This Fire*, from the band's debut album, was used as the signature tune in the Netflix Japanese animated series *Cyberpunk: Edge Runners*.

FALCONNETTI

Queensbury lad Matt Fortune (drums) and his mate Mark Midgely (bass) had worked together in previous bands Drench (1994) and Seal Team Six (1994-97). Their work with this eventually seven-piece experimental post-rock group produced an atmospheric landscape of sounds on their five CDs.

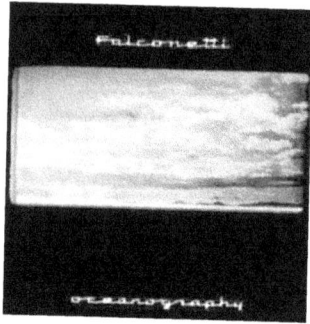

In 2003, they released three CDs on the Halifax-based Ryburn Recordings; the EP *Oceanograph*, the singles *Kino* and *Falconetti Vs The Enemy*. The EP *Finisterre* came out in 2005, again on Ryburn.

The History Of Skyscrapers EP was given away free at the band's final gig at the Holy Trinity Church in Leeds on March 29, 2008. Matt and Mark, continued to work together in the noughties, first with the Black Lanterns and then with their current band Burning Flag.

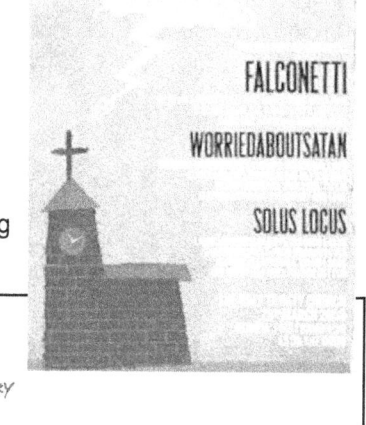

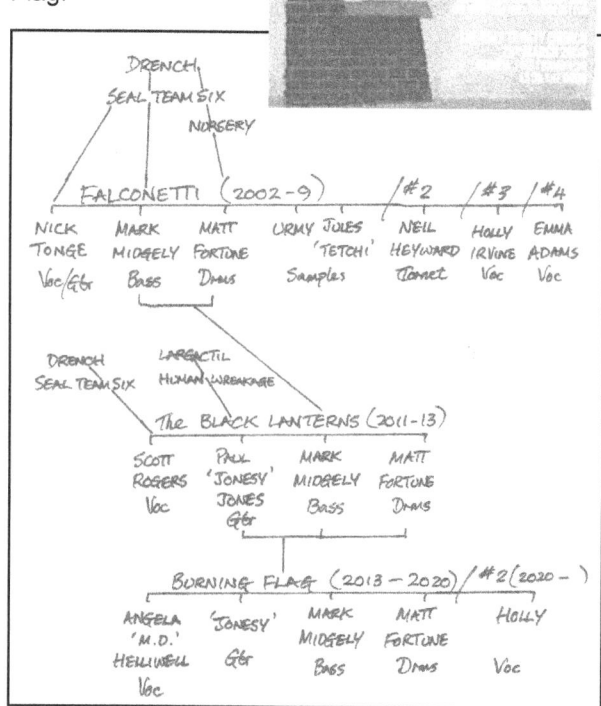

1 IN 12 CLUB GIGS: FEBRUARY-APRIL 2002

Saturday, February 2 – An all-dayer with The Deal/ HHH/ Send More Paramedics/ Buzzkill/ The Devils/ Driven Down and the band from Leeds 6, ex-Canvas (metalcore pioneers) Humanfly.

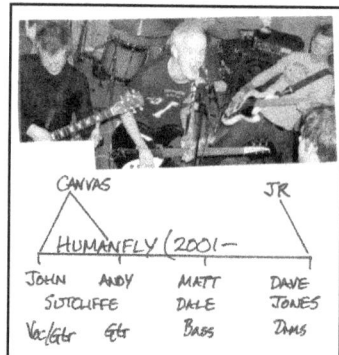

Tuesday, February 19 -US band Paths Of Destruction / State Of Filth / Monkey Tennis

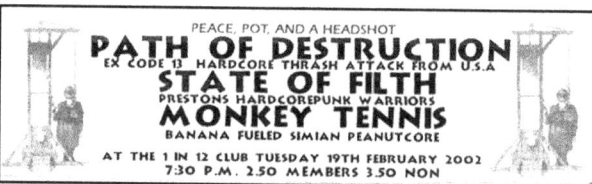

Thursday, February 28 – Gabrqeqqes Wish /Kwai Chang Caine/ Belle Vue/ Overtone

Friday, March 1 – Local metal band Circus

Friday March 8 – Baba Yaga

Friday, March 15 – The Inspectors / Paradox City / Virus House

Saturday, March 16- An Alldayer with Boxed In / Belligerent Declaration / Fig 4.0 / Narcosis / Khang/ Sex Maniacs / Beer Beast / Losing The Battle / Like A Kind Of Matador

Friday, March 22 – Two ska bands Finapple / Flukeshot Frenzy

Friday, March 29 – Greasy Monkeys / Grande / Tink

Thursday, April 4 – For the second year running the US band

Songs Of Zarathustra / Metrophon from Germany/ L.Sid / Like A Kind Of Matador

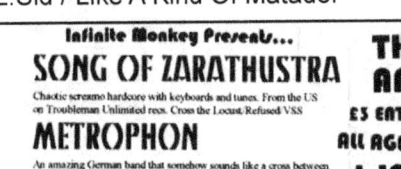

Friday, April 5 – From Poland Dezerter /French band La Fraction / and Scotland's Scatha

Dezerter formed in Warsaw, Poland in 1981, they were a highly regarded punk trio, whose debut album came out in 1989 on the Poljazz label. They had been due to play the 1 In 12 back in 1993 but were refused entry into the UK, this time they were only playing three UK gigs, the other two in Birmingham and London.

Friday, April 12 – The Inspectors

Saturday, April 14 – US band Dead & Gone, playing a return gig at the club, they last played on April 14, 1996, with support from John Holmes /D-Rail

During March 2002, the local fascist Young National Front website started to post photos entitled *'Spot The Red Scum In Bradford'* as reported by the *Telegraph & Argus*. Originally there was some concern about how they managed to get the photos of Bradford activists, but it was clear they had simply pinched them from the 1 In 12 & KDIS websites.

Following vigorous protests, the NF website was closed down and much of their information was out of date anyway, indicating that their operation was from outside Bradford.

MAYDAY 2002

This year's annual Mayday parade took place on a Wednesday, against a backdrop of an intransigent Police force who initially refused permission for the march to go ahead. After five days of pressure from The 1 In 12 Club, two MPs, the Law Centre, and enquires from the T&A and Guardian newspapers, plus the threat of the march going ahead anyway, the Police finally backed down and the parade/march to Centenary square was allowed.

ANGOLA 3

On Thursday, May 2, two US Black Panther members Robert King Wilkerson and Althea Francois gave a talk in the evening about the Angola 3. Three men Herman Wallace, Albert Woodfox and Robert King Wilkerson had all been wrongly convicted and locked down for nearly three decades in the maximum security Angola Louisiana State Penitentiary. The three Black Panther members were targeted by the administration at Angola (just north of Baton Rouge), for organising their fellow inmates, teaching some how to read and write, doing legal work, stopping rapes and sex slavery, and working across race lines and other divisions designed to keep 4,000 men under control.

While Woodfox and Wallace were still in prison, Robert King Wilkerson was released in February 2001, and since then had toured the world to raise awareness of the brutality, corruption, racism, and injustice of the US Criminal justice system.

Friday, May 3 – Dutch band Seeing Red / Shikari / Scalplock

Saturday, May 4 – The Hugh Reed Experience aka Hugh Reed & The Velvet Underpants

This Glasgow band had been around since 1990 and had supported Debbie Harry formerly of Blondie, on her solo tour of the UK in 1993.

Over the Mayday weekend the 1 In 12 footie team, held their annual tournoi, organised by Rob 'Kito' Hallowes at pitches in Hipperholm, Halifax.

Friday, May 10 – Palehorse /Narcosis/ Beecher /Tangaroa

Saturday, May 18 – Finnish band Forca Macabre / Scarborough's Active Minds / Boxed In / Kismit HC / Nailbiter / State Of Filth / 'rong 'uns

1 IN 12 CLUB AGM

Some interesting reports from the various Club collectives:- Publishing Collective – the initial 250 copies of the reprint of Harry Goldthrope's *Room At The Bottom*, sold out pretty quickly, breaking even. Club member Matt Hannam had written six chapters of a proposed twenty-four, on the history of The 1 In 12 Club and people are still living in hope and expectation of its eventual publication.

The Peasants Collective was still producing food on the allotments for the Club's cafe, and a new collective formed to re-activate 1 In 12 Records, hopeful of a new release on the horizon. (16)

Finally, the Quiz Team got to the final of the Airedale Plate on May 7, and the Games Team got promoted to the first division of the Monday night friendly league. Individual titles went to Club members Dave 'Beer Beast' and Bill Pritchard.

1 IN 12 CLUB GIGS: JUNE-JULY 2002

Saturday, June 1 – Local indie band Facelift

Sunday, June 2 – An all-day street party to celebrate fifty years of opposition to the Monarchy.

In the evening, Chumbawamba played a surprise gig and hand out

the limited edition free CD single *Her Majesty* (17).

The following month the Chumbas give an exclusive interview to the local BCB community radio station, on their thoughts and connections to Bradford.

Sunday, June 9 – US band Atrolous Madness / Cluster Bomb Unit from Germany / The Devils

Saturday, June 15 – Heavyfest II with London bands Sloth / Evil Knievel /Glasgow's Marshan / Blackrock / Supereagle / Sonic Lord / John Holmes

and Sex Maniacs from Leeds / and Bradford bands Khang / Silverburn and The Enchanted.

CHAPTER 2   2001 - 2003

Friday, June 28- Canadian band Black Hand / Thirty Seconds... / Fig 4.0 / D-Rail

Saturday, July 6 – Dagda from Ireland / Losing The Battle / Boxed In

Friday, July 12 – Sin Dios from Spain / Boxed In / Active Minds / Great Refusal

Saturday, July 20 – Rawcous Festival all-dayer with US band Total

Fuckin' Destruction / Palehorse/ Labrat / KervorKian Solution / Tangaroa / Silverburn / Gulla Bruja / Losing The Battle / State of Filth / Narcosis / Era

Friday – Sunday, July 26-28 –Three-day festival with Sweden's DS-13 and Norway's Kaospilot.

1 IN 12 CLUB GIGS: AUGUST-OCTOBER 2002

Friday, August 24 – Broadfest All-dayer

Thursday, September 12 – Skipton's Driven Down

Friday, September 13 – A benefit gig for the 2003 Manchester Ladyfest, with US all-girl group The Radical Cheerleaders / with all-girl bands Valere from Manchester and Flamingo 50 from Liverpool

Radical Cheerleaders were anti-capitalist, feminists from Minneapolis, who'd started in October 1998, two of their catchy chants were, *'We're sexy, we're cute, we're radical to boot,'* and *'Two, four, six, eight, F**K the Police state'*. Their track *Sound Of* appeared on the 2002 compilation *Constructive Engagement*. Before long there were more 'radical cheerleaders' forming all over America from Florida to Memphis, New York, and Atlanta. (18)

Saturday September 21- Baba Yaga

Saturday, September 28 - US band Pageninety Nine / The Devils/ Army Of Flying Robots / Send More Paramedics

Saturday /Sunday, October 5 &6 – Fast Fest #1 Two-day all-dayers, featuring two Dutch bands Reaching Forward and Vitamin X plus Finnish band Wasted.

Friday, October 11 – The Leeds Cops & Robbers collective presented US band Trans Am from Washington DC doing one of only three UK gigs.

They blend Chicago-style rock into a mechanical Krautrock framework and throw in early '80s sounds for good measure. Supported by Leeds band Bilge Pump and Wakefield's Itch.

Saturday, October 19 – Paradox City / The Inspectors

Sunday, October 20 – For the second year running Zann from Germany / Babies 3 / Losing The Battle

Friday, October 25 – Swiss band Anti-Maniax / Fig 4.0/ Mingers / Indicators

1 IN 12 CLUB GIGS: NOVEMBER-DECEMBER

Friday, November 22 – Dub Reggae from the UK Players

Friday, December 6 – (The Curse of..) Zounds (classic 1980s anarcho-punx) / Baba Yaga

Saturday, December 7 – An all-dayer with Truth In My Hands from Italy / John Holmes / Khang / The Inspectors / State Of Filth / Beligrent Declaration / Losing The Battle/ Burn All Flags / Itch / Driven Down / Indicator.

BRADFORD FESTIVAL 2002

In the House of Commmons, on April 15, an Early Day Motion (EDM) was tabled by six local Labour MPs; Terry Rooney, Gerry Sutcliffe, Marsha Singh, Chris Leslie, Ann Cryer, and Alice Mahon. The text of the motion stated, *'...the City recognises the contribution of the National Film & Photography Museum (the most visited museum outside London), Ilkley Literature Festival and Bradford Festival have made to the cultural life of the district.'*

A seventh Labour MP, Alan Simpson (Notts. South), added his name to the motion.

That year's festival was sparsely attended, and described as poor, which resulted in more criticism of the newly recruited organisers Zap Productions, based in Brighton.

Bradford Festival was previously organised and run externally for Bradford Council by a non-profit organisation, the Bradford Festival Company.

Zap Productions had been awarded the 2002 festival contract by Bradford's Conservative-led council, which had irked local community groups as Brighton was also bidding for the European Capital of Culture 2008.

On Thursday, June 6, 2002, a 'classic rock night' at Pennington's (formerly the old Mecca ballroom) on Manningham Lane, hosted 1970s Welsh rock trio Budgie. The band had some great song titles from their early albums, like *Breadfan, Hot As A Dockers Armpit,* and *In The Grip Of A Tyre Fitter Hand.*

On Friday, June 14, the 1960s / 70s pop chanteuse Petula Clark, famous for her 1964 No 2 hit single *Downtown,* played at St George's Hall on the final night of her 24-date *Ultimate Tour.*

Photo by Philip Meehan

WHARF RATS

This eight-piece alternative/rock band included troubadour Richard Marriot (pictured) on guitar and vocals and Bobby Weaver on bass. The band, who boasted two saxophonists and two percussionists, played a gig at The 1 In 12 Club on June 6, 2003.

After the unfortunate death of their drummer Alex Slater (who'd been in Last In The Brain Q) in 2002, Hidea Harding, daughter of former Eaten Alive By Insects guitarist Phill Harding, was brought in to take the drum stool.

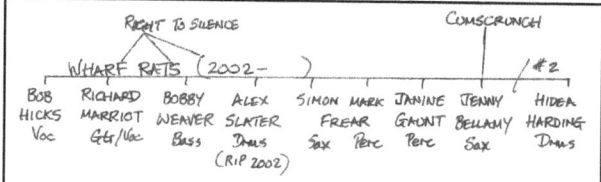

GINGER FRINGE FESTIVAL

Sunderland-born Ian Austin ran the popular Bradford cellar bar MacRory's Bar from 1991 to 2004. Situated beneath the Beechfield Hotel on Easby Road, the venue put on bands every Wednesday and Sunday night and hosted numerous jam sessions that often took place on Saturday afternoons.

From the late 1990s onwards, there was an annual Ginger Fringe Festival (named after

Ian's distinctive hair colour) that took place in the pub's car park. Each year, the event featured a number of bands and artists who appeared regularly at the venue, including Somebody's Brother (pictured above), Chantel McGregor (above right), and Shiny Beast (below).

The car park was usually packed with MacRory's regulars and those drawn by the great atmosphere. The festival was a free event, but money raised from raffles and collections was donated to the mental health charity *Mind*.

SOUP BOWL PRESS

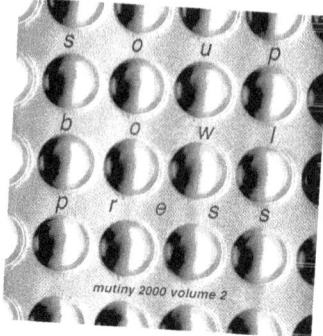

The second and, as it proved, final compilation album from the Mutiny 2000 collective was *Soup Bowl Press*. Once again, the CD was a collection of tracks from bands and artists involved with the Mutiny 2000 Studio and label based on the top floor of The Mill on Thornton Road. It was billed as a Mutiny 2000 / Righteous Sound production and mainly recorded, produced and compiled by Rob Heaton, Matt Webster and Jont.

The album featured:

Moota. Two tracks from their *Music From The Big Blue Vein* album. Full band performance of *Shiny Little Man* and an acoustic take on their song *Dangerous* featuring Bela Emerson on Cello and Sean Dillon on acoustic guitar.

Elvis Taxi another Rob Heaton produced track.

Bitter Dreamers were a one-off studio project fronted by Denny Austin from Somebody's Brother, featuring Timmy Nutall on drums, Jont on bass, Matt on lead guitar, and John Gray on sax with mouth organ on the intro played by Rob Heaton.

Frantic. Dub Kitchen singer/songwriter Fran Jones backed by former New Model Army drummer Rob Heaton, Sean Dillon on bass, Harris on guitar and saxophonist John Gray.

Steve Hanson, self-produced solo artist.

Rob Heaton's **Gardeners Of Eden** with two tracks from his unreleased album. *Bradford 6 A.M.* features Bela Emerson on cello with vocals from Leanne Hall (both from The Hiphuggers), and *America Atomica* featuring Moses Basquait on sitar.

Kwai Chang Caine - Their track *Pussy Galore* almost led to the album being banned due to a pastiche of the *James Bond Theme* being used as the middle 8.

Transu - a project produced by DJ Chad Meade, and future Gentlemen's Pistols members James Atkinson and Simon Mawson.

Jazz Mutiny drummer Rob Heaton, bassist Jont and saxophonist John Gray with Dave Ledgard on the track *Tandouri Jam*.

Zed. White Knuckle Ride is a track taken from their *Mutiny 2000* album, recorded in 1997 and featuring Rob Heaton on maracas and Harris on harmonies.

Sometime in September 2002, Gary Cavanagh began working on the research for the first volume of what became the *Bradford's Noise Of The Valleys* series, after working on around eight to ten preliminary rock family trees.

Leeds' early punk/alt-country band The Mekons (pictured above) marked their twenty-fifth anniversary by playing at the Irish Centre on York Road, Leeds on Thursday, November 21, supported by Chumbawamba and The Three Johns. The band played three more celebratory gigs that month, in Brighton, London, and Cardiff.

Local heroes New Model Army (Justin Sullivan pictured above) played a homecoming gig at Pennington's on Manningham Lane, on December 16, supported by the band Air Hammer.

SIMON ELLIS

Bradford-born keyboard player and producer won a Brit Award in 2002 for co-writing and producing the S Club 7 hit *Don't Stop Moving*. He had been recruited in 1997 by Simon Fuller for his 19 Entertainment agency to be musical director for the Spice Girls. He had previously been a member of Ellis, Beggs & Howard before being musical director for D:Ream and a touring member of East 17.

Simon was a keyboard player and/or musical director for tours with S Club 7, Britney Spears, Westlife, and Spice Girl Emma Bunton.

HIS GIRL FRIDAY

This local three-piece was formed in 2003 and comprised Darren Ellis, Rikinder Panesar and Samuel Exon. By 2004 they had been joined by guitarist Alex Richardson and had renamed themselves The Forge.

HIS GIRL FRIDAY / THE FORGE

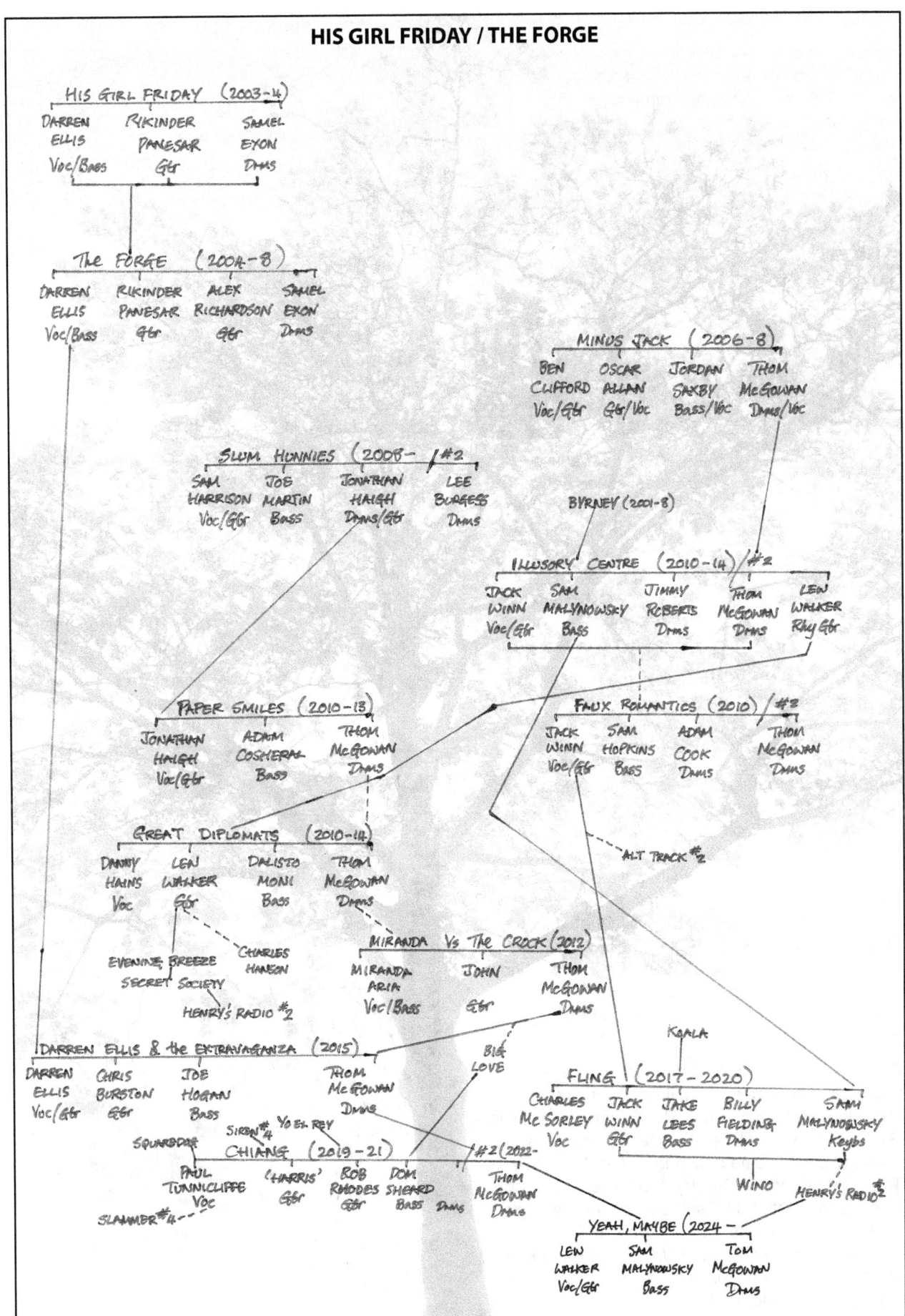

LOOM

A local duo of former T&A colleagues music journalist Simon Ashberry on bass and vocals and ex-Trip & Stumble member John Rigby on guitar, vocals and programming.

They were active on the local scene between 2000 and 2003, playing venues like The Love Apple and MacRory's Bar. For some gigs, they were joined by occasional vocalist Naomi Calhoun.

Loom released one self-titled 8-track CD album.

BRADFORD EMBASSY

"London's newest diplomats crunched on their cheese and onion crisps (more than likely Seabrook's from Allerton) and curd tart yesterday, as their doors swung open to revel the exotic charms of ....Bradford. Stung by a vintage outbreak of metropolitan amnesia over the whereabouts of their city, the Yorkshire visitors hired West End premises, screwed up a brass plaque and opened the first official Bradford Embassy." Quoted in the *Guardian* newspaper on September 19, 2002, as Bradford spokesperson 'ambassador' Lord David Puttnam and 'cultural attache' ex-YTV *Calendar* presenter Richard Whiteley, promoting the city's *European Capital Of Culture* 2008 bid.

Bradford was shown to be at a disadvantage as it was up against higher profile competing cities - Oxford, Brighton, Liverpool, Belfast, and Newcastle/Gateshead. A survey of a thousand Londoners revealed that 90% had no idea where Bradford was! The bookies' moved Bradford from twelfth to fourth in the running after the Guardian article, although the title eventually went to Liverpool. In 2025, Bradford became the fourth *UK City Of Culture*, a more recent designation intended to bring culture-led regeneration to the area.

LAIKA DOG / MALIBU STACEY

Born in November 2002, in the depths of the moors around Keighley, Terrorvision vocalist Tony Wright's new band Laika Dog named themselves after the first dog in space (sent up by the former USSR).

They released their debut CD *Forever And A Day*, and the CD single *What's Your Soul*, on their 10410 Recordings label in 2005.

Laika Dog's next release was the CD album *Mercury* in 2007, followed by their third album *Laika Dog* and the CD single *Monkey Song* in 2011.

Terrorvision bassist Leigh 'Cluey' Marklew formed Malibu Stacey in 2002. They played at The 1 In 12 Club on September 19, 2003, supported by local punkers The Inspectors.

In 2003, Malibu Stacey released the four-track CD *I Was Made For Lovin' You* on their own label. Their ten-track album *On Heat*, and a further CD single, *Invasion*, followed in 2004 on Townsend Records.

CHAPTER 2 — 2001-2003

TERRORVISION / CLOUDED FISH / LEAFEATER / LAIKA DOG / MALIBU STACEY

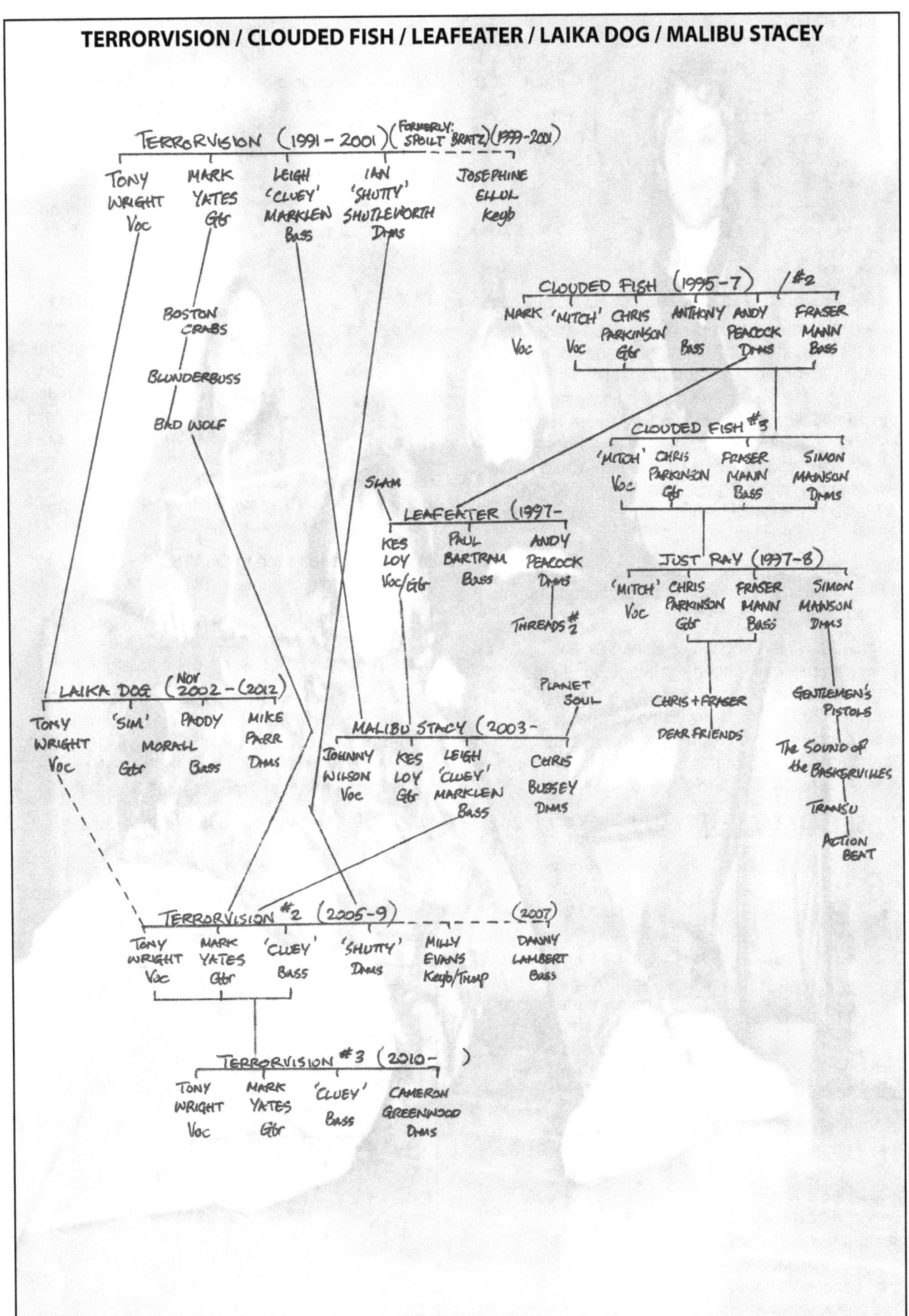

GIRLS ALOUD

The five-piece all-girl group Girls Aloud were formed in the summer of 2002 when thousands of hopefuls auditioned for the new TV reality show- Popstars: The Rivals. Twenty made it to the final stages of the competition before the final five were chosen – Sarah Harding (Manchester), Nicola Roberts (Liverpool), Nadine Coyle (N. Ireland), Cheryl Cole (Newcastle), and a 20-year-old studying English & Media at Leeds Univerity, Kimberley Walsh from Allerton, Bradford.

Irish svengali Louis Walsh was appointed their manager, working alongside the production team Xenomania.

The debut Girls Aloud single *Sound Of The Underground* was rushed out in time to top the Xmas 2002 single charts, eventually going gold. Between 2002-2009, they would go on to be the most successful girl group in UK history, with twenty-one top 10 singles, including four No 1's, five No 2's, three No 3's, and three No 4's.

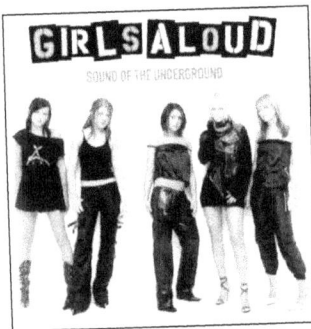

Their debut album *Sound Of The Underground* went to No 2 in the charts, as did the May 2003 single *No Good Advice* from the same album. The girl's fourth single, a cover of the Pointer Sisters' *Jump,* also reached No 2 in the charts and was used in the soundtrack of the Richard Curtis film *Love Actually*.

In November 2004, they recorded the official *Children In Need* single *I'll Stand By You* which went straight to No 1. They recorded five albums; their second, *What Will The Neighbours Say?*,

came out in 2004, followed by *Chemistry* (2005), *Tangled Up* (2007) and *Out Of Control* (2008).

During the group's hiatus in 2010, Kimberley Walsh embarked on an acting and presenting career, becoming a presenter on the music talk show *Suck My Pop*, and presenting that year's coverage of the BAFTA awards.

Her acting career began in 2011 when she played the part of Prissy Polly in the film *Horrid Henry: The Movie*. In 2012, she made her London West End theatre debut playing Princess Fiona in *Shrek: The Musical*, and also during that year took part in the popular BBC 1 TV show *Strictly Come Dancing*, becoming joint runner-up.

In 2015, she returned to the West End stage, playing the role of June in *Elf: The Musical*.

In 2016, Kimberley married her long-time partner Justin Scott, formerly of boy band Triple 8. They have three sons; Bobby, Cole, and Nate.

Kimberley's two sisters are both actresses. Sally Walsh played Lyn Hutchinson on Yorkshire TV's long-running soap *Emmerdale* between 1997-2000, while Amy Walsh appeared on the same show playing the character Tracy Metcalf from 2014.

In 2022, the remaining group members reunited for *Breast Cancer Awareness Month*, in honour of Sarah Harding who had died of the disease in September 2021, aged 39. They also joined forces with Primark to design a range of nightwear in memory of their former bandmate.

THE KEIGHLEY SCENE

In February, *Keighley News* columnist David Knights reported on the release of a compilation called *Working Class Heroes*. The CD featured bands from Keighley, Bradford, and Halifax. The bands from K-Town were The Undecided, Monutak, Soulfish, Circus, and Fake Uzi (hip hop artist).

RANDOM HAND

This young Keighley band formed in 2002, with political and socially conscious lyrical themes in the musical style that fused ska and reggae with metal, hip hop, and dub.

They thrived on the local scene, playing regularly at most venues and notably at The 1 In 12 Club, where band members became Club members. Between 2003 and 2008, they played nine times (at least once a year), with other local bands. Their first demo CD, *Buy This, Copy It...*, was released in 2003, and the CD EP *On The March* in 2004. They supported bands like Bad Manners, The Beat, and Skindred.

By 2007, they'd released their debut CD album, *Change Of Plan*, on Riot Music and signed a publishing deal with indie publisher Bomber Music. In 2008, they played a twenty-date UK

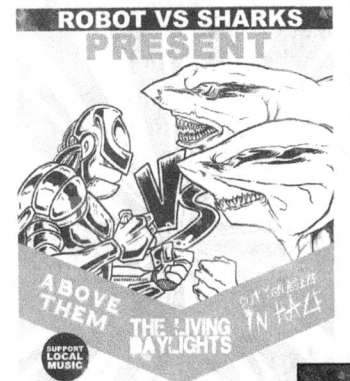

tour, then went to the American west coast to tour with Voodoo Glow Skulls.

Their second album, *Inhale / Exhale*, came out in February 2009 on Rebel Alliance Records and the band toured for twenty dates that month to promote the album. By the end of the year, they'd played around 100 shows.

Their 2011 album *Seething Is Believing* (2011) was the last to feature original guitarist Matthew Crosher and the second with drummer Sean Howe.

Their *Live In K-Town* album, recorded on New Year's Eve 2012, came out in 2013.

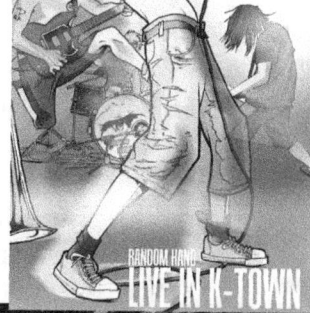

The band's bassist Joe Tilston organised around half a dozen gigs at The 1 In 12 Club under the title *Robot Vs Sharks* between 2012-13. He also released his own singer/songwriter album, *Embers,* on the Fellside label in 2013.

The last two Random Hand gigs at The 1 In 12 Club were in August 2019 and August 2022.

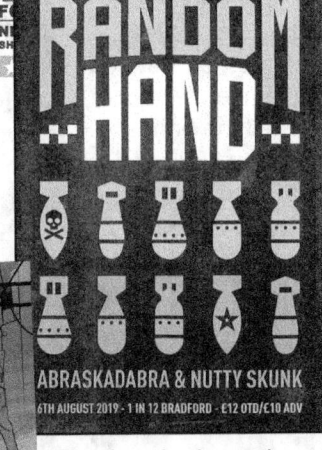

The band released a new album, *Random Hand,* and toured in 2023.

THE RETURN OF SKELETAL FAMILY

The revival of the underground Goth scene in America and Europe led to a resurgence of labels like Cherry Red. This meant that many of the original 1980s Goth bands' back catalogues were brushed off and re-released.

Skeletal Family's 1984 number one indie chart album, *Burning Oil*, was reissued on the Cherry Red off-shoot Anagram Records.

After more than a decade apart, three of the original Skeletal Family members; guitarist 'Stan' Greenwood, bassist Roger 'Trotwood' Nowell, and singer Anne-Marie Hurst announced a comeback gig at the Cockpit venue in Leeds, for Thursday, December 5, 2002, with fellow original member Ian 'Spud/Karl Heinz' Taylor on keyboards and saxophone and former drummer Martin Henderson.

Unfortunately, Anne-Marie backed out of the gig and the band had to fly in Skeletal Family #6 (1985-87) singer Katrina Phillips from the USA for the night. The band's set, including their hits *Trees, So Sure, She Cries Alone, Promised Land,* and *Restless* was played to a packed room with support from Keighley's Operator Six and Breene. (19)

During 2003, the band continued with former Smack Dolly vocalist Claire 'BB' Bannister fronting the band, playing a hometown gig at Victoria Hall, Keighley, on Saturday, December 27. Claire fronted the band between 2003 and 2009 and was the vocalist on their albums Sakura (2005)

and *Songs Of Love, Hope & Despair* (2009), both on Gepek Records.

The band's original vocalist Anne-Marie (the 'Queen Of Goth') was back in the fold for a gig at the Gasworks, Bradford on Saturday,

October 31, 2009, supported by local rockers Harlequyn. The band was billed as 'Anne-Marie Hurst' during this time and featured Stan and Trotwood with new drummer Rob Caswell and additional guitarist Owen Richards, playing a mixture of songs by Skeletal Family and Anne-Marie's post-Skeletal's band Ghost Dance. They played The 1 In 12 Club with Operator Six on Monday, December 27, 2010.

In November 2011 they released the album *Day Of All Days* on Jungle Records, recorded at Paul Weller's Black Barn Studios. Bassist Trotwood had been Paul Weller's guitar tech since the early 2000s.

The band reverted to the name Skeletal Family and gigged at home, in Europe and America with great success until Anne-Marie left in 2016.

Cherry Red Records released the five-CD boxed set compilation *Eternal* in 2016.

From 2017 to 2020 vocal duties were taken up by Hannah Small before former Exoterik vocalist Anneka Latte joined the band in 2021 (pictured above).

In 2023, their album *Light From The Dark,* recorded at Black Barn Studios, was released on CD and vinyl by Chapter 22 Records.

CHAPTER 2 — 2001 - 2003

SKELETAL FAMILY / ANNE-MARIE HURST / OPERATOR SIX / GHOST DANCE

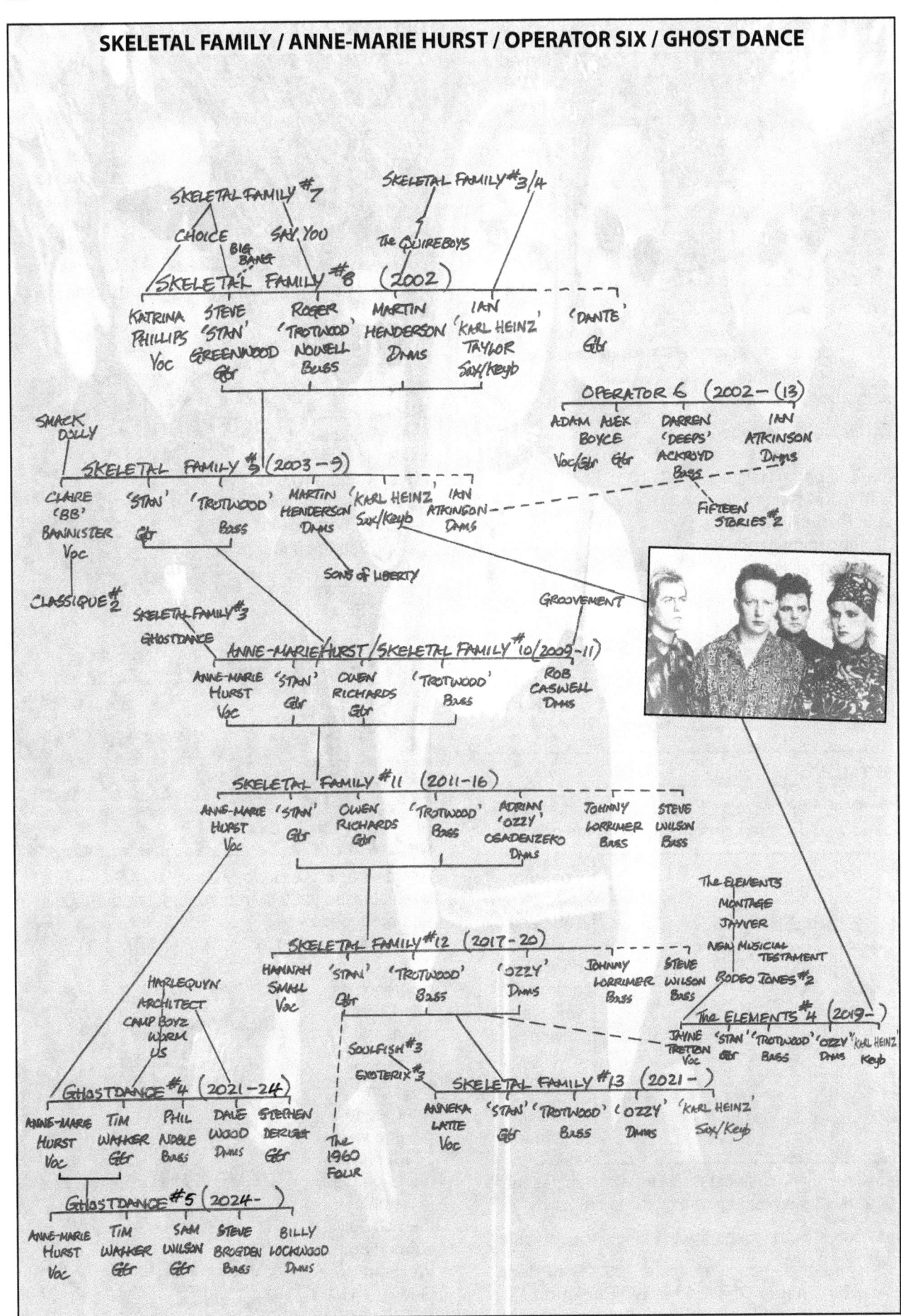

THE PIPERS

Formed in 2002, The Pipers were essentially a trio with guest accompaniment. Their debut release that year was a three-track CD single, *Tortoise / Submarine / The Faraway Tree*. In 2004, they released the five-track CD EP, *Alien*, on their own Handsome Dog Records.

On Saturday, October 9, 2004, they played at the Zoo bar in Halifax with fellow Keighley acts Exoterik and Jeff, all supporting headline band Modeliste.

In 2007, the band released their three-track CD EP *Medicine Cabinet*.

```
The PIPERS (2002 - (4))
JAMES      IAN       LEEY      DON      BOB       JULIE
ATKINSON   CLARKE              WARD     HOWELL    DARLING
Voc/Bass   Gtr       Drums     Trump    Ten.Sax   Celtic Harp
```

FATAL JOY

Originally a four-piece, Fatal Joy were another new band who'd started performing live in the previous year. In February, they parted company with their bassist and drummer who were having a baby together.

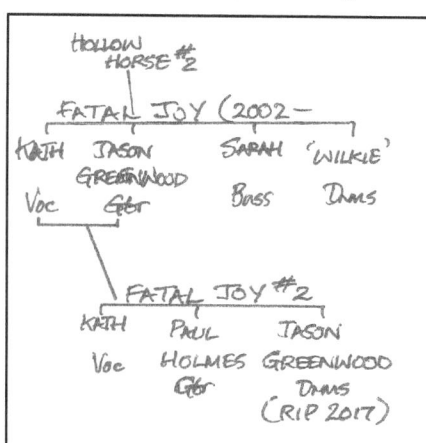

The band continued as a trio after recruiting guitarist Paul Holmes with Jason Greenwood switching from guitar to drums.

In 2003, they released the CD single *It's Too Late*.

Other Keighley bands around in 2002; **Fat Priest, Deepfill, Theory Of X**, and **Brave Radiation**.

OPERATOR SIX

Also formed in 2002, this Keighley outfit boasted a bluesy, British rock sound and were past winners of *Britain's Best Unsigned Band* award.

Their debut EP, *Talisman*, was released in 2007 and recorded at Paul Weller's Black Barn Studios. In 2009, a twenty-date UK tour saw them play Leeds twice, Keighley and Baildon once, as well as supporting Ocean Colour Scene on four dates.

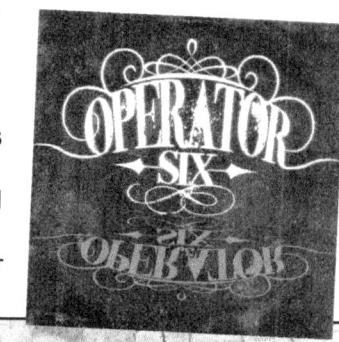

A three-track CD, *Buddy / Dear You / Cameras*, was released in 2011, recorded at Loom Studios, and produced by Steve Whitfield. A final CD single, *Somebody's Mind*, was released in 2013.

The band returned to gigging in 2015, playing the Exchange in Keighley, then on July 2, supporting Paul Weller at St George's Hall.

In 2003, Conor Nicholson, a Bradford lad from Clayton, became the editor of weekly music magazine the *New Musical Express (NME)*, a job he retained until 2009.

THE PRIESTLEY CENTRE

The Priestley Centre had formerly been the Civic Playhouse in 1929, but in 1966 changed its name to the Bradford Playhouse & Film Theatre. After a fire in 1996, it reopened as the Priestly Centre For The Arts. Many famous Bradford actors like Billie Whitelaw, George Layton, Bernard Hepton and BBC's *Hello, Hello* comedy star Gordon Kaye had all trod the boards at the theatre in their earlier days.

In the 1990s, the theatre ran into financial difficulties, owing around £14,000 to creditors. Poor box office receipts and a lack of grants ended with the council's funding running out in 1996.

Tom Priestly (son of JB Priestley) a film editor on such films as *Deliverance* and *Dunkirk*, returned in 1994 to try and save the venue. Although deemed by the Home Office to be of national importance and containing a Delius manuscript, JB's diaries, and racks of vintage designer dresses, the theatre's archive had to be put up for sale.

Local newspaper, the *Telegraph & Argus*, ran a campaign to help keep the theatre alive and raised £11,000. This was added to by a further £14,000 from Bradford Council to try and secure the theatre's future.

Unfortunately, as the *T&A* headline for January 8th, 2003, *The Final Curtain*, forewarned, the theatre was set to close on January 20th.

By now a registered charity, it had struggled with the estimated debts of £60,000. Chairperson Glen Boldy said: *"...the board will recommend that the 430 theatre members agree to liquidation, leading to the disposal of the theatre building on Chapel Street, Little Germany."*

Later, a new board secured a £40,000 bank loan and relaunched the venue as The Priestley. In 2008, after another financial crisis, there was a further relaunch with another new board in place. It still stands today, now called the Bradford Playhouse.

JUSTIN SULLIVAN SOLO CD SINGLE

On January 13, 2003, the artist formally known as Slade The Leveller, frontman of New Model Army, released his debut solo CD single, *Twilight House / Sooner Or Later / Headlight (Live)* on the band's Attack Attack label. As with most NMA releases, the single cover was a painting by Joolz Denby.

At the start of 2003, **His Girl Friday, The Silence**, and **The Solicitors** were the emerging local bands.

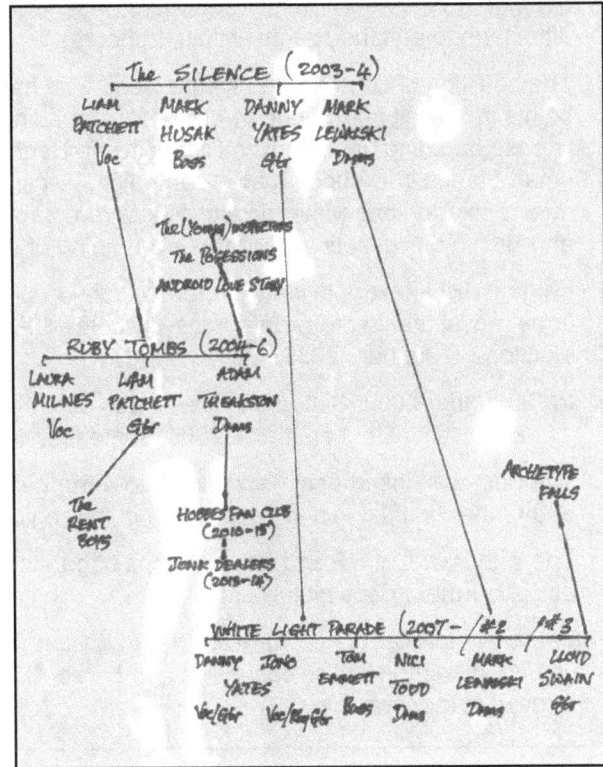

TORTOISE WALTZ

This local rock-metal band was formed in 2003 by guitarist Tony Wildwood, formerly of The Enchanted, and ex-Bloodstream drummer 'Vinny' Philpotts.

Their track *Gnarley Dude* appeared on the 2003 Voltage Records compilation CD of the same title. The band gigged extensively on the local scene and supported Toetag from Norway at The 1 In 12 Club on October 9, 2003. On their second appearance at the Club, on October 8, 2004, they supported Firebird.

Members moved on to other projects in 2005 after the band's demise.

THE IRAQ WAR

By January 2002, US President George W Bush was calling Iraq, Iran, and North Korea the 'Axis of Evil' and co-oped the UN resolution 14:41, on the inspection of Iraq's possible WMD sites. The prospect of the invasion of Iraq, using the faulty info from the MI6 'dodgy dossier' regarding Weapons of Mass Destruction, loomed closer.

UNSCOM's (United Nations Monitoring, Verification & Inspection Commission) chief weapons inspector Hans Blix stated that there were no weapons of mass destruction, contradicting Bush.

UK Prime Minister Tony Blair supported the claims of the sexed-up MI6 dossier and joined Bush in advocating 'regime change', thus taking Britain to war.

One million people attended an anti-war demo in London, on February 15, 2003, with the chant of 'not in my name'.

On March 18, Iraq's President Saddam Hussein rejected the US ultimatum to quit the country within 48 hours.

The coalition of countries led by the US/Britain had deployed over 180,000 troops to the jumping-off points in Kuwait and Saudi Arabia, before invading Iraq on March 20, 2003. The war started with the intense bombing of strategic military sites in Baghdad, by satellite-guided missiles and hi-tech remote smart bombs in a 'shock & awe' campaign. Within twenty-two days, ground troops captured Bagdad after a six-day-long battle. The oil fields were captured too, with minimal damage, and protected for US and British oil workers to start the re-pumping of the precious oil.

With no exit strategy in play, the reconstruction of the country (a goldmine for Cheney and Rumsfeld's firms) advocates a proxy democracy, with the CPA (Coalition Provisional Authority) in charge, until elections in January 2005.

In December 2003, Saddam Hussein was captured by US special forces at a farm in an underground 'bunker'. He was put on trial in 2005, sentenced to death, and hanged.

The post-war 'insurgency', spiralled into a Sunni-Shi-ite sectarian civil war, leading to the rise of ISIS and further confusion and devastation in the region.

The withdrawal of US and British troops began in 2009, with the Brits pulling out of Basra in the south, and all further troops by the end of 2011.

The financial cost of the war was over $2 trillion. The human cost was 36,000 US troops killed or wounded and the British casualties numbered 179 dead. Over one million Iraqis were killed or injured as a result of the invasion. (20)

PARADISE LOST 20TH ANNIVERSARY

The pioneering Bradford/Halifax doom/gothic band, Paradise Lost played a homecoming 20th Anniversary gig at Rio's on Woodhead Road, on March 28, 2003, supported by Tapping The Vein.

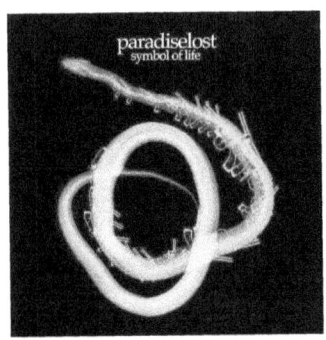

The band had signed a deal with Gun Records and released their ninth studio album, *Symbol Of Life*, in 2002.

In April 2003, the BBC released a compilation album of Paradise Lost radio sessions on their Strange Fruit label. The *At The BBC* CD comprised the band's sessions from the *Friday Rock Show*, the *Rock Show* and a live set from December 1993 at Liverpool Royal Court for the *Sunday Rock Show*.

Four of the original lineup are still on the go, despite going through several drummers in their continuing career. They released their 16th album, *Obsidian*, in 2020.

THRESHOLD SHIFT RISE AGAIN

After a ten-year hiatus, Bradford punk band Threshold Shift reformed in 2002 with drummer Paul 'Chillo' Child and former Convulsions guitarist Phil Hey joining founder singer/guitarist Mick Barrett and bass player Kenny Armitage.

They were booked to support punk 'supergroup' Dead Men Walking, a band featuring former members of The Cult, Theatre Of Hate, Sex Pistols, Stray Cats and The Alarm, at Pennington's on October 16, 2003. However, when Threshold Shift turned up at the venue, they were told no support band was needed as the main act did two sets. This didn't go down well with the band's supporters as over 300 tickets had been given out by Threshold Shift. Dead Men Walking were heckled by the audience and a stool was thrown onto the stage, knocking over guitarist Billy Duffy's amp during the intro to Pretty Vacant. The event made the headlines in the T&A. (21)

Threshold released the album *Trees*, CD EP *'65* (2005), *...Another Fine Mess* (2007), and *Live In Rio*, recorded live at Bradford's Rio when they supported Stiff Little Fingers in 2006.

In 2011, they teamed up with Bradford poet

Nick Toczek, for the *Britanarchy* CD EP recorded at Mutiny Studios.

After bassist Kenny left the band, the other three members continued as Chutzpah with bassist Martyn Birchill.

Threshold Shift reformed once more for an appearance at the Black Bull, Bradford, on January 4, 2014, which was announced as the band's last ever gig, *'we mean it this time!'*

In 2015, Phil Hey and Martin Birchill teamed up with guitarist Dave Wainfor and drummer Warren Garner to become stoner rock band Too Many Chiefs.

They played local venues and allayers including a Harley Dawson rally in at the Bull's Head in Baildon, in August 2015. A self-titled online album was made available on Bandcamp in December 2015, produced by James Atkinson.

Too Many Chiefs morphed into Psychlona who went on to have success on the desert rock/stoner festival circuit and released four vinyl LPs by 2024.

But if you thought you'd seen the last of Threshold Shift, you were wrong!

The band made a comeback in 2019, this time with Alex Marlow on guitar.

They played Scarborough Apollo on Saturday, August 24. As part of the Bradford By The Sea event, alongside Gods Of Hellfire, TPS, Abbey Falls and Crash Scene Flowers.

Threshold played at the Underground on Saturday, December 7. The band had a series of gigs lined up for 2020 that were cancelled due to the outbreak of Covid-19 and decided not to continue.

THE 1 IN 12 CLUB 2003
GIGS: JANUARY - APRIL

Monday, January 27 – Pale Horses / Narcosis / Vehemence

Sat & Sun, February 1 & 2 – A Two-day benefit gig of brutal and heavy bands including Charger (the Stoke-on-Trent sludge-metal band formed in 1995, who released their *Confessions Of A Man Mad Enough To Live Amongst Beasts* album in April 2003 on Peaceville Records) / Dukes Of Nothing / Mistress / Humanfly / Khang / Army Of Flying Robots / Parade Of Enemies/ Pale Horse / Snowblood / Send More Paramedics / Bilge Pump / Losing The Battle / D-rail / and Humans The Size Of Microphones.

Sunday, March 9 – Beecher / Eden Maine / Jairus / Emotive Exposed

Saturday, March 29 - An all-day anti-war benefit.

Saturday, April 4 - Firebird / Sloth / Khang / Godsize

Firebird were the heavy stoner-blues rock trio, led by ex-Napalm Death / Carcass geezer Bill Steer.

Friday, April 11 - Blockdown

Friday, April 18 - Ninepound Note / Bobby Six Killer / Saving Lenny / Pier 62 / Five Finger Discount / Fair Weather Solution

NINEPOUND NOTE

This young local five-piece ska-punk band toured the UK for three weeks, with augmented extra brass members making them a nine-piece, in two Nissan Micras. They self-released a ten-track CD album *Chips For Tea* in 2003.

Sax player Dave Hogan went on to play with another local band, The Deed Poll from 2005-07.

Their trumpet/alto sax player John Longbottom went on to write for the UK's favorite rock magazine *Kerrang!*, and wrote an article entitled *In Defence Of Ska-Punk* in 2018.

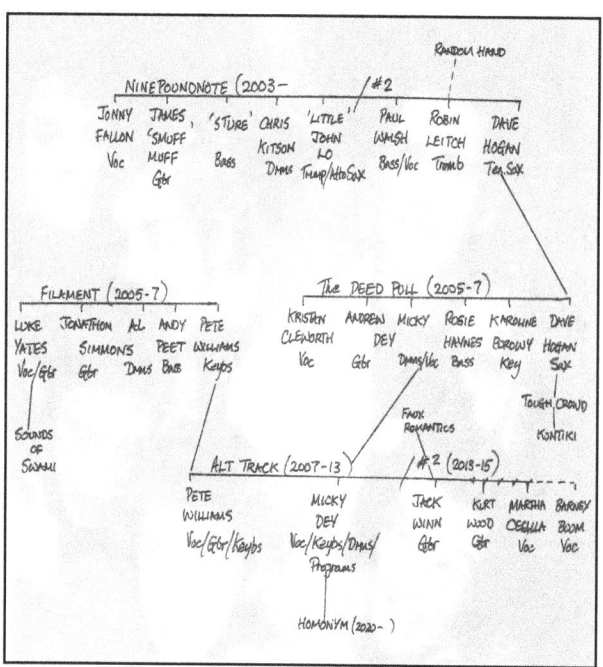

CHAPTER 2 — 2001 - 2003

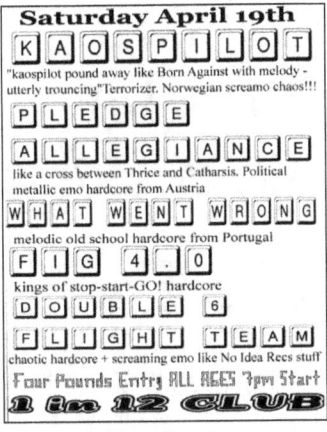

Saturday, April 19 – Norwegian band Kaos Pilot / Pledge Allegiance (from Austria) / What Went Wrong (from Portugal) / Fig.4.0 / Double 6 Flight Team

Saturday, April 26 – Anodyne (from USA) / French band Tantrum / Plague Of Zoltan / D-rail

Sunday, April 27 – Iceland's Minus / Beecher / Kevorkian Solution / D-rail

MAYDAY

The annual Mayday march from Infirmary Fields to Centenary Square took place on Thursday, May 1, and culminated with 1 In 12 members returning to the Club for a drink.

The next night, on May 2, the Club hosted local acts Kwai Chang Caine / Bookworms / Uncle Skinny.

Saturday, May 3 – Zounds (the return of 1980s anarchos whose 7" single *Demistification* gave bands and small labels a DIY guide to making their own vinyl records) supported by Bradford/Newcastle band Boxed-In and the first of two appearances by Belfast oi band Runnin' Riot.

Wednesday, May 7 – US hardcore band Severed Head Of State (who were

promoting their latest album, *Anathama Device* on Hardcore Holocaust Records) / Runnin' Riot

Sunday, May 11 – Seven Machine / Burst Rondo / Godsize / Isor

Thursday, May 15 – Leif Ericson / Radio Alice / The Mingers / Red Star Parade (from Leeds) / Losing The Battle

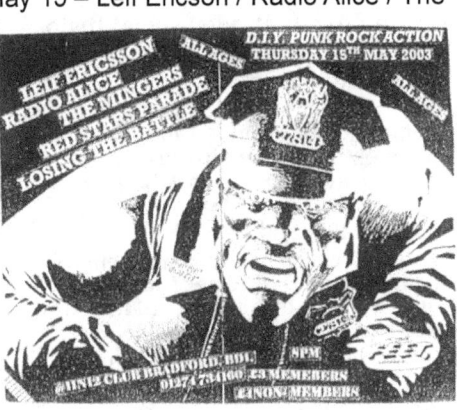

Saturday, May 17 – Violent Minority / Indicators

BRADFORD ANARCHIST GROUP

The Bradford Anarchist group was started by young local activists, who used The 1 In 12 Club as their base and mailing address. The group organised around anti-war and anti-fascist activities and produced small leaflets and the A4 double-sided *Stateless* bulletin leaflet.

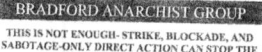

BIRTH OF BRADFORD'S NOISE OF THE VALLEYS

On May 30, 2003, the Telegraph & Argus newspaper ran an article entitled *Go Down In Music History* about a proposed book by local historian Gary Cavanagh.

A further article appeared in Keighley News the next month entitled *Gary In Hunt For Old Rockers* and advertised an informal meeting at the Red Pig pub on July 30, 2003.

Go down in music history

ROCK & POP
with DAVID BARNETT

Okay – name ten big Bradford rock acts over the past 30 years. If you've counted off Terrorvision, Smokie, Kiki Dee and Tasmin Archer and have ground to a halt, then social historian Gary Cavanagh's new project is definitely for you.

Gary, a university lecturer and founder member of Bradford's 1 in 12 Club, has taken on the exhausting task of documenting every single rock band to spring from the city's well of talent between 1966 and 1987.

His work, which he is hoping to publish along with a CD of some of the best music to come out of Bradford in that 20 year period, is a direct sequel to Derek Lister's celebrated book Bradford Rock and Roll, which covered the years 1956 to 1965 and is still considered an invaluable guide to the city's rich rock heritage.

Gary is putting together the follow-up to Lister's book in the style of the 'rock family trees' cartoon that used to grace the pages of the NME, and his research has thrown up some fascinating little treasures.

"So far I've got something like 353 bands documented," said Gary. "I started off just dabbling in it for my own interest, but as I got deeper into it I realised just how many bands Bradford had through that period."

Gary has consulted Derek Lister over some of the bands that didn't make it into his book, and the original author has given his blessing to the new project.

His research covers a fascinating time in musical history – from rock 'n' roll through psychedelia, heavy metal, funk, soul and punk. Old favourites such as New Model Army are there, of course, as well as lesser-known outfits such as The Accent and Shadowfax.

To show the fruits of his labour so far, Gary has organised a "viewing" of the research at the 1 in 12 Club for Thursday, June 12. It will take place from 8pm at the 1 in 12 Club on Albion Street, and anyone who has an interest in Bradford's music scene is invited to come along. There will be live music from B.A.J. – one of the bands Gary has researched – and a chance to peruse the family trees and add your own annotations.

When the project is finished, Gary is hoping to find a local publisher to distribute the book and help preserve his research for posterity.

He has also been getting permission from many of the old acts to use their music in a CD which will accompany the written volume. In some of the cases it'll be the only time you get the chance to hear the music – one track by The Accent was released by Decca Records in 1967 and currently changes hands among collectors of rare vinyl for upwards of £400.

Meanwhile, you can earn yourself a mention in the book by helping Gary out with his investigations into some of the bands which he is struggling to either find information about or track down original members.

For example, if were you ever in The Blue Sounds, The Lyric Show Group or, heaven help us, Silas Warthelmet's Battering Ram? What about Hepworth's Good Impression, Pig Pen or Straw? And if you remember being in Hot Buttered Leg, Man Ray's Haircut or Ministry of Fear, then like the 1960s you probably weren't there.

Anyone who can help Gary is promised an acknowledgement in the book and you can either go along to the open night on June 12 or write to him care of the 1 in 12 Club, 21-23 Albion Street, Bradford BD1 2LY.

Gary in hunt for old rockers

by David Knights

OLD rockers never die — they simply hang up their guitars and nip down to the pub.

And that's where they will meet the man who is chronicling the history of Keighley's music scene.

They will tell Gary Cavanagh all about the rock and pop bands which thrived in the town during the 1960s, 1970s and 1980s.

Then he will include the information in his comprehensive overview of Bradford and Keighley's musical history.

Gary, a university lecturer, hopes his book will include every band active in the district between 1966 and 1987.

But he needs to know more about outfits such as Ginger Wheelbarrow, Plastic Dream Machine and The Cobblers.

Gary is compiling an accompanying CD which will feature long-lost tracks by some of the better-known bands. As a founder of Bradford's 1 in 12 Club, a haven for fledgling bands, Gary is well placed to carry out the project.

He is also running a ten-week History of Pop Music course, in Keighley, for the Workers Educational Association. Gary has developed several rock "family trees" detailing local musicians' progress through various bands.

But he admits there are blank spaces on these trees and several bands he needs to know more about. To this end he has organised a get-together for Keighley musicians on Wednesday, at 8pm, in the Red Pig, Church Green.

He wants to meet anybody who was involved in rock or folk bands during the three relevant decades.

Gary will present the research he has already carried out in the hope he can spark discussion.

He said: "We can cross-reference what people know. I want to fill in the blanks — there are sure to be some bands I've missed."

Gary particularly wants to know about The Thimbleriggers — whose original single was recently released on CD — and The Nomads, who are still well-known locally. Other bands on his wish list include The Beat Squad, the Key Men, the Quarrymen, Jovial Crew, Threefold, Jackfield Farm and Mountain Ash. Gary is also trying to track the careers of people like John Loveday, whose band John's Followers played in Europe, Tony and Keith Tretton, and folk singer Linda Russell.

CHAPTER 2   2001 - 2003

GIGS: JUNE - JULY

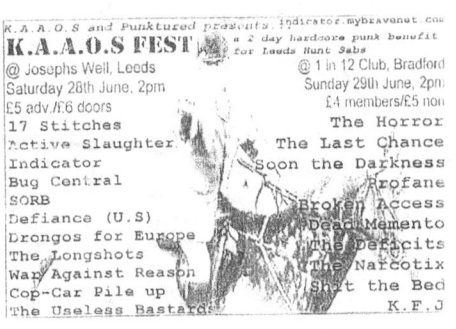

Wednesday, June 4 – Tear It Up / Sex Maniacs / The Devils

Friday, June 6 – Wharf Rats

Saturday, June 7 – The Evolution Tour

The tour featured over twenty bands on a twenty-seven-date tour of the UK, sponsored by Totalrock.com. Those who played the Club that night were: Skindred - the nu-metal/reggae rock band from Newport, Wales who were managed by local lad Andy Farrow of Northern Music Co. Their vocalist Benji Webbe had previously been in the band Dub War (1993-99). Skindred's debut album *Babylon* was reissued in 2003 by RCA Records.

Shellshock – a four-piece band from Watford, with a hybrid mix of nu-metal/hardcore and drum'n'bass, their debut album was due out in September.

Project Abner - promoting their All My Love EP

These three bands were supported by Through Silence.

Thursday, June 19 – The Varukers / US band Star Strangled Bastards / Japanese outfit Tetsuarry / Valhalla Pacifists / Indicators

HEAVYFEST III

The third event organised by the *None More Heavy*

promotions team took place on Saturday, June 21. Amongst the ten bands playing that day were Birmingham's Mistress and Sally, Nottingham's My War, Helvis and Ninedenine, Glasgow's Ultimodragon, Doncaster's Black Mariah, and the trio of bands - Khang, Bloodstream and Enchanted all from Bradford.

Sunday, June 29 – A Benefit for the Hunt Sabs with The Horror / Last Chance / Soon The Darkness / Profane / Broken Acess / Dead Memento / The Deficits / The Narcotix / Shit The Bed / KFJ

Saturday & Sunday, July 5-6 – An Infinite Monkey two-dayer.

Thursday, July 17 – What Happens Next? / Army Of Flying Robots / Jinn / The Horror

Saturday, July 19 – Lice & Sheep

Thursday, July 24 – Informers

Sunday, July 27 – December Revolution

Monday, July 28 – Hot Property

GIGS: AUGUST - OCTOBER

Friday, August 1 – Baba Yaga / Flamingo 50 / Mrs Pilgrim / Snail Racing

Sunday, August 3 – From Holland Barnhouse Effect / Broken Access / Last Chance / D-rail / Mingers / Losing The Battle / Charlie Don't Surf / Valhalla Pacifists

119

2001 - 2003 BRADFORD'S NOISE OF THE VALLEYS VOLUME 3 PART 1

Friday, August 8 – Cosmo / Bookworms / Bry Outlaw / Uncle Skinny / Muppet

Thursday, August 14 – Foruta

Sunday, August 17 – Zillan / Broken Off from Scotland

Thursday, August 28 – Japanese band I Excuse / two Finnish bands Manifesto Jukebox and Wasted / Radio Alice

Saturday, August 30 – For the second time that year - The Varukers / Radio Alice etc

Sunday, August 31 – Active Slaughter / Flute Target / Fukhate Propaganda

Saturday, September 13 – A Carpe Noctum night with Libertina (UK dark wave) vs Projekt (goth metal)

Sunday, September 14 – Chapmanbury featuring Battle Royal from Germany / The Horror / Bilge Pump / Dragon Rapide / Brown Owl / Eleven Fiftyeight

Friday, September 19 – Malibu Stacey / The Inspectors

Saturday, September 20 – Violent Minority / The Indicators

Friday, September 26 – Cut Out Hero

Saturday, September 27 – Local Keighley metal band Diavolo

Friday, October 3 – Local group Bryney

Thursday, October 9 – Toetag from Norway / Charlie Don't Surf/ Tortoise Waltz

Germany

Friday, October 17 – A BISAN benefit with Random Hand / Kwai Chiang Caine / Bookworms

Friday, October 12 – Two US bands American Heritage and Remains of The Day / Keitzer from

Friday, October 31 – US band Drop Dead - making their third appearance (April 1995 & October 1998 previously) at the Club. Their guitarist Ben Barnett had lived in Bradford for a year or so in the late 1990s, as he was in a relationship with a female Club member.

Supported by Scalplock / Jinn / Radio Alice / Broken Access / Patient Zero

GIGS: NOVEMBER - DECEMBER

Friday, November 14 – The return to the Club of esteemed punk-poet Attila The Stockbroker.

Saturday, November 15 – Knifed / Sex Manics / Eleven 58 / Broken Access / The Holy Riff

Saturday, November 22 – One Hundred Dollar Cigar

120

Saturday, November 29 – Local noise merchants Violent Minority, supported London's anti-fascist/animal welfare band Active Slaughter who were promoting their debut album *Ave A Butchers*, released that year.

Saturday, December 6 – Gertrude / Flamingo 50 / Thrash Brigade / Violent Minority, playing their fourth gig of the year at the Club.

Friday, December 12 – Floodstain / Khang / Monster Killed By Laser

Thursday, December 18 – Two Icelandic bands I Adapt and Hrydjuverk plus Red Star Parade / Broken Access / The Nothing

Friday, December 19 – Ninepound Note / Random Hand / Strike 59 / The Stickybacks

Saturday, December 20 – December Revolution

At the end of 2003, fourteen bands from all over Europe and six from the USA had graced the Albion Street stage.

DARWIN

This local outfit featured Matt Barraclough, Drew Jones and Tony Smith. They had two tracks, *More Than You Will Ever Know* and *On Air*, featured on the Voltage Studios 2002 compilation CD, *AQ: Aural Quagmire*. They released one CD album, *Under Supervision*. The band played at the Brewery Tap in Idle, on June 7, and then a final gig on September 6, 2003, at The Coniston, again in Idle.

LOS GUYS

Formed in 2003 by former members of local bands Indiqa and Elsie Moon, Los Guys went on to release two albums, *La Noche de San Jaun* and *Last Of The Redunos* in 2006.

They were winners of *mp3unsigned.com*'s Band Of The Year in 2004 and 2005 and appeared on Yorkshire TV's *Calander*. Los Guys debuted at the Glastonbury festival in 2005 and were the official band of the *High Times* magazine's Cannabis Cup 2004 at the global Marijuana Music Awards.

Band member Jim Henderson also happens to be the second cousin of The Cult's guitarist Billy Duffy.

BRADFORD INTERNATIONAL FESTIVAL 2003

2003's Bradford Festival took place between June 12 and June 22. The first free gig in Centenary Square took place on Friday 13, featuring local acts Imani Hekima, Johnny & The Poorboys, Wilful Missing, Seven Hours, Azam Khans, and Midnight Special.

A further gig on Friday 20 featured Blue Arsed Flies, Loki, Iration Steppas, and ex-Detrimental member Indergoldfinger.

The Peel Park Mela was held over the weekend of 21-22. Alongside the market, fun fair, women's marquee and children's entertainment, the Global Mela Stage featured, on Saturday: Apache Indian (pictured above), local act RDB, Lemar, Gubi Savhu and Black Star Liner.

On the same stage on Sunday were Fundamental (pictured) and Mighty Zulu Nation, Safri Boyz, Milkit Singh, Omar Pugite, Baka Beyond, Dark Lord Black Star, and Shilpi Baruri.

Other Festival activities included street theatre, events at The Mill, gigs at The Love Apple, including the Fresh Milk new talent showcase night on Thursday, 19, and a Celtic Folk And Rock Night at St George's Hall on Friday 20, June.

GENTLEMEN'S PISTOLS

This Leeds / Bradford band was formed in 2003 as a duo, by ex-Clouded Fish drummer Simon Mawson and former guitarist in Voorhees #6 and the Horror, James 'Atko' Atkinson who were both engineers at Mutiny recording studios based at The Mill on Thornton Road. Their first demo CD was recorded at Mutiny in 2005, a studio that various bands including The Eagles, The Dolphins, Flex, Violent Reactions, Asomvel, Mob Rules, Dr Cyclops (Italy), and Perplex Flesh used over the years.

The duo were joined by bassist Douglas McLaughlan and played only one gig before Simon Mawson was replaced by Adam Clarke in 2004.

By the time their debut 7" single was released, the band was now a four-piece with the addition of guitarist Chris Rogers. *Just A Fraction* revamped 1970s style rock, and was released in 2006 on the Leeds-based Art Goes Pop label.

This was followed by a second 7" *The Lady*, again in 2006, this

time on Rise Above, the label run by ex-Napalm Death vocalist Lee Dorrian.

Drummer Adam Clarke left the band before the release of their debut album, and was replaced by Stuart Dobbins Their self-titled debut album came out in 2007, on the American label Candlelight Records.

That same year the Gentleman's Pistols appeared twice at The 1 In 12 Club, on Friday, July 13, supporting Finnish band Pharoah Overlord, then on November 11, supporting Pharoah Overlord's alter-ego Circle.

In 2009, the band released their third 7" single *Sherman Tank / Frustration*, on their own Rare Blood label. Their fourth 7" single *I Wouldn't Let You / Butcher, Baker,*

Candle Stick Maker was released in 2011, as was their second album *At Her Majesty's Pleasure,* both on Rise Above.

In August 2011, the band had an article in the Japanese glossy heavy-metal magazine *BURRN!*, and made it to number 11 in the mag's import album top 20 chart.

Their third album, *Hustler's Row,* was released in October 2015 on the German Nuclear Blast label. As well black vinyl, the album was also released in a limited run of 300 in white vinyl in a gatefold sleeve.

TRIAL

Another young band formed in 2003 were Trial, who existed on the scene until 2005.

Two of its members, vocalist/guitarist Patrick Dowson and drummer Jed Forward, then formed the trio Monty Casino (2005-09) with Jed's brother Kai on bass.

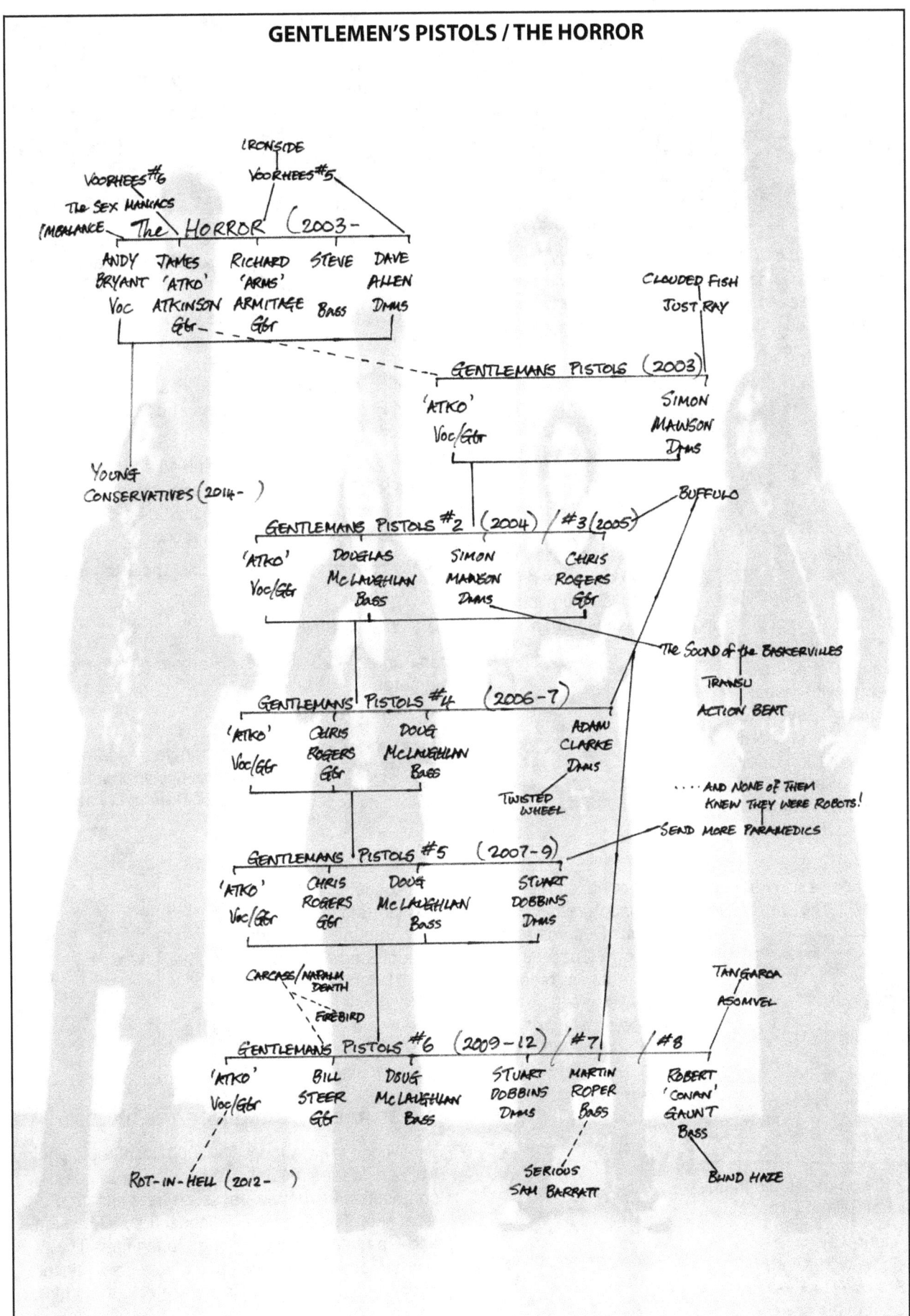

THAT FUCKING TANK

Formed around 2003, this duo comprising Andy Abbott (guitar) and James Islip (drums), went on to appear on eleven releases in their career. Originally based in Leeds, they both moved to live in the Saltaire/Shipley area.

They released four albums (one on vinyl) and seven 7" singles/EPs, three of which were splits.

Their first CD EP, *A Document Of The First Set*, was released in 2004 on the Leeds-based label Jealous Records. Two split 7" singles followed in 2005; the first with Grabba Grabba Tape, the second with Monster Killed By Laser. Both bands had recorded covers of King Crimson tracks - *Red* by TFT and *Larks Tongues In Aspic (Part 2)* by MKBL.

The next year, That Fucking Tank released the vinyl LP, *The Day Of Death By Bono Adrenalin* on Jealous Records and their own Obscene Baby Auction Records. The 7" single *The Awesome Magnet* came out in 2007, and their *Tankology* album was released on CD in 2009 on the Nottingham label Gringo Records.

A four-way split 10" single with Kong, Sheild Your Eyes, and Castrovala appeared

in 2011, followed by two albums on CD; *TFT* (2012) and *A Document Of The Last Set* (2013), both on Gringo Records. Their final release was the 7" single *China Tour* in 2015, again on Gringo.

During their existence, the duo played and toured regularly in the UK and Europe, playing at least five times at the 1 In 12 Club between 2005-2015.

In 2007, they headlined the Woollen Wig Out Festival at The New Beehive on Westgate, with other local acts Harmacy, Fourteen Corners, Kill Manticore, Le Tournoi, Tixxx, The Hipshakes, Pixel Pixel Pixel and Laura Groves and Serious Sam Barrett.

From 2011 to 15, Andy organised and ran the excellent Threadfest using various venues across the city, showcasing an eclectic range of local, UK, and international bands and artists.

Andy continues to perform solo under the moniker Elizabeth'

NEW GIRL SINGERS

In August 2003, two new Bradford girl singers emerged.

NATALIE GOODAIR

Natalie, a fourteen-year-old from Low Moor, was one of five youngsters to reach the final of *Dream Idol* at Leeds City Varieties.

SALLY DAWSON

On August 9, Sally, a twenty-six-year-old from Cottngley and graduate of the Idle drama school Stage 84, appeared on the BBC's *Fame Academy* show with twenty-five other singers. She was a good friend of Girl's Aloud singer Kimberly Walsh and her sister Sally Walsh.

PULSE RADIO'S BATTLE OF THE BANDS

On Wednesday, August 13, 2003, local radio station Pulse held the final of its *Battle Of The Bands* competition at Jumpin' Jacks in Great Horton. Four local acts, The Gift, The Touchsecured, Cohesion, and Finapple had won through to the final. The winners opened at that year's Myrtle Park concert, supporting Busted and Gareth Gates in front of a crowd of over 25,000.

CHAPTER 2 — 2001-2003

THAT FUCKING TANK / THE TRIAL / MONTY CASINO

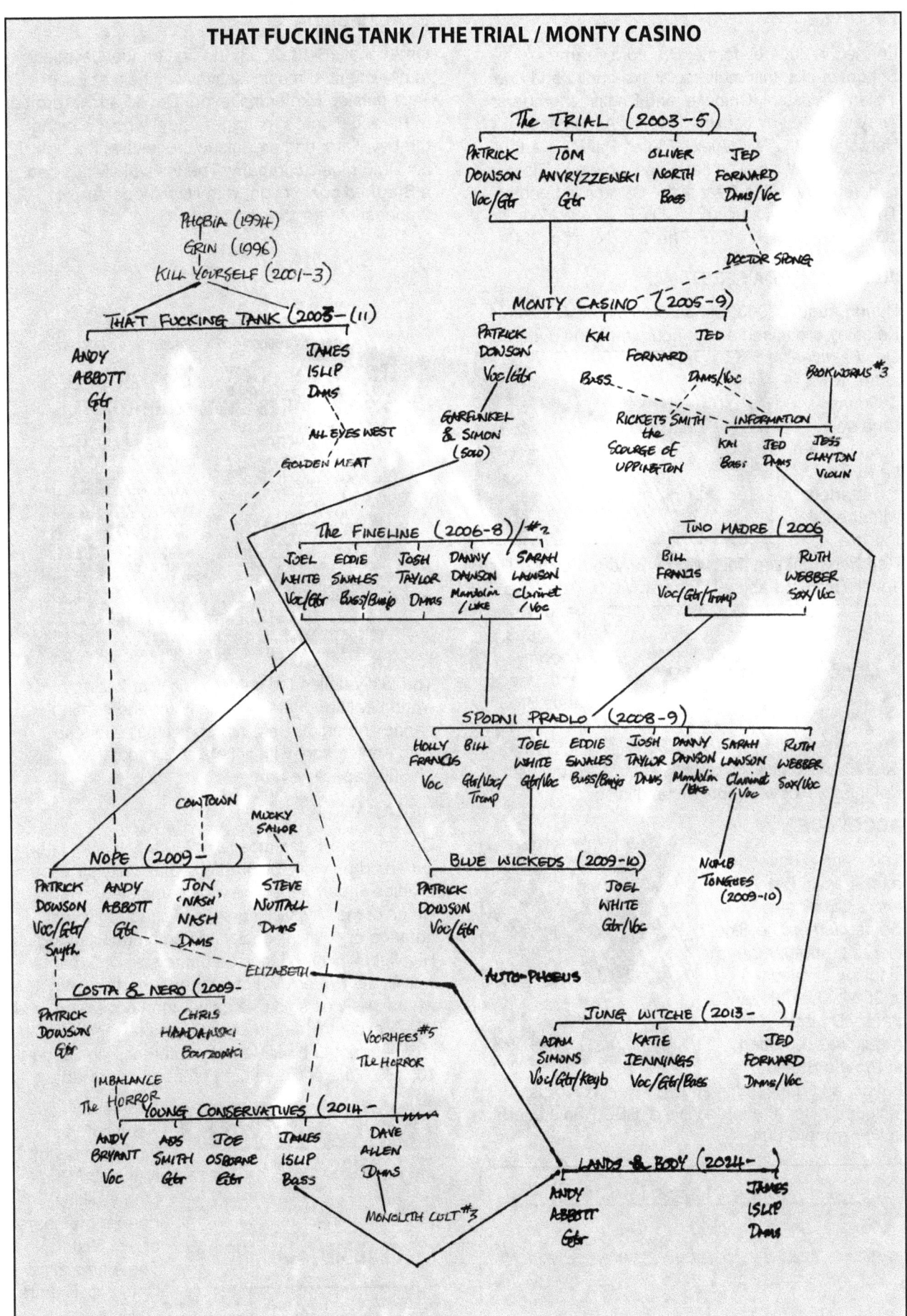

FINAPPLE

Formed in 2001 by former Bradford Grammar School pupils, this multi-racial ska-punk band had Indian, Pakistani, Chinese, and English members. They were led by cousins Thomas Almas and Haroon Rashid, with Alexis Ridler, Patrick Martin, and Daniel Wong. The band had played at Rio's and had supported The Beat at the Cockpit in Leeds. They released a four-track CD EP, *A New Hope*, in 2002, then the CD album *The Good Stuff* in 2004.

JUDGEMENT DAY FESTIVAL

During August 2003, Simon Clark of *We Rock* in Keighley organised a nine-hour, ten-band *Judgment Day Festival* at the Town & Country Club on Manningham Lane. The day started with the Ilkley four-piece Red Eye Funktion, followed by Bradford bands The Touch (pictured above), Tortoise Waltz, Accolade, Brand New Analogues, Random Hand, Leeds bands Brody, The Downfall, and Saw Throat with Keighley's Reeved (above) headlining.

ACCOLADE

This band produced a ten-track CD demo and a CD single, *Something In The Sky*, in 2002. Another demo single was released in 2004. Their eleven-track CD album, *Long Night*, was recorded at Pravda Studios, Leeds, and released in 2006 on Reef Records. It included a song recorded live at BBC Radio Leeds in December 2004.

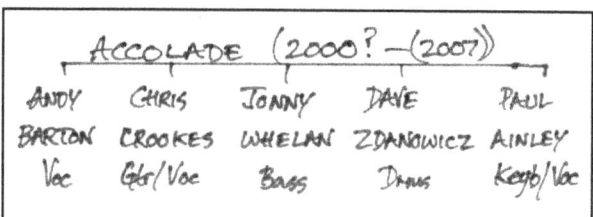

BEAUTIFUL DAYS

On August 16-18, 2003, the first annual Levellers family-oriented music festival was held at Escot Park outside Exeter in Devon. Dave Farrow (brother of Paradise Lost's manager Andy) who managed the Levellers, had organised the festival through his DMF Music company. The festival always had a Bradford connection, with New Model Army, amongst others, playing regularly.

The festival blended indie music with folk and world beats and featured many up-and-coming bands and artists. In 2023, they celebrated the 20th Anniversary with tickets selling out the 17,500-capacity event.

URBAN WALK

On Saturday, September 24, 2003, Gary Cavanagh led an urban walk for Bradford University's Peace Studies department. The walk completed a rough circuit of the city, visiting sites of Bradford's vast heritage of political, social and community struggles. Highlights included the site of the sale of a man's wife at the Butter Market (Darley Street) in 1837, where she was sold to a delver for a sovereign, and 36, Peckover Street in Little Germany, the site of the Independent Labour Party's conference on January 13, 1893, the effective birth of the Labour Party.

Events at Pennington's included Kastoff Kinks and Dead Men Walking, (former members of Sex Pistols, The Alarm, Stray Cats and Theatre Of Hate.)

THIS ET AL

A local four-piece indie-rock band, formed in 2003, who played regularly around Bradford venues and did four UK tours between 2003-08. They produced seven singles during that time. Their first release, *Previews* (2004), was a CDr with two songs, *He Shoots Presidents / Catscan* followed by the four-track EP *Demos* (2004), again on CDr.

The band's next release was the 7" single *Wardens / Rotary Queen* (2005) on Leeds label Jealous Records. A further 7", *You've Driven For Miles.... / All You'll Ever Be Is A Dancer*, followed later that year on the Sony Music subsidiary Double Dragon.

Their fifth release was the 7"/ CD *Sabbatical* (2006) again, on Jealous Records and mixed by Choque Hosein formerly of Leeds band Salvation.

The sixth single *Of Natural Importance / The Mother Position* (2007) on FC Recordings, preceded their debut album *Baby Machine* (2007) containing six previous tracks from their singles.

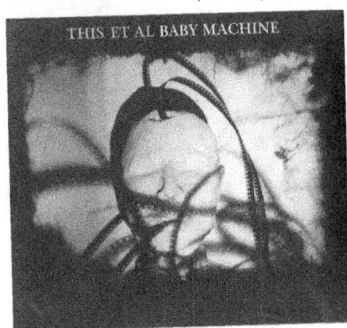

The album was recorded and mixed by the Somatics Richard Green (who had been in the late 1990s NME darlings, Ultrasound). It was released on Broken Pixel Records and distributed by Cargo Records.

Following a line-up change as Chris Wall replaced Gavin Bailey on bass, in July 2007, This Et Al released their the four-track 10" *The Figure Eight EP (Figure Eight / Medicine Hammer / Ice Age / (The Tale Of) Frosty Jackson)* on Leeds label On The Bone Records in 2008.

The band had also released two split singles with the bands, !Forward Russia! and Adzuki.

Their guitarist Ben Holden also did the design and layout for the Bradford fanzine *Mono* (2006-08).

BRADFORD IN FOCUS

In 2003, Bradford Council published the book *Bradford In Focus*, which was a rich photographic history based on photographs by Tim Smith.

It was described as, *'A vivid celebration of the present-day city, in four sections: Work / Landscape / People / Leisure.'*

The book included shots of iconic Bradford landmarks and picturesque countryside locations.

FILM FESTIVAL

Between November 16 and 23, 2003, the second *Peace Studies Film Festival* was held at Bradford's Priestley Centre and Hebden Bridge's Picture House. The aim of the festival was to heighten awareness of contemporary issues, by showing a range of films that documented and analysed areas on human rights, social justice and conflict. Films included Ken Loach's *Bread & Roses* (2000) which was about the struggles of a Mexican family who arrive in Los Angeles, the Brazilian film life in a favela, *City Of God* (2002), and the drama *Buffalo Soldiers* (2000,) starring Joaquim Phoenix and Ed Harris.

THE KEIGHLEY SCENE

The new band **Glamnation** was formed in 2003 by ex-members of Rhino. Vocalist Tony 'Krimmson Velvet' Brennan later fronted So It Goes (2006-9), before re-activating Glamnation #2.

On Saturday, September 6, 2003, at Keighley's Victoria Hall, a mini festival took place organised by K-town-based Real Music Promotions, featuring headliners Bradford metallers Bloodstream, K-town's Diavolo and Wasted Earth from Preston. Spokesperson Simon Clark for the promotions team said... *'we hope to do more mini-festivals in the Bradford /Halifax area.'*

Two other gigs at Keighley's Victoria Hall later that year are of note. On Friday, November 7, local soul band Soulfish (1998-2007) played a headline gig supported by a bunch of 18-year-olds from Keighley/Bingley called **Second Cousin**.

The following Saturday, November 15, local promoters We Rock organised a gig at the venue with Bradford band Honeytoad headlining supported by Worm, Downfall and Keighley band Breene.

EXOTERIK

This Keighley-based rock/indie band was formed in 2003, by partners singer Anneka Latta and guitarist Tom Fay. Anneka had played saxophone and sung backing vocals in the local band Soulfish.

They were joined by drummer Steve Riley (formerly of local bands Teenage & the Wildlife, Lively Arts, Since The Accident and Mapp) and original bassist Richard Burns (also formerly of Mapp, Since The Accident, Aim and Class Type Bees).

Exoterik played a gig at Halifax's Zoo Bar on Saturday, October 9, 2004. Also on the bill were Modeliste and two other Keighley bands, The Pipers and Jeff.

The band produced two self-released CDs.

The first, *Don't Swallow* (2008), was an eleven-track album recorded at the Sound Division Studios in Riga, Latvia and Grooveland Studios in Lahti, Finland. It was mastered by Morten Stendahl at the Redroom Studios in Trondheim, Norway.

Their second was the ten-track album, *Butterfly In Your Hand* which came out in 2009 and was recorded at the Lodge in Northampton.

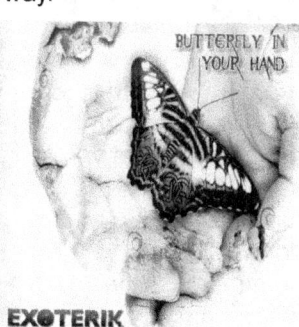

In November 2010, the band joined fellow Keighley band Skeletal Family (at the time

gigging under the name of singer Anne-Marie) on a two-date tour of Sheffield and Liverpool.

In 2012, Tom and Anneka released the album *Beauty In Chaos* as Fay & Latta. It was co-produced with former Exoterik member Richard Burns who also provided bass guitar and programming.

The album also featured Harrogate-born former Electric Light Orchestra and Violinski violinist Mik Kaminski who played on five tracks.

Since, 2021, Anneka has been touring the UK, Europe and the USA, as the lead singer of Skeletal Family, appearing on the band's 2023 album *Light From The Dark*, recorded at Paul Weller's Black Barn Studios.

DON GAUDIOSI & HUSH

Riddlesden singer/guitarist Don Gaudiosi had been in local Keighley band Suffering In Silence in the 1980s. They released two 7" singles in 1985; *Girls On The Dancefloor / Remember This* on Leeds label Off Beat Records, and *Sea Of Red / The Very Last*

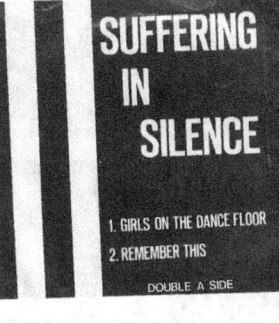

Time on SIS Records, which was recorded at Bradford's Flexible Response Studios.

After being in a few more local bands in the 1980s and 1990s, Don teamed up with legendary local drummer Pete Kaberry, formerly of NWOHM band Dawnwatcher, to form Grip (1994-96) and Rockheads (1997-98).

In August 1999, Don did a one-off charity gig for Leukaemia research at Keighley's Victoria Hall. He also produced a three-track CD under the name of Hush with some of the musicians who backed him at the gig. One of the songs, *Eleanor,* was about his daughter, the other tracks were *Technology 2, and* a cover of the Eddie & The Hot Rods standard *Do Anything You Wanna Do*.

Hush were now firmly established, and gigging extensively locally, including a gig at The Royal public house in Clayton on April 25, 2003. They released their debut fifteen-track CD album *Streets Of Gold* the same year, on their Groovy Entertainments label.

The CD contained the three tracks mentioned

above, as well as three covers - American band REM's *The One I Love*, Australian's Crowded House's *Fall At Your Feet* and The Jam's *In The Crowd*, amongst original titles.

Promoting the CD, the band did a home town gig at the Snooty Fox on Friday, December 12, 2003.

BLACK HORSE FAIRY

In 2009, after a change in the line-up, the band released the ten-track CD album *Lost Soul*, again on their own label. All the songs on the CD were written by Don or co-written with the guitarist Paul Green.

Both albums were recorded at Beaumont Studios in Huddersfield and produced by Steve Whitfield.

Drummer Pete Kaberry went on to join the five-piece band Black Horse Fairy in 2011. The line-up initially included former Shakes frontman Ashley Cartwright on guitar.

They put out the thirteen-track CD album *Dark Stars*, which was recorded at Jam On Top Studios in Keighley in 2014. The band went under aliases on the release: Fanny Ferris (Yvonne Gillson) on vocals, Franklin Gothic (Jeff Rowland) on guitar, Archie Blackwell (Cartwright) on rhythm guitar, the Earl of Doncaster (Graham Lloyd) on bass and Count Kundalini (Pete Kaberry) on drums.

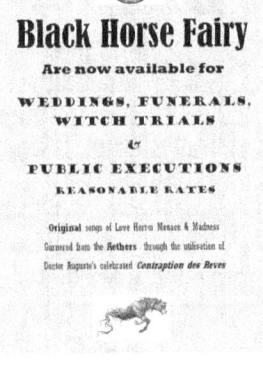

Black Horse Fairy continued for a while as a four-piece after

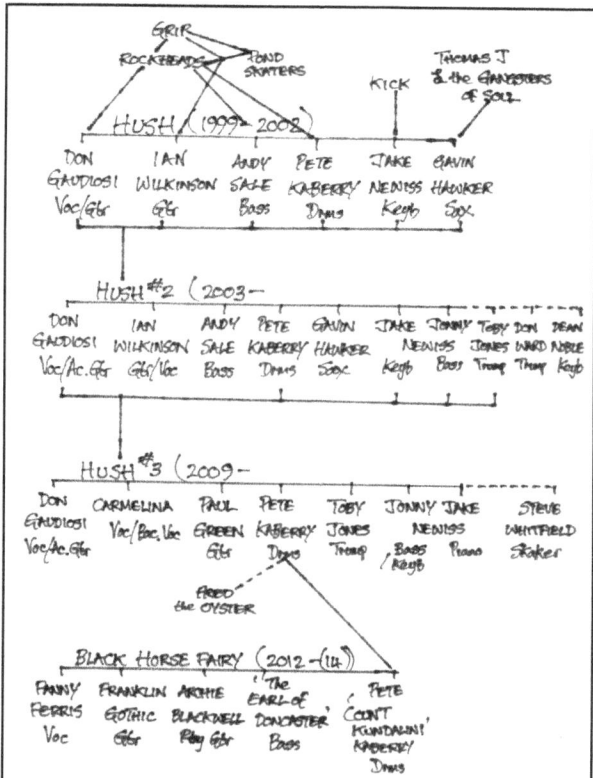

the death of Ashley Cartwright in 2016.

In 2021, the duo of Yvonne and Graham celebrated their tenth anniversary with the release of a new album called *Entanglement*.

CHAPTER 3: BRADFORD FOLK 1999-2009

Folk music was originally the oral tradition of the people, songs of the everyday life of the rural peasantry and industrial working class. Usually in the form of ballads or 'broadsides' that represented the collective 'folk' memory, printed on cheap paper and sold by vendors for a ha'penny to 1d a sheet.

These were hawked around London and new urban populations in the fast-growing industrial areas of the country from the late 1790s to the 1890s. Ballads, in some sense, were the best popular illustration of the times, often rude and expressive of the political struggles of the day, their absence would have made the UK's social history incomplete.

Two latter-day examples are reproduced below, first *The Ballad Of Enterprise Low Moor, Bradford* by Benny Howell.

The Ballad Of Enterprise Low Moor, Bradford

*A simple enough address,
Nothing apparently to impress,
Yet I'll leave you to decide,
It is an address, that is known,
Not just nationally, but its fame,
Was and could be still, renowned,
Absolutely, world-wide.
It identifies an industrial site,
Surrounded by a ten foot high wall of stone,
Like an island on its own,
Set in the middle of Low Moor,
It commenced its commercial duty,
in the 18th Century, inherited from a former chapter of monks,
Not just for the natural unspoilt beauty,
but to employ the residents of Low Moor,
Its people attracted from the mines and woollen mills,
To use their natural skill to manufacture iron from the natural ore.
So successful were they, that it is true to state, that the business went from good to great,
And happy to relate, it is true to say that its reputation, soon began to soar,
Best Yorkshire iron, was soon the toast of Low Moor.
Few only were the households that did not provide a worker for this firm,
now known locally Quite simply as the Forge!
It seemed like no time at all that for extra Workers they now called, as a result of The extra labour recruited it increased in size,
The works now ever extended was supplementing to manufacture,
Engineering machines and yes, even the materials of war.
Inside those stone surrounding walls was no retreat of sanctity
But a beehive of activity as the flow of their lathes,
And machine drills, plus products needed for Bradford's Woollen Mills.*

The second example of a latter-day ballad, *It's A Mean Old Scene* written by Peter Coe during the 1984-85 miner's strike. His inspiration for the title was the old 1970s graffiti on All Saint's Road in Great Horton.

It's a Mean Old Scene

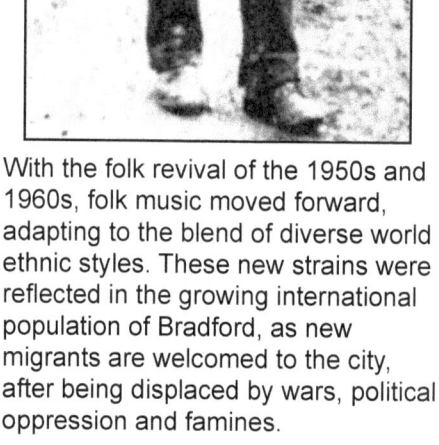

Monday morning, stand in line; four million forms for you to sign.
You're unemployed, so take your time. It's a mean old scene.
Land of hope and tarnished glory, my old man once voted Tory,
But now he tells a different story. It's a mean old scene.
'It's a mean old scene' was written on the wall;
'It's a mean old scene', don't you hear me when I call?
It's a mean old scene.

Plaster's cracking on my ceiling, windows leak and paper's peeling;
Rent arrears, but I'm appealing. It's a mean old scene.
And the landlord's knocking at my door; lost my job, can't pay no more,
And now I'm one of the idle poor. It's a mean old scene.

Oh relatives 'phone, no use lying; husband's left and the kids are crying,
Solicitors write but you keep replying. It's a mean old scene.
And I've taught kids from Pakistan, Bangladesh and Vietnam,
For strangers in a foreign land. It's a mean old scene.

Oh unemployment cures inflation; fanatics breed assassination;
Indifference leading to starvation. It's a mean old scene.
It's the same in many a northern town, mills and shipyards run aground;
We built them up, you knock them down. It's a mean old scene.

Now a mining man is worth his hire but the National Coal Board still conspire.
Come on, MacGregor, and light my fire. It's a mean old scene.
Civil servant's indignation, leaking secret information;
Got six months from a grateful nation. It's a mean old scene.

With the folk revival of the 1950s and 1960s, folk music moved forward, adapting to the blend of diverse world ethnic styles. These new strains were reflected in the growing international population of Bradford, as new migrants are welcomed to the city, after being displaced by wars, political oppression and famines.

Firstly, this chapter must revisit the local folk scenes covered in the previous two volumes, to update and produce information on artists either omitted or mentioned in those books.

FOLK RARITIES

JANET JONES

Keighley folk singer Janet Jones' two 1974 LPs on the Welsh-based Folk Heritage label, Sing To Me Lady and Janet Jones, are both now highly collectable. The

twelve tracks on her second LP are mostly covers of well-known traditional tunes, plus some hits singles from that time. Janet's fragile and dreamy voice is mingled with her acoustic guitar and is backed by two additional guitarists and a keyboard player.

She was often portrayed as Yorkshire's answer to Mary Hopkins, but that's where the similarity ends, as Janet's songs talk of pollution and other social issues.

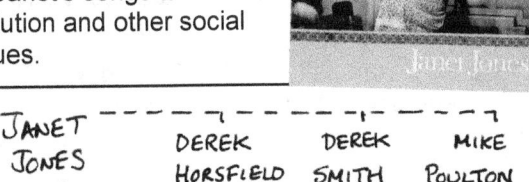

"Although mainly considered as a solo artist, she is also a member of the 8 strong Yorkshire Folk Company, supreme winners of the 1972 Dales Folk Festival at Gargrave. The company, who use many unusual traditional instruments, include Penda's Way from Leeds, New Heritage and Bernard Fawcett. They have a varied repertoire and use an amusing 'jig doll' in some of their songs. The doll's arms and legs jerk to the music and it's a traditional form of street entertainment." (7)

Recently, both of Janet's albums have been re-released on Big Pink Music, a company based in South Korea.

JANET JONES			
74	Midas MR 005	SING TO ME LADY (LP) 200
74	Midas MFHR 059	JANET JONES (LP, released on Folk Heritage label) 200

THE JOVIAL CREW

Formed in 1966, The Jovial Crew were a very popular Keighley folk group who played widely on the north of England folk circuit during the late 1960s and early 1970s. They were often joined on stage by guests like fellow Keighley artist Janet Jones as well as Rosie Hardman, Brian Lazonby, Christine Fairbairn and Derek & Dorothy Elliot, amongst many others, in sing-songs to finish the evening's entertainment.

Their only LP, the self-titled *The Jovial Crew*, was released in 1971. It was recorded by Folk Heritage Recordings at Cheadle Hulme, Cheshire and the one hundred copies pressed soon sold out.

The group also appeared on the 1973 *Folk Heritage* compilation LP on Windmill Records, with the track *Johnny Lad* which was engineered and produced by Alan Green of Folk Heritage Recordings at

| 73 | Windmill WMD | FOLK HERITAGE .... 30 |

the Mid-Wales Sound Studios. The other artists appearing on this now very collectable LP were; Folkways, Combine Harvester, Blue Water Folk, Horden Raikes, Folkal Point, The Yardarm, Parke, Gallery, Paul & Glen, Mike Raven & Joan Mills and The Blue Horizon.

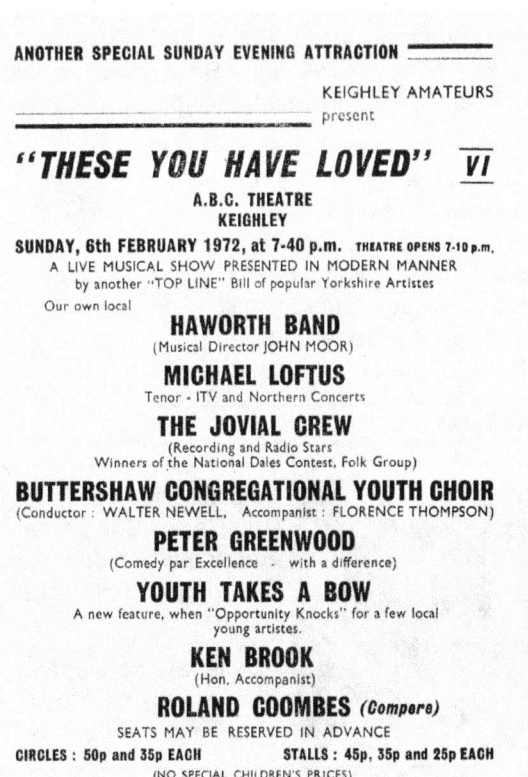

Since the publication of *Bradford's Noise Of The Valleys Volumes One & Two* records by other local folk acts have also risen dramatically in price in the *Record Collector Rare Record Guide*.

```
JAN DUKES DE GREY
70  Decca Nova (S)DN 8      SORCERERS (LP) .................................................. 250
71  Transatlantic TRA 234   MICE AND RATS IN THE LOFT (LP, gatefold sleeve) ........ 250
```

These include both albums by Jan Dukes de Grey; *Sorcerers* and *Mice And Rats In The Loft*, the Moonkyte album *Count Me Out*, and the 1975 single, *Hourglass / War Orphan*, by Moonchild which was

```
MOONKYTE
71  Mother SMOT 1   COUNT ME OUT (LP, with insert, cover has a die-cut spire) ........ 400
```

released on the local Look Records label based in Golcar, Huddersfield.

LOOK RECORDS

Look Records was among only a few independent record labels in West Yorkshire in the mid-1970s. It was started by brothers Dave and Bob Whitely and Stephen Goddard at their studio, September Sounds.

Early releases on the label were mainly local Kirklees area brass bands and choirs, like the two LPs they put out in November 1979; *Marching With Hepworth,* by The Hepworth Band, and *The Village Of Song,* by The Bolstertone Choir.

Look Records also released records by a few local Bradford artists, like the previously mentioned Moonchild single, the now highly collectable 1976 LP *Death Letter* by folk/blues guitarist Roger Sutcliffe (LKLP6038) and folk artists The

```
MOONCHILD
75  Look LKSP 5010   Hourglass/War Orphan (Brother Of The Day) .................. 20
```

Yorkshire Miracle 7" single *The Camra Song /The Redeemin' Grace* in 1977, featuring local Shelf lad Tim Moon.

The label also dipped its toe in the new local punk/new wave scene

```
SUTCLIFFE, ROGER
Death Letter ............................ Look LKLP6038RS ........... 1976  £30
```

by releasing the debut single by The Negatives, *Stakeout / Love Is Not Real* (LKSP 6478), and the EP single *Mr. Somebody* by Skipton band Muggins Blight, both in 1979.

Two more sought-after LPs were released on Look Records; Welfare State's *Songs* (LKLP6347) in 1978, and The Elements 1981 album *Elementary* (LKLP6649). Keighley band The Elements later morphed into goth legends Skeletal Family after a change of singer.

BARBARA YOUNG

In 1981, Barbara Young, the first wife of Cleckheaton-based folk artist Kevin Young, released her thirteen-track solo LP, *No Game At All*, on their own Corridor Records label. The LP was recorded at Bingley's JSG Studios and also featured her husband on backing vocals and guitar.

THE QUARE FELLAS

Formed in Dublin in 1963, originally as the ballad group The Jolly Tinkers, before renaming themselves after the Brendan Behan play, *The Quare Fellas*.

In 1965 they were settled in Halifax and were playing regularly at The Princess Ballroom dance hall in the town, with six dates there between March and July.

The group recorded two LPs on CBS Records, *At Home* (1969) and *A Fond Tale* (1970), before splitting up.

Sean McGuinness went on to become a founder member of the world-famous Dublin City Ramblers, considered Ireland's best ballad and folk group.

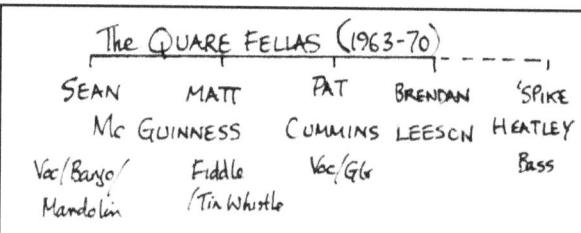

Courtesy of the Telegraph & Argus, April 27, 1968.

There is no need to call for quiet at this club... there is always rapt attention. The mood was caught in these pictures by DEREK CHAPMAN as the audience listens to David A. Farrar (far left) and (right) Patricia Anne Bastow and James J. Dibb.

Singing the songs of the centuries

Like the cottagers of old they gather to sing and to hear the songs of the people... but they gather not in a cottage beside a peat fire, but in the top room of a pub in the heart of 20th century Bradford. "They" are the members of Bradford Folk Club and JOHN HEWITT talked with them of the music that fascinates...

The pint glasses of bitter stood untouched; the murmur of conversation died, leaving the room unnaturally quiet.

Unaccompanied, amateur folk singer Richard Stephenson stood on the edge of the miniature stage, eyes closed, his head thrown back, his foot tapping, swaying a little ... a stance adopted by the old cottagers who sang songs to the family gatherings round the peat fire.

The tune was as slow and measured as an English plough-horse — a monotonous half-chant, dreamy and mysterious. The words, an Easter song which has survived five centuries:

"Go down, go down into yonder town,
And sit in the gallerie
And there you will see sweet Jesus Christ
Nailed to a tall oak tree."

It is an odd sensation, hearing a fragment of everyday musical history brought back to life in the top room of Bradford's Commercial Hotel in James Street.

Twenty years ago it would only have interested erudite collectors; now it is one of the bright coins in the varied currency of what is known as Folk.

Members of the Bradford Folk Club, which meets every Sunday evening at the Commercial, take their folk songs seriously. The big boom in the folk idiom five years ago brought clubs springing up like fresh corn.

But now the Bradford Folk Club is sternly traditional and looks on commercialism with disdain. "Bob Dylan was a genuine folk artist," one enthusiast told me "but the fame and money spoilt him."

In Bradford it all started with skiffle. The Topic Club was formed, and you could hardly get through doors for washboards and tea-chests. But as skiffle died, folk took over and stayed, surviving the pressures of the pop charts.

Tastes at the Topic, which is still going strong, grew too popular for the more traditional fans who broke away to hold separate sessions.

As numbers dwindled they moved into the smaller room at the Commercial (capacity is 47) and the Bradford Folk Club was born.

The Easter Sunday audience sat quietly sipping their drinks. As the evening wore on and stools became scarce one or two squatted on the floor. Most were under 20, all were intent.

"Several of our regulars have gone off camping or hiking. Usually we get a capacity audience," said secretary 22-year-old Miss Lesley Naylor. "We could do with a bigger room now. The trouble is they are pulling down the old pubs and building new ones without small rooms like this.

"You need a full room to create the right atmosphere. Atmosphere is very important. What I like about this folk club is that is so friendly. If you know a song you can just get up and sing — nobody is offended if you are out of tune. If you can't sing you can just sit and join in the choruses."

Overshadowed by Leeds—perhaps the major folk centre in the north — the Bradford club cannot afford big name personalities. They rely on their own members and local amateurs who do the rounds, singing at clubs in neighbouring towns.

One of these is Irish Jim, a smooth, charming 26-year-old Irishman living in Bradford. He roundly abuses his audiences especially when they are half-hearted about the choruses and then passionately sings a handful of Irish rebel songs:

"When first I came to London in the year of '39
The city looked so pretty and the girls were so divine
Till the polis got suspicious and they soon gave me the knock,
I was charged with being the owner of an old alarm clock."

"The point is," explained Jim, "the clock was full of gelignite."

"I am a rebel myself," he added, "but not the grenade-throwing type; rather a John Osborne rebel." His real name is James Anthony Anthony Hayden ("The Bishop made a mistake at my confirmation") and he was born in County West Meath, Eire.

"I learnt rebel songs at school. My uncle had a ceilidh band and played on Radio Eireann and my father played the accordion and tin whistle all over Ireland. But I just sing.

"I left home at 17 and came over to England. I was brought up to believe the English were a bunch of cretins but I found they were just people like ourselves. But I am all for a bit of animosity. It adds spice to life.

"I don't usually sing for Irish audiences. They stamp and tend to be very hysterical. I once sang at Leeds to the Irish Clan Nu Eireann. They wouldn't let me sit down for three-quarters of an hour.

"I don't come to the Bradford club every Sunday. I sing when I feel like it. That's the only way to sing folk songs I don't like the audiences at Leeds. They go to folk clubs because they think it is the thing to do."

Fingering the lapel of his expensive lounge suit, complete with immaculate laundered shirt and smart tie, he added, "People expect folk singers to wear scruffy sweaters and jeans, so I come in this suit. It annoys some people."

The time came for Paul Tattersall to play. Known to everyone as "Dad," he lives at Five Lane Ends and has been interested in folk music for over 20 years.

President of the club, he inaugurated Friday evening sessions for beginners. When sufficient singers fail to turn up "Dad" can be relied upon to take up his guitar and fill the evening.

"I sing blues mostly, perhaps because I identify with the underprivileged people who composed them:

"When you are on your feet again everyone wants to be your long-lost friend;
It's mighty strange without any doubt, Lord
Nobody knows you when you are down and out."

"I first became interested in folk music through studying English history," he said. "People talk about folk music being commercial, but it has always been commercial. They used to make up songs for the broadsheets which were sold in the streets."

Fifteen years ago he tried his hand at collecting folk songs. Equipped with a 20lbs mains taperecorder, he tramped the Dales from Grassing to Hawes.

"I found one old man at Starbotton who had the most fantastic guitar I have ever seen. It was ancient and covered in mother-of-pearl. He taught me an Elizabethan dance and I have spent about ten years trying to play it like he did.

"There must be folk songs in Bradford still to be collected before they are forgotten. Some years ago the Halifax museums published a booklet giving hundreds of local folk songs about the Napoleonic Wars—the boys who left their girl-friends, those who were pressed into service—but their mistake was they didn't put the music with them.

"It's a pity really that Bradford didn't have the same foresight. But there must be industrial folk songs which have never been set down. I only wish I had time to search for them."

STEVE TILSTON

Singer-songwriter Steve Tilston was born in Liverpool and then reared in Leicestershire. He worked as a graphic designer before taking up music in 1971. He recorded his debut album *An Acoustic Confusion* while living in Bristol. His second album, *Collection*, came out on the Transatlantic label in 1972 and was produced by Shel Talmy. The track *Falling* was released a a single from the album.

By the late 1980s, Steve and his family had relocated to Yorkshire and settled in Oakworth, Keighley. He was soon playing regularly at the town's Bacca Pipes Folk Club and the Topic Folk Club in Bradford.

Between 1989-2012, Steve played the Topic at least ten times. He frequently performed with Keighley singer Maggie Boyle (of Gracenotes) and they appeared at the Topic twice as a duo, in 1989 and 1990. They recorded two albums together, 1992's *Of Moor And Mesa* and *All Under The Sun* in 1996.

Steve released around twenty solo albums and set up his Run River label in 1987. He worked with John Renbourn's Ship Of Fools band on their only album in 1988. He had formed his own Hubris Records in 1995 and by 2003 had moved into a 'melodic jazz' style with the album *Such & Such* which featured saxophonist Andy Sheppard. Over the years, many of Steve's songs have been recorded by a range of folk artists, such as Delores Keane, Peter Bellamy, Bob Fox and Fairport Convention.

His daughter Martha, based in London, is a folk artist in her own right, while his son Joe Tilston, based in Keighley, is a member of the town's ska-punk band Random Hand.

STEVE TILSTON			
71	Village Thing VTS 5	AN ACOUSTIC CONFUSION (LP)	35
72	Transatlantic TRA 252	COLLECTION (LP, textured gatefold sleeve)	18
77	Cornucopia CR 1	SONGS FROM THE DRESS REHEARSAL (LP, with Rupert Hine/John Renbourn)	25
83	TM PROP 4	IN FOR A PENNY IN FOR A POUND (LP, with Peter Bardens)	15

THE YORKSHIRE MIRACLE

The Yorkshire Miracle band, fronted by Shelf lad Tim Moon, released the 7" single *The CAMRA Song / Redeeming Grace* on the Goldcar label Look Records in 1977, recorded at Filibuster Studios in Brighouse. The A-side, an ode to the *Campaign For Real Ale (CAMRA)*, was a singalong for the CAMRA coach trips.

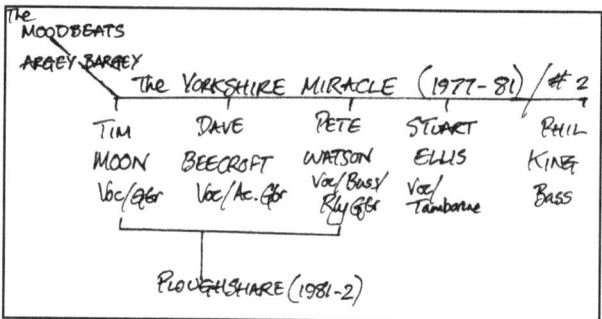

ARRIN

This progressive folk-rock trio formed while they were students in Bradford. In 1988, they self-released a debut cassette album, *Spirit Of Arrin*, recorded at Flexible Response Studios. In June 1989, they played two Bradford gigs; the Fox & Pheasant and the Merry Mason.

By the time of their next release, Arrin were a duo of Andrea and Richard, now married and living in Mayenne, France. Their eleven-track CD *Reel Or False* included the tracks *Spirit Of Arrin* and *Lie Detector Blues*. They also released a four-song CD EP, *4 Titres Demo*, and, in 2007, the album *Frith*.

A further album, *When You Think You're A Pig*, followed in 2011.

CHAPTER 3: BRADFORD FOLK   1999 - 2009

GARY BOYLE

In 1990, Gary Boyle's Crosstown Traffic were playing imaginative interpretations of classic Jimi Hendrix numbers. Gary had been a friend and gigging partner of Hendrix in the late 1960s.

Gary Boyle was born in Bihar, India and moved with his family to England when he was eight in 1949. By his late teens, he was playing small clubs, and working with artists like Millie Small and in Dusty Springfield's band The Echoes before becoming a member of Brian Auger & The Trinity.

In 1969, after attending Leeds College Of Music, he briefly joined Dorris Henderson's folk rock band Eclection. In the early 1970s, he was an in-demand session musician with the likes of Keith Tippett, Mike Gibbs, Mike Westbrook and Stomu Yamashta.

In 1973, he formed the influential jazz fusion group Isotope, with whom he made three albums, *Isotope, Illusion* and *Deep End* which came out in 1976. When they disbanded he pursued a solo career, releasing *The Dancer* album in 1978.

LEEDS TRADES CLUB
21 SAVILE MOUNT·LS7
HENDRIX meets JAZZ with GARY BOYLE'S CROSSTOWN TRAFFIC
FRI 16th NOV · £3.50

By the late 1980s, Gary was settled in the Skipton area and had formed Crosstown Traffic.

In 2006, he joined Keighley singer and flautist Maggie Boyle (no relation) in the trio Sketch, who released a CD the following year.

JON HARVISON

Jon Harvison is based in Seeton, Keighley. He became a solo folk singer-songwriter in the mid-1980s after the demise of the jazz-rock band Montage. Jon had been writing his own compositions since 1975 while at Bingley College.

He soon built a reputation as an accomplished performer and was complimented as *"one of the country's most powerful artists with his dynamic voice which contrasts nicely with his neat guitar work."* (2)

Jon was a regular on the local and national folk circuit playing at the Topic, Bacca Pipes and Skipton folk clubs. He set up his own Drive-On Record label and released at least five CDs, *Still Water, Alibi Of Innocence, Knight's Gambit, High Diving* and 1995's *Lonely As The Moon* - a thirteen-track album recorded at the Old Bridge Studio in Ilkley.

Jon continues to perform and play his music as well as being a local guitar tutor.

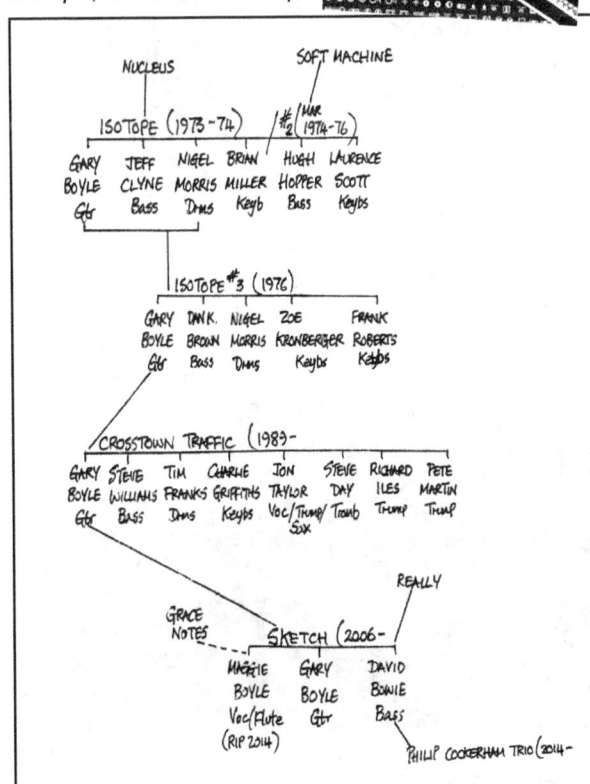

FIONA-KATE ROBERTS

Since 1995, this multi-talented Oxenhope harpist has performed with many people like folk artists Maggie Boyle & Steve Tilston, Loobie, Alchemy and the Irish bands Wild Geese, Clannad and The Chieftains.

In 1999, Fiona-Kate and her 13-year-old daughter Phillipa, who'd taught herself to play the harp, played a concert at East Riddlesden Hall on Bank Holiday Monday, May 3.

Fiona-Kate played a rare triple harp, which was specially made for her. It was an instrument traditionally popular in Wales but was originally designed in Italy in the 16th century.

"It's incredibly difficult to play," said Fiona-Kate, *"It's got three sets of strings. The two outer ones are like the white notes on a piano and the inner set are like the black ones."* (3)

She has over thirty harps, each with its own name and a hand-painted design. She makes her harps from birch plywood. Her first harp was made from recycled materials, including a stairwell tread, and was named 'Angal' by her children.

On August 21, 2009, Fiona-Kate played a special concert at the Victoria Hotel in Keighley, as part of the *Red & White Roses Tour* for visiting Austrian musicians touring the North. Local folk singer Liz Narey accompanied her as did Freespirit who hailed from Vienna and played 'folk & roll' with bouzouki, mandolin and guitars.

Since then, she has jammed informally with rock giants Led Zeppelin and Gun'n'Roses, with Zeppelin guitarist Jimmy Page inviting her to play at a wedding and U2's Bono has sat at her feet listening to her play.

LATE 1970s – 1998 GIGS AT THE TOPIC FOLK CLUB

While based at The Star pub on Westgate, The Topic played host to most of the local artists like

the aforementioned Fiona-Kate Roberts, Roy Bailey, Steve Tilston, Scarlet Heights, Roger Sutcliffe, Jon Harvison, Stuart Crampton, Ian Smith, Liz Jenkinson & Jon Carey, Los Zimmos, Bev Sanders, Gracenotes, Peter Norman & Norrie Spence, The Hall Brothers and Bingley's Liz Narey.

On December 8, 1987, New Model Army's singer Justin Sullivan played a rare gig as 'Slade The Leveller' supported by poet Joolz (pictured right) and Rev Hammer.

The Topic at this period also hosted some of the cream of British folk artists including: Martin Carthy, June Tabor, Martin Simpson, Bob Pegg, Vin Garbutt, Hamish Imlach, The Watersons, Nic Jones, Gary & Vera Aspey, Geoff Higginbottom, Leon Rosselson, John Kirkpatrick, Mike Chapman, Dave Burland, Isaac Guillory, Tony Capstick, Harvey Andrews, Wizz Jones, Dave Swarbrick & Simon Nicol, Magna Carta, The Spinners, Steve Phillips,

Peter Bellamy, Cyril Tawney, Rab Noakes, Andy Irvine, The Oyster Band, Ewan MacColl & Peggy Seeger, Dick Gaughan (pictured), Alan Hull, Clive Gregson & Christine Collister, Keith Christmas, Jake Thackray, Rory McLeod, Janet Russell, and Kathryn Tickell to name just a few.

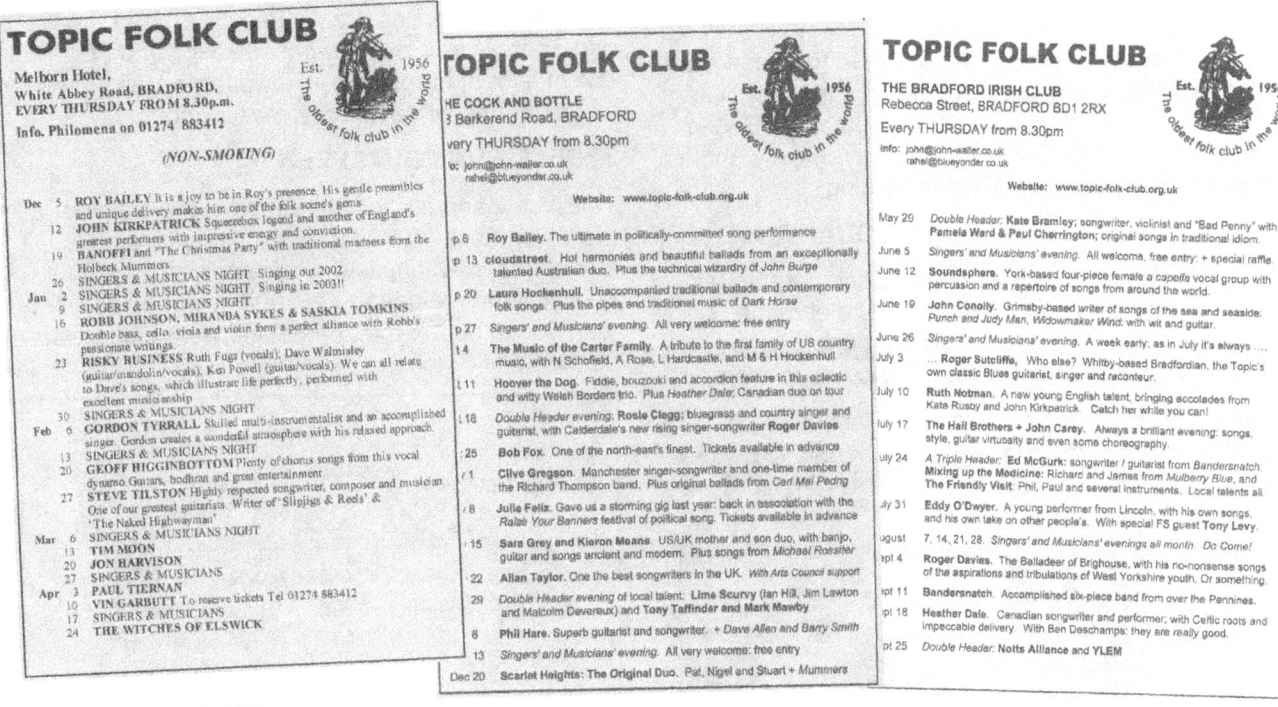

TOPIC FOLK CLUB

Established in 1956 and named after the Topic record label, the Topic Folk Club is the longest-surviving weekly-run folk club.

It has survived and adapted to the changing shifts in styles in the thirteen venues (listed below) it has made its home in during its over sixty-year existence.

The club continues to present artists from the locality, the UK and the rest of the world at the weekly Thursday night events. During the period 1999-2009, it was based at The Melborn pub on White Abbey Road (1994-2005) and then The Cock & Bottle (2006-2008).

From 2008 to December 2013 the Topic Folk Club was based at The Irish Club (formerly John Dillon Club) on Rebecca Street, off Westgate. It then moved to Glyde House on Little Horton Lane in 2014 where it remained until 2023.

In 2024, the Topic moved to Shipley, first at The Groove Pad, then to Hullabalou.

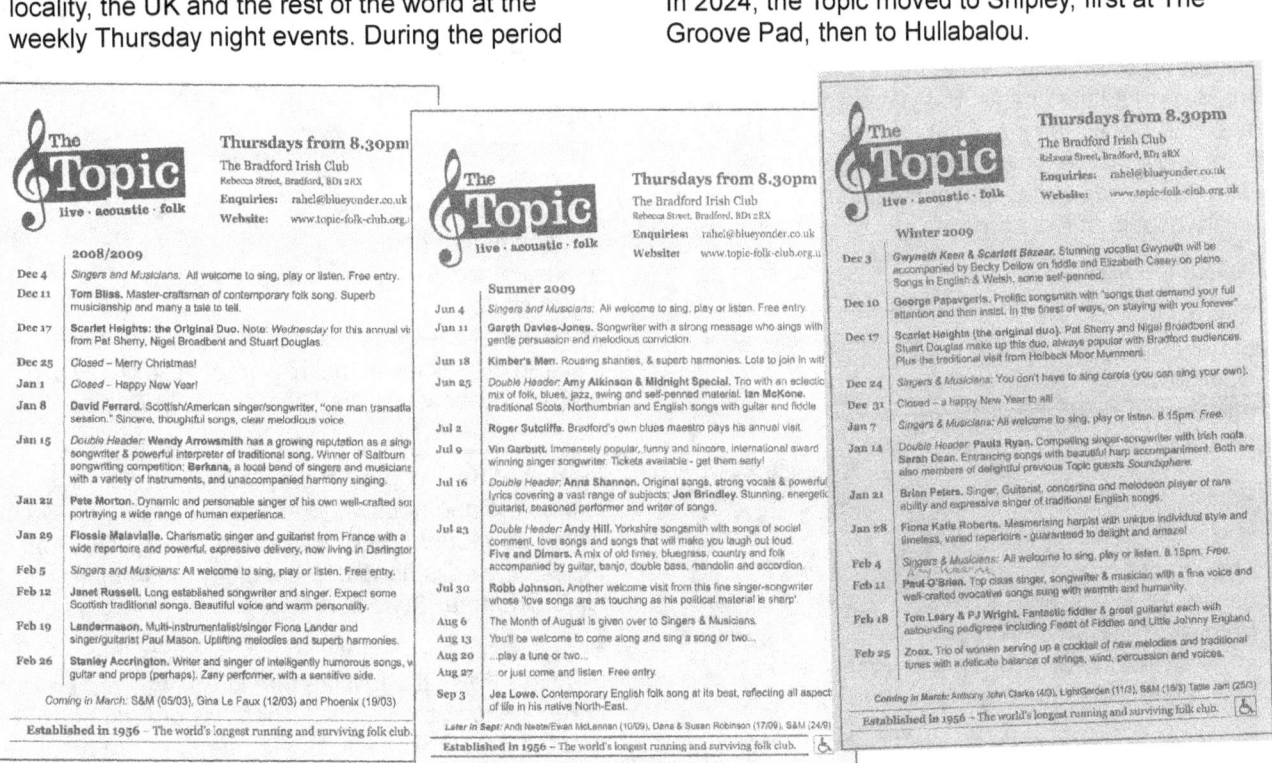

1999- 2009

At the start of this period, the Bradford folk scene was as healthy and vibrant as it had ever been. Old local folk stalwarts like Scarlet Heights, Wild Geese and Roger Sutcliffe were still playing regularly and a new breed of local talent was emerging.

GAEL FORCE AT CENTENARY SQUARE

On Saturday, February 20, 1999, Centenary Square saw the start of the first month-long celebration of Irish culture, with music and dance performed by members of the Bradford Irish Music Association.

It marked 150 years since the Irish famine of the 1840s, which brought a wave of Irish immigrants to the city.

Local MP Marsha Singh was a major influence on getting the celebrations off the ground, asking Bradford Council why there were no celebrations to mark St Patrick's Day (March 17) despite the Irish being one of the largest minority ethnic groups in the city. He said, *"We had ignored St Patrick's Day and the Irish community ...it's a multi-cultural society and everyone's festivals should be celebrated."* (4)

The Bradford Irish community can trace at least 60,000 Bradfordians back to Ireland and the majority of settlers came 150 years ago during and after the Great Famine. Over the years the Irish kept a low profile, being absorbed into the area with thousands of descendants taking their place in every aspect of Bradford life.

HONEYHOLE

This duo of Anna Daiches and Becky Garnet formed in August 1997. Their name comes from a street in Todmorden where they met when Anna was doing a solo gig organised by Becky.

They released the eight-track CD album *Tasty* on their own Trash Cat label, based in Shipley.

The duo's influences are diverse, from Janis Joplin and Sheryl Crow to blues-based songs and the use of a lot of harmonica. They adapted their set to whatever and whoever they are playing for.

ZYDECO FUNK BUTCHERS

This local band formed in 1999 from the ashes of the Cajun Aces (1993-99) and included Malcolm Manning of *Mannings Musicals* shop on Westgate on violin and melodeon. By 2001, they had dropped the Zydeco part of their name and were going out as the Funk Butchers.

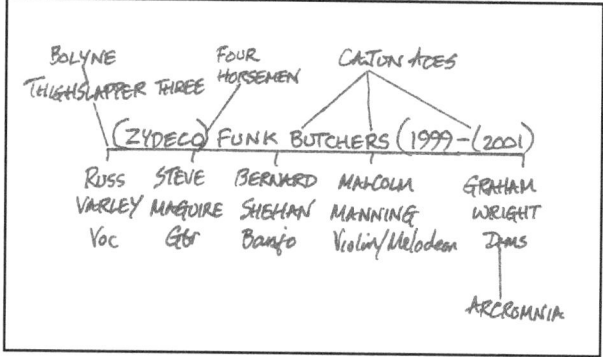

FOWK TALES

In November 1999, folk duo Dave Webster and Julie Partis (nee Dunbar) compiled thirteen songs celebrating the city through its people which they called *Bradford Fowk*. Six centuries of Bradford history proved the inspiration for a unique collection of folk songs that paint a musical picture of the city and its colourful characters. Many of the songs were inspired by articles in the *Telegraph & Argus (T&A)* and its predecessor, the *Bradford Daily Telegraph*.

"We spent a long time at Bradford Central Library looking at back copies of the T&A. It was the interesting and unusual stories that caught our eye, which we thought could make into songs," said Mr. Webster, who is head of technology at Bradford Girls Grammar School. (5)

Songs about the First World War soldiers 'the Bradford Pals', the mill fire that killed two firemen in 1889, the love story ballad *The Lass of Eldwick Hall* and the Bradford character Ivegate Kate are among the collection.

CHAPTER 3: BRADFORD FOLK 1999 - 2009

Dave and Julie have been performing together since 1972 and were part of the folk trio **Bracken** with Graham Ford.

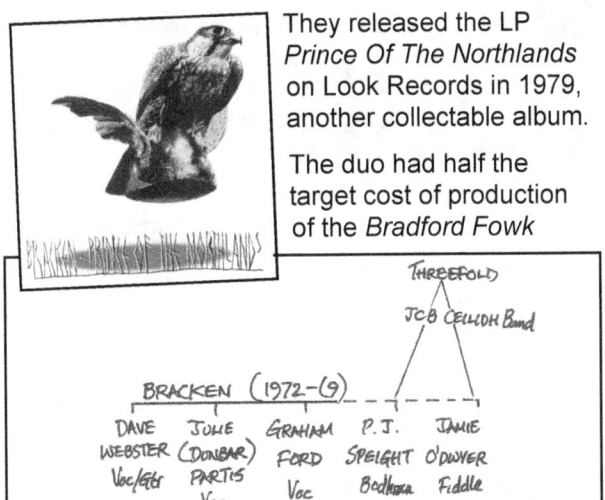

They released the LP *Prince Of The Northlands* on Look Records in 1979, another collectable album.

The duo had half the target cost of production of the *Bradford Fowk* CD sponsored by the Bradford & Bingley Building Society. Monies raised were donated to the *Imperial Cancer Research Fund*.

HALEY SISTERS

The Haley sisters, Jo-anne and Becky, were from the village of Harden, near Bingley, and first appeared in 1989 playing original Americana and country folk as The Applejack Trio with Kevin Raymond. From 1990, the pair played all over the UK as a duo before becoming a trio with the addition of Brian Smith in 1993. In 1996, after gigs in Ireland and Europe, they were voted the *Best UK Group* at the *Great British Country Music Awards*.

In 1997, they released the album *Angels Break Free* on the Peterborough Comet Records label.

The eleven-track CD was recorded and engineered by Mick Noonan, former bassist of local rock band Tuxedo, at his Potz'n'Pans studio off Manchester Road. Among the musicians helping the sisters on the album were Bradford lad Brendan Croker, guesting on vocals on the track Lovin' All Night, and the Pudsey country-rock guitarist Stu Page.

Their second album, *To Be With You Tonight*, came out in 2004, followed by the subsequent albums *No Boundaries*, *Vicissitude*, *When I Reach The Place I'm Going*, *Sweetest Gift* (a compilation) and *Always By My Side*.

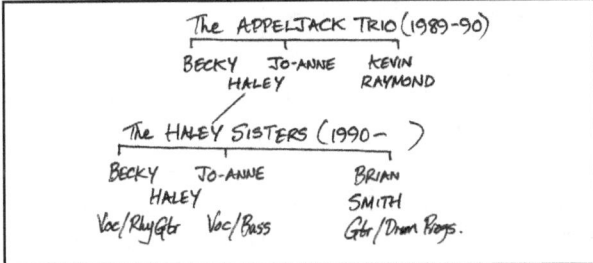

RDB (RHYTHM DHOL BASS)

Formed in 1997, Bradford's own RDB were a bhangra/hip-hop/Bollywood group made up of three Sikh brothers; Manjeet, Surjeet and Kuldeep. They began singing at their local gurdwara (temple), assisting their father who played the harmonium and tabla in front of the local Sikh community.

This experience helped the brothers to blend Western genres with the traditional Punjabi beats and vocals, producing a passionate mix of technology and experimentation.

They soon gained a worldwide reputation with a roadshow that played festivals, weddings, birthdays and special events and included a stunning visual light show. Their first CD album, *Sounds Of The*

North, came out in 2002 on the Leeds-based Untouchables Records. This was followed the next year with their second CD, *Unstoppable,* and then the album *Three* in 2005, all on the same label. Many of the group's songs were written by the brother's father, Harjog Singh.

In 2003, they won the *Best Club DJ Bhangra* at the *UK Asian Music Awards*. Over the years, the lads have worked on many Indian film soundtracks, such as *Singh Is Kinng* (2008), *DeDana Dan* (2009), and *Bullet Raja* (2013). They have collaborated musically with artists like Snoop Dogg, T-Pain, Indy Sagu and Gubi Shandu as well as influencing artists like Jay-Z and Britany Spears.

In 2007, a fourth album, *Vaisakhi-The Birth Of Khalsa*, was released on their own Three label.

Sadly, after being diagnosed with a brain tumor, Kuldeep died in May 2012. Shortly after his brother Manjeet announced that he was pursuing a solo career, leaving Surjeet to carry on the legacy of RDB. He now leads a team of singers, performers and composers.

JASON McNIFF

Shipley lad Jason McNiff is a modern singer/songwriter in the folk mould, with a skilful fingerpicking guitar style. He came to prominence after moving down to London, and was '...first observed co-hosting The Easycome Club in Peckham with Andy Hang Dog, and had a ragamuffin demeamour.' (6)

In 2000, he released his debut CD album, *Off The Rails*, on London's Snowstorm Records. The label's tagline was

'*semi-acoustic for the people*'. Jason was accompanied on the album by Andy Hang Dog on guitar, accordion and backing vocals, Geoff Spence on drums and Simon Stewart on violin.

More albums followed on the Snowstorm label, *Nobody's*

Son (2003), *Another Man*, and the 2008 album *In My Time*.

In 2011, he released the album *April Cruel* on the Fledg'ling label, recorded at Bark Studios. It included *Students Of Love*, a song about a failed marriage set in Northcliffe Woods, near Shipley.

In 2015, Jason released his sixth album, *God Knows Why We Dream*, as Jason McNiff & The Lone Malones on the Tombola label. A three-star review of this album appeared in *Mojo* magazine #256

(March 2015) where reviewer Andy Fyfe noted '*...he makes no bones about his love of Bob Dylan*' and labelled Jason the Yorkshire Bob Dylan.

The album *Joy And Independence* (2018) on At The Helm Records was followed in 2021 by *Dust & Yesterday* on the Tombola label.

On July 9, 2022, Jason played a hometown gig at The Heritage Venue at Black Dyke Mills in Queensbury.

KEITH CHRISTMAS AT THE TOPIC

On April 27, 2000, 1970s singer/songwriter Keith Christmas appeared at the Topic Folk Club at the Melborn. Keith had first recorded his debut LP, *Stimulus*, on RCA Victor in 1969, followed by the album *Fable Of The Wings* (1970) on B&C Records.

His highly acclaimed next album *Pigmy* (1971), also on B&C Records, brought him support slots on tours with King Crimson and Ten Years After. He changed labels to Manticore for his next two albums, *Brighter Day* (1974) and *Stories From The Human Zoo* (1976), Keith continued to release sporadic albums in the 1990s and up until 2019.

TIM MOON

In early September 2000, local folk artist Tim Moon released the new CD album *Anger & Kisses* on Inner Motion. Tim played over fifty instruments, including his mobile phone, on the album's twenty-two tracks.

Two tracks from the album were later recorded by other folk artists. His song about the late folk singer Peter Bellamy, *Black Concertina*, was recorded by *Mercury Music Award* winner Norma Waterson. The other track, *Breathless* (a virtual anthem at the Bacca Pipes Folk Club in Keighley), was used by guitarist Lee Collinson as the title track on his latest album.

Tim also contributed the track *Swift As The Wind* to the 1999 Compilation CD *Winged We Were: A Tribute to The Incredible String Band* which had a limited run of only 546 copies.

PERFORMANCE EXPRESS

On Monday, October 9, 2000, a music and drama group called Performance Express At The Crazy Horse Saloon released a CD single *Mental Health Day / Wings Of A Dream* as a soundtrack to that year's *World Mental Health Day*. The single had already gained international recognition, with mental health organisations in Australia requesting permission to use it there.

In December, the local band Wild Geese held an Irish party at the Melborn, on White Abbey Road.

KEIGHLEY FOLK SCENE

Many local and visiting folk artists/groups were still performing at the Bacca Pipes folk club, in the centre of Keighley.

KITCHEN SONGS

Maggie Boyle, singer and accomplished flute and bodhran player with the acapella group Grace Notes, started her kitchen songs project, tag-lined,

'music from the hearth and the heart'. She visited singer-songwriters and interviewed them in their kitchens up and down the country.

Sadly, Maggie passed away in 2014.

FAY HIELD

This local Keighley lass was a traditional folk singer. Her first recorded output was on the 1999 privately pressed CD *The Haworth Set* by BACCApella – a group of singers from the Bacca Pipes Folk Club singing sixteen Christmas carols. She appeared with the three members of Grace Notes (Maggie, Lynda, and Helen) as well as

contributors Mollie Binns, Jenny Scott, Carolyn Gill, Anne McGarth, Jim Ellison, Sian & John Pedrick, Joel Griffiths, Mal Jardine, Jim Lawton, Alan Rose, David Williams, Mike Hockenhull and Tim Moon.

She formed The Witches of Elswick with her student friend Bryony Griffith from Huddersfield and Becky Stockwell. They released two albums, *Out Of Bed* (2003) on Fellside and *Hell's Belles* (2005) on Selwyn Music.

Fay's debut solo album *Looking Glass* came out on the Topic label in 2010 and was mainly traditional songs and ballads. Her fifth album *Wrackline*, also on Topic, was released in 2020.

Her partner Jon Boden, from Chicago, USA, was formerly with the group Bellowhead.

Besides her folk career, Fay was a Senior Lecturer in Ethnomusicology at the University of Sheffield.

EDDIE LAWLER

In 2001, Saltaire-based folk artist Eddie Lawler, made a musical appeal for Bradford Beck to be cleaned and restored to its former glory as part of Bradford's *Capital Of Culture* bid. The beck had run under the city since Victorian times when it was diverted below ground.

Eddie, a part-time lecturer, wrote the ditty *Bradford Beck* which includes the lyrics: *'I'm culverted and tunnelled out of sight and out of mind and when I briefly re-emerge I'm verged with warning signs.... I'm real West Yorkshire water and I ought to be clean, be a pleasure and be seen.'*

In 2015, Eddie released a twelve-track CD album called *Bradford Canal... and Other Tales* which was recorded at the Dove Sound Studios, Bradford. The opening track was entitled *The Ballad Of Little Beck*.

KARL DALLAS

London-born Karl Dallas was a folk singer (performing as Fred Dallas 1959-60), a music

journalist in the 1970s for *Melody Maker* and a writer, who came and settled in Bradford in 1989.

In 1955, he wrote the song *The Family Of Man*, which was recorded by The Spinners in 1964.

As Fred Dallas with Betty Dallas in 1959, he had three tracks; *Strontium 90, Doomsday Blues* and *Hey Little Man* on the Topic Records compilation *Songs Against The Bomb*, which also had tracks by Ewan McColl & Peggy Seeger, Ramblin' Jack Elliot and Leon Rosselson.

In 1960, Fred and Betty contributed two tracks; *The Conscript's Farewell* and *The Smithfield Market Fire*, to the 10" HMV compilation LP *Rocket Along*, which included tracks by Shirley Collins, Cyril Tawney and Jimmy MacGregor.

In 1963, Karl published the magazine *Folk Music* which carried wide-ranging and informative articles. He later published a magazine called *Folk News*.

In the 1970s he wrote two books; *Singers Of An Empty Day* (1971), and *The Cruel Wars* (1972). In 1975 he helped to compile the boxed four LP set of folk and folk/rock music *Electric Muse* on Island / Transatlantic Records with Robin Denselow, David Laing and Robert Shelton.

In March 2002, Karl held an exhibition at the Priestley Centre called *The Shapes Of Sounds* - a range of Karl's black and white photographs of 1960-1970s musicians he'd worked with and befriended, including close friend Frank Zappa. These atmospheric photos were combined with excerpts from taped interviews.

In 2003, during the build-up to the Iraq war, Karl joined other peace activists on a double-decker bus as human shields.

In 2007, Karl was discussed in an online debate on *Living Tradition*'s letters page under the title *Where Have All The Folk Songs Gone?* The debate juxtaposed the origins of the folk tradition with the *'...ascendancy of the 'anything goes', non-policy club not only affected the performance of traditional song but led to a situation where it was, and is, possible to spend an evening at a folk club without hearing a folk song. The traditional repertoire: ballads, sea songs, canisters, bawdry songs of working-class life and love, were replaced by Victorian tear-jerkers, music hall ditties, pop songs of the past and those dreary all-round-the-year carols.'* Also, *'the term 'finger-in-the-ear' became one of abuse, even though cupping the hand over the ear in order to stay in tune without the guidance*

CHAPTER 3: BRADFORD FOLK 1999 - 2009

of an instrument, is an age-old device used by singers from Bucharest to Belfast and can be found in woodcut illustrations of street ballad-sellers throughout the ages.' (7)

Sadly, Karl passed away at the age of 85 in June 2016.

ROY BAILEY

Folk troubadour Roy Bailey was a regular at the Topic Folk Club, including gigs on December 5, 2002, and September 2006.

He was a former resident of Bradford during the late 1960s and early 1970s when he lived in Shipley with his wife Valerie and daughter Katherine. He taught sociology at Bradford University.

Roy and his wife Val released the album of children's songs called *Oats & Beans & Kangaroos* on the Fontana label in 1968, accompanied by Leon Rosselson on guitar, banjo and accordion.

His debut solo album came out in 1971 on the Trailer label, set up by producer Bill Leader in 1969.

Over the years, he released around twenty-six albums and was on the Fuse label from 1975. He released three further albums with Leon Rosselson; *That's Not The Way It's Got To Be* (1975), *Love, Loneliness & Laundry* (1976), and *If I Knew Who the Enemy Was* (1979).

Roy also released the album *Writing On The Wall* with the late Labour MP Tony Benn in 2004.

Roy was a committed socialist and was a patron of the Sheffield-based organisation *Raise Your Banners*, which organised the November 2009 weekend at Bradford's Kala Sangram Centre. Roy was joined on stage performing *Turning Silence Into Song* by Leon Rosselson, Martin Carthy, Frankie Armstrong, Janet Russell and Sandra Kerr. He passed away in November 2018.

CHUMBA FOLK

In 2002, Armley-based anarcho-band Chumbawamba released their eleventh album *Readymades*, recorded at their studio in The Mill, on Thornton Road, Bradford. The thirteen-track album, released on their own Mutt Records, had two Bradford-related numbers: *One Way Or The Other* is a song about the 1930s unemployed workers who ran a club on Quebec Street, off Thornton Road, and *Song For Len Shackleton*

Bradford-born footballer **Len Shackleton** joined Bradford Park Avenue at seventeen, before moving to Newcastle United in 1946 for £13,000. He scored six goals on his debut, in a 13-0 victory over Newport County at St. James Park. Len was a highly skilled inside forward, nicknamed the Crown Prince of English football. Although he was a talented footballer, Len only won five England caps, between 1945-54, as his on-field antics didn't impress the selectors.

After joining Sunderland for £20,000 in 1948, he played the rest of his career at Roker Park, scoring 98 goals in 320 games for the Wearsiders. An ankle injury ended his career in 1957. Len passed away at the age of 78, in November 2000.

Chumbawamba's *Readymades* album mixed their pop-dance sound with a folk sample on every track, using a multitude of artists including Dick Gaughan, Kate Rusby, Coope Boyes & Simpson and the late Lal Waterson.

In 2003, Chumba's guitarist Boff Whalley's book *footnote* was published by the Hebden Bridge Pomona Press. The book was a trawl through

his life from being brought up in Burnley, Lancashire, to the forming of Chumbawamba, moving to Armley, Leeds, squatting, anarchism/activism, EMI and nearly having a No 1 single with *Tubthumping*.

The same year, the band re-released their 1988, 10" folk-based acappella mini-album, *English Rebel Songs 1381-1914,* on CD. The new release added the extra track *Coal Not Dole* to the twelve-song album, updating the title to *English Rebel Songs 1381-1984*.

A trimmed-down acoustic line-up of Boff, Lou Watts, Jude Abbot and Neil Ferguson toured the UK and Europe throughout 2005-06. Their twenty-one date 2006 UK tour took them to Leeds City Varieties on Sunday, February 5, where they unveiled their latest album *A Singsong And A Scrap* on the No Masters label.

'The new acoustic album is a collection of songs, pure and simple. Songs with a radical voice, songs with the signature four-part harmonies and the catchy choruses, but songs nevertheless.'

In 2007, the full eight-piece band played Glastonbury Festival.

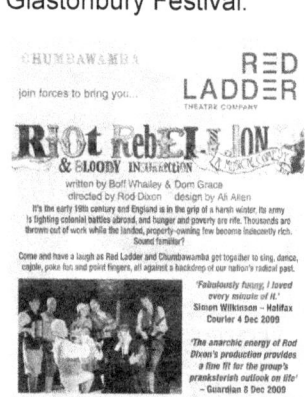

Their next album *The Boy Bands Have Won*, came out in 2008. The twenty-five acoustic folk-style tracks featured appearances from The Oysterband, Barry Coope and Roy Bailey.

In late 2009, the band toured northern England with the self-penned pantomime, a comedy musical entitled *Riot, Rebellion & Bloody Insurrection* with the Yorkshire-based Red Ladder Theatre Co.

THE HALL BROTHERS

Bradford brothers Duncan and Nick Hall had been performing together since around 1991. Their first releases were the two CDs; *Time And Tragedy* and *Dark Waters*. Both appeared on the Confidential Records label, based in Snaith, East Yorkshire, in 2003.

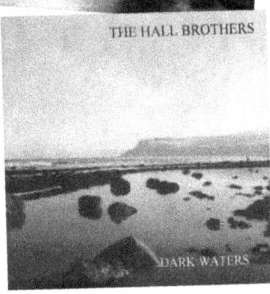

In 2004, their thirteen-track album *Songs From The Shore* was released on Tumulus Records. It was recorded at Host Studios in Chapletown, Leeds and engineered and produced by Andy Bell of Spike Productions. Six of the tracks were self-penned compositions, alongside *House Carpenter* - a traditional song dating from at least 1685 which had been covered by Bob Dylan and inspired the brothers' version. That same year, Nick released his solo CD *The Golden Time* on Confidential.

In 2006, to commemorate the 90th anniversary of the Battle Of The Somme in July 1916, they released a CD single called *The Bradford Pals*. The single featured children from Holybrook Primary School.

The Hall Brothers, with violinist John Carey, played The Topic Folk Club on July 17, 2008, and again on November 14, 2014.

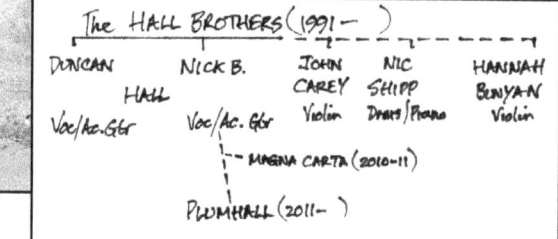

In 2011, Nick joined up with Michelle Plum, a singer who appeared on some Chumbawamba albums, to form Plumhall. Their debut single, *Learning How To Talk*, was written by the Chumba's Boff Whalley.

A four-track CD, *Live At The Courthouse*, recorded on Saturday, December 17, 2011, appeared in 2012. Their debut album, *Thundercloud*, was released in 2014, followed by *The Ghost Of Noise* in 2020.

The Hall Brothers still perform together and played a home town gig at the heritage venue in Black Dyke Mills on Saturday, October 1, 2022.

SHAUN T HUNTER

Cleckheaton lad Shaun T Hunter had been around as a singer-songwriter since 1990.

His debut release was the CD *For Adults And Brave Children* on Luu-it Recordings in 2003, recorded at Carl Stipetic's In-A-City Studios in Manningham. Carl performed keyboards, guitar, bass, and drums on all of the fifteen tracks on the album.

Shaun was honoured at the first Independent Leeds Music Awards and released two CDs in 2007, *The Great Departure* and *Flying Not Falling*.

Around 2017, Shaun evolved into his alter-ego, the nu-vaudevillian folk-opera character

The Captain Of The Lost Waves. That year he released the first of three CDs under the title *Hidden Gems*.

Hidden Gems Chapter 1 was recorded at Factory Street Studios in Dudley Hill, Bradford, and released on the Brigand Broadcasting Company label.

In 2018 he released a vinyl compilation LP called *Synthesis*. The album featured tracks from *Hidden Gems Chapter 1* and the follow-up, *Hidden Gems Chapter 2 - Circus Of Morality* which was released on CD the following year. *Chapter 2* featured Carl Stipetic on bass and keyboards amongst a host of guest musicians and was recorded at Trapdoor Studios, Bradford. *Hidden Gems Chapter 3 - Mysterium Tremendum* followed in 2022.

The artwork on all three *Hidden Gems* CDs was done by Damian Clark, who also played synthesiser on some tracks.

WILFUL MISSING

This five-piece folk-rock band formed in Bradford in 2003. They contributed the track *Ghosts* to the *Mono* magazine's compilation CD in 2006.

Their debut CD was the five-track mini album *Vast Atlantic* on Sheffield-based label Voodoo Toodler in 2009. Another EP, *Loose Ends*, followed the next year.

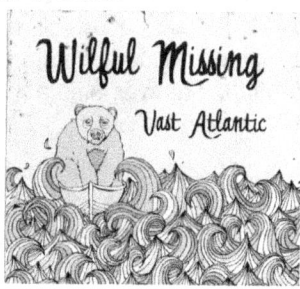

Their eleven-track debut album *Molehills Out Of Mountains* came out in December 2011. It was released as a limited edition vinyl LP on Little Attic Records. It was also released as a promo CD with alternative cover artwork.

Wilful Missing were championed by BBC Radio 2 and 6 Music DJs Steve Lamacq and Tom Robinson and performed several live sessions for BBC Radio Leeds. In 2011, four of their songs were featured on the BBC television series *Waterloo Road*.

Their next two albums were *Scarborough Fair* (2013) and *Unsinkable Sailor* (2016).

As a solo musician, he released the CD *Boxed*, recorded at Huddersfield's Beaumont Street Studios, in 1995. This was followed by *The Furrowed Field*, a CD collaboration with Keighley-based female group Grace Notes, Steve Tilston, and The Wilson Family, on the Norwich-based DJC label, released in 2000.

Two further CDs came out on his own Demon Barbers Sound label, *Under The Influence* (2009) and *The Old Songs* (2011), both with Mike Wilson of The Wilson Family.

The Demon Barbers' debut album, *Uncut*, came out on CD in 2002, and their second CD album, *Waxed*, in 2005.

The next year, they were on the bill at The Levellers' annual *Beautiful Days* festival in Exeter, Devon.

Their CD EP *+24db* appeared in 2008.

In 2009, they won the *Best Live Act* at that year's BBC Radio 2 Folk Awards. In 2010, the group released another CD album, *The Adventures Of Captain Ward*. After a tour in China in 2013 they put out another album, *Disco At The Tavern*, in 2015.

By 2022, Damien was the only original member.

THE DEMON BARBERS

On Sunday, December 7, 2003, The Demon Barbers played their regular once-a-month, live rehearsal at Bradford's Love Apple cafe/bar. This Huddersfield-based folk-rock group was led by Keighley resident Damien Barber and Bryony Griffith, who was also a member of Witches Of Elswick.

Damien was brought up in Norfolk, and from an early age was steeped in the English folk tradition. He took the bold decision to become a professional folk musician at the end of the 1980s.

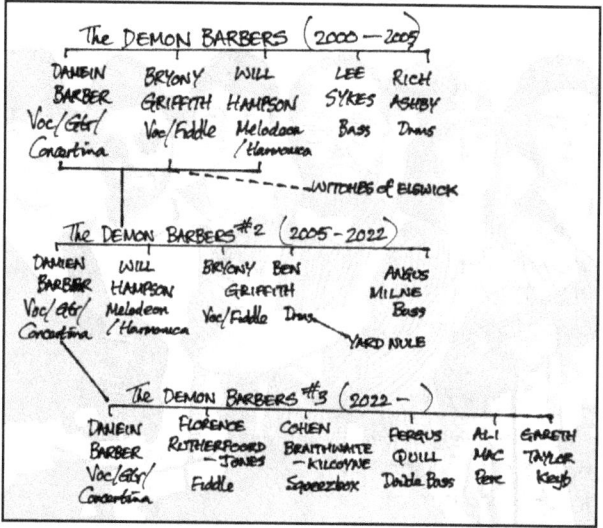

CHAPTER 3: BRADFORD FOLK 1999 - 2009

NIGEL GARRY (BROADBENT)

Former Scarlet Heights bassist Nigel Broadbent worked solo as Nigel Garry from around 2004.

He worked the clubs and pubs with classic pop songs of the 1950s onwards, mixed with comic and Irish songs. He had spent two years playing to holidaymakers in the hotels and bars on the east coast of the Spanish island of Majorca.

Nigel played a gig at John Pennington's Octagon Club in Sandbeds, Keighley on Sunday, January 18, 2015. In 2022, he appeared on 'the floor spot' at the Topic Folk Club's latest venue the Groove Pad in Shipley.

THE MELBORN

The Melborn Hotel, just off White Abbey Road, hosted the Topic Folk Club on Thursday nights for eleven years (1994-2005). The venue also held regular gig nights on Friday and Saturday, as well as Sunday open-mic sessions. Monday nights hosted landlord Eamon's informal acoustic sessions and there was a jazz night on Wednesdays.

Other venues that put on Acoustic or Folk nights in the local area, were Bacca Pipes Folk Club in Keighley, Bradford's MacRory's Bar and The Grove Inn in Leeds.

The much missed Melborn and (below) a jam session at MacRory's Bar. (Picture: Richard Ingham)

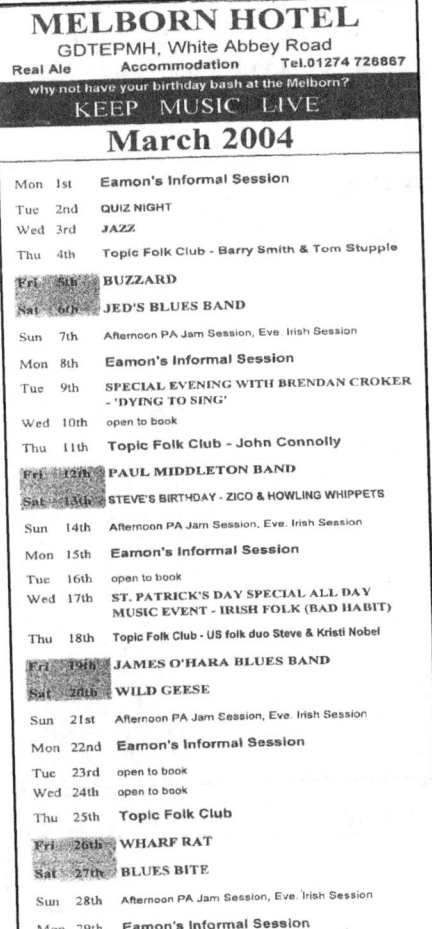

FOLK AT THE 1 IN 12 CLUB

Over the years The 1 In 12 Club had been primarily known as a venue that promoted punk and indie-rock bands, though many folk artists played during this period.

On Thursday, June 10, 1999, Swedish folk-punksters, The Tequila Girls returned for a second gig at the Club, supported by local band The Next World.

On March 4, 2001, Norwegian band The Greenland Whalefishers played, supported by The Blue Arsed Flies. The Greenland Whalefishers were from Bergen and had formed in 1994, playing in a folk-punk style in the Celtic tradition. The band released their debut album *The Mainstreet Sword* in 1996. They returned for a second gig at the Club on Friday, June 25, 2004.

Singer/Songwriter Robb Johnson, regarded as one of the UK's finest political folksters, returned to the Club, having played in the 1990s and had appeared on *A Nightmare On Albion Street: Worst Of The 1 In 12 Club Volume 11* in 1992.

In 2001, he was supported by local folkie Tim Moon. He played again on Wednesday, October 22, 2003, on the same bill as Tim Moon, Wilful Missing, and The Bookworms. On this occasion, Robb appeared as a part of a trio with Miranda Sykes (double bass/cello) and Saskia Tomkins (viola/violin). Robb returned for a further gig on Thursday, May 29, 2008.

In 2002, Zimbabwean thirteen-piece band Hohodza played, drawing heavily on their traditional Zimbabwean musical roots and culture. Formed in 1992, they were led by Portia P Gwanzara and were largely self-taught, using traditional instruments like the mbira and marimba. They had recently relocated to the UK.

On Friday, November 7, 2003, veteran agitprop folkie Leon Rosselson graced the Club's stage, supported by Tim Moon.

On Thursday, February 12, 2004, the 1 In 12 hosted a gig by Canadian Geoff Berner & Friends. Geoff was from Vancouver and had previously fronted the Canadian punk band Terror Of Tiny Town.

His debut EP *Light Enough To Travel* was released in 2000 on the Sudden Death Record label.

On Thursday, June 3, 2004, American David Rovics headlined, supported by ranter Attila The Stockbroker and a band called The Drunken Maidens. Attila would return to the Club on Friday, November 24, 2006, with support from Baba Luck and local artist Captain Hotknives.

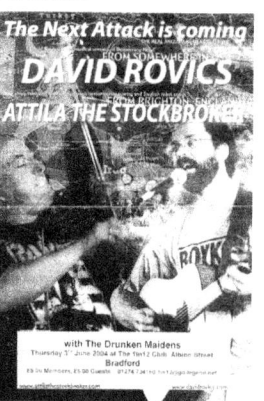

Australian folk singer Penelope Swales played on Friday, July 16, 2004, as part of the promotion for her latest CD *Monkey Comfort* on Black Market Records. Penelope was from Melbourne but was now based in Victoria and was also a legal aid lawyer and activist.

UNFINISHED DRAWINGS

This alt-folk trio hailed from the Crosshills/Skipton area and graced the Club's stage on Saturday, December 10, 2005. In 2006, they released their debut CD album, *Audio Project*, which included a cover version of Scottish band Biffy Clyro's song *Justboy*. The trio released another ten-track CD, *If You Can't Do It For Yourself, Do It For Me,* in 2007.

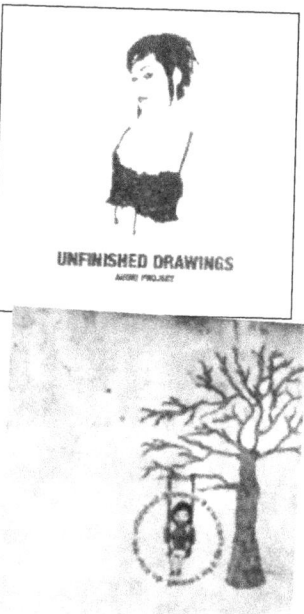

On Sunday, November 16, 2008, the trio returned to The 1 In 12 Club, supported by young Bingley alt-rock band The Marmozets.

CHAPTER 3: BRADFORD FOLK 1999 - 2009

On Saturday, March 18, 2006, Manchester lad Bernard Kelly played. He was a friend of Graham Fellows, whose alter ego *Jilted John* had reached the number 4 spot in 1978 with the self-titled song. Bernard had been the inspiration for Jilted John's nemesis Gordon, who is mentioned in the lyric, *'Gordon is a moron'*. Besides singing his own compositions, Bernard was also a painter and illustrator of some renown.

On Monday, May 8, 2006, French avant-progressive folk-funk duo Vialka, played, supported by local musician Rob Holden, guitarist in local rock outfit Threads. Vialka were formed in 2002 by Eric Boros (guitar/vocals) and Marylise Frechville (drums/vocals) and they came from *'the deepest regions of France'*.

A young local singer/songwriter named **Abi Lovelle** played at the 1 In 12 on Friday, May 12, 2006.

Over the next few years, Abi was a regular on the local circuit, playing often at the Love Apple.

CAPTAIN HOTKNIVES

Chris Smith, aka Captain Hotknives, had previously been a bassist in a few bands, most notably Chest (1991-96). After their demise, he joined Union Wireless, then Urban Originals (1998-2000), before going solo around 2005.

Chris' keenly observed, irreverent humour won him many fans and instantly popularity on the local scene. He was a regular face at The 1 In 12 Club, playing over seven times during 2006-9. He was on the bill for an Anti-Fascist benefit on Saturday, December 16, 2007, with Danbert Nobacon (from the Chumbas), Bookworms, Action Directe, and local bands Monty Casino, The Fineline and Aspirin. He has continued to play and host events at the 1 In 12 over the years.

On August 5 & 6, 2006, Captain Hotknives was among the artists who took part in the two-day festival called *Worthstock*, near Cullingworth. Over 300 people attended the festival, watching local bands including Random Hand, Breene, Dusty Not Digital, Susskind, Aspirin, Reeved, and Hoover Dams. Profits from the event went to the local Manorlands Hospice.

He has released at least four CDs on his own Fiver Deal Discs; *The Pigeons Told Me*

To Shoplift, I Hate Babies, Blarney Stoner and *The Squidgy Black Album*.

151

SKETCH

Music
Sketch join in anniversary celebrations

■ Sketch at the 1 in 12 Club

A new trio featuring musicians Maggie Boyle, Gary Boyle and Dave Bowie is playing the 1 in 12 Club as part of its 25th anniversary celebrations.

Described as "an exuberant cocktail of traditional and contemporary folk with a splash of jazz", the trio, called Sketch, features Maggie Boyle on vocals, flute and bodhran, Gary Boyle (no relation) on guitar and Dave Bowie on double bass.

Maggie's catalogue of recordings and live appearances includes work with the Chieftains and she also provided the title-track vocals for Harrison Ford blockbuster Patriot Games.

Gary's career began in the 1960s and his first big gig was with Dusty Springfield. He has also worked with

the likes of Brian Auger and Julie Driscoll, John Etheridge and much-lauded jazz fusion band Isotope.

His six solo albums won him critical acclaim, The Dancer winning the Pop/Jazz Award at the Montreaux Jazz Festival. Gary now teaches at the Liverpool Institute of Performing Arts, set up by Sir Paul McCartney.

Dave is described as "primarily a soul boy, looking for the groove". A 25-year association with sax player Snake Davis and guitarist Mark Creswell established him as probably the UK's only Northern Soul bass player. He has worked with Martha Reeves and Edwin Starr, among a legion of other Motown stars. His early career was managed by Andy Kershaw and included a single with TV presenter Carol Vorderman!

A whimsical career path has included punk/art band The Mekons, the Ukulele Orchestra of Great Britain, tango and Cuban charanga. He plays with symphony orchestras and chamber groups in Leeds and York.

● *Sketch are at the 1 in 12 Club tomorrow. For details ring (01274) 734160.*

A folk-jazz trio, formed in 2006 by Keighley's Maggie Boyle on flute and vocals, guitarist Gary Boyle and David Bowie (not the mega-famous superstar of *The Laughing Gnome* and *Space Oddity* fame, but the former bassist with 1980s Leeds band Really).

They performed at the 1 In 12 as part of the Club's 25th anniversary celebrations on June 4, 2006.

On Sunday, July 2, 2006, the trio played at the Alhambra Studios as part of the city's *Big Summer* festivities with folkies Martin Simpson and Rory McLeod.

Sketch released a CD in 2007, while Gary Boyle returned to play a gig at the 1 In 12 on July 14, 2007, accompanied by Lorraine Cockburn.

SEX PATELS

A group of musicians originally formed to play music for one of Alice Nutter's plays, led by local folky Tim Moon. The group also included Bri Outlaw from local rock act Threads and Chumbawamba's Harry Hamer on percussion.

The loose collection of musicians, using traditional Asian instruments, easternised punk meets bhangra covers of old punk/new wave favourites. A line-up of 25 'Patels' collaborated on their *Never Mind The Bollywood, Here's The Patels* CD. It was recorded at Woodman Studios in Elland, in May 2006, and released on their Aik-Do-Teen-Char Records label.

SEX PATELS

Their other self-released and self-titled fourteen-track CD included a version of Ian Dury & The Blockhead's *Hit Me With Your Rhythm Stick* and the Dead Kennedy's *Holiday In Cambodia*.

The group were championed by BBC Radio 1's Nihal and were regulars on the festival circuit. They often appeared locally between 2006-09. The Sex Patels played at the 1 In 12 on January 27, 2007, with Spanner and Jesus Bruiser, then again on Friday, September 8, 2008, with Lynch Mob, Captain Hotknives and a solo set by Rob Holden, guitarist of Threads.

They also played a Christmas show on Wednesday, December 17, 2008, at the New Roscoe pub in Leeds where they were supported by DJ Jill Gondwanasound.

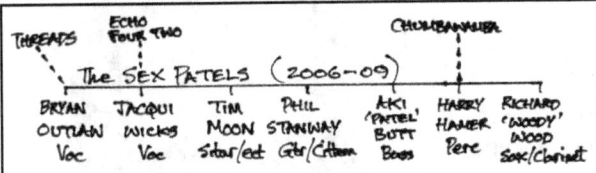

THE FAMILY ELAN

Originally formed as a trio in 2005 by Chris Hladowski, formerly of local bands Mundane and Scatter, by 2007 they had expanded to include Chris' sister Stephanie. As a band they experimented with a psych meets folk/world music vibe, and produced two CDs, *Stare Of Dawn* (2007) on the Chicago label Locust Music, and *Bow Low, Bright Glow* (2010) on Alt. Vinyl.

Their first gig at the 1 In 12 was on September 4, 2009, with Zun Zun Egui. They played at least twice more; on February 25, 2011, with Stig Noise, Viaika, and That Fucking Tank, and on May 26, 2012, with Black Moth and Trio VD.

In 2013, The Family Elan performed in collaboration with some local South Asian musicians at Bradford University's MoBU music programme, and *Threadfest VI* in 2015, both organised by That Fucking Tank's Andy Abbott.

JAMES DEY

James was born in Halifax but was raised in Bradford. His singer/songwriting style was reminiscent of people like Badly Drawn Boy and Damien Rice. In September 2005, a collection of his songs appeared on his debut CD *Landing Lights*. Accompanying him on the album were his brother John, on guitar and trumpet, Andy Sykes on violin and Lisa Mallaghan on backing vocals.

JULIE FELIX

On November 8, 2006, while the Topic Folk Club was based at The Cock & Bootle, British-based American singer/songwriter Julie Felix was the guest artist. Julie was born in 1938, in Santa Barbara, California, and had met Leonard Cohen on the Greek island of Hydra while travelling around Europe in 1962. Julie signed a three-album deal with Decca Records in the UK, in 1964.

She had two top thirty hit singles in 1970, *If I Could (El Condor Pasa)* reached No 19 in April and *Heaven Is Here* reached No 22 in October, both on Rak Records.

Julie passed away in March 2020, aged 81.

TWO MADRE

The lo-fi folk duo of Bill Francis (vocals/guitar) and Ruth Webber (sax, keyboards and vocals) formed in 2006.

They played a gig at the Love Apple on Sunday, January 27, 2007, with Irish act My First Tooth, Leeds' The Rosie Taylor Project and local act Zuzu's Petal.

In 2008, the duo merged with local band The Fineline to form Spodni Pradlo.

LAURA GROVES

Only 18 years old in 2006, Shipley-born Laura Groves grew up in a musical household as both her parents, Eleanor and Dominic, played the saxophone. Laura played her first live gig at the Love Apple on Sunday, June 11, 2006, with Jeremy Warmsley and Napoleon III. Her influences were Joni Mitchell and Regina Spektor. Her vocal style was reminiscent of Kate Bush, Janis Ian, and Martha Wainwright. Alongside playing her own material, Laura was known to cover Bob Dylan and Radiohead songs.

Laura's first limited edition 7" single, *I Am Leaving*, was released in 2007 on Saliva Records, while she was at Sheffield University studying English and music. She played regularly at the Love Apple and Shipley's Boathouse. On Friday, May 25, 2007, she took part in the *BD1 Live* gig at St George's Hall, sharing the stage with Duels, Analog Bombs and Monty Casino.

In 2008, she signed to the XL Recordings label, home of Radiohead and The White Stripes, releasing her debut album under the artist name of Blue Roses. The next year, as Blue Roses, she released a 7" single *Doubtful Comforts* and the 12" EP *Does Anyone Love Me Now?* Two further 12" were recorded for XL Recordings in 2013 and 2015.

By, 2023, having returned to calling herself Laura Groves, her album *Radio Red* was released on the Bella Union label.

Laura Groves
★★★★
Radio Red
BELLA UNION. CD/DL/LP

Yorkshire singer-songwriter finds her own frequency.

On Sky At Night, the starstruck opening track of *Radio Red*, Laura Groves sounds like she's in a self-contained observatory, looking out into the cosmos and trying to pick up the right emotional signals – "getting you on my wavelength," as she sings dreamily. With the touch-sensitive, jazz-edged balladry of I'm Not Crying and Sarah, it doesn't initially seem too hard to tune into where Groves (formerly known as Blue Roses) is transmitting from, but if the buttons marked 'Kate Bush' and 'Joni Mitchell' are worn smooth, *Radio Red* has a free-floating lushness that generates its own little whirl of stardust. There's a touch of *Cupid & Psyche 85* glimmer to Make A Start and Good Intention (featuring Sampha); Any Day Now carries a lot of tension in its keyboards. Expansive, restless, subtly volatile, *Radio Red* is intriguing enough to keep it locked.

Victoria Segal

CHAPTER 3: BRADFORD FOLK — 1999 - 2009

JAZZ & BLUES / WORLD MUSIC

Jazz and blues, as well as any world music styles, are covered in this section as part of the folk traditions from around the globe.

JIMMY CLIFF

Jamaican ska/reggae singer Jimmy Cliff lived in the UK for around fifteen years, mostly in London, but for a short period during the late 1960s, Jimmy lived in Bradford with his brother on St Paul's Road, Manningham. He is perhaps best remembered for his captivating role in the 1972 film *The Harder They Come* and its soundtrack album.

BLUES LEGEND DIES

Legendary American Blues guitarist/singer John Lee Hooker quietly died in his sleep on June 21, 2001, aged 83, within days of his last gig. One of the authentic blues icons, he was born on the Mississippi Delta, and plied his trade in 'jook joints' before settling in Detroit, Michigan, in 1947.

He recorded tracks like *Boogie Chillen'* (1948), *Crawlin' King Snake* (1949) and the million-selling *I'm In The Mood* (1951) for the Modern label. By 1955, he was under exclusive contract to Chicago's Vee Jay Records, and in 1960, he appeared at the Newport Folk Festival.

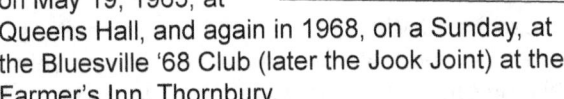

In the early sixties, he recorded *The Folk Lore of John Lee Hooker* and had big hits with *Boom, Boom* (1962) and *Dimples* (1964).

John Lee Hooker played Bradford twice, on May 19, 1965, at Queens Hall, and again in 1968, on a Sunday, at the Bluesville '68 Club (later the Jook Joint) at the Farmer's Inn, Thornbury.

John Lee Hooker and other black American blues artists were a big influence on the British blues-rock scene of the 1960s, influencing the likes of Eric Clapton, Jeff Beck, Jimmy Page and Peter Green.

JOOLS HOLLAND

Former Squeeze pianist Jools Holland appeared at St George's Hall on Saturday, November 20, 1999, with his Big Band. The line-up included guest vocalists Chris Difford (a former bandmate in Squeeze) and Sam Brown, the daughter of rock'n'roll star Joe Brown. Sam had a No 4 hit single with *Stop* in February 1989.

ANNIE WHITEHEAD

As part of the Bradford Festival, the UK's premier female modern jazz trombonist Annie Whitehead played at the Chicago Rock Cafe, on Great Horton Road, on Wednesday, July 4, 2001.

She was promoting her latest CD album, *Naked*, released on the Voiceprint label.

The drummer on the album was Liam Genockey, who had previously been the drummer in the 1970s band Zzebra, a band which also included ex-Love Affair vocalist Gus Yeadon and bassist John McCoy, later of the band Gillan.

AL DIMEOLA

On November 15, 2002, the jazz fusion guitarist, formerly of US band Return To Forever, played a solo set at St George's Hall, Bradford, promoting his album, *Flesh On Flesh*.

PETER GREEN

St George's Hall played host to legendary British blues guitarist Peter Green on February 4, 2003.

He replaced Eric Clapton, in John Mayall's Bluesbreakers in 1967, before leaving with bassist John McVie to form the original Fleetwood Mac (below). The band had hits with *Albatross, Black Magic Woman* and *Oh Well (Parts 1 & 2)*.

The current tour was to promote his new album *Reaching The Cold 100* on Eagle Records.

Unfortunately, Peter could no longer play the solo parts on the old hits, leaving another guitarist from his band, the Peter Green Splinter Group, to play all the solos.

ZOOT MONEY

At Haworth Social Club on Saturday, March 22, 2003, George 'Zoot' Money gave a rare solo performance on the keyboards. He entertained the crowd with a mix of the 1960s R'n'B and soul standards he once played with his 1960s Big Roll Band and his psyche band Dantalian's Chariot.

A farewell gig for pianist Dave Skinner was held at Jazz at the Priestly Centre on Friday, September 3, 2003.

MIDNIGHT TRAIN

Local blues band Midnight Train were still plying their trade in their fourth incarnation as the 21st century dawned.

Originally formed in 1966 by local vocalist/harmonica player Grahame 'Grom' Kelly, they built up a strong following around the northern gig scene, before their demise in 1968.

Grom moved to London to join progressive rock band Junior's Eyes for a few years. He sang lead vocals on their album *Battersea Power Station* (1969) and their singles *Woman Love / White Light Part 2, Circus Days* and *Star Child,* all produced by Tony Visconti.

Junior's Eyes, led by guitarist Mick Wayne but without Grom backed David Bowie on a BBC radio session and members played on early Bowie tracks including *Space Oddity*.

Grom returned north to front a handful of bands between 1970 and 1981.

He reactivated Midnight Train in 1982 with guitarist Steve Isherwood, bassist Brian Duffissey and John White on drums. Later members included John Sheppard (drums), Pete O'Grady (keysboards), Lee Abbott (bass) and Miriam Walton (piano). The band entertained blues enthusiasts all over the country until they hung up their picks in 2007.

CHAPTER 3: BRADFORD FOLK — 1999 - 2009

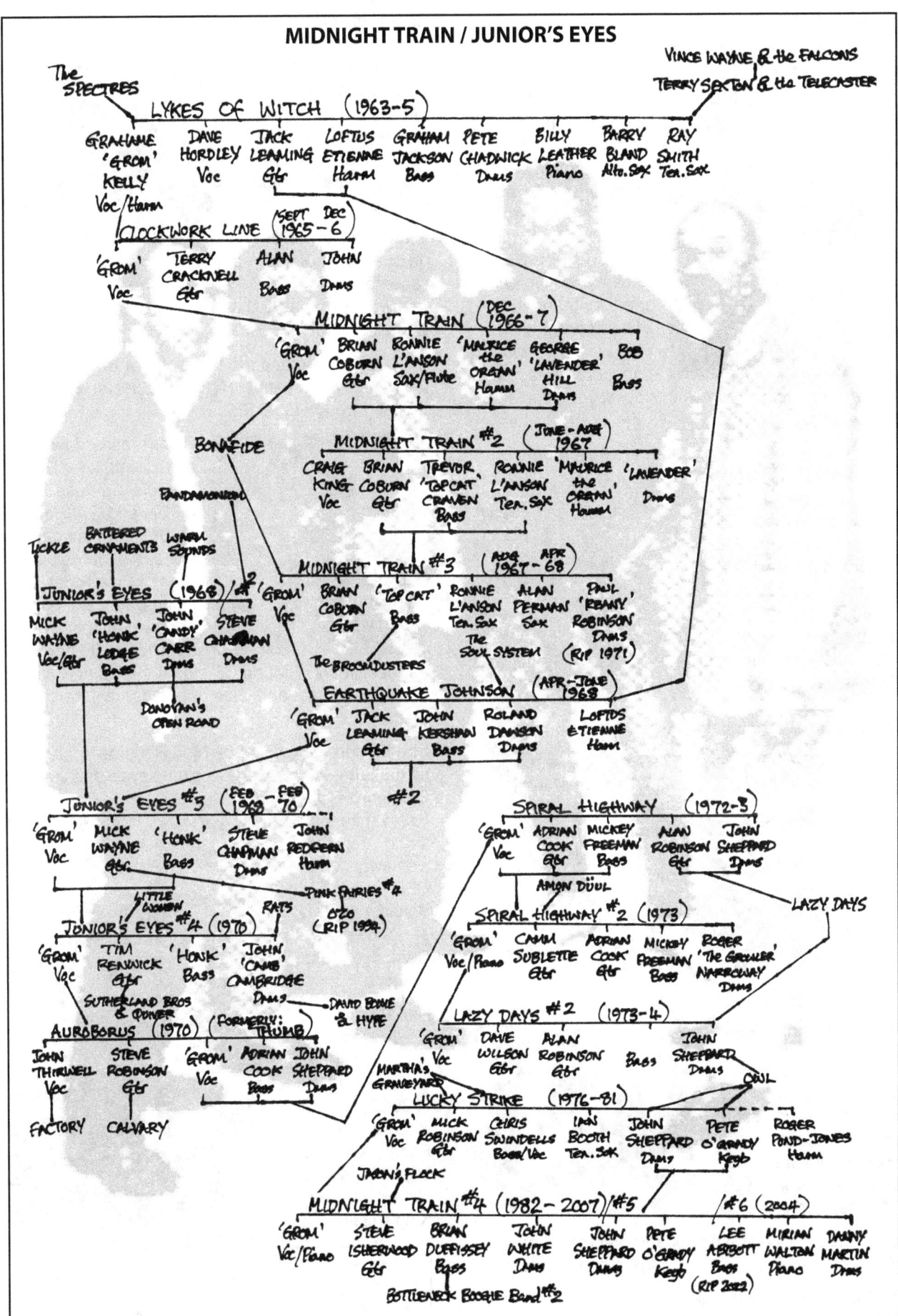

CLARE TEAL

Born in Kildwick, on the outskirts of Keighley in 1973 Clare was out of step with most of her generation, becoming obsessed with jazz music from the 1930s and '40s. *'For years jazz was a private passion, she spent long periods of her teens in the attic practising with a phonograph (record player) and her grandmother's collection of jazz 78 records.'* (8)

After gaining her music degree at Wolverhampton University, Clare worked in a Lanchashire studio, learning about studio technology. She recorded and released her debut album *Nice Work* in 1995 on the Purple Lemon label. Not finding the success she craved, she worked in a variety of jobs before working in the advertising business.

Clare revived her career with the help of Alan Bates who ran the Candid Productions label. He released her next three albums *That's The Way It Is* (2002), *Orsino's Songs* (2002), and *The Road Less Travelled* (2003).

Her cover of The Mamas & The Papas classic *California Dreaming*, which appeared on her *Ornino's Songs* album, was championed by BBC Radio presenter and chat show host Michael Parkinson.

In September 2003, she appeared at that year's Scarborough Jazz Festival, playing on the Friday.

In 2004, Clare signed the biggest recording contract for a British jazz singer when she signed to the Sony Music label. They heavily promoted her *Don't Talk* album which topped the jazz charts and reached the top twenty in the UK album charts.

Clare became British Jazz Vocalist of the Year in 2005, a feat she repeated in 2007, 2015 and 2017. As well as this, she was also the BBC Jazz Vocalist of the Year in 2006.

In 2006 she became the presenter of BBC Radio 2's Monday night show *Big Band Special* which she hosted through to 2013.

Clare recorded two more albums for Sony, *Paradisi Carousel* (2007) and *Get Happy* (2008), both the usual mix of standards by the likes of Cole Porter and Irving Berlin alongside her own compositions, co-written with her partner Amanda 'Muddy' Field. At this point, Clare had lived in Bath and Glastonbury for over ten years.

She formed her own label, Mud Records, for her next album, 2011's *Hey Ho*, and played that year's Cleethorpes Jazz Festival. In the same year, Clare was awarded a *Gold Badge* by the British Academy of Songwriters, Composers and Authors.

Her albums *And So It Goes* and *Jing, Jing-A-Ling* both followed in 2013 on Mud Records. On Friday, November 10, 2017, she played at Ilkley's King's Hall.

158

ALAN WORMALD BAND

Jazz-prog guitarist Alan Wormald, a contemporary of Allan Holdsworth, played in many bands during the late 1960s and early 1970s. His most successful band was First Aid, who released their only album *Nostradamus* on Decca Records in 1977. It is now very collectable.

By 1994, Alan was playing with funk outfit Shakatak live on the road, and appeared on a few of their albums, like *Beautiful Days* in 2005. He also played guitar for singer/impressionist Joe Longthorne. From 2004, he ran his own four-piece jazz fusion combo, which included Mick Wake who'd drummed in local bands since the 1960s. As the Alan Womald Band, they played mainly covers of artists like Steely Dan, Billy Cobham, Stevie Wonder, Robin Ford, Cream, and did a stunning version of Fleetwood Mac's *Oh Well*.

They played locally all over the north, especially in Leeds and Bradford, at venues like Bingley's Brown Cow and regularly at the Black Bull in Clayton. Alan taught guitar to Leeds lad Julian Barratt, who went on to create the cult BBC TV show *The Mighty Boosh* with Noel Fielding.

After their keyboard player Steve 'Stretch' Price left the band, they reverted to a trio. After Mick retired, a young new drummer joined, plus Alan's wife and friend on backing vocals. This line-up continued until the passing of the talented bassist Simon Goulding in 2020. Sadly, Alan also passed away in 2021 after returning home from a tour with Shakatak.

Local Pink Floyd tribute band Off The Wall played a stunning show at Halifax's Piece Hall, on Saturday, August 7, 2006.

Just over a month later, on September 16, 2006, Halifax hosted ex-Soft Machine guitarist John Etheridge at the Square Chapel, supported by Kit Holmes.

John was promoting his latest solo album *I Didn't Know* (2004), on Dyad Records.

HUDDERSFIELD JAZZ

Huddersfield Jazz Society arranged a series of concerts in the cellar bar at the Lawrence Batley Theatre, from September to November 2006. Among those performing were the Tim Kliphuis Quartet, Alison Neale Quartet, Andy Panayi Quartet, and the Peter Churchill Trio with saxophonist Bobby Wellins and Jacqui Dankworth, daughter of Johnny Dankworth and Cleo Laine.

JED'S BLUES BAND / MAUREEN GALVIN

Jed Turner had been in local bands including Isengaard, Electric Bon, Ghandarva and Midas, since 1968.

In 1977, he formed the first incarnation of his long-running Jed's Blues Band. The line-up was fluid, with members coming and going over the years.

On Wednesday, April 4, 2007, Jed agreed to do a benefit gig at the Love Apple for social activist Maureen Galvin who had recently passed away as they were Maureen's favourite group. Funds raised went towards helping Maureen's son, Kieran keep living in the family home. (9)

Jed passed away in 2014.

THREADS ORCHESTRA

A jazz-fusion ensemble formed by a group of Bradford University students who released a six-track CD called *Portrait Of A Nation* in 2008, part funded by Bradford Council.

Threads Orchestra played live at the 2009 Bradford Mela in Peel Park. They released a second CD, *Threads*, in 2011. A further CD, *'Ranch' - Music by Jonathan Brigg* came out in 2012, a collection of compositions written by Bradford-born pianist and composer Jonathan Brigg.

JONATHAN BRIGG

Jonathan Brigg was born in Bradford in 1984. He studied music at the University of Manchester, then at York University where he took his doctorate in composition.

As a pianist and composer, his work defies easy categorisation. He is heavily influenced by jazz, postminimalism and American ultramodernism. He composed extensively for jazz-classical combo Threads Orchestra and performed at the London Jazz Festival with his own group, Stoop Quintet.

As composer in residence at Ely Arts Festival, he regularly wrote for the festival orchestra and performed a solo piano concert of original works. He has worked with numerous composers, including Hugh Harris, lead guitarist in pop-rock band The Kooks.

Jonathan now lives in Stroud, Gloucestershire.

WELCOME HOME SEXY

Welcome Home Sexy promoted a series of jazz gigs at the New Beehive on Westgate.

CHANTEL McGREGOR

Bradford-born blues-rock guitarist Chantel McGregor had been given a guitar and lessons at age seven by her parents. In the family home, she had grown up with a background of rock music, like Led Zeppelin, Black Sabbath and Fleetwood Mac's Rumours, which she loved and later covered songs from the album.

From around the age of twelve, Chantel's parents would accompany her to many local jam sessions held in pubs like the Black Bull in Clayton, the Melborn and MacRory's.

At those events, she would digest the various styles of the local guitarists, which helped her development. Chantel attended Leeds College Of Music, while still gigging around the country. In 2008, she gained a first-class honours degree in Popular Music.

Chantel played at the *Leeds Bradford Guitar Show* at Pudsey Civic Hall on Sunday, September 13, 2009..

By 2011, she had released her debut CD album *Like No Other*, on her own Tis Rock Music label. That same year, Chantel was named the *Young Artist of The Year* at the British Blues Awards. The next year she won the *Best Female Vocalist*. In 2013, she won *Best Female Vocalist* for the second time and also the *Guitarist Of The Year* award.

In 2015, she released her second album, *Lose Control*, produced by her bassist Livingstone Brown who had also produced her debut LP. The three-track CD *Take The Power / Southern Belle / Walk On Land* was released as album promo.

On May 12 that year, she appeared live on stage in Centenary Square as part of the Bradford Festival celebrations. On July 12, 2019, she returned to do the same. She also released her *Bury'd Alive* live album, recorded at the Apex in Bury St. Edmunds.

In 2020 she released a reworked cover of *Stupid Love* by Lady Gaga, on the LA-based Cleopatra Records label. She also became a regular weekly presenter on Hard Rock Hell Radio with her show, *Chantel's Monday Brunch Club*.

During Covid-19, she performed a live weekly show from her shed singing and playing acoustic guitar, later with Jamie Brooks on keyboards. Two CD albums, *Shed Sessions Vol 1 & 2* came out in 2021, again on her Tis Rock Music label.

Also that year, she released the single *I Will See*, which she co-wrote and recorded remotely with David 'Nova' Nowakowski of Bradford band Scars On 45, who was now living in Colorado, USA.

On June 21, 2024, Chantel played a rare hometown gig at Tapestry Arts Centre in Dudley Hill.

In 2025 she undertook a UK tour to promote her new rock-oriented album, *The Healing*.

Chantel McGregor Band (2011–) #2					
Chantel McGregor	Livingstone Brown	Chris Taggart	Colin Sutton	Thom Gardner	Jamie Brooks
Voc/Gtr	Bass/Keyboards	Drums	Bass	Drums	Keyb

As the year 2008 dawned, the Topic Folk Club (now based at the Irish Club, off Westgate) still hosted the usual local suspects like Scarlet Heights, The Hall Brothers and Roger Sutcliffe, but the city also saw a new breed of artists emerging.

JO DUNWELL

This local singer-songwriter won the 2007 Pulse Radio's *Battle Of The Bands*, thus securing a support slot with local boys Terrorvision at their rare hometown gig in Saltaire in January 2008.

On February 14, 2008, Jo played the new Shipley venue the PM Lounge Bar with Abi Lovelle, Laura Shackleton and keyboardist Imani Hekim, formerly of the 1980s ska and reggae band Spectre.

BERKANA

Formed in 2002 as a duo of Neil Benton and Terry Armitage, Berkana became a three-piece in 2007/8 when they were joined by Wakefield folk singer Lou Finch. They played a range of instruments and performed folk in traditional and contemporary styles with some self-penned material. They played the Topic Folk Club at least twice in 2008 and appeared at the Cleckheaton Folk Festival in 2009, 2010 and 2011. Later they added a fourth member, Tony Taffinder.

Berkana is the rune symbol B for the birch tree goddess and represents the female qualities of fertility, the mother, healer and midwife.

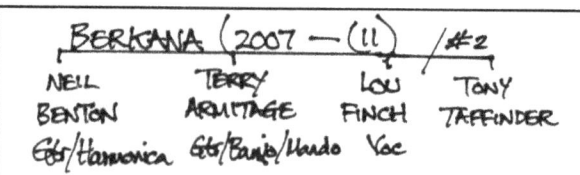

HUIGAN QUARTET

A local jazz ensemble that started life as a trio in 2008, led by pianist John Higgins, before becoming a quartet when John's brother Mark joined on alto saxophone.

THE 309S

This local quintet played 'hot fiddling dance music', incorporating cajun, creole and Louisiana roots music with rock'n'roll, Texan swing jazz, jump blues, jive and rockabilly.

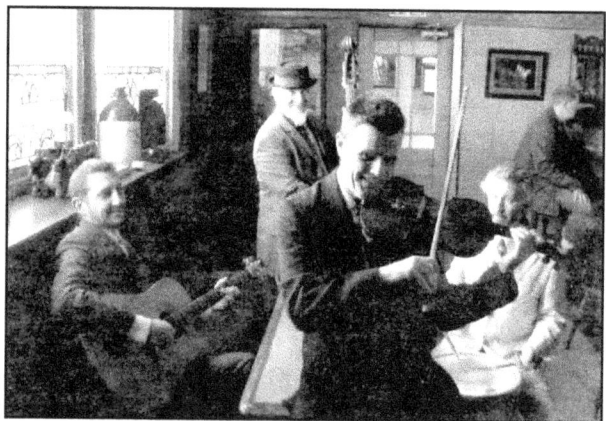

Since they formed in 2008, they have performed at various festivals, including The Cheltenham Jazz Festival, Colne Blues Festival, Saltaire Festival and Haworth 40s Weekend. They have played The 1 In 12 Club a couple of times; a private party on May 29, 2015 and a *Funk'n'Soul* night on March 4, 2016.

The quintet played at the Shrewsbury Folk Festival at the end of August 2024.

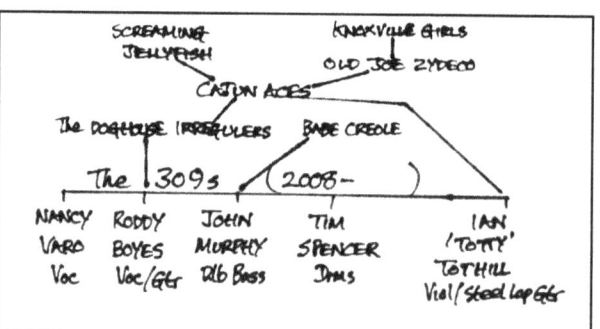

THE BAD SHEPHERDS

Bradford lad Adrian Edmondson, known for his role as Vyvyan in the BBC comedy series *The Young Ones*, had already tasted musical fame as part of the spoof rock band Bad News alongside fellow members of The Comic Strip comedy team; Rik Mayall, Nigel Planer and Peter Richardson. After buying a mandolin when drunk, Ade taught himself some basic chords and started to play folk versions of the punk songs of his youth.

He quickly enlisted Uilleann pipes player Troy Donockley, a former member of 1980s folk-rock outfit You Slosh. (10)

They became a trio with the addition of all-Ireland fiddle champion Andy Dinan, with guest members joining them in the studio and on live dates.

After a UK tour in 2008, they released their debut CD album *Yan, Tyan, Teathra, Methera* in 2009 on Monsoon Music. The album title was ancient Cumbrian dialect for *One, Two, Three, Four*. The songs on it were folk versions of punk/new wave standards by The Clash, The Jam, The Undertones, Squeeze and Talking Heads. Their second album, *By Hook Or By Crook*, came out in 2010, after which the band had a two-year hiatus.

They returned in 2013 with a twenty-four-date tour of the UK and a six-date tour of Australia to promote their third album, *Mud, Blood & Beer*. They played Glastonbury Festival and appeared at The Beautiful Daze Festival in 2014, before Ade announced the band's end on his Facebook page in October 2016.

Ade's other musical endeavours included playing Brad Majors in a West End run of *The Rocky Horror Show* in 1990, singing with The Bonzo Dog Doo Dah Band on their 2006 reformation tour and their 2007 album *Pour l'Amour Des Chiens*.

He formed the Idiot Bastard band with the Bonzo's Neil Innes and comedians Phill Jupitus, Rowland Rivron and Simon Brint in 2010 playing a mixture of covers and their own comedy songs

ROGER DAVIES

Other West Yorkshire towns produced many new folk artists, like Brighouse lad Roger Davies, a folk singer/songwriter who created songs about everyday life and local characters.

His debut release was *Littletown* in 2004, followed by the *Northern Trash* album and three track 7" of the same name in 2006, on the Huddersfield label Headroom Records.

Roger's traditional folky-blue style won him lots of acclaim. On his CD releases, there were many songs about the Bradford area, with titles like *Bradford Girl*, *Judy Woods*, *Sunbridge Road* and *Bradford Born 'n' Raised*. His third album, *The Busker*, came out in 2009, followed by several more CDs, *Songs In*

Plain English (2012), the double CD *The Yorkshire Songwriter* (2014) (a re-release of his previous albums

Northern Trash and *The Busker*), *Local Radio* (2014), *Live At The Topic Folk Club* (2016) and *Roger Davies & His Band* (2018).

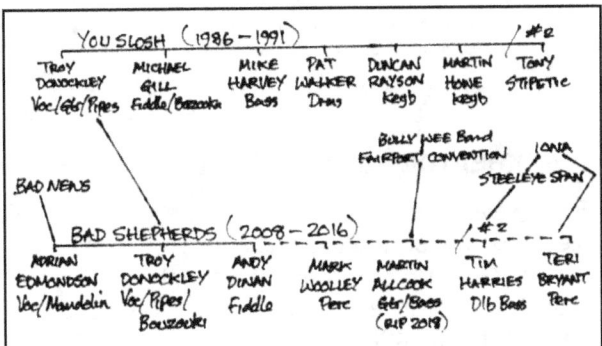

Roger has played Bradford's Topic Folk Club numerous times over the years. He played at The Priestley Theatre in Little Germany on December 15, 2013, with Serious Sam Barrett, Mary Hampton and Bradford-based singer/songwriter Gerrard Bell-Fife.

After impressing members of UK folk legends Fairport Convention, Roger was offered the support slot on their twenty-six-date tour of the UK in 2015. That same year, on April 22, he appeared with Plumhall, Jon Harvison, Nick Toczek, Liz Narey, Karl Dallas, Pete Coe and Den Miller for an evening's entertainment at the Germany Church on Great Horton Road.

Roger is a graduate of the Batley School of Art and is a highly acclaimed contemporary painter. He had an exhibition at the Smith Art Gallery in Brighouse, on December 2024.

QUEENSBURY MUSIC FESTIVAL

On Saturday and Sunday, March 7-8, 2009, the Queensbury Music Festival took place with events in the afternoon and evening at Victoria Hall and the local Conservative Club. It was co-sponsored by Bradford Council and the Old Spot, the Cullingworth small brewery. Artists appearing included local boys Pat Sherry & Stuart Douglas (ex-Scarlet Heights), The Hall Brothers and Brighouse's Roger Davies.

BEEHIVE POETS

Local venue the New Beehive Inn, on Westagate, ran a series of poetry workshops around this time.

New Beehive Inn, Westgate, Bradford, BD1 3AA

Bradford West Area Committee Community Chest   BRADFORD

BEEHIVE POETS & BRADFORD POETRY WORKSHOP
- Readings from visiting poets – 2nd Monday at 8.30 pm
- Read-arounds – 1st & 3rd Monday at 8.30 pm
- Bradford Poetry Workshop – 4th Monday. at 8.30 pm
- *For critical and constructive comment on your poetry; please bring 6 copies and a pair of ears!*

For more information about the workshop contact Bruce Barnes: bruce.poetbradford@blueyonder.co.uk Telephone: 01274 223665

CLECKHEATON FOLK FESTIVAL

For the twenty-second year running, the Cleckheaton Folk Festival took place on the weekend of July, 3-5, 2009. The event was sponsored by Kirklees Council, and a weekend ticket cost £50/£40.

CHAPTER 3: BRADFORD FOLK   1999 - 2009

SALTAIRE LIVE

A series of concerts took place between September and December 2009, at Saltaire's Victoria Hall, with an additional concert at St George's Hall on Saturday, October 17, featuring Bellowhead.

JONATHAN TAYLOR

Singer-songwriter Jonathan Taylor was based in Frizinghall during 2008/09, and released four self-produced CDs on his own label, Brittuncli Music. The first

Picture by Mike Green

was *Songs Of The Fete De La Musique (Luddenden Music Festival)* (2008), followed by *Partisan* (2008) which was dedicated to the memory of the partisans, Sargeant Frank Thompson and members of the Special Operations Executive (SOE), in Bulgaria 1940-45.

2009's *The Holocaust Denier* was recorded in Bulgaria and the UK with local folk artist Tim Moon guesting on track 4, playing cello, accordion, flute and balalaika.

Jonathan's *A Useful Fool* came out in 2009.

Jonathan was born in Warwick and had moved to West Yorkshire in his teens, living in Calderdale then Bradford from the ages of nineteen to forty, before settling in Bulgaria.

While in Bulgaria, he received some great press and TV coverage and garnered a loyal following. In 2013, he released the CD *Priest - Forget The Past (The Blacksail Studio Sessions)*.

Jonathan was the second cousin of the late Bob Johnson, guitarist with Steeleye Span.

RAISE YOUR BANNERS

Raise Your Banners started life in Sheffield in 1995, as a commemoration of the *Industrial Workers Of The World (IWW)* member Joe Hill who was executed in 1915. (11)

John Tams' *Unity (Raise Your Banners High)* was the inspiration for their name. The festival was a celebration of political song with festivals and subsequently held every two years.

In 2001, the organisers released a nineteen-track CD, featuring performers who had appeared at the festivals in 1995, 1997, 1999 and 2001. The aim was to: *'celebrate political song and to give the exponents of such music an opportunity to meet, sing and join with the many people who are committed to this music and want to enjoy themselves.'*

Artists appearing on the CD included Roy Bailey, Dick Gaughan, Tom Robinson, Robb Johnson, Frankie Armstrong, Billy Bragg and thirteen others.

In 2007, the festival was held in Bradford between the 5th and 17th of November at various venues including St George's Hall (9th), Topic Folk Club (then at the Cock & Bottle pub) where American folky Julie Felix played on the 8th,

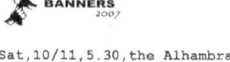

Alhambra Studios (10-11th), the New Beehive (10th and 17th). The 1 In 12 Club held an open mic night to celebrate the music of the 'Wobblies' - the nickname of IWW members.

The organisers also

released another CD that year, entitled *Not In My Name*, a response to the wars in Iraq and Afghanistan. A one-off gig was held at Manningham Mills on May Day, 2009.

The festival returned to Bradford in November 2009, with the Kala Sangam Centre being the main venue.

Other events were held at The Beehive, Treehouse Cafe, Topic Folk Club, Bradford Resource Centre and The 1 In 12 Club, where a couple of gig nights and a special film night were held.

On Friday the 6th, Chumbawamba, Bleeding Hearts, Tracey Curtis and Gary Kaye appeared at Kala Sangam. At the same venue, the following day

was a radical book fair, a choir concert and an event named *Turning Silence Into Song* with Roy Bailey, Leon Rosselson, Frankie Armstrong, Martin Carthy, Sandra Kerr and Janet Russell. The evening finished with a concert of twelve choirs at Bradford Cathedral.

Sunday continued with the radical book fair and a special closing concert, with Claire Mooney, The Hall Brothers, Sex Patels and Imani Hekima.

REFERENCES

The local Bradford evening newspaper the Telegraph & Argus provided a lot of the material for the research, particularly in the early chapters, the rest was gleaned from many other local sources, some of which are listed below, and the personal recollections of some of the people involved in the Bradford music scene during the relevant period.

CHAPTER 1: 1999-2000

1. John Braine (1922 – 1986) was born in Westgate, Bradford and brought up in sunny Thackley. He worked as a librarian in Bingley. He is perhaps best know for his 1957 novel *Room At The Top* which was made into a successful film starring Laurance Harvey, two years later. He wrote eleven other works of fiction, including the sequel *Life At The Top* (1962) and scripts for *Man At The Top* (1970-71), a Thames Television drama based on his lead character Joe Lampton.

2. In October 2001, Slobodan Milosevic, the third Serbian president, was charged by the International Criminal Tribunal with war crimes (including genocide and crimes against humanity) in connection with the wars in Bosnia, Croatia and Kosovo. After, a five-year trial, where he defended himself, Milosovic died of a heart attack in his cell in The Hague on March 11, 2006.

> Dear Kerrang!
> I am writing to complain about the shitty review you gave Khang's album, Worship The Evil in Kerrang #891. You gave it a measly two Ks. I'm from Bradford and I also know the band.
> I also know that they worked really hard on the album and the vocalist Bryan worked really hard on practicing his vocals. The album is certainly not 'ruined' by Bri's vocals, quoted by Mr Dave Everley.
> Worship The Evil is a brilliant album, it might be a bit short for an album and it might not be everybody's cup of tea but I think it's a great album.
> **Rory, Bradford.**

3. Conquest Of Steel cartoon (pictured right).

4. Letter sent to *Kerrang!* rock magazine by Rory Cavanagh (left).

5. P.76 *Franz Ferdinand & The Pop Renaissance* – Hamilton, Harvey Reynolds & Hearn (2005)

6. On the Friday night, the main raffle prize was a reconditioned Mini car, donated by car mechanic and midfield player Ged Chatfield...who promptly won it in the draw...

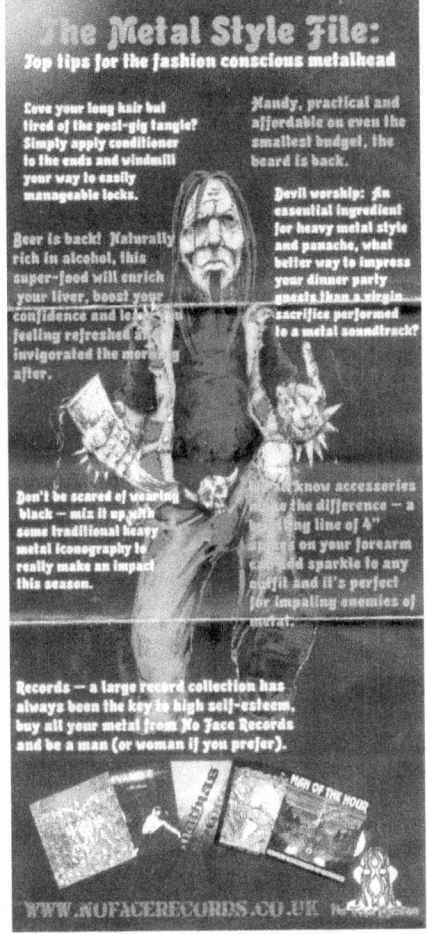

7. Stated on the label's website.

8. The winning trophy was a 'lovely painted plastic toilet seat', handmade by members of the Lunnatics. The teams could have done with the toilet seat during the tournament, as in the toilet block, there were just hard white ceramic units without seats.

9. The BAFC donated money. £1600, was handed over at the Cultural Union in Pristina.

10. *Decade Of Dissidence* was the last 1 In 12 release, Gary Cavanagh had a hand in the production.

11. P.6-9 *Big Issue In The North* #259 May 1999.

12. One of Gary's old school friends, Chris Overend (RIP 2016), wrote the occasional article for the *City Gent*.

13. A letter in the *T&A* (right).

Unforgettable holiday on our own doorstep

SIR - I have just had an unforgettable three-week holiday. I went alone but had company every day – strangers, long lost relatives, old friends and new.

We enjoyed good food and drink, superb free entertainment, chatted, danced, were educated. As an added bonus, the weather was glorious and I didn't have to find accommodation.

For those who haven't guessed, the holiday was Bradford Festival, about which I could write a book. But briefly, the highlights for me were:–

● Routes of Resistance – an historical walk through Bradford – informative, interesting. I look forward to more such events.

● Fanfare Ciorcalia – Romanian gipsy music. What a performance! Please bring them back.

● Levi Ta-fari whose delivery of his brilliant poetry was spellbinding, and who was so nice to me when I went to thank him.

● Mind The Gap – whose enthusiasm was infectious.

The most memorable impression was the friendly, happy atmosphere in Centenary Square, where all ages, races and abilities gathered together in a common enjoyment. The MC and stewards did a great gob with good humour and diplomacy. Well done, Bradford. Roll on Festival 2000.

Mrs Mary Loy, Fairway Grove, Bradford 7.

14. Info supplied by email from Tony Brennan.

15. Besides the original, there was US band No Use For A Name and Italy's Contropotere's versions.

16. *The Star* 8.2.2001

17, *Asian Eye T&A* 10.7.2000

18. Without Prejudice's tree can be found on P130 in *BNOTV Volume 2*.

CHAPTER 2: 2001-2003

1. *Metro* 17/04/2001

2. Pickled Eggs Records' first release was the 7" single *Black & Blue* by the Leeds band The Mekons (EGG1)

3. A generation of Bradford-born writers in the 1970s-80s, included Duncan Kyle who had worked at the *T&A*. His first novel was entitled *A Cage Of Ice*. He published at least another eight novels, including the 1983 spy thriller *The King's Commissar* on Fontana.

4. Gary had begun his research into *BNOTV 1* (2009) in early 2000. By February 2001, with over 20,000 words written, he met up with Matt Webster at MacRory's bar to prepare for starting work on the book using Matt's computer and layout skills. The WEA course at the Club was the first time that he had publicly shown his first ten 'family trees' as part of his ongoing research.

5. Adam was the son of Gary's former bandmate in Phobia, drummer Keith Theakstone.

6. Chumbawamba wrote the song *Bradford Bad Lad* as an exclusive track for the 1 In 12 compilation double album – *Wild & Crazy Noise Merchants....Worst Of The ...Vol.9/10*.

7. Easton Cowboys article (right)

8. *T&A* July, 2001.

9. The Taliban under Mullah Mohammed Omar in control of the Afgan capital Kabul imposed a brutal police state in an effort to build 'Khilifah' as the Sharia law government for the Islamic world with its hardline misoginistic policies.

10. p.26 *Guardian Weekender* 29/12/2001.

11. p.210 Richardson

12. *The Guardian* 22/05/2002

13. Another Bradford lad, Danny Tetley of Windhill, Shipley got to the last seventy-five.

14. Quoted by media correspondent Matt Wells in *The Guardian* 6/02/2002.

15. Leeds United fan James Brown played in the short-lived band The Butter Cookies who supported Blackpool's The Membranes at The 1 In 12 Club gig at the Market Tavern in May 1985.

16. p.80-1 in op cit Hamilton, Harvey (2005).

17. It took until 2012 for the next 1 In 12 records release, the 7" single *I Still Hate Thatcher / Sing A Happy Song* by Andy T (Cat No 12017).

18. The song *Her Majesty* was a cover of The Beatles ditty that appeared as the final track on their *Abbey Road* album.

19. p.19 *Clamor* #10 magazine, Sept-Oct 2001.

REFERENCES 1999 - 2003

20. A bizarre robbery took place during the set by the band Breene. A guy just jumped up on the stage, grabbed the lead microphone from its stand, jumped back into the crowd and took off.

21. Tania Branigan/ Martin Wainwright in *The Guardian* 19/09/2002.

22. Theshold Shift article, *T&A* 16/10/2003 (pictured below)

Anger as band is banned

by CAROLINE WRIGHT
Chief Reporter

Angry fans reacted with fury after their band was told at the 11th hour: "Sorry, you can't go on stage!"

A stool was thrown and smashed into equipment on stage at Pennington's after indie outfit Threshold Shift did not get to play their support act.

They had been booked to support Dead Men Walking – the band made up of former Cult, Sex Pistols and Alarm members – on its nationwide tour.

But Dead Men, on a 31-date tour, never play with support and were stunned when they arrived to find the local band ready to go on.

Threshold Shift had given out 300 tickets to loyal fans for the gig at the Manningham Lane club.

The fans started shouting abuse and a stool was thrown at the stage during the performance.

Club owner John Pennington said he was considering offering Threshold Shift another date. "I have a lot of sympathy with them and I have made great inroads to get another support slot for them," he said.

Threshold Shift had rung him asking if they could support Dead Men Walking – which includes Glen Matlock from the Sex Pistols and Billy Duffy from The Cult who formed in the city.

Mr Pennington said: "I was trying to support a local band and was thinking 'no problem'. I checked the contracts and it is a bit of a grey area. There was nothing in them about supports.

"The next thing the band were saying they would not go on. I could have insisted but then the main artist would not have appeared. Then a chair was thrown at an amp and smashed it all and everyone fell out."

Threshold Shift band member Paul Armitage said: "The first we heard of any problems was when we turned up to sound check at 5.30pm on the evening of the gig as requested.

"We tried to reason with Dead Men Walking explaining that we had been booked by the owner of the club and had 400 people en route from all over Yorkshire. They were adamant that only they were going to appear on stage that night."

Fan Jo Elsom, from Idle, said: "I am gutted that a Bradford band were not allowed to play in a Bradford venue."

Jack Gray, agent for Dead Men Walking, said: "We do not have support bands for any concert. We do two sets and if there was a support it would go on for ever and ever. If there is no support, then management need permission from the management of the artist if they want to provide one. Without checking with us, we were unaware until the day of the show."

● Threshold Shift are next appearing at The Coniston, Idle, on Saturday, November 1.

CHAPTER 3: BRADFORD FOLK 1999-2009

1. *Keighley News* 1977

2. John Harvison's biog sheet.

3. *T&A* 22/04/1999

4. *T&A* 20/02/1999

5. *T&A* 17/11/1999

6. Nick West in *Propaganda Magazine* #21, Oct/Nov 2011

7. *Living Tradition* homepage, 2007. Jim Carroll, Pat McKenzie (County Clare)

8. Interview in *Jazz UK* magazine #45, May/June 2002

9. Maureen Galvin's obituary (right).

10. You Slosh were a folk-rock act in the 1980s/'90s who produced two albums, *Glorious Racket* (1989) and *Lift Me Up* (1991), both on On Them Records.

11. The International Workers Of The World (IWW) was a USA trade union organisation, also known as 'the wobblies'.

Maureen Galvin

Maureen Galvin, who has died of a brain tumour aged 52, instigated the Women's Walk as part of the Bradford Festival in 2000. It celebrated the impact that women had had on the city. To introduce it, she wrote about the mill girls who had stormed male-only pub tap rooms in 1910, and about the women who had fought against the exploitation of pornography and strip shows in the 1970s: "Bradford has a glorious history of women's achievements."

Maureen was part of that. She arrived there in the 1980s to work in the careers service, and chaired a branch of the public service workers' union, Nalgo. When that service was privatised, Maureen was in the front line of opposition to the change. When the service made her redundant, citing the time she spent on union duties, she went to a tribunal and won. She then chaired the voluntary sector branch of the MSF, the manufacturing, science and finance union, taking on intractable cases. Astute, well prepared and witty, she handled debates with aplomb and business with efficiency.

Her political life encompassed many organisations. She was involved with a club set up in the 1980s by members of the local claimants' union to create a social scene for the low waged and unemployed; she was involved with the Bradford Resource Centre, which worked with individuals and community and trade union groups. She loathed the British National party and was a solid supporter in campaigns with the black community.

With the local trades councils women's subcommittee, she organised day schools on new technology, part-time workers, and maternity rights, and supported the National Abortion Campaign, Women Against Pit Closures, Hindle Wives, and Rape Crisis.

Maureen was born in Nuneaton, Warwickshire, and educated at Nuneaton high school for girls and Wolverhampton Polytechnic, where she took a BA in English. Before moving to Bradford, she lived in Sittingbourne, Durham and Leeds.

In December 2006, she was diagnosed with an inoperable tumour: she stayed sharp and realistic for months, and with the help of her son Kieran, friends and carers she lived at home until the end. Kieran, her mother and sister survive her.
Ann Nicholls

Maureen Galvin spent her life in support of the women and organisations of her adopted city, Bradford

The Ballad of Joe Hill *by Alfred Hayes and Earl Robinson*

I dreamed I saw Joe Hill last night,
Alive as you or me
Says I, "But Joe, you're ten years dead,"
"I never died," says he.
"I never died," says he.

"In Salt Lake, Joe," says I to him,
Him standing by my bed,
"They framed you on a murder charge,"
Says Joe, "But I ain't dead,"
Says Joe, "But I ain't dead."

"The copper bosses killed you, Joe,
They shot you, Joe," says I.
Takes more than guns to kill a man,"Says Joe, "I didn't die,"
Says Joe, "I didn't die."

And standing there as big as life
And smiling with his eyes
Says Joe, "What they forgot to kill
Went on to organize,
Went on to organize."

"Joe Hill ain't dead," he says to me,
"Joe Hill ain't never died.
Where working men are out on strike
Joe Hill is at their side,
Joe Hill is at their side."

From San Diego up to Maine,
In every mine and mill -
Where working men defend their rights
It's there you'll find Joe Hill.
It's there you'll find Joe Hill.

I dreamed I saw Joe Hill last night,
Alive as you or me
Says I, "But Joe, you're ten years dead",
"I never died," says he.
"I never died," says he.

BIBLIOGRAPHY

Other invaluable reference material includes the following publications:

Record Collector's Rare Record Guide (2016- 2022)
Girls Aloud - Dreams That Glitter: Our Story (2008) Bantam Press
Music Master: Price Guide For Record Collectors 2nd Edition, Nick Hamlyn (1992), Waterlow
Franz Ferdinand & The Pop Renaissance, Hamilton Harvey (2005), Reynolds & Hearn Ltd
A History Of The Middle East 2nd Edition, Peter Mansfield (2003), Penguin
A Touch On The Times: Songs Of Social Change 1770-1914, Roy Palmer (Ed) (1974), Penguin
What Terrorists Want: Understanding The Terrorist Threat, Louise Richardson (2005), John Murry
Punk Rock: An Oral History, John Robb (2006)
Losing Control: Global Security In The 20th Century, Paul Rodgers (2000), Pluto
Clamor #10 Sept/Oct 2001 fanzine

And a special mention for Pete Frame's *Rock Family Trees (1979-93) Omnibus*. Pete's family trees have adorned a multitude of magazines, articles and record sleeves over the years and were a major source of inspiration for my own hand-drawn trees which adorn this book.

INDEX OF BANDS ON TREES

A

Abyss 46
Accolade 126
Action Beat 107, 123
Active Slaughter 72
Adolescents UK 71
Aftermath 49
After The Massacre 23
Afternoon Gentlemen 33
Albeit 17
All Eyes West 125
Alan Wormald Band 159
Alpine Movement 19
Alt Track 105, 116
Amon Duul 157
Amphetameanies 75
And None Of Them Knew They Were Robots! 123
Animal Day Sessions 17
Another Cinema 15, 19
Android Love Story 28, 113
Anti-System 13, 67, 95
Applejack Trio 141
Apple Moths 13
Architect 111
Archetype Falls 113
Arcromnia 140
Argey Bargey 136
Arkham Witch 25, 26, 49
Arrin 136
Asomvel 123
Aste 75
Astral Trip 28, 29
Atavist 25
Auroborus 157
Auto-Phoeus 125
Aviator Ray 13

B

Baba Yaga 86
Baby Harp Seal 86
Bad News 163
Bad Shepherds 163
Bad Wolf 79, 107
Babe Creole 162
Backslider 46
Bantus 27
Battered Cod 72
Battered Ornaments 157
Beats Working 27
Beer Beast 13
Beginning Of The End 33
Belle & Sebastion 75
Belonging 21
Ben Peel & The Wool City Folk Club 15
Berkana 162
Berlin 46
Bervas 19
Bibles FC 13
Big Bang 46, 48, 111
Big Fish 13
Big Love 17, 28, 105
Black Falcon 23, 79, 95
Black Feathered Feet 29
Black Horse Fairy 46, 130
Black Lanterns 98
Blacklist 47
Blind Haze 123
Blisters/Karelia 75
Blister Factory 95
Blood Robots 82
Bloodstream 25, 26, 28, 49, 86, 95
Bloom 17, 50
Blue Denim 27
Blue Wickeds 125
Blunderbuss 26, 79, 107

Bobby Charltons 48
Bolyne 140
Boneshakers 48
Bonifide 157
Bonnie 'Prince' Billy 75
Bookworms 84, 125
Boston Crabs 107
Bottleneck Boogie Band 157
Boxed-In 82
Bracken 141
Brand New Analogues 48
Brazil 73
Breene 47, 72
Brendan Croker & The 5 O'Clock Shadows 44
Broomdusters 157
Buffulo 123
Bullweek 13
Bully Wee Band 163
Burning Flag 98
Burning Witch 25
Byrney 105

C

Cajun Aces 140, 162
Calvary 157
Camp Boyz 111
Canvas 98
Capt Haddock & The Fishy Fingers
Carcass 123
Cardiacs 13
Catharsis 82
Cath O'Connor Sound 86
Chainsaw 46
Chantel McGregor Band 161
Charles Hanson 19, 105
Cheap'n'Nasty 48
Chiang 17, 29, 105

INDEX

Chief 72
Choice 111
Chorus Of Ruin #3 25, 49, 79
Chris + Fraser 107
Chris Sharp Project 64
Chumbawamba 153
Chutzpah 95
Circulus 79
Circus 47, 72
Citusk 47
Clare Teal Band 158
Classique 47, 49, 111
Clockwork Line 157
Clouded Fish 86, 107, 123
Cocktail Shakers 27
Colenso Parade 19
Collusion 25
Come To Grief 23
Conquest Of Steel 21, 95
Costa & Nero 125
Couldn't Care Less 13, 95
Cowboy Chords 48
Cowtown 125
Criminal Damage 71
Crosstown Traffic 137
Crows Blood 79
Cumscunch 102
Cyber Circus 23

D

Danse Society/The Society 13
Darren Ellis & The Extravaganda 17, 105
Das Tor 28
David Bowie & Hype 157
Dawn of Elysium 23, 49, 79, 95
Dawnraiser 95
Dawnwatcher 46
Dead Resurrected 23, 52, 79, 86, 95
Dead To This World 86
Dead Wrong 86
Dear Friends 107
Deed Poll 116
Demon Barbers 148

Demonix 49
Department M 28
Devils 34
Diavolo 49
Dinosaur Pile-Up 28
Dirty Work 48
Disciples BC 33, 82
Doctor Spong 125
Doghouse Irregulars 162
Dolphins 17, 28
Domestic Enemies 84
Donovan's Open Road 157
Doom 23, 33, 82
Drastics 95
Drench 17, 98
Driven Down 92
Dr Keating's Clamp 52
Dub Kitchen 11
Duckstab 33

E

Earthquake 28
Earthquake Johnson 157
Ebola 82
Echofire 95
Echo Four Two 153
Egomania 19
Eiger 17
Electric Wizard 23
Element 79
Elements 111
El Loco 64
Elsie Moon 15
Elizabeth 125
Embryo 75
Embittered 82
Enchanted 25, 26, 86
Endless Torment 26
Endtimes 23, 79, 86
Epitaph 25
Ethel & The Heroes 47
Evening Breeze 105
Excalibur 47
Exoterik 47, 48, 111

Eyesore Angels 25, 47, 49

F

FM 64
Factory 157
Fade Like Rockets 52
Fairport Convention 163
Falconetti 17, 98
Fallacy 13, 49
Fall Guys 27
Family Elan 75
Far Fetched 48
Fargo 46
Fatal Joy 112
Faux Romantics 105, 116
Fifteen Stories 47, 72, 111
Filament 47, 116
Fineline 125
Firebird 123
Five Previous Owners 48
Flat Back Four 50
Fling 19, 105
Flukeshot Frenzy 72
Forge 105
Forestry Commission 10
Forty Thieves 79
Foul Play 23
Four Fighters 86
Four Horsemen 140
Foxes Faux 25, 47
Franz Ferdinand 75
Fred The Oyster 130
Full Tilt 46

G

Galores 14, 15, 17
Garden Of Rememberance 49
Garfunkel & Simon 125
Gentlemen's Pistols 107
Get Guns 47
GFA 11
Ghostdance 111
Give Up All Hope 33, 82

Glamnation 2, 46
Goad 64
God's Of Hellfire 13, 23, 25, 26, 49
Golden Meat 125
Gold, Frankensense & Discdrive 27
Goo 47
Gore 26, 86
Grace Notes 137
Grain 79
Great Diplomats 17, 105
Great Refused 33
Green 17, 28
Green Car Legacy 29
Grieve 52
Grip 130
Grin 125
Groovement 111
Gruel 33, 82, 86

H

#Crime 11
Hacksilver 82
Haley Sisters 141
Hall Brothers 146
Handful Of Dance 67
Hangman 29
Hardcore Pirates of Doom 49
Harlequyn 111
Harmacy 28
Hawkeyes 28
Headstone 26, 49, 95
Henry's Radio 19, 105
Highway To Hell 49
High Parasite 79
High Street 52
Himself 17
His Girl Friday 105
Hobbes Fan Club 17, 28, 113
Hollow Earth 23, 25, 49
Hollow Horse 112
Holy Mirimba 44
Homonym 116
Honey Toad 23, 48, 49
Hoodoo Operators 52

Horror 123, 125
Hospital Food 95
Hot Spiced Bananas 95
Howlin' Johnny & The Devils Rejects 48
Howlin' Johnny & The Full Moon Blues Band 48
Humanfly 98
Human Wreakage 98
Hunting Party 46
Hush 130
Hypernoid 26
Hypnosis 21

I

IdiotBox 13, 25, 28, 95
Illusory Centre 105
Imbalance 123, 125
Immigrants 71
Incest Brothers 82
Indianic 47
Indiqa 15
In Dying Grace 25
Infomation 125
Inner Turmoil 52
Inside Out 27
Iona 163
Iron Monkey 23
Iron-On Maiden 79
Iron Rat 23, 25, 49, 79, 95
Ironside 123
Ironstorm 49
Iron Void 79
Isotope 137

J

Jacacanda 44
Janet Jones 133
Japanese Voyeurs 28
Jason's Flock 157
Jasper 46
Jayver 111
JCB Ceilidh Band 141

Jigsaw Culture 21, 26, 95
Jimmy Savile's Wheelchair 84
Jinn 82
John Holmes 33, 82
Johnny Gray Band 13
Johnny & The Poorboys 48
Jonny & The Rizlas 13
JR 98
Junior's Eyes 157
Jung Witche 125
Junk Dealers 28, 29, 113
Juratory 95
Just Ray 107, 123

K

KMP 33
Kaboss 46
Kaesmel 15
Kettlewitch/Skullcrusher 49
Khang 23, 33, 79, 86
Kick 130
Kill To Gain 25, 49
Kill II This 29
Kill Yourself 125
King Booty 15
Kiss My Axe 46
Kito 82
Knoxville Girls 162
Knoxville Saints 48
Koala 105
Kontiki 116
Krakatoa 23, 46
Kubera 29
Kwai Chang Caine 13, 95

L

Laboratory Noise 17
Laika Dog 107
La La & The Boo Ya 15
Lamp Of Thoth 49
Land & Body 125
Lapdog 65
Largactil 17, 98

Lazarus Blackstar 23, 25, 33, 49, 79
Lazy Days 157
Leafeater 107
Lenin Black 13
Let 'Em Burn 25, 26, 49
Le Tournoi 28
Liam Newton Psychonaut Experience 86
Life Destruction 72
Little Egypt 64
Little Women 157
Lizard Tongue 23, 52, 95
Liz Wright Band 27
L'Orchestre Du Café 75
Los Guys 15
Lounge 79
Loved Ones 19, 44
Love Not War 95
Lowlife UK 13, 95
Lucky Strike 157
Lykes Of Witch 157

M

Mad Jax 52
Magic Theatre 10
Magna Carta 27
Maladiction 82
Malibu Stacey 107
Mammoth Tank 95
Manfat 82
Mannix 49
Mantra 17
Mapp 48
Martha's Graveyard 157
Mariko (Resin) 61
Matrak Attakk 95
Means Of Escape 86
Medula Nocte 23
Midnight Train 157
Militia 72
Minefield 95
Minute Manifesto 82
Minus Jack 105
Miranda Vs The Crock 105

Molotov Cocktails 28
Monolith Cult 23, 79, 86, 95, 125
Montage 111
Montauk Island 49
Month Of Birthdays 86
Monty Casino 125
Moodbeats 136
Moota 15, 67
Morbid Humour 67, 71
Mortal Terror 82
Motley Crudos / Losing The Battle 33, 86
Motorvators 13
Mr Mak / Daisy Cutter 14, 29
Mucky Sailor 125
Mwstard 86
My Dying Bride 23
My Name Is Satan 33
Mysterious Footsteps 71

N

1919 15, 19
1960 Four 111
NNN 13
Nalle 75
Napalm Death 123
Naranja 17
Neckbrace 70
Necromancer 25
Necromancy 71
Negatives 71, 95
Negativz 71
Nerve Agents 71
New Direction 48
New Opera 27
New Model Army 71
New Musical Testament 15, 111
Nexus 49
Ninepoundnote 72, 116
No Eager Men 95
Noisegate 23
Nope 125
Nosebone 72
Nowt 13, 67, 95
Nucleus 137

Numb Tongues 125
Nursery 17, 98

O

Oakenthrone 23, 29, 79, 86
Officer Dibble 27
Old Joe Zydeco 162
Old School Enemy 52, 79, 95
One By One 82
One Ensemble 75
One Zone 82
Ooberman 10
Ooberon 10
Operator Six 47, 111
Out from Animals 72
Owl 157
Owt 15
Owter Zeds 44
Ozbest 26
Ozo 157

P

Panama Jack 46
Panamonium 157
Paper Smiles 105
Paralell or 90 (PO90) 27
Peached Out 17
Pepperjam 44
Philip Cockerham Trio 137
Phobia 125
Pink Fairies 157
Pipers 112
Planet Soul 107
Plastic Letters 13
Ploughshare 136
Plumhall 146
Pocket Watch 47, 72
Pond Skaters 130
Possessions 26, 28, 113
Pro Forma 75
Prolefeed 82, 95
Prophecy 21
Psychlona 79, 95

INDEX

Psycho Slinkys 29
Purity Cries 25, 26, 95

Q

Quantico 9
Quare Fellas 134
Quireboys 111

R

Rainbow Bridge 46
Random Hand 47, 72, 116
Rats 157
Real Fucky-Fucky 75
Real Life
Really 137
Red Room 17
Reefer 15
Reeved 95
Reflex 71
Rent Boys 113
Rhino 46
Rhythm Seeds 44
Rickets Smith The Scourge Of Uppington 125
Right To Silence 102
Ripoff UK 71
Rockheads 130
Rodeo Jones 111
Rose Of Avalanche 13
Rose Bay Willow Band 86
Rot-In-Hell 123
Ruby Tombs 28, 113
Ruin 33

S

Sand 28, 29
Sasquatch 26
Satanic Malfunctions 95
Sawn Off 82
Say You 111
Scatter 15, 75

Scatter (2)
Screaming Jellyfish 162
Screamachine 46
Seal Team Six 17, 98
Secret Circuits 28
Secret Society 105
Seer's Tear 21
Send More Paramedics 123
Serenity 23
Serious Sam Barratt 123
Seven Machine 26
Sex Maniacs 23, 123
Sex Patels 23, 79, 86, 153
Shades Of Grey 46
Shakatak 159
Shakes 46, 48
Shiney Beast 67
Signia Alpha 13
Silence 113
Silverburn (Burn Horizon) 23, 79
Siren (Neon Angels) 15, 105
Six Feet Under 71
Skeletal Family 47, 111
Sketch 137
Skitvarld 23
Slack 13, 67
Slam 107
Slammer 105
Slum Hunnies 105
Smack Dolly 111
Snuff Rock 13, 71, 95
Soft Machine 137
So It Goes 46
Solicitors 27
Solstice 23, 49
Son Of Boar 52
Sons of Liberty 111
Somebody's Brother 19, 44, 67
Soul System 157
Soulfish 48, 111
Sound Of The Baskervilles 107, 123
Sounds Of Swami 47, 72
Spectre 25
Spectres 157
Speed 48

Spiral Highway 157
Spodni Pradlo 125
Squaredog 105
Stagefright 46
Stalingrad 33
Stalking Horse 28
State Of Filth 33
Stiff Weaponz 49
Stillborn Unicorn 95
Stormer (Method) 64
Stormin' Normans 46
Strange Arrangement 72
Street Regal / Albion St 25, 84
Stutter 71
Suffer 33, 82
Suicide By Cop 23, 95
Sunfish Doo 13
Supercollider 23, 25
Susskind 25
Sutherland Bros & Quiver 157
Swakara 48
Swamp 52
Swamp Flower 71
Symphonika 10

T

309s 162
Talon 46
Tangaroa 123
Tefra 21
Telestar Ponies 75
Temple Balls 79
Terrorvision (Spoilt Bratz) 107
Terry Sexton & The Telecasters 157
That Fucking Tank 125
That Man There 13
Thighslapper Three 140
Third Stone Satelite (One Louder) 25
This Et Al 13, 28
Thomas J & The Gangsters of Soul 44, 130
Threads 23, 33, 79, 82, 86, 107, 153

INDEX

Threefold 141
Three Men & A Bass 19, 44
Threshold Shift 71
Throne Of Nails 21
Thundering Hearts 48
Thuser / Mundane 75
Tickle 157
Too Many Chiefs 95
Too Much 159
Tortoise Waltz 23, 25, 26, 28, 33, 86
Tough Crowd 116
Toyz 19
Transatlantic Alien 72, 86
Transu 107, 123
Trauma Unit 72
Traveling Bilberries 48
Trench 13
Trial 125
Tribe 26
Twisted Wheel 123
Twister 5 50
Two Madre 125
Two Wings 75

U

Ubik 19
Unbalanced 52
Undecided 47
Unfinished Drawings 150
Unicorn Love 33
Us 111

V

VR 23
Vagrants 71
Valafar 25, 49
Vampire Death 25, 47
Vardo Nine 52
Varukers 33, 95
Vegetable Section 71
Vex 19
Vince Wayne & The Falcons 157
Violent Minority 72

Voorhees 13, 23, 123, 125
Vye 27

W

Wankys 33, 82
War All the Time 33, 82
Warm 29, 79
Warm Sounds 157
Water 17
Wayriders 72
We Are Theives 28, 29
We'll Die Smilling 72
Wet Paint 47
Wharf Rats 102
Whatevers 64
When Giants Collide 23
When Idols Fall 49
White Hot & Blue 46
White Light Parade 113
Wild Trash 23, 26, 49, 71, 95
Wilful Missing 148
Windy Mills 13
Wino 105
Witches Of Elswick 148
Witchknot 86
Woes 72
Wolves In Winter 23, 79
Word 27
World Chaos 25
Worm 111
Wrong Band 27

X

Y

Yard Nule 148
Yeah, Maybe 105
Year Dot 13
Yo El Rey 29, 105
Yorkshire Miracle 136
You Slosh 163

Young Conservatives 123, 125
(Young) Inspectors 28, 113
Yummy Fur 75

Z

Zap Gun Virus 15, 19
Zed #4 13, 67
Zoundeakite 47
(Zydeco) Funk Butchers 140

AFTERWORDS

Gary Cavanagh was born in Clayton, Bradford, and is a founder member of Bradford's 1 In 12 Club, a former university tutor in history and politics, and a local historian and archivist.

He has been a life-long Bradford City supporter and one time City Junior. If it hadn't been for that niggling knee injury...

Former vocalist with legendary local rock gods Phobia, he has been involved in the local music scene since the mid-1970s and was instrumental in the production of the 1 In 12 Club compilation album series.

Gary has appeared on ITV's *Calender* news programme and local radio stations including Radio Leeds and BCB to promote the books, as well as giving talks on local music history at various seats of learning.

Matt Webster hails from Thackley, Bradford, and has been a drummer in numerous local bands since the early 1980s, including The Convulsions, The Nerve Agents, Swamp Flower, Western Dance, Primate, The Bottleneck Boogie Band, Nowt, Grim, Zed, The Horton Carpets, Kwai Chang Caine, Lenin Black, Plastic Letters and Signia Alpha. Also known as Matt Nazgul and Pete, Matt is a graphic designer and recording engineer/producer, and co-founder of Mutiny 2000 Studios/Records.

He was an occasional music reviewer for the Bradford Star in the early 1990s during his time working in the Pre-Press Department at the Telegraph & Argus where he also used to sneak various bits onto the *Rock On* page when no-one was looking. Matt was the original co-presenter of the Bradford Beat show on BCB from 1995 to 1999. He is currently recording and releasing fabulous vinyl albums with his recording band, Signia Alpha.

bradfordnoise.com

Acknowledgements

Thanks to Nick Toczek for his forward.

We are grateful to the following for permission to reproduce certain articles: *Telegraph & Argus* Perry Austin-Clark, Peter Orme, Jim Greenhalf, Emma Clayton, Odele Ayres, *Keighley News* (David Knights) and *Record Collector's Rare Record Guide*.

Thanks to Pete Chapman for his faith and continued support.

This book would have been virtually impossible without the help, support and contribution of the following:
Rory Cavanagh, Patrick Dowson, Hayden Wilcox, Alec Marlow, Tony Brennan, Neil Blanchett, Lee Baines, Ian Tilleard, Rik Ironmonger, Wayne Hustler, Lee Durham, Mickey Dey, Jonny Knewell, Rob Kershaw, Nagbea, Marek 'Fritz the Cat' Skoczylas, Neil Roddis, Malcolm Jackson (RIP 2018), Darren Parkinson, Rob 'Kito', Chris 'Captain Hotknives' Smith, Paul Durkin, Andy Wells (RIP 2023), Joanne Gallagher, James 'Atko' Atkinson, Thom McGowan, Karl Townend, Craig Sheenan, Dom Sheard, Tom Chapman, Paul Mason, Nathan Moses, Tim Walker, Rich Savage, Fran Jones, Robb Philpotts, Micky Knowles, Mark 'Varik' Teal, Mark 'Keany' Kean, Dean Martindale, Stuart Hillman, Liam Newton, Susan Kasher, Gordon Wilkinson, Clive Hughes, Peter 'Skinny' Finan Mick Spencer, Chris Burstun, Darren Ellis, Nick Millbank, Daz Miah, Porl 'Lemmy' Lane, LewWalker, Jack Winn, Dwayne Robinson, Howard Rickards, Jon Harvison, Chris Hladalowski, Joel White, Gareth Pugh, Ian Tothill, Bri Outlaw, Phil Hey, Andy Smith, Andy Irvine, Alex Gray, Steve Vincent, Mark 'Jim' Henderson, Bridgit Izod, Matt Fortune, David Hemingway, Ben Goodwin, Mick Wake, Jamie Robinson, Bri'Doom' Talbot, Andy Rukin, Tony Ryan, Lindsay Burns, Sean O'Sullivan, Richard Brass, Jed Forward, Eddy & Lorraine Kyrk, Simon Mawson, Mik Davies, Dave Shevyn, Luke Oliver, Martin Sturdy, Graeme 'Mushy' Muschamp, Steve Ward, Dave Wainfor, Craig Williams, Nigel & Emma Mason, Mark 'Cranny' Cranmer, Jonathan Gregson, Steven 'Johna' Johnson, Britt Jagger, Steve Vincent, Steve 'Paddy' Forsythe, Mike Holden, Andy Cactus, Phil Hobson, Graham McAndrew, Joe Warren, Phil Hobson, Sean Denning, Geoff Ashford, Richard Blakelock, Jon Hanslip, Trev Thomas, Sarah Carey, Ashley Quinn, Andy Burden, James Islip, Billy Fielding, Chris Sharp, Stu & Eve Firth, Sam Malynowsky, Neil 'Sak' Saxton, Keith Jowett, Phil Dean, Liz Austin, Anthony Burlison, Brian Lumb, Erin Kasher-Cavanagh, Sharon Helliwell.

From Keighley:-Stan Greenwood, 'Trotwood', Joe McEvoy, Kurt Wood, John Gow, Joe Tilston, Bruce & Linda Russell, Luke Parker, Simon 'Strange' Rourke, Ben Snowden, Billy Barton, Steve Wilson, Pete Kaberry, and David Knights for the photo archive of bands from *Keighley News*

Also, a special big Thanks to Janet Mawson for all her help and research on John's Followers and other Keighley artists and who has produced numerous superb local Entertainment 'Story Boards', also Gina Birdsal, and all at Keighley Local Studies Library.

David 'Sned' Sneddon for digitised 1 In 12 gig flyers archive.

Consultant for: Folk Chapter: Liz Narey.

Local Record shops: Jumbo, Leeds (Matt Bradshaw (top lad) and the rest of the staff), Wall Of Sound, Leeds (under Crash Records)Elliot Smaje for support and help, Mark et al at Vinyl Tap (Distro & shop), Huddersfield, Five Rise Records, Bingley, Gareth at Grind'n'Groove, Keighley and Chris Connelly at Cargo Studios (Rochdale).

Special Thanks to Martin Levy at Bradford University's Library's Special Collections Archive. And finally, all the Staff at Bradford Local Studies Library, past and present, for all their help and support.

RIP

Lest we forget. To all the fallen musicians who are no longer with us: Rest In Peace.

Year	Names
1968	Malcolm Clark
1971	Paul 'Reany' Robinson
1972	Tony Murphy
1976	Alan Waller
1977	John Boyle
1982	Fred Lagley
1983	Colin Ciprian
1985	Brendan Crowe
1988	Zero Singsby
1989	Colin Houghton
1990	Cindy-Ann Lee • Royston Wood
1991	Chris 'Beany' Bean • Martin Griffin • Dennis McCafferty
1992	Susan Fassbender
1993	Dave Beale
1994	Sean Mansley • Mick Wayne
1995	Steve Peyton • Darren Dickenson • John Hebron • Alan Barton
1996	Ged Grace
1999	Chris Groves • Mick Allison • Paul Marshall • Austin Danks • Richard Castle
2000	Allen Dinning • Alan Scott • Brian 'Spike O'Brien' Holt • Jim Hayden
2001	Brian Furnley • Andy Tyson • Steve 'Rocker' Blakeley • Terry 'Dadio' Moran
2002	Alex Slater • Mike King • Johnny Morrow • Mikey 'Roots' Pryce
2003	Roger Hepworth • Dave 'Murph' Mirfield
2004	Rob Heaton • Dave Lee (Sound) • Malcolm Nixon
2005	Chris Taylor • Josh Grundy • Jackie Talent • Wayne Southworth • Mick Brassington
2006	Dave Wilcox • Dave Brady • Garry O'Connell • Howard Burnette
2007	Wild Willi Beckett • Clive Royston • Andrew Wright • Robert Bailey
2008	Mike Berry • Kevin O'Brien • Steve Mason • Tony Palmer • Duncan Wilson
2009	Chris Richmond • Colin Howdin • Harvey Mitchel • Steven 'Swells' Wells
2010	John 'Grubby' Mason • Jonathon Swift • Dave Parkinson • Malcolm 'Mac' Murry
2011	Simon 'Snibs' Currer • Michael Aryes • Richard Skelly • Kuldip Manak
2012	Paul Smith • Pete Bell • Garry Whitfield • Alex Eaton • Adam Bennett • Kuldeep Singh • Rick (Birkett)Hayward
2013	Gerald Smith • Graham Cook • Huw Lloyd-Langton • Milan Lad • Darren Maud
2014	Martin 'Protag' Neish • Jed Turner • Maggie Boyle • Sam Carlisle
2015	Crispian Baker • Ian 'Tosh' Ward • Steve Hussein • Mary Johnson • Jim Towson
2016	Ashley Cartwright • Karl Dallas
2017	Allan Holdsworth • Rodney Bewes • Mark Tighe • Peter 'Bod' Haworth • Steve Wood • Joe Augustine • Jason Greenwood
2018	Malcolm Jackson • Richard Bolton • Rob Moore • Andy Watkins • Roy Bailey • Mick (Novak) Kershaw
2019	Andy Ashton
2020	Dan Durrant • Mike Sagar • John Jankovictz • Milo Zivanovic
2021	Barbara Moore • Terry Utterly
2022	Jules Vasylenko • Simon Goulding • Lee Abbott • Mick Raven • Gavin Wilkinson
2023	Gary Quinn • Alan Wormald • Tony McPhee • Brendan Croker • Bobby Oladujoye • Andy 'Tiddy' Wells • Benjamin Zephania • John Hyatt
2024	Kendra Farrar (nee Pashley) • Kay Russell • Robert 'Spyda' Leak • Bill Byford
2025	Tommy Hunt • John Fox • Vince Deary

...and to any others not listed above.

No one really ever dies.

1966 - 1982   BRADFORD'S NOISE OF THE VALLEYS - THE MUSIC

VOLUME 1 THE MUSIC CD 1

BNOTVCD001 1966-1976

1. *Allen Pound's Get Rich* - Searchin' In The Wilderness (Pound) © 1966 Toby Music
2. *The Accent* - Red Sky At Night (Davies/Beetham/Hebron/Birkett) © 1967 Getaway Songs
3. *The Outer Limits* - Great Train Robbery (Christie) © 1968 MCS Music Limited
4. *Love Affair* - Once Upon A Season (Michael Jackson) © 1968 Universal/Dick James Music Ltd
5. *Welfare State* - Silence Is Requested In The Ultimate Abyss (Coleman/Welfare State) © 1969 Copyright Control
6. *'Igginbottom* - Golden Lakes (Holdsworth) © 1969 Universal / Dick James Music Ltd
7. *Junior's Eyes* - White Llight (Wayne) © 1969 Onward Music Ltd
8. *Free Expression* – Nightmares (Peaker) © 1970 Terry Peaker
9. *Barbara Moore* - Hot Heels (Moore) © 1971 De Wolfe Ltd
10. *Jan Dukes de Grey* - The Cheering Crowd (Noy) © 1970 Derek Alan Noy
11. *Jonathan Swift* - Clever Headed Spell (Swift/Hamilton) © 1971 Jelly Music Ltd
12. *Moonkyte* - Blues For Boadicea (Stansfield) © 1971 Endomorph Publishing
13. *Rick Hayward* - Weasel (Hayward) © 1971 Blue Horizon
14. *Martin Carter* - British Man O'War (Trad.Arr. Carter) © 1972 Copyright Control
15. *Mountain Ash Band* - The Outcast (King/Cripps) © 1975 Witches Bane Music
16. *John Verity Band* - Hitch-hiker (Verity) © 1973 Carling Music Corp
17. *Lazy Days* - Wait For Me (Wilson/Shepard) © 1973/2001 Holyground
18. *Dave Lee Sound* - Down The Line (Montgomery/Petty/Holly) © 1975 MPL Communications Ltd
19. *Smokie* - Back To Bradford (Norman/Spencer) © 1975 Universal Music Publishing
20. *Phoenix* - Easy (Verity) © 1976 Nereus Music
21. *Kukulkan* - Lady Heatwave (Kukulkan) © 1976 Copyright Control

VOLUME 1 THE MUSIC CD 2

BNOTVC002 1977-1982

1. *First Aid* - Shape Of Things To Come/Nostradamus/Epilogue (Excerpts from Nostradamus) (Wormald/Parsons) © 1977 Palace Music
2. *The Negatives* - Stake Out (Robinson/Palmer/Stubbs) © 1979/2000 Tandiz Music Ltd
3. *Ulterior Motives* - Another Lover (Russell/Toczek) © 1979 Motive Music
4. *Eaten Alive By Insects* - John Wayne's Jacket (Phill Harding/Paton) © 1979 Copyright Control
5. *The Scene* - Hey Girl (Ian Harding) © 1980 Hole In The Wall Records
6. *Mysterious Footsteps* - White Dread (Stobbs) © 1980 Copyright Control
7. *The Invaders* - Japanese Dreams (Invaders) © 1980 Copyright Control
8. *Rhabstallion* - Chain Reaction (Thompson) © 1980 EMI Music Publishing Ltd
9. *Dawnwatcher* – Spellbound (Dawnwatcher) © 1980 Copyright Control
10. *New Model Army* - The Cause (Sullivan) © 1981 Intersong Music Ltd
11. *Chronic* – No Time (Chronic) © 1981 1Noise12 Publishing
12. *Living Dead* – Procession (Living Dead) © 1981 1Noise12 Publishing
13. *Southern Death Cult* - Moya (Live) (Astbury/Burrows/Jepson/Nawaz) © 1981 Warner Chappell Music Ltd
14. *Dial* - In Love This Year (Dial) © 1981 1Noise12 Publishing
15. *Fall Guys* - New Start (Fall Guys) © 1981 1Noise12 Publishing
16. *The Vindaloos* – Problems (Vindaloos) © 1982 1 Noise12 Publishing
17. *Height* - Looking Through Glass (Sadofski) © 1982 Useful Music

*Individual CD covers show for illustration purposes only. *The Music 1967-1987* comes in a vinyl sleeve with one cover insert, shown middle.
Compilations © 2009 Bradford Noise. Licensed by MCPS.
All tracks used courtesy of the original artists and copyright of the original recordings belongs to their individual owners.
All rights of the producer and the owner of the recorded works reserved. Unauthorised copying, hiring, public performance and broadcasting of this record prohibited.

BRADFORD NOISE RECORDS

VOLUME 1 THE MUSIC CD 3

BNOTVCD003 1982-1984

1. *Skeletal Family* - **Trees** (Greenwood/Hirst/Nowell) © 1982 Kassner Associated Publishers
2. *Holy Holy* - **The Judge** (Holy Holy) © 1982 Copyright Control
3. *1919* - **Storm** (Tighe/Tilleard/Reed/Madden) © 1983 Big Life Music Ltd
4. *Requiem* - **Spartan Life** (Requiem) © 1983 1Noise12 Publishing
5. *Stacc* - **Children Of The Night** (Stacc) © 1983 Copyright Control
6. *Anti-System* - **Service/1000 Rifles** (Nolan/Watts) © 1983 Centa Music
7. *The Negativz* - **Mental Case** (Pete Stobbs) © 1984 Pox Island/Mutiny 2000
8. *The Convulsions* - **Media Punx** (Webster/Armitage) © 1983 Mutiny 2000
9. *Seven Antelopes* - **Eat People** (Seven Antelopes) © 1983 1 Noise 12 Publishing
10. *Malcolm Hansson* - **The Naked Truth** (Hanson) © 1983 Copyright Control
11. *Spectre* - **Ideal Home** (Spectre) © 1984 1Noise12 Publishing
12. *Men From The Mountains* - **Trembling** (Harding/Bough/Waddington) © 1984 1 Noise 12 Publishing
13. *The Word* – **Immaculate** (The Word) © 1984 Menace Music
14. *Morbid Humour* - **Oh My God** (Parts 1&2) (Morbid Humour) © 1984 Copyright Control
15. *The Nerve Agents* - **To And Fro** (Sheeran) © 1984 Home Brewed Music
16. *Vegetable Section* - **Fruitcake Jake** (Arron/Canmer) © 1985 1 Noise 12 Publishing
17. *Swamp Flower* - **Swamp Flower** (Ingham/Leith/Webster) © 1985 Home Brewed Music
18. *Joolz* - **Audience Participation** (Denby) © 1982 1Noise12 Publishing
19. *Seething Wells* - **Tetley Bittermen** (Stephen Wells) © 1982 1 Noise 12 Publishing
20. *Wild Willi Beckett* - **Privilege** (Beckett) © 1982 1 Noise 12 Publishing
21. *Little Brother* - **Land Of The Rising?** (Stockell/Austin) © 1982 Sixty Three

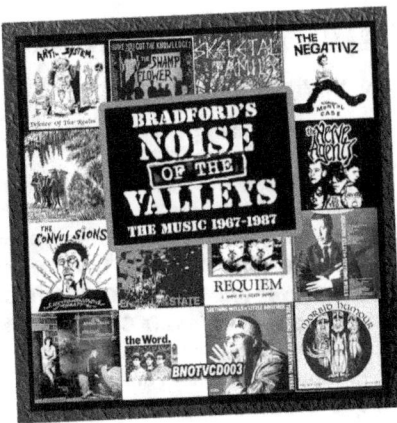

VOLUME 1 THE MUSIC CD 4

BNOTVC004 1985-1987

1. *Brendan Croker & The 5 O'Clock Shadows* - **Hard Times** (Skip James) © 1985 Wynwood Music Co Inc
2. *Domestic Enemies* - **Tiny Minds** (Domestic Enemies) © 1985 1 Noise1 2 Publishing
3. *Boys From The East* - **Young & Beautiful** (Boys from the East) © 1985 1 Noise 12 Publishing
4. *Passmore Sisters* - **Strong For Europe** (Taylor/Sadofski/Lee/Richardson) © 1985 1 Noise 12 Publishing
5. *Still Life* - **She Don't Care** (John/Burns/Walker) © 1985 1Noise12 Publishing
6. *Doctor & The Inmates* - **Never A Rebel** (Beckett) © 1985 QTA/Mutiny 2000
7. *The Skidmarks* - **Dirty Old Man** (Skidmarks) © 1986 Copyright Control
8. *Britanarchists (Nick Toczek & Spectre)* - **Sheer Funk** (Toczek) © 1986 Nick Toczek
9. *The Best Way To Walk* - **Unbelievable** (Ware/Flynn/Bryson/O'Conner) © 1986 Sony Music Ltd
10. *Happiness Ad* - **Geburrah** (Rob Moore) © 1986 Copyright Control/Flexible Response
11. *Psycho Surgeons* - **Give A Man A Badge** (Beckett) © 1986 QTA/Mutiny 2000
12. *Western Dance* - **This Perfect Day** (Andrews) © 1987 Home Brewed Music
13. *Verity* - **Are You Ready For This?** (Verity) © 1983 Verity Music
14. *Siren* - **American Girl** (Cook) © 1984 Distant Cousins
15. *Bobo* - **Tall Talk & Rocking Horse Tales** (Bobo) © 1985 Copyright Control
16. *Excalibur* - **I'm Telling You** (Solynskyj/McBride) © 1985 Solynskyj McBride
17. *Voyager UK* - **Don't Hold Back** (Voyager) © 1985 Copyright Control
18. *Tuxedo* - **Set Me Free** (Clarke/Erdos/Lumb/Noonan) © 1986 Copyright Control
19. *Baby Tuckoo* - **I'm Your Man** (Armitage/Barrott/Saxton/Smith/Sugden) © 1986 Derek Savage Music Ltd
20. *Harlequyn* – **Caroseul** (Mother/Walker) © 1987 Copyright Control
21. *Somebody's Brother* – **Soweto** (Austin/Lord/Neen) © 1987 Tinza
22. *The Crowd* – **You'll Never Walk Alone** (Rogers/Hammerstein) © 1985 EMI Music Publishing Limited

*Individual CD covers show for illustration purposes only. *The Music 1967-1987* comes in a vinyl sleeve with one cover insert, shown middle.
Compilations © 2009 Bradford Noise. Licensed by MCPS.
All tracks used courtesy of the original artists and copyright of the original recordings belongs to their individual owners.
All rights of the producer and the owner of the recorded works reserved. Unauthorised copying, hiring, public performance and broadcasting of this record prohibited.

BRADFORD NOISE RECORDS

1964 - 1987   BRADFORD'S NOISE OF THE VALLEYS - THE MISSING MUSIC 1 & 2

THE MISSING MUSIC

BNOTVCD005 1964-1987

1. **The Thimbleriggers** - Beg, Borrow Or Steal (Thimbleriggers)
   © 1964 Copyright Control
2. **The Financial Tymes** - All Or Nothing (Marriot/Lane)
   © 1964 Aquarius Music Ltd
3. **The Cresters** - Put Your Arms Around Me (Vandyke) © 1964 TRO Essex Music Ltd
4. **Barbara Moore** - I Found Love (Moore) © 1967 Maxwood Music Ltd
5. **The Outer Limits** - Just One More Chance (Christie) © 1967 Ambassador Music ltd
6. **The Accent** - Winds Of Change (Davies/Hebron/Beetham/Birketts)
   © 1967 Peterman & Co Ltd
7. **Ellison's Hogline** - Funk Bag (Ellison's Hogline) © 1968 Copyright Control
8. **The Bradfords** - Bonnie & Clyde (Georgie Fame) © 1971 Copyright Control
9. **Kiki Dee** - Someone To Me (Dee) © 1974 Rocket Music Ltd
10. **Hebric** - Three Drunken Maidens (Traditional) © 1976 Public Domain
11. **Shadowfax** - Really Into You (Unnuk) © 1979 Copyright Control
12. **Dedringer** - Maxine (Dedringer) © 1981 Copyright Control
13. **Catch 22** - Bantam Anthem (Catch 22) © 1985 Copyright Control
14. **Diamond Light** - Fly Me Wind (Steven Long/Diamond Light) © 1983 Copyright Control
15. **Susan Fassbender** - Twilight Cafe (Fassbender/Russell) © 1980 Bocu Musioc Ltd
16. **The Elements** - Kill Yourself (Taylor) © 1981 Keith Ian Taylor
17. **Teenage & The Wildlife** - Get The Hell Out Of Here (Teenage & The Wildlife) © 1981 Copyright Control
18. **The Shakes** - I Kill God (Cartwright) © 1981 Copyright Control
19. **Muggins Blight** - Mr Somebody (Muggins Blight) © 1981 Copyright Control
20. **Getting The Fear** - Last Salute (Nawaz/Burrows/Jepson/Hampshire) © 1984 Chappell Music Ltd / Universal Music Publishing
21. **Ghost Dance** - When I Call (Marx) © 1986 Copyright Control
22. **Zodiac Mindwarp & The Love Reaction** - Planet Girl (Manning) © 1987 Warner Chappell Music Ltd

THE MISSING MUSIC 2

BNOTVC006 1972-1987

1. *Jonathon Swift* - Lonely Trip (Swift) © 1972 Rondor Music Ltd / Mum & Dad Music
2. *Swan Arcade* - The Battle Of Sowerby Bridge (Trad/Boyes/Brady/Brady) © 1972 Northworks
3. *Roger Sutcliffe* - Death Letter Came This Morning (Trad/Sutcliffe/Newborn) © 1976 Copyright Control
4. *Highly Likely* - Whatever Happened To You (Hugg/La Frenais) © 1973 Mann Music Publishers Ltd
5. *Smokey* - A Day At The Mother-In-Law's (Silson) © 1975 Rak Music Publishers Ltd
6. *Midnight Hearse* - We're Gonna Have A New World Champion (Jowett/Jones/Jowett) © 1976 Copyright Control
7. *Welfare State* - Come Away, Come Away (Holland/Trad) © 1978 Copyright Control
8. *Middle 8* - Misadventure (Cass) © 1980 Copyright Control
9. *The Invaders* - Girl's In Action (Invaders) © 1979 Copyright Control
10. *Cameras In Cars* - Avoid A Void (Sadofski/Beckham) © 1980 In Cinc Music
11. *Harsh Words* - Busy Man (Mann) © 1980 1 Noise 12 Publishing Inc
12. *Edible Marquetry* - Dust (Edible Marquetry) © 1981 1 Noise 12 Publishing Inc
13. *Radio 5* - True Colours (Cotton/Haran/Hayes/Groves) © 1981 PLD Ltd
14. *New Model Army* - Bittersweet (Sullivan/Morrow) © 1983 Watteau Music / Intersong
15. *Hindle Pickets* - Part Of The Union (Hudson/Ford) © 1984 Peermusic UK / TRO Essex
16. *Siren* - Deceiving Lies (Neen/Cook) © 1984 Distant Cousins
17. *Excalibur* - Come On And Rock (McBride/Solynskyj/Hawthorn) © 1985 Sus Music
18. *Western Dance* - Scream Out (Sheeran/Andrews) © 1986 Home Brewed Music
19. *John Verity* - Two Hearts Burning (Verity/Thompson) © 1987 Verity Music / Gus Songs
20. *Bad News* - Bad News (Fuego/Brint) © 1987 Channel 4 / Chappell Music Ltd

Compilations © 2011, 2013 Bradford Noise. Licensed by MCPS.
All tracks used courtesy of the original artists and copyright of the original recordings belongs to their individual owners.
All rights of the producer and the owner of the recorded works reserved. Unauthorised copying, hiring, public performance and broadcasting of this record prohibited.

BRADFORD'S NOISE OF THE VALLEYS - THE MUSIC VOL 2   1988 - 1998

VOLUME 2 THE MUSIC CD 1
BNOTCD007 1988-1996

1 **The Godfathers** - Birth, School, Work, Death (Coyne/Coyne/Dollimore/Mazur/Gibson) © 1988 SM Publishing (UK) Limited
2 **Seven Dead Americans** - Night Of The Living Dead (Wood/Lyon/Clarke/Hooper) © 1988 Copyright Control
3 **The Spurs** - Soldier (Horsfall) © 1988 Horsfall
4 **Thundering Hearts** - Caught Red Handed (Thundering Hearts) © 1988 Copyright Control
5 **Little Brother** - SS Spies (Stockell/Austin/Stockell) © 1988 Sixty Three
6 **Symphony In X** - Dreams Never Die (Cattlin/Cass) © 1989 Madigan/King/MacDonald
7 **Pride** - Mercenary Man (Madigan/MacDonald/King) © 1989 Madigan/King/MacDonald
8 **Kage Engineering** - Whistling (Binder/Binder/Shaw/Saddington) © 1989 Artlos Music
9 **The Hollow Men** - White Train (Hosein/Taylor/Roberts/Owen/Cragg) © 1989 Hollow Men
10 **Dubh Chapter** - Touch And Go (Mann/Quinn/Staunton/Staunton) © 1990 Universal Music MGB
11 **The Wonderful Thing Called Tiddles** - Where Has Everybody Gone? (WTCT) © 1990 1 Noise 12 Publishing
12 **The Miracle Mile** - What Became Of Monty (Nemes/Jones) © 1990 Nemes/Jones
13 **The Orange World Of Titan** - Big Baby (Whittaker) © 1990 Whittaker
14 **Poppy Factory** - 7x7 (Cotton/Binns/Dale) © 1991 Universal Music Publishing
15 **The Headmen** - Reach The Sky (Eskriett/Pattern/Slater/Keene) © 1991 Copyright Control
16 **For What** - Clear (For What) © 1994 Voltage
17 **Summum Bonum** - Exploding Raindrops (Mitchell) © 1994 Copyright Control
18 **Comic Book Heroes** - Changing (Comic Book Heroes) © 1995 Copyright Control

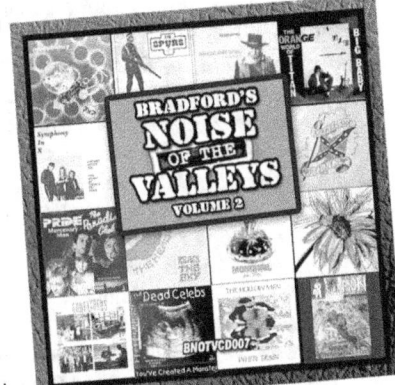

VOLUME 2 THE MUSIC CD 2 - FOLK / BLUES / WORLD MUSIC
BNOTVCD008 1988-1998

1 **Jane Harrison** - If You Leave Me Now (Cetera) © 1988 Universal Music Pub/Spirit Music Pub
2 **Kevin Young** - Hello Little One (Song For Adam) (Trad./Young) © 1988 Young
3 **Old Joe Zydeco** - Zydeco Gris Gris (Trad./Tothill) © 1989 1 Noise 12 Publishing Inc
4 **The Everly Sisters** - Inside/Outside (Harris) © 1989 1 Noise 12 Publishing Inc
5 **Heart Of Darkness** - The Storm (Jackson/Ram) © 1989 1 Noise 12 Publishing Inc
6 **Uncle Ted Grundy** - Sacred Cow (Chapman) © 1989 1 Noise 12 Publishing Inc
7 **Not Precious** - Nightmares (Hill/Bayliss) © 1989 1 Noise 12 Publishing Inc
8 **Mary & Chris** - Dam(n) Your Eyes (Halliwell) © 1990 Oval Music Ltd
9 **Natural Rhythm** - Bluebeat & Ska (Boyce) © 1991 Kassner Associated Pub
10 **Roger Higgins** - Take Me Back To Mississippi (Higgins) © 1994 Higgins
11 **Cajun Aces** - Chere Joues Roses (Trad./Cajun Aces) © 1994 Copyright Control
12 **Crone** - Rain (Crone) © 1994 Crone Music
13 **Scarlet Heights** - The Scarcity Prayer (Sherry/Broadbent) © 1995 Scarlet Music
14 **Shiny Beast** - Ed Wood (Hennessy) © 1996 Mutiny 2000
15 **Milan Lad** - Witch Hazel (G Stewart) © 1995 Swall World Records Limited
16 **Loobie** - It Fascinates Me (Maclean) © 1996 Limetree Arts & Music
17 **Phil Gilbert** - Gideon Here (Gilbert) © 1997 Second Chance Music
18 **Grace Notes** - The Quiet Land Of Erin (Traditional) © 1998 Copyright Control

This compilation © 2013 Bradford Noise. Licensed by MCPS.
All tracks used courtesy of the original artists and copyright of the original recordings belongs to their individual owners.
All rights of the producer and the owner of the recorded works reserved. Unauthorised copying, hiring, public performance and broadcasting of this record prohibited.

BRADFORD NOISE RECORDS

1990 - 1998   BRADFORD'S NOISE OF THE VALLEYS - THE MUSIC VOL 2

VOLUME 2 THE MUSIC CD 3
BNOTVCD009 1990-1998

1. *Tasmin Archer* - **Sleeping Satellite** (Archer/Beck/Hughes) © 1992 Beck/Nettwerk One Music Ltd
2. *Psycho Surgeons* - **Panic On!** (Beckett/Gambles/Hoey/Kirkley) © 1990 QTA/Mutiny 2000
3. *Bomb Everything* - **Just Like Mine** (Cooper/Prytherch) © 1990 Imagem London Limited
4. *Slammer* - **What's Your Pleasure?** (Annecchini/Gagic/Tunnicliffe/Zivanovic) © 1991 Slammer
5. *Station West* - **Love Calling** (Station West) © 1991 T-Bone Records
6. *Threshold Shift* - **Cardboard City** (Threshold Shift) © 1992 Threshold Shift
7. *Egomania* - **Cool, Calm And Collected** (Gibbons) © 1994 Copyright Control
8. *Paul Mother* - **Till Dawn** (Bolan) © 1993 Spirit Music Publishing Limited
9. *Grim* - **Grim** (Watson/Bennett) © 1995 Mutiny 2000
10. *Screaming Life* - **Away** (Screaming Life) © 1995 Copyright Control
11. *Rollercoaster* - **Modern Man** (Rollercoaster) © 1995 Copyright Control
12. *Far Fetched* - **Clumsy** (Cichy) © 1994 Copyright Control
13. *Chest* - **Angels** (Chest) © 1996 Copyright Control
14. *Lional Blairs* - **Wishing Your Life Away** (Stubbs/Pickard) © 1996 Copyright Control
15. *Blister Factory* - **Coming Good** (Blister Factory) © 1996 Copyright Control
16. *Vochi* - **Please** (Vochi) © 1996 Naracen Musik
17. *Embrace* - **All You Good Good People** (McNamara/McNamara) © 1997 EMI Music Pub Ltd
18. *The Auxiliary Of Real Men* - **Brown Love** (Bateson) © 1998 Copyright Control
19. *Fundamental* - **Godevil** (Qureshi) © 1998 Copyright Control

VOLUME 2 THE MUSIC CD 4
BNOTVCD010 1990-1998

1. *Zed* - **Easy Does It** (Watson/Nolan/Farrar) © 1990 QTA/Mutiny 2000
2. *Loud* - **D Generation** (McLaughlin) © 1990 Universal Music Publishing Ltd
3. *Primate* - **Break My Fall** (Andrews) © 1992 Mutiny 2000
4. *Bobby Charltons* - **Bastard Town** (Quinn) © 1991 Copyright Control
5. *The Big Bang* - **Gangland** (Big Bang) © 1990 Copyright Control
6. *Wicked Rich* - **Rebel** (Wicked Rich) © 1990 Copyright Control
7. *Mr Meana* - **Social Elite** (Mr Meana) © 1991 Mean Music
8. *Architect* - **Set Me On Fire** (Cunningham/Walker) © 1992 Voltage Records
9. *Krakatoa* - **Poison** (Krakatoa) © 1992 Copyright Control
10. *New Model Army & Tom Jones* - **Gimme Shelter** (Jagger/Richards) © 1993 Abkco Music Ltd/Onward Music Ltd/Westminster Music Ltd
11. *Tiny Monroe* - **VHF855V** (Wilow) © 1994 Wilow
12. *Psyche* - **Skimming Stones** (McKendrick/Chrisanthou) © 1994 Flux Music
13. *Blood Orange* - **Why** (Blood Orange) © 1995 Copyright Control
14. *Ripcord* - **You (Anytime, Anyplace, Anywhere)** (Ripcord) © 1995 Copyright Control
15. *Facelift* - **It's Alright** (Facelift) © 1996 Copyright Control
16. *Twister 5* - **Barbara** (Twister 5) © 1996 Copyright Control
17. *Terrorvision* - **Perseverance** (Marklew/Shuttleworth/Wright/Yates) © 1996 Touch Tones Music Ltd
18. *Bullweek* - **Superglue Star** (Sheeran) © 1996 Copyright Control
19. *Slack* - **In Our World** (Nolan) © 1996 Copyright Control
20. *Nowt* - **Another Bloody Blustry Day In Bradford** (Hennessy/Bennett) © 1998 Mutiny 2000

This compilation © 2013 Bradford Noise. Licensed by MCPS.
All tracks used courtesy of the original artists and copyright of the original recordings belongs to their individual owners.
All rights of the producer and the owner of the recorded works reserved. Unauthorised copying, hiring, public performance and broadcasting of this record prohibited.

BRADFORD'S NOISE OF THE VALLEYS - THE MUSIC VOL 2   1988 - 1998

VOLUME 2 THE MUSIC CD 5 - HARDCORE / METAL / THRASH

BNOTVCD011 1988-1998

1 *Toranaga* - Bastard Ballads (Toranaga) © 1988 Copyright Control
2 *Sore Throat* - Eric Pickles Is A Fat Tory Bastard (Sore Throat) © 1989 1 Noise 12 Inc
3 *The Next World* - Respect The Earth (Ward/Roue) © 1989 1 Noise 12 Publishing Inc
4 *One By One* - Shop Me (One By One) © 1990 1 Noise 12 Publishing Inc
5 *Health Hazard* - Not Just A Nightmare (Health Hazard) © 1992 1 Noise 12 Publishing Inc
6 *Wartorn* - Armed Response (Wartorn) © 1992 1 Noise 12 Publishing Inc
7 *Paradise Lost* - Gothic (Mackintosh/Holmes) © 1991 Imagem London Limited
8 *Chorus Of Ruin* - Dreaming Of Indigo (Chorus Of Ruin) © 1993 Avantegarde Music
9 *Solstice* - The Revenant (Solstice) © 1993 Copyright Control
10 *Ironside* - Skincrawl (Ironside) © 1993 Copyright Control
11 *Witchknot* - Pianist Envy (Witchknot) © 1994 Copyright Control
12 *Dark Embrace* - Dark Embrace (Dark Embrace) © 1995 Copyright Control
13 *Dawnraiser* - Holy Lies (Dawnraiser) © 1996 Copyright Control
14 *Serenity* - The Way I Bleed (Serenity) © 1996 Holy Records
15 *Doom* - (We Hate The) Brew Crew (Talbot/Dickens/Croft/Gladock) © 1996 1 Noise 12 Publishing Inc
16 *VR* - Intolerance (Ward/Roue/Talbot) © 1995 1 Noise 12 Publishing Inc
17 *Voorhees* - Fucker (Leck/Readman/Rogman-Jones/Nichols/Gillham) © 1996 1 Noise 12 Publishing Inc
18 *Stalingrad* - The Politics Of Ecstacy (Allison/Claxton/Snell/Wood) © 1996 1 Noise 12 Publishing Inc
19 *Hardware* - What Race Are You? (Hardware) © 1996 Copyright Control
20 *Purity Cries* - Division (Purity Cries) © 1998 Copyright Control

VOLUME 2 THE MUSIC CD 6 - DANCE

BNOTVCD012 1990-1998

1 *Unique 3* - Rhythm Takes Control (Brown/Collins/Parke/Cargill) © 1990 The Int Music Network
2 *Push Button Technology* - Just 4 U (PBT) © 1992 Copyright Control
3 *Rodeo Jones* - Shades Of Summer (Copland/Plato/Tretton) © 1993 Tretton/Plato/Copeland
4 *Monument* - I Like It (Guitar Mix) (Edit) (Annecchini/Cargill/Khan) © 1994 Copyright Control
5 *Mystic Light* - In Casa Bella (Funk Mix) (Edit) (Annecchini/Cargill/Khan) © 1994 Copyright Control
6 *Glamorous Hooligan* - New Age Pension (Annecchini/Cavanagh) © 1995 Universal Music Pub
7 *Detrimental* - Babylon (Detrimental) © 1994 Copyright Control
8 *Dayiah* - Storm Clouds (Dayiah) © 1995 Thrd Eye Music
9 *Sansaar* - Bind Us Together (Global Scale Mix) (Bolloten/Rootsman) © 1995 Third Eye Music
10 *King's Highway* - Temple Of Light (Low Rider Mix) (Rootsman/Davemet) © 1995 Third Eye Music
11 *Strongpoint* - Perilous Time (Stop The War Mix) (Rootsman/Monument) © 1995 Third Eye Music
12 *Rootsman* - Old Pan Killer (Rootsman) © 1995 Third Eye Music
13 *Doctor Man* - Comin' In Style (Doctor Man) © 1996 DMP
14 *Pianoman* - Blurred (Albarn/Coxon/James/Rowntree/Dabney) © 1996 Universal/MCA Music Ltd/Garber Music Ltd
15 *Angeles* - Hi Horse (Edit) (Welsh/Cartledge) © 1998 Cartledge/Proof Songs Limited

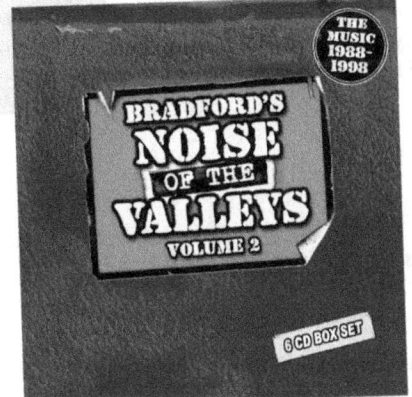

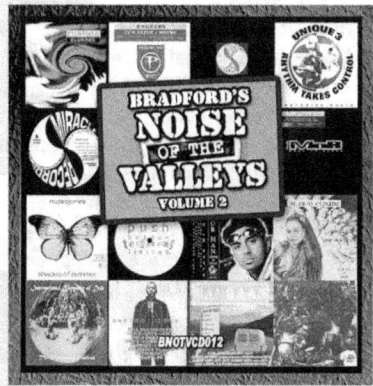

This compilation © 2013 Bradford Noise. Licensed by MCPS.
All tracks used courtesy of the original artists and copyright of the original recordings belongs to their individual owners.
All rights of the producer and the owner of the recorded works reserved. Unauthorised copying, hiring, public performance and broadcasting of this record prohibited.

BRADFORD NOISE RECORDS

1966 - 1998   BRADFORD'S NOISE OF THE VALLEYS - THE MISSING MUSIC 3 & 4

THE MISSING MUSIC 3

BNOTVCD013 1966-1988

1. *Champion Jack Dupree* - Third Degree (Boyd) © 1966 Decca Record Copmany Ltd
2. *Jude Brown Band* - Green Light (Brown) © 1967 Copyright Control
3. *Tree* - Secrets (Tree) © 1969 Copyright Control
4. *Root & Jenny Jackson* - Lean On Me (Vann/arr. Morehouse) © 1969 Copyright Control
5. *Jan Dukes De Grey* - Sorcerers (Jan Dukes De Grey) © 1969 Copyright Control
6. *Janet Jones* - November 1837 (E. Bronte/Jones) © 1976 Copyright Control
7. *Liz Narey* - Ships Out Of Sligo (Narey/Collens) © 1982 Copyright Control
8. *Ocean* - It's Alright (Quinn) © 1975 Copyright Control
9. *Phobia* - One More Vice (Skelly) © 1976 1 Noise 12 Publishing Inc
10. *Vex* - Project Alien Emotion (Tyson/Pickard/Ironmonger/Binns) © 1980 Copyright Control
11. *Dawnwatcher* - Firing On All Eight (Barton/Richardson) © 1980 EMI Music Ltd
12. *Baby Tuckoo* - Things (Baby Tuckoo) © 1984 Copyright Control
13. *Allan Holdsworth* - Tokyo Dreams (Holdsworth) © 1983 Warner Bros Records Inc
14. *Joolz* - War Of Attrition (Joolz/Jah Wobble) © 1983 Copyright Control
15. *Anti System* - Take A Look At Life (Anti System) © 1984 Copyright Control
16. *Anjana* - Nachna Pia (Kuldip Manak/Sat Paul) © 1985 Copyright Control
17. *Jab Jab* - Pity (C&J Augustine) © 1985 Rip Off Records
18. *Guido* - I'm Alone (Peters/Fahy/Fortune/Maal) © 1986 Prism Records Ltd
19. *Secret People* - China (Denby/McKendrick/Siddall) © 1987 Zomba Music Publishing Ltd
20. *Sloan Square East (Hansaid)* - Hands Reach Out (Dirkin/Dutson-Bromley/Otychel/Isles/Zielinski) © 1988 Sloane Square East
21. *Bradford Kids* - Christmas Song (Bradford Kids) © 1988 Copyright Control

THE MISSING MUSIC 4

BNOTVC014 1989-1998

1. *Twice Around The Houses* - Early Learning (Horton/TATH) © 1989 Copyright Control
2. *Arise* - Agouti (Wood/Lyon/Clarke/Hooper) © 1993 Copyright Control
3. *Gorgeous* - The Chill (Maude) © 1993 Copyright Control
4. *Mash-M* - Collateral Damage (Mash-M) © 1993 Copyright Control
5. *Beer Beast* - Ilkley Moor (Trad arr. Beer Beast) © 1995 Copyright Control
6. *Liberty Scream* - Control (Liberty Scream) © 1995 Copyright Control
7. *Mannix* - F.O.C. (Mannix) © 1995 Copyright Control
8. *Trip And Stumble* - The Ovaltinies (Harry Hemsley) © 1994 Copyright Control
9. *Smokie featuring Roy 'Chubby' Brown* - Living Next Door To Alice (Who The F*** Is Alice?) (Chinn/Chapman) © 1995 State Music Ltd / Chinnichap Publishing Ltd
10. *Anita Madigan* - The Dalai Lama (Loves You All) (Madigan/King) © 1995 On The Floor
11. *Blade* - Love And War (Allen) © 1995 Copyright Control
12. *Rattlesnake Shake* - Some Like It Hot (Rattlesnake Shake) © 1989 Copyright Control
13. *Lost Weekend* - Is It Love? (D Thompson) © 1996 ASP / EMI Music Publishing Ltd
14. *Zed* - White Knuckle Ride (Watson/Baker/Webster) © 1997 Mutiny 2000
15. *Dragster* - Meteorite (Dragster) © 1997 Copyright Control
16. *My Dying Bride* - It Will Come (My Dying Bride) © 1996 Peaceville Records
17. *Worm* - Cybersex (Arnfield/Walker) © 1998 Voltage
18. *L'Orchestre Du Cafe* - Dark Eyes (Borodin) © 1998 Copyright Control

Compilations © 2017, 2019 Bradford Noise. Licensed by MCPS.
All tracks used courtesy of the original artists and copyright of the original recordings belongs to their individual owners.
All rights of the producer and the owner of the recorded works reserved. Unauthorised copying, hiring, public performance and broadcasting of this record prohibited.

BRADFORD'S NOISE OF THE VALLEYS - THE MISSING MUSIC 5 & 6   1966 - 1996

THE MISSING MUSIC 5

BNOTVCD015 1966-1996

1. *Three Good Reasons* - Nowhere Man (Lennon/McCartney) © 1966 Sony/ATV Music Publishing
2. *Linda Russell* - We've Got A Need For Each Other (Trad: Martin/Miller) © 1969 Lollipop Music Corp
3. *Hogsnort Rupert's Original Flagon Band* - Pretty Girl (Luther) © 1970 Ardmore & Beechwood Ltd
4. *Rivington Pike* - Wish A Little Love (Ashford) © 1972 Decca Records Co Ltd
5. *Kindness* - Lonely Long Lady (Kelly/Norman/Silson/Uttley) © 1973 Luddington House Music
6. *Jovial Crew* - Johnny Lad (Trad: Jovial Crew) © 1973 Multiple Music
7. *Janet Jones* - Silver Coin (Jones) © 1974 Winter Music Ltd
8. *Moonchild* - Hour Glass (Ray Sherwin) © 1975 Look Records
9. *Hebric* - Blow The Candles Out (Trad: Hebric) © 1978 Copyright Control
10. *The Collection* - Spinning Wheel (DC Thomas) © 1976 EMI Music Publishing Ltd
11. *Kiki Dee & Elton John* - Don't Go Breaking My Heart (Ann Orson/Carte Blanche) © 1976 Universal Music Publishing Ltd
12. *The Donkeys* - Four Letters (Ferguson) © 1979 Ferguson
13. *Silver Screen Girls* - Photographs (Whitaker) © 1980 Siren Records
14. *Excel* - Rock Show (Smith/Taylor) © 1980 EMI Music Publishing Ltd
15. *The Invaders* - Rock Methodology (Sidelnyk) © 1980 Maxwood Music Ltd
16. *Stormtrooper* - Grind 'n' Heat (Thompson/King/Wilkinson/Wadkin) © 1980 EMI Music Publishing Ltd
17. *Titan* - Imaginary Lady (Whitaker) © 1983 Leola Music Ltd
18. *Rebecca Storm* - The Wrong Girl (Walmsley/Findon) © 1986 EMI Music Publishing Ltd
19. *Talulah Gosh* - Beatnik Boy (Fletcher/Price/Scott/Fletcher/Momtchiloff) © 1986 Bucks Music Group Ltd
20. *Clocks & Clouds* - Have A Heart (For The Children) (McAndrew/Griffin) © 1989 Ha Ha Records
21. *The Godfathers* - She Gives Me Love (Coyne/Coyne/Dollimore/Mazur/Gibson) © 1989 SM Publishing (UK) Ltd
22. *Legend* - Cry For Me (Denning/Richardson) © 1993 Reckless Rhino Records
23. *Clouded Fish* - Expect (Clouded Fish) © 1996 In Yer Face Records

THE MISSING MUSIC 6

BNOTVCD016 1970-1997

1. *Rodney Bewes* - Dear Mother, Love Albert (Hugg/Bewes) © 1970 Carling Music
2. *Tempest* - Brothers (Hiseman/Holdsworth) © 1973 Tempest Music
3. *Argent* - Rock 'n' Roll Show (Argent) © 1975 Verulam Music
4. *Tommy Hunt* - One Fine Morning (Eddy Adamberry/Tony Craig) © 1976 Peer Music
5. *Pheonix* - Mississippi Neckbone (Rodford) © 1976 Nereus Music
6. *Stormer* - My Home Town (Brassington/Hughes/David) © 1978 Brasshog Music/David Martin Music
7. *Fassbender-Russell* - Stay (Fassbender/Russell) © 1981 Bocu Music Ltd
8. *Boys From The East* - Eastern Eyes (Clayton/Rahman/Rajwadi) © 1984 Copyright Control
9. *Skeletal Family* - She Cries Alone (Greenwood/Hurst/Nowell) © 1984 Kassner Associated Pub
10. *The Answering Machine* - Night Time Radio (Walker/Burns/John) © 1987 Playground Sounds
11. *New Model Army* - Green & Grey (Sullivan/Heaton) © 1989 Attack-Attack Music
12. *The Headmen* - Kissed To Pieces (Eskriett) © 1990 Very Positive Music
13. *New Musical Testament* - Joy (Zinyuku/Reid/Deacon) © 1992 Survival Records
14. *Rootsman* - Tremors (Bollenton) © 1996 Third Eye Music
15. *John Harvison* - Mask (Harvison) © 1995 Drive On Records
16. *Grim* - Fuckin' Weird Mate (Bennett/Hennessy) © 1997 Mutiny 2000 Records

THE SPORTS SECTION

17. *Trevor Hockey* - Happy 'Cos i'm Blue (Dienham/Lewthwaite/Sealey) © 1970 Kassner Associated Pub
18. *Bradford City AFC* - You Know We're Going To Win (Gordon Lorenz) © 1987 Lorenz/Cornerways Music
19. *Joe Johnson* - Bradford (Bouncing Back) (D Lawrence) © 1987 The Bacon Empire Publishing Ltd
20. *Bradford Bulls feat. Robbie Paul & Anita Madigan* - Run With The Bulls (Madigan/King/Paul) © 1996 On The Floor Records

Compilations © 2017, 2019 Bradford Noise. Licensed by MCPS.
All tracks used courtesy of the original artists and copyright of the original recordings belongs to their individual owners.
All rights of the producer and the owner of the recorded works reserved. Unauthorised copying, hiring, public performance and broadcasting of this record prohibited.

1968 - 1996 BRADFORD'S NOISE OF THE VALLEYS - THE MISSING MUSIC 7 & 8

THE MISSING MUSIC 7
BNOTVCDCD017 1968-1996

1 *Love Affair* - **A Day Without Love** (Phillip Goodhand-Tait) © 1968 Universal/Dick James Music
2 *Rick Hayward* - **Find Yourself Sometime** (Hayward) © 1971 Uncle Doris Music
3 *Steve Tilston* - **Falling** (Tilston) © 1972 Logo Songs Ltd
4 *The Dave Lee Sound* - **Instant Loneliness** (Duncan) © 1975 Universal Music Publishing
5 *Jasper* - **She's Not There** (Argent) © 1978 Marquis Music Co Ltd
6 *Roy Sunholm* - **East To West** (Roy Sunholm) © 1981 Dizzy Heights Music Publishing Ltd
7 *Another Cinema* - **Hallucinations Spires I** (Another Cinema) © 1984 Altered States
8 *Nick Toczek with Burial* - **Stiff With A Quiff** (Toczek/Burial) © 1984 Copyright Control
9 *Single File* - **Out In The Traffic** (Westhead) © 1984 Main Line Record Co
10 *The Passmore Sisters* - **All I Need Is Change** (Sadofski/Taylor/Roberts/Grace) © 1987 Sharp
11 *Brendan Croker & The 5 O'Clock Shadows* - **Lonely Boy In Town**
    (Trad. Arr. Croker/Shadows) © 1987 Endomorph Music Publishing
12 *Jah Bertie* - **Isn't it Lovely Girl** (Keith Goldson) © 1978 Graffiti Records
13 *New Horizon feat. Janet Gordon* - **Here With You**
    (Fontaine/Gordon/McFarlane) © 1989 Quatro World Music
14 *Desoto* - **Turn Your Love Around** (Poole) © 1990 Universal Music Publishing
15 *Dub Kitchen* - **Criminal Justice** (Fran Jones) © 1994 Copyright Control
16 *Slammer* - **Insanity Addicts** (Slammer) © 1990 Copyright Control
17 *Vanishing Point* - **I'm Gonna Win** (Tattersfield) © 1990 EMI Music Publishing Ltd
18 *Bedlam* - **The Plague** (Bedlam) © 1991 Copyright Control
19 *Monorail* - **Between Here & Somewhere** (Fretwell) © 1996 Edel UK Records Ltd

THE MISSING MUSIC 8
BNOTVCD018 1968-1996

1 *John's Followers* - **Crystal Mountain** (Andy Pickles) © 1968 Copyright Control
2 *Zenith Band* - **So Far Away** (Avington Ledwidge) © 1970 Carlin Music Delaware LLC
3 *Catherine Howe* - **Hot Night** (Howe) © 1975 Carlin Music Delaware LLC
4 *Roger Sutcliffe* - **Slow Drag** (Traditional) © 1976 Copyright Control
5 *The Yorkshire Miracle* - **The Redeeming Grace** (Tim Moon) © 1977 Look Records
6 *Bracken* - **Land O' The Leal** (Traditional) © 1979 Copyright Control
7 *The Negatives* - **We're From Bradford** (Robinson/Stobbs/Palmer) © 1980 Tandiz Music Ltd
8 *Kit Rolfe* - **The Wizard** (Rolfe/Pottinger) © 1980 Heath-Levy Music Co Ltd
9 *Ocean* - **Don't Want You To Love Me** (Cairns/Lee) © 1980 Little Black Plastic Records
10 *Chainsaw* - **Lonely Without You** (Chainsaw) © 1980 Copyright Control
11 *Rockabilly Rebs* - **Boothill Boogie** (Strain/Scholey/Lynch/Harrison/Harrison)
    © 1981 Nervous Publishing
12 *Tea House Camp* - **To Kill: Stab In The Back** (Scurrah/Staunton) © 1985 Real Men Records
13 *The Word* - **Schoolboy Saint** (Bahr/Cotton/MacDonald/Singh) © 1985 Abstract Dance
14 *Happiness Ad* - **Love Can Be Cruel** (Burli/Moore) © 1985 Queensbury Music
15 *FM* - **I Belong To The Night** (S Overland/C Overland) © 1986 Warner Chappell Music
16 *Voyager UK* - **Rock This Town** (Wells/Thompson/Markovic) © 1987 Sacen / Wells
17 *Excalibur* - **Lights Go Down** (Solynsky/Hawthorn/Blades/Sykes/McBride) © 1990 Active Records
18 *Primate* - **Open Your Head** (Sheeran/Andrews) © 1995 Mutiny 2000 Records
19 *Poppy Factory* - **Fabulous Beast** (Cotton/MacDonald/Dale) © 1992 Universal Music Pub.
20 *Detrimental* - **Informer** (Lallaman/Goldfinger) © 1995 Cooking Vinyl / BMG Music Publishing
21 *Bad Dudes* - **Make A Move On Me** (Hobson) © 1996 Copyright Control

Compilations © 2023, 2024 Bradford Noise. Licensed by MCPS.
All tracks used courtesy of the original artists and copyright of the original recordings belongs to their individual owners.
All rights of the producer and the owner of the recorded works reserved. Unauthorised copying, hiring, public performance and broadcasting of this record prohibited.

THE MISSING MUSIC 9
BNOTVCD019 1981-1997

1. *Susan Fassbender* - Merry-Go-Round (Russell/Fassbender) © 1981 Bocu Music Ltd
2. *Modes For Mutants* - Slant Chant Rock'n'Roll (Mds For Mtnts) © 1981 Copyright Control
3. *Southern Death Cult* - Fat Man (SDC) © 1982 Copyright Control
4. *Swamp Flower* - Shackles On The Mind (Webster/Ingham/Leith) © 1985 Mutiny 2000
5. *Annie & The Aeroplanes* - A Million Zillion Miles (A & Arplns) © 1988 Copyright Control
6. *The Apple Moths* - Fred Astaire (Apple Moths) © 1990 Copyright Control
7. *Cabbage Head Kidz* - Brian's White Jacket (Ian & J Hodge/CHK) © 1990 Copyright Control
8. *Arrin* - Lie Detector Blues (R Heaney) © 1995 Copyright Control
9. *Tasmin Archer* - Give In With Grace (Archer/Hughes) © 1996 EMI Records Ltd
10. *Tiny Monroe* - She (NJ Wilow) © 1996 London Music Ltd
11. *Bullweek* - Green (Bullweek) © 1997 Copyright Control
12. *Chest* - Aniseed (Chest) © 1997 Copyright Control
13. *Barbara Moore* - Bright & Shining (Moore) © 1981 EM Records
14. *Belle & The Devotions* - All The Way Up (Curtis/Sacher) © 1984 CBS Records
15. *Janet Cook* - Strike Anthem (Cook/Gruber/Cook) © 1986 Copyright Control
16. *Rebecca Storm* - Mr Love (R Russell/W Russell) © 1986 Willy Russell Music / Warner Bros
17. *Kiki Dee* - Stay Close To You (P Caffrey/G Lamb) © 1987 EMI Records Ltd
18. *The Hollow Men* - The Moon's A Balloon (Hollow Men) © 1990 BMG Eurodisc Ltd
19. *Rodeo Jones* - Get Wise (Plato/Copland/Tretton) © 1991 A&M Records Ltd
20. *Naseeb* - Tera Dil (Malik/Maky) © 1991 Copyright Control

This compilation © 2025 Bradford Noise. Licensed by MCPS.
All tracks used courtesy of the original artists and copyright of the original recordings belongs to their individual owners.
All rights of the producer and the owner of the recorded works reserved. Unauthorised copying, hiring, public performance and broadcasting of this record prohibited.

BRADFORD NOISE RECORDS

Bradford's Noise Of The Valleys The Music 1967-1987 4 CD Set (2009)	BNOTVCD001
	BNOTVCD002
	BNOTVCD003
	BNOTVCD004
The Missing Music (2010)	BNOTVCD005
The Missing Music 2 (2011)	BNOTVCD006
Bradford's Noise Of The Valleys Volume 2 The Music 1988-1998 6 CD Set (2013)	BNOTVCD007
	BNOTVCD008
	BNOTVCD009
	BNOTVCD010
	BNOTVCD011
	BNOTVCD012
The Missing Music 3/4 Double Pack (2014)	BNOTVCD013
	BNOTVCD014
The Missing Music 5 (2017)	BNOTVCD015
The Missing Music 6 (2019)	BNOTVCD016
The Missing Music 7 (2023)	BNOTVCD017
The Missing Music 8 (2024)	BNOTVCD018
The Missing Music 9 Indie / Pop (2025)	BNOTVCD019
Bradford's Noise Of The Valleys Volume 3 Folk / World Music 1999-2009 (2025)	BNOTVCD020
Bradford's Noise Of The Valleys Volume 3 1999-2003 Double Pack (2025)	BNOTVCD021
	BNOTVCD022
Leeds Noise Of The Valleys CD 1 (2023)	LNOTCD001
Leeds Noise Of The Valleys CD 2 (2024)	LNOTCD002

2001 - 2009   BRADFORD'S NOISE OF THE VALLEYS VOLUME 3 PART 1 THE MUSIC

BNOTVCD020 1999-2009 FOLK / WORLD MUSIC

1 *Creation Roots* - Let Jah Music Play (Fontaine/McFarlane/Gordon/Musgrave) © 1999 Ariwa Music
2 *Angelo Palladino* - Charlie's Lament (Palladino) © 2000 Right Music
3 *Jason McNiff* - Through With Love (McNiff) © 2000 McNiff
4 *Shaun T Hunter* - Billy (Hunter) © 2003 Hunter
5 *The Hall Brothers* - Shanty (D Hall) © 2004 Maori Music
6 *The Demon Barbers* - The Ballad Of Minepit Shaw (Roberts/Barrand) © 2005 Copyright Control
7 *James Dey* - Landing Lights (Dey) © 2006 Dey
8 *Abi Lovelle* - Just Like Lovers (Lovelle) © 2006 Copyright Control
9 *Captain Hotknives* - The Pigeons Told Me To Do It (Smith) © 2006 Copyright Control
10 *Rhythm Dhol Bass* - Teray Bin (Kadija/Harjog-Singh) © 2003 Copyright Control
11 *Sex Patels* - Ghost Taal (Ghost Town) (Dammers) © 2006 BMG Rights Management
12 *Threads Orchestra* - Zulfikar 2 (Secret Chiefs 3/Arr. Robinson) © 2006 Copyright Control
13 *Alan Wormald Band* - I Wish (Wonder/Wonder) © 2006 EMI Music/Jobette Music/EMI Music Publishing Ltd
14 *Clare Teal* - Get It On Sam (Teal/Fields) © 2008 Teal/BMG Rights Management
15 *Laura Groves* - Can't Sleep (Groves) © 2008 Domino Publishing Company
16 *Wilful Missing* - Night Parachuting (Kipling/Freeman/Smout/Viqueira/Lawrence) © 2009 Sunshine HQ Ltd
17 *The Bad Shepherds* - Yan, Tyan, Tethera, Methera (trad arr Bad Shepherds) 2009 Non-Copyright Work

This compilation © 2025 Bradford Noise. Licensed by MCPS.
All tracks used courtesy of the original artists and copyright of the original recordings belongs to their individual owners.
All rights of the producer and the owner of the recorded works reserved. Unauthorised copying, hiring, public performance and broadcasting of this record prohibited.

BRADFORD NOISE RECORDS

BRADFORD'S NOISE OF THE VALLEYS VOLUME 3 PART 1 THE MUSIC   2001 - 2003

BNOTVCD021 INDIE / ALTERNATIVE 1999-2003

1. *Ooberman* - Millions Suns (Kelly/A Flett/Popplewell/Churney/S Flett) © 1999 Universal/MCA Music Limited
2. *Indiqa* - Your Favourite Word Is Mine (Indiqa) © 1999 Copyright Control
3. *New Model Army* - Leeds Road 3 am (Sullivan/Dean) © 2000 Sullivan/Dean
4. *The Gardeners Of Eden* - Motherfucker (Heaton/Rhodes) © 2000 Intersong Music Limited
5. *Frantic* - Move Me (Jones/Heaton) © 2000 Righteous Music/Warner Chappell Music
6. *Year Dot* - Girlington (Sheeran) © 2000 Mutiny 2000 Records
7. *Elvis Taxi* - Hypocrite (Riley) © 2000 Copyright Control
8. *Embrace* - Hooligan (McNamara/McNamara) © 2000 EMI Music Publishing Ltd
9. *Parva* - Good Bad Right Wrong (Hodgson/Wilson/White/Rix/Baines) © 2002 Copyright Control
10. *Moota* - All Or Nothing (Appleyard) © 2002 Mutiny 2000 Records
11. *Kwai Chang Caine* - God Luv Ya (Sheeran) © 2002 Mutiny 2000 Records
12. *IdiotBox* - No Disco (IdiotBox/Bolton) © 2002 Copyright Control
13. *Zico* - Lovers (Brauns) © 2002 Brauns
14. *The Pipers* - One Track Mind (Clarke/Atkinson/Lee) © 2004 Copyright Control
15. *The Horton Carpets* - Driven (Watson) © 2003 Mutiny 2000 Records
16. *Franz Ferdinand* - This Fire (Huntley/McCarthy/Thompson/Hardy) © 2004 Universal Music Publishing Ltd
17. *Threshold Shift* - Chillin' Out (Threshold Shift) © 2005 Copyright Control
18. *This Et Al* - Can You Speak European? (Widdop/Holden/Wilson) © 2007 Sentric Music Ltd
19. *Skeletal Family* - Chop Chop (Lorrimer) © 2009 Copyright Control

This compilation © 2025 Bradford Noise. Licensed by MCPS.
All tracks used courtesy of the original artists and copyright of the original recordings belongs to their individual owners.
All rights of the producer and the owner of the recorded works reserved. Unauthorised copying, hiring, public performance and broadcasting of this record prohibited.

2001 - 2003 BRADFORD'S NOISE OF THE VALLEYS VOLUME 3 PART 1 THE MUSIC

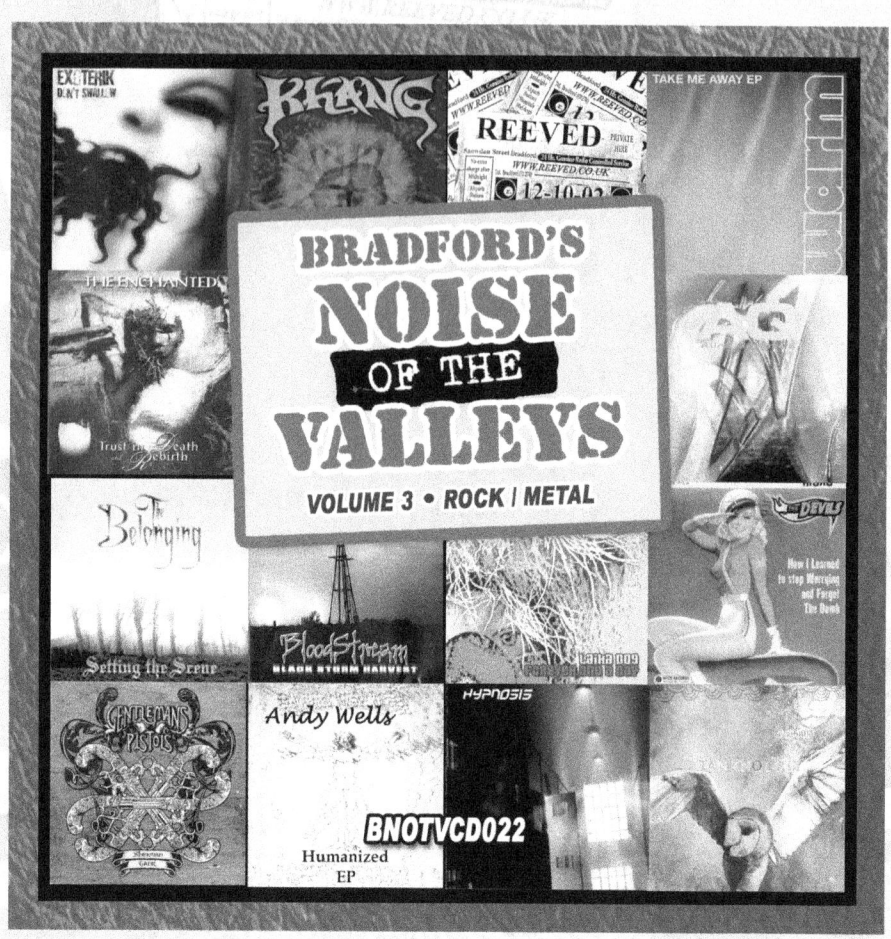

BNOTVCD022 ROCK / METAL 1999-2003

1 *Warm* - **Feel It In The Music** (Hamilton) © 2000 Skylark Recordings
2 *Darwin* - **On Air** (Barraclough) © 2002 Copyright Control
3 *Khang* - **(You Make Me So) Godamn Heavy** (Khang) © 2002 Bionic Conker Recordings
4 *Reeved* - **Solo** (Reeved) © 2002 Copyright Control
5 *The Enchanted* - **Soulburn** (Enchanted) © 2002 Sinister Realms
6 *Bloodstream* - **Blood & Sand** (Bloodstream) © 2002 Sinister Realms
7 *Tortoise Waltz* - **Gnarley Dude** (Tortoise Waltz) © 2002 Copyright Control
8 *Andy Wells* - **Waiting For The Night** (Wells) © 2003 Wellsongs
9 *Siren* - **Feel For You** (Siren) © 2003 Copyright Control
10 *The Devils* - **Cuddle** (Devils) © 2003 Copyright Control
11 *Conquest Of Steel* - **Steel Is The Law** (Conquest Of Steel) © 2003 Copyright Control
12 *Silverburn* - **Godlike & 10 Miles Wide** (Silverburn) © 2005 Copyright Control
13 *The Belonging* - **Dreaming Of Darkness** (Belonging) © 2005 Copyright Control
14 *Hypnosis* - **Unopposed** (Hypnosis) © 2005 Copyright Control
15 *Laika Dog* - **Daddy What's Your Soul?** (Wright) © 2005 10410 Recordings
16 *Exoterik* - **Watch You Bleed** (Fay/Latta/Parry/Riley) © 2008 Sentric Music Limited
17 *Gentlemen's Pistols* - **Frustration** (Gentlemen's Pistols) © 2009 Copyright Control
18 *That Fucking Tank* - **Keanu Reef** (Abbot/Islip) © 2009 Copyright Control

This compilation © 2025 Bradford Noise. Licensed by MCPS.
All tracks used courtesy of the original artists and copyright of the original recordings belongs to their individual owners.
All rights of the producer and the owner of the recorded works reserved. Unauthorised copying, hiring, public performance and broadcasting of this record prohibited.

BRADFORD NOISE RECORDS

LEEDS NOISE OF THE VALLEYS CDS   1968 - 1996

LEEDS NOISE OF THE VALLEYS CD 1

LNOTVCD001 1978-1987

1. *The Mekons* - Never Been In A Riot (Allen/Corrigan/Greenhalgh/Lycett/White/Langford)
   © 1978 BMG Rights Management (UK)
2. *Gang Of Four* - Love Like Anthrax (Allen/Gill/King/Burnham) © 1978 EMI Rights Management
3. *Delta 5* - Mind Your Own Business (Delta 5) © 1979 Rough Trade
4. *The Expelaires* - Sympathy (Don't Be Taken In) (Gregory/Harper/Adams/Harper/Wolfenden)
   © 1980 PLD Music Ltd
5. *Music For Pleasure* - The Human Factor (Peace/King) © 1980 Copyright Control
6. *Soft Cell* - Tainted Love (Ed Cobb) © 1981 Intersong Music/Jobete Music Ltd
7. *Girls At Our Best!* - Fast Boyfriends (Girls At Our Best!) © 1981 Happy Birthday Music
8. *The Volunteers* - Francis (Volunteers) © 1981 Voluntary Music
9. *Dance Chapter* - Backwards Across Thresholds
   (Bruton/Hadfield/Dumbar-Dempsey/Bruton) © 1981 Beggars Banquet
10. *Sisters Of Mercy* - Alice (Sisters of Mercy) © 1982 Copyright Control
11. *March Violets* - Grooving In Green (Ashton/Denbigh/Elliott) © 1983 Tritec Songs Ltd
12. *The Three Johns* - Lucy In The Rain (Brennan/Hyatt/Langford) © 1984 Domino Publishing Co Ltd
13. *Chumbawamba* - The R'n'R Factory Strike (Chumbawamba) © 1984 Agit-Prop
14. *Red Lorry Yellow Lorry* - Hollow Eyes (Red Lorry Yellow Lorry) © 1985 Red Rhino
15. *The Batfish Boys* - The Tumbleweed Thing (Ashton/Denbigh/Elliott) © 1985 Tritec Songs Ltd
16. *Akimbo* - So Long Trouble (Wilson/Wilson) © 1985 Wilson Wilson
17. *Zoot & The Roots* - Love Bug (Gilderdale/Ewing) © 1985 Song Management Ltd
18. *Upside Down* - Dead Man's Clothes (Upside Down) © 1987 Uneasy Listening
19. *Salvation* - Thunderbird (Salvation) © 1987 Prism Music
20. *Son Of Sam* - Nature's Made A Mistake (Bishop) © 1987 Sixty Three
21. *Age Of Chance* - Who's Afraid Of The Big Bad Noise? (Elvidge/Howson/Perry/Taylor)
    © 1987 Age Of Chance Ltd

LEEDS NOISE OF THE VALLEYS CD 2

LNOTVCD002 1980-1988

1. *Alwoodly Jets* - Long Time Lonely (Rigby) © 1980 Pineapple / Chappell Music
2. *The Motivators* - Miss Demeanors (The Motivators) © 1980 Copyright Control
3. *Side Effect* - Chain Reaction (Side Effect) © 1980 Copyright Control
4. *Household Name* - World Paranoia (Household Name) © 1981 Copyright Control
5. *Equivalent VIII* - Burning Down (Equivalent VIII) © 1981 Copyright Control
6. *Edward's Voice* - Falling From Another High Building (Edward's Voice)
   © 1982 Cherry Red Music Ltd
7. *Victims Of Romance* - Abigail's Party (Victims Of Romance) © 1984 Copyright Control
8. *Surfin' Dave & The B'Nee Teas* - Exchange & Mart (Coleman) © 1984 Coleman
9. *Indiscriminate Hoax Fund* - Bulkhead (Indiscriminate Hoax Fund) © 1985 1-Noise-12 Pub Inc
10. *The Mighty Clifton Brothers* - Eldridge (Mighty Clifton Brothers) © 1985 1-Noise-12 Pub Inc
11. *The Blood Brothers* - We Steal (The Blood Brothers) © 1985 1-Noise-12 Publishing Inc
12. *The Jazz Hipsters* - Elvis's Quiff (The Jazz Hipsters) © 1985 1-Noise-12 Publishing Inc
13. *The She-Hees* - Hello (Ritchie) © 1985 Universal / MCA Music Ltd / Concord Music Publishing LLC
14. *Matamba* - Nowhere To Run (Matamba) © 1985 1-Noise-12 Publishing Inc
15. *The Chorus* - Chimeras (Parkes/Hand/Solowka/Finnis) © 1985 AAZ Records
16. *The Sinister Cleaners* - Wallflower (Liggins/Middleton/Parkes/Smith) © 1986 AAZ Records
17. *Len Liggins* - Bye Bye Brenda (Liggins) © 1988 Liggins
18. *The Mission* - Serpent's Kiss (Adams/Brown/Hussey/Hinkler) © 1986 Universal Music Publishing
19. *Sally Timms & The Drifting Cowgirls* - Long Black Veil (Wilkins/Danny) © 1986 Copyright Control
20. *Pink Peg Slax* - Li'l Jean (Pink Peg Slax) © 1988 Copyright Control
21. *The Ukrainians* - Vasya Vasyl' Ok (Trad Arr: David Gedge) © 1988 Gedge

Compilations © 2023, 2024 Bradford Noise. Licensed by MCPS.
All tracks used courtesy of the original artists and copyright of the original recordings belongs to their individual owners.
All rights of the producer and the owner of the recorded works reserved. Unauthorised copying, hiring, public performance and broadcasting of this record prohibited.

BRADFORD NOISE RECORDS

www.ingramcontent.com/pod-product-compliance
Lightning Source LLC
Chambersburg PA
CBHW081101070526
44583CB00018B/2507